[redacted]

[redacted]

PHENOMENOLOGY OF UNIFIED THEORIES

– from standard model to supersymmetry –

PHENOMENOLOGY OF UNIFIED THEORIES

– from standard model to supersymmetry –

Dubrovnik, Croatia, Yugoslavia
May 22-28, 1983

Editors: H Galić, B Guberina & D Tadić

World Scientific

Published by

World Scientific Publishing Co Pte Ltd.
P O Box 128
Farrer Road
Singapore 9128

ISBN 9971-966-12-3

Printed in Singapore by Singapore National Printers (Pte) Ltd.

QC173
.7
P467
1984
PHYS

PHENOMENOLOGY OF UNIFIED THEORIES
- from standard model to supersymmetry -

Dubrovnik, Croatia, Yugoslavia
May 22-28, 1983

International Scientific Committee: D. Bailin (United Kingdom), S.D. Drell (U.S.A.), E. Fischbach (U.S.A.), G. Furlan (Italy), H. Fritzsch (F.R. Germany), G. Marx (Hungary), L.B. Okun (USSR), R.D. Peccei (F.R. Germany), H. Pietschmann (Austria), A. Salam (Italy/United Kingdom)

National Advisory Board: M. Blagojević and Z. Marić (Belgrade), M. Rosina and M. Mihailović (Ljubljana), Z. Stipčević (Sarajevo), D. Tadić (Zagreb)

Organized by: Prirodoslovno-matematički fakultet, University of Zagreb and Rudjer Bošković Institute, Zagreb, Croatia, Yugoslavia

Local Organizing Committee: D. Tadić (head of the Committee), H. Galić, B. Guberina, S. Pallua (scientific secretary), I. Picek, K. Pisk, J. Trampetić, D. Vranić

Topical Lectures:

R. Barbieri (Pisa)
V.S. Berezinsky (Moscow)
M. Davier (Orsay)
J.F. Donoghue (Amherst)
E. Fiorini (Milano)
E. Fischbach (Lafayette)
H. Fritzsch (München)
V.A. Kuzmin (Moscow)
P. Lipari (Syracuse)
V.A. Novikov (Moscow)
R.D. Peccei (München)
E. de Rafael (Marseille)
G.G. Ross (Didcot)
H.R. Rubinstein (Rehovot)
G. Senjanović (Upton)
V.I. Zakharov (Moscow)

Seminars:

A. Barroso (Geneve)
F. Csikor (Budapest)
J.O. Eeg (Oslo)
B. Guberina (Zagreb)
I. Picek (Zagreb)
M. Quirós (Madrid)
P. Senjanović (Zagreb)
J. Szwed (Krakow)
J. Trampetić (München)
Z. Was (Krakow)
G. Zoupanos (Geneve)

Sponsored and/or supported by:

- European Physical Society
- British Council, United Kingdom
- Deutsche Forschungsgemeinschaft, F.R. Germany
- U.S. National Science Foundation, U.S.A.
- UNESCO
- International Centre for Theoretical Physics, Trieste, Italy
- Istituto Nazionale di Fisica Nucleare, Italy
- International School for Advanced Studies, Trieste, Italy
- Yugoslav Academy of Sciences and Arts - Section for Mathematical, Physical and Technical Sciences
- Self-Managing Community of Interest for Science of S.R. Croatia
- Union of Societies of Mathematicians, Physicists and Astronomers of S.F.R. Yugoslavia
- Society of Mathematicians, Physicists and Astronomers of S.R. Croatia
- Prirodoslovno-matematički fakultet, University of Zagreb
- Rudjer Bošković Institute, Zagreb

FOREWORD

The main intention of this Conference was to provide a broad overview of the phenomenological aspects of unified field theories. It is gratifying that at the time of the Conference important ingredients of electroweak theory, W and Z bosons, were finally found. Besides emphasizing solid experimental foundations for theoretical speculations, the Conference also strived to leave enough space for the creative theoretical imagination from which new fundamental ideas and insights might emerge.

The choice of the Conference town, Dubrovnik, was influenced by the long scientific and cultural tradition of this town, which is the most glittering gem of our Adriatic coast.

The Conference was supported and sponsored by many international, Yugoslav and Croatian institutions in various ways (see the list).

The organization of the Conference was very much helped by the International Scientific Committee and the National Advisory Board.

We take this opportunity of expressing our gratitude to the members of all the bodies mentioned above.

The organization of the Conference would not have been possible without our valiant secretaries M. Galeković and V. Čičin-Šain. In the preparation of these Proceedings we had invaluable help from B. Fanton.

Organizing Committee

CONTENTS

LOW ENERGY WEAK INTERACTIONS AND THE QUARK MODEL

John F. Donoghue

Department of Physics and Astronomy
University of Massachusetts
Amherst, Mass. 01003
U.S.A.

ABSTRACT

I describe the present understanding of the weak interactions of hadrons within the standard model. In particular, the progress which has been made through use of the quark model is reviewed, including topics in semileptonic and nonleptonic $\Delta S=1$ decays, parity violation in nuclei and hypernuclear decays.

I. Introduction

The purpose of this talk is to summarize what is known about the application of the standard model to low energy weak interactions. Put in other words, how do we go from the cryptic symbols

$$SU(3)_c \times SU(2)_L \times U(1)$$

$$\binom{\nu_e}{e}_L \quad \binom{\nu_\mu}{\mu}_L \quad \binom{\nu_\tau}{\tau}_L \qquad e_R, \mu_R, \tau_R$$

$$\binom{u}{d_c}_L \quad \binom{c}{s_c}_L \quad \binom{t}{b_c}_L \qquad u_R, c_R, t_R, d_R, s_R, b_R$$

which characterize the standard model, to the physical processes which are observed everyday in the lab

$$\Lambda \to p\pi^-$$

$$\Lambda \to pe\nu$$

$$\vdots$$

$$K \to 3\pi$$

$$K \to 2\pi$$

$$\vdots \qquad ?$$

In describing this transition use will be made of symmetries and, when symmetries are no longer predictive, of the quark model. The weak properties of purely leptonic processes are straightforward within the standard model, and so the emphasis will be on semileptonic and nonleptonic reactions.

There are many applications of these ideas to "classic" areas of weak interaction phenomenology such as

- semileptonic decays
- $\Delta S=1$ nonleptonic decays
- parity violation in nuclear physics
- hypernuclei
- radiative $\Delta S=1$ decays
- Ω^- physics .

In these cases, the fundamental structure of the weak interactions is rarely in doubt, and the interest lies in trying to accurately describe the reactions. To the extent that this is successful the methods can be applied to the study of new and not yet understood processes such as CP violation, right handed currents, proton decay, etc.

II. General Features of Hadrons

Most of the calculations depend primarily on the most basic features common to all quark models. For example when a dimensional number is being computed, most often the scale is set by the hadronic size. That scale we know from experiment to be about one fermi or 1/(200 MeV). For example, the charge radii of hadrons[1] are

$$\left.\langle r^2\rangle^{1/2}_{EM}\right|_{PROTON} = .9 \text{ fm}$$
$$\left.\langle r^2\rangle^{1/2}_{EM}\right|_{\pi} = .62 \pm .04 \text{ fm} . \quad 1)$$

The quarks confined to this scale are necessarily relativistic. The uncertainty principle lets us estimate an average momentum for quarks as

$$p \sim \sqrt{3}/R \sim 350 \text{ MeV} . \quad 2)$$

(The $\sqrt{3}$ is for the 3 spatial dimensions.) This is comparable to quark masses or energies. A more direct indication of the relativistic nature of quarks comes from the spectrum. Nonrelativistic systems are characterized by excitation energies small compared to the constituent masses. In the hadronic spectrum typical excitation energies are 300 → 500 MeV, comparable to or larger than quark masses. Despite being confined, the quarks in hadrons appear to be quasi-free. Theoretically there is perhaps the most difficult feature of the quark model to understand, but there is no evidence for strong correlations between quarks, or for more complex structure of hadrons. The quantum number structure appears to be well described by simple spin and color wavefunctions. The evidence for this is that quark model calculations generally work.

One of the specific models which has been extensively used is the MIT bag model.[2-5] This model describes a two phased system, the external phase being the vacuum, and the interior being the region where the quarks exist. It is derivable from a Lagrangian[5]

$$\mathcal{L} = (\mathcal{L}_{QCD} - B)\, \theta(\bar{q}q) \quad . \quad 3)$$

L_{QCD} is the Lagrangian of Quantum Chromodynamics and B is a constant positive energy density for the interior of the bag. The order parameter is $\bar{q}q$, as would be expected from chiral theories. Variation of this Lagrangian leads to the usual equations of motion inside the bag, plus boundary conditions on the surface.

The most commonly used approximation is to fix the bag to be spherical. In this case the quark's 4-component Dirac wavefunction has the form

$$\psi = \begin{pmatrix} i\,u\chi \\ \ell\,\vec{\sigma}\cdot\hat{r}\chi \end{pmatrix} e^{-iEt} \qquad 4)$$

with χ being a two component Pauli spinor and the upper and lower components (u and ℓ) being spherical Bessel functions

$$u = Nj_0(pr)$$
$$\ell = -Nj_1(pr) \qquad 5)$$

and for nearly massless quarks

$$E \approx p \approx \frac{2.04}{R} + .48\, m_q + \ldots \qquad 6)$$

The standard parameters are $R \approx 1$ fm and the light quark masses $m_q = 0 \rightarrow 33$ MeV.

Another model used frequently is the harmonic oscillator quark model. Here the (two component) wavefunction falls off exponentially

$$\psi = N\, e^{-1/4\,\alpha r_{ij}^2} \qquad 7)$$

with α being the oscillator strength. One relevant feature here is the question of the best oscillator strength for calculations of weak processes.[7] Hadron spectroscopy favors $\alpha^2 = 0.17$ GeV^2, but this leads to a charge radius which is too small ($\langle r^2\rangle^{1/2}_{EM\ PROTON} = .51$ fm). In some processes this could lead to an overestimate of the effect of the "wavefunction at the origin". Adjusting the charge radius to agree with experiment yields $\alpha^2 = 0.049$ GeV^2. Aside from this scale problem, the calculated results of the two models often agree fairly well.

Tadić and Trampetić[8] and Isgur and Hyne[9] have recently calculated relativistic corrections within this model. These are significant and improve the agreement with experiment in many cases, including the charge radius.

III. Semileptonic Hyperon Decay Form Factors

Processes involving both leptons and hadrons are described by the weak Hamiltonian

$$H_w = \frac{G_F}{\sqrt{2}} \left(aJ_\mu^{\Delta S=0} + bJ_\mu^{\Delta S=1}\right) \bar{\psi}_\ell \gamma^\mu (1+\gamma_5)\psi_\nu \qquad 8)$$

with G_F derivable from muon decay

$$G_F = 1.16632 \times 10^{-5}\ \text{GeV}^{-2}\ . \tag{9)}$$

In the 6-quark GWS-KM model, $a = \cos\theta_1$ and $b = \sin\theta_1 \cos\theta_3$ so that $a^2 + b^2 \leq 1$. At the quark level the currents are

$$J_\mu^{\Delta S=0} = \bar{u}\gamma_\mu(1+\gamma_5)d \tag{10)}$$

$$J_\mu^{\Delta S=1} = \bar{u}\gamma_\mu(1+\gamma_5)s\ .$$

At the hadronic level the matrix elements of the currents are described by many form factors[10]

$$\langle B'(p_2)|J_\mu|B(p_1)\rangle =$$

$$\bar{u}(p_2)\{f_1(q^2)\gamma_\mu - \frac{if_2(q^2)}{m_1+m_2}\sigma_{\mu\nu}q^\nu + \frac{if_3(q^2)q^\mu}{m_1+m_2} \tag{11)}$$

$$+ g_1(q^2)\gamma_\mu\gamma_5 - \frac{ig_2(g^2)}{m_1+m_2}\sigma_{\mu\nu}q^\nu\gamma_5 + \frac{ig_3(q^2)q^\mu\gamma_5}{m_1+m_2}\}u(p_1)$$

with $q_\mu = (p_1 - p_2)_\mu$. T invariance requires that all these form factors be real. Let us look at each of these and see how they arise in the quark model.

$f_1\gamma_\mu$: The vector form factor is known from the CVC hypothesis and SU(3) to be given by

$$f_1(0) = if_{ijk} \tag{12)}$$

where i,j,k = 1,2,...8 refer to the SU(3) structure of the external states ($B \to i$, $B' \to j$ and $J_\mu \to k = 1 + i2(\Delta S=0)$ or $k = 4 + i5(\Delta S=1)$. In the quark model this is calculated by studying the time component of the vector current

$$f_1 = \langle p|\int d^3x\ \bar{u}\gamma_o d|N\rangle \tag{13)}$$

plus generalizations to other states. These reproduce CVC in the SU(3) limit.

SU(3) breaking for the vector form factor is known to be only second order in the SU(3) breaking parameter. In the quark model this is explicitly borne out by calculation, but nevertheless some exists. In the bag model[11], the mismatch in the s and u wavefunctions, due to the s quark mass, lowers $\Delta S=1$ transitions by about 3 percent with respect to the $\Delta S=0$.

$\dfrac{-if_2\sigma^{\mu\nu}q_\nu}{m_1+m_2}$: This is the "weak magnetism" form factor and it is also known from CVC and SU(3)

$$f_2(0) = if_{ijk}f + d_{ijk}d$$

$$f = K_p + \frac{1}{2} K_n = 0.84 \quad 14)$$

$$d = -\frac{3}{2} K_n = 2.86$$

$$f/d = .29$$

K_p and K_n are the anomalous magnetic moments of the proton and neutron. In the quark model it can be calculated by a magnetic-moment-like weighting of the vector current

$$\frac{f_1 + f_2}{2M_p} = \langle p|\frac{1}{2}\int d^3x\ \vec{r} \times \bar{u}\vec{\gamma}d|N\rangle\ . \quad 15)$$

This will also reproduce CVC in the SU(3) limit if the parameters are adjusted to fit the magnitude of the proton's magnetic moment. If this is done, there is also the quark model prediction of

$$f/d = .31 \quad 16)$$

in excellent agreement with experiment. In the case of this, and all subsequent form factors, SU(3) breaking is first order and generally is larger than the vector case.

$g_1\gamma_\mu\gamma_5$: The axial vector current may also be parameterized by SU(3)

$$g_1(0) = if_{ijk}F + d_{ijk}D \quad 17)$$

but its magnitude is not predicted. Measurement of neutron beta decay yields

$$g_1^{np} = F + D = 1.254 \quad 18)$$

and studies of hyperon decay seem to indicate (see below)

$$\frac{D}{D+F} = .65\ . \quad 19)$$

The magnitude can be obtained using PCAC in the form of the Adler-Weisberger relation[12]

$$1 - \frac{1}{g_1^2} = \frac{4m_N^2}{\pi g_{\pi NN}^2}\int_{m_N+m_\pi}^{\infty} dW\ \frac{W}{W^2 - m_N^2}\ [\sigma_{\pi^+p}(W) - \sigma_{\pi^-p}(W)] \quad 20)$$

which yields $g_1 = 1.25$.

A different approach is direct calculation in the quark model

$$g_1 = \langle P_\uparrow|\int d^3x\ \bar{u}\gamma_3\gamma_5 d|N_\uparrow\rangle\ . \quad 21)$$

In nonrelativistic models one obtains the SU(6) prediction

$$g_1^{np} = \langle \tau^+ \sigma_3 \rangle = 5/3 \ . \qquad 22)$$

In relativistic models this is always reduced by the effect of the lower component in the wavefunction.[13] In the notation of Eq.

$$g_1 = \frac{5}{3} \int d^3x (u^2 - \frac{1}{3} \ell^2) \qquad 23)$$

where the wavefunction normalization condition is

$$1 = \int d^3x (u^2 + \ell^2) \ . \qquad 24)$$

In the bag model the values for g_1 range from 1.09 → 1.3 with the experimental value easily obtainable. Similar results hold in relativistic versions of the harmonic oscillator model. The SU(3) structure is predicted to be

$$\frac{D}{D+F} = 3/5 \qquad 25)$$

again in reasonable agreement with experiment.

The Adler Weisberger relation and the quark model may seem very different, yet there is some systematic relationship between the two.[14] Both yield 5/3 in the nonrelativistic limit. For the Adler Weisberger relation this involves imagining a world when $M_\Delta \approx M_N$ and all of the resonances except the Δ decouple from πN scattering. As relativistic binding effects are turned on both decrease from 5/3 at about the same rate.

$- \dfrac{i g_2 \sigma^{\mu\nu} q_\nu \gamma_5}{m_1 + m_2}$: This is the "weak electricity" or "second class axial" form factor. Use of G-parity plus SU(3) predicts $g_2 = 0$ (i.e. it is "second class"). Here is one case where the quark model should be better than SU(3), and g_2 is predicted to be sizable.[15] It is calculated like an electric dipole moment

$$\frac{g_2}{m_1 + m_2} + \frac{1}{2}\left(\frac{1}{2m_1} - \frac{1}{2m_2}\right) g_1 = \langle B_{2\uparrow} | - i \int d^3x \ z A_0 | B_{1\uparrow} \rangle \ . \qquad 26)$$

In a nonrelativistic model, this expression yields

$$= \frac{1}{2} \left(\frac{1}{2M_s} - \frac{1}{2M_u}\right) g_1^{SU(6)} \qquad 27)$$

while in the bag model

$$= g_1^{SU(6)} \int d^3x (u_s \ell_u - u_u \ell_s) \ . \qquad 28)$$

The ratio of g_2 to g_1 is almost universal for $\Delta S=1$ transitions

$$\frac{g_2}{g_1} \begin{array}{ll} = 0.30 & \text{(bag model)} \\ = 0.60 & \text{(nonrelativistic)} \ . \end{array} \qquad 29)$$

So far there is no measurement of this, but one should be possible in the near future.

The other two form factors f_3 and g_3 are almost always unimportant because their effect is proportional to the lepton mass. In the bag model[16], for $\Delta S=1$ transitions the scalar form factor f_3 is

$$\frac{f_3}{f_1} = \frac{g_2}{g_1} \quad . \tag{30}$$

The pseudoscalar form factor g_3 is an example of what the quark model cannot calculate because it is due to the pion pole. Luckily PCAC saves the day

$$g_3 = g_1 \frac{(m_1 + m_2)^2}{m_\pi^2} \quad . \tag{31}$$

Thus we have achieved at least a general understanding of the origin and size of the various current matrix elements.

IV. π and K Decay

In addition to hyperon decay, the charged weak currents are responsible for the semileptonic processes $\pi^+ \to e^+\nu$ and $K^+ \to \mu^+\nu$. Here the relevant matrix elements are

$$\begin{aligned} \langle 0|A_\mu^{\Delta S=0}|\pi^+\rangle &= i f_\pi p^\mu \\ \langle 0|A_\mu^{\Delta S=1}|K^+\rangle &= i f_K p^\mu \end{aligned} \tag{32}$$

with

$$f_\pi = 130 \text{ MeV}; \quad f_K = 160 \text{ MeV} \quad . \tag{33}$$

These are also calculable in quark models, although not as simply. In the bag model (see ref. 4 for a fuller discussion)

$$\begin{aligned} f_\pi &= \frac{.5\sqrt{2}}{R_\pi} = 200 \text{ MeV} \\ f_K &\approx f_\pi \end{aligned} \tag{34}$$

while nonrelativistic models generally yield a larger value

$$f_\pi \approx 400 \text{ MeV} \tag{35}$$

and provide a worse estimate of

$$f_K/f_\pi = \sqrt{\frac{m_\pi}{m_K}}\, \psi_0^K(0)/\psi_0^\pi(0) \approx .5 \tag{36}$$

(i.e. the "van Royen-Weisskopf paradox"[17]). The bag model description contains an interesting feature which resolves the van Royen Weisskopf paradox and also will be important later in nonleptonic decays. The amplitudes which determine f_π involve a cancellation between the upper and lower components of the wavefunction (it is proportional to $u^2 - \ell^2$). This lowers the result down towards the experimental value (and presumably explains why the bag f_π is lower than the nonrelativistic f_π). The origin of this cancellation is clear; it is related to the "helicity suppression" of $\pi \to e\nu$ with respect to $\pi \to \mu\nu$

$$\frac{\Gamma(\pi \to e\nu)}{\Gamma(\pi \to \mu\nu)} = 1.2 \times 10^{-4} . \qquad 37)$$

The latter occurs because helicity conservation forbids the production of two free massless fermions by vector or axial vector currents if they are in a spin zero state. The ratio of Eq. 37 is then suppressed by a factor of m_e^2/m_μ^2 over naive phase space considerations. For confined quarks helicity is not as well defined a quantity but the annihilation of $q\bar{q}$ by an axial current still shows this type of cancellation. As the quark mass increases the cancellation becomes weaker and the numerator factor in the calculation compensates for the dependence on the kaon mass in the denominator, keeping f_K roughly equal to f_π.

V. Why Worry About SU(3) Breaking?

There is both an experimental and theoretical answer to the above question. In experiment, it is common for the SU(3) values of f_1, f_2, and g_2 to be assumed in the analysis of g_1/f_1. SU(3) breaking then affects the experimental results. If SU(3) breaking is present (as it appears to be; see below) many entries in the Particle Data Tables are therefore in fact wrong, and, if one does not know the correlation of the various assumptions with the result, the experimental result may be without any value anymore. There are strong correlations. The UMASS-BNL group working on $\Lambda \to pe\nu$ have found that[18]

$$\left.\frac{g_1}{f_1}\right|_{\Lambda \to pe\nu} = 0.715 + .25\,\frac{g_2}{f_1} \qquad 38)$$

which, if g_2 is as large as expected, can produce effects well outside the statistical errors. To avoid this one should either quote all correlations or use the model independent parameterization provided by Garcia and Kielanowski[19].

One of the important theoretical issues in semileptonic processes is the determination of the KM angles. SU(3) breaking can limit the precision of this enterprise. Fits with small SU(3) breaking can reproduce the data as well or better than the usual Cabibbo fit, but sometimes with different values of "$\sin\theta_1 \cos\theta_3$". There is some theoretical uncertainty in this value due to lack of knowledge about the form of the breaking, the size of which is difficult to assess at present.

VI. Status of Semileptonic Decays

There have been several good high statistics results in recent years. In particular the rates

$n \to pe\nu$
$\Lambda \to pe\nu$
$\Sigma^- \to \Lambda e\nu$
$\Sigma^- \to ne\nu$

are all known to better than 5% and data analysis is still ongoing for some of these reactions.[20,21]

One of the results of this is that the standard Cabibbo fits to the data (assuming SU(3)) no longer works well.[22,23] The χ^2/DOF is an abysmal 31/11. The reason seems to be SU(3) breaking, which after all is expected. It is just that experiment is now better than SU(3). The fit to the KM angle depends slightly on the details of the method but yields

$$\begin{aligned} &\cos\theta_1 = 0.9739 \pm 0.0025 \\ &\sin\theta_1 \cos\theta_3 = 0.225 \pm 0.002 \\ &\cos^2\theta_1 + \sin^2\theta_1 \cos^2\theta_3 = 0.999 \pm 0.005 \,. \end{aligned} \tag{39}$$

The latter two have an additional unknown theoretical uncertainty due to the lack of knowledge of the true pattern of SU(3) breaking. One feature is worth commenting on is that SU(2) x U(1) as a renormalizable gauge theory is being tested in these results because it would not be possible to obtain this close to a good fit if it were not for the radiative corrections[24,25], in particular those where the ultraviolet divergence is cut off by the Z° mass.

There are in addition some anomalies in the data which do not appear easily cured by allowing small SU(3) breaking. One is the electron asymmetry in $\Sigma^- \to ne\nu$, which was measured[26] to have the value $\alpha_e = +0.35 \pm 0.29$, which disagrees with the SU(3) value $\alpha_e = -0.69$. Another is a set of inconsistent values for g_1/f_1 in $\Lambda \to pe\nu$. Studies of the Dalitz plot yield a world average of $g_1/f_1 = 0.703 \pm 0.019$. However[27] measurements of various asymmetries always yield a lower g_1/f_1

$$\begin{aligned} &\alpha_e \Rightarrow g_1/f_1 = 0.28 \begin{smallmatrix} +0.35 \\ -0.11 \end{smallmatrix} \\ &\alpha_\nu \Rightarrow g_1/f_. = 0.42 \begin{smallmatrix} +0.07 \\ -0.06 \end{smallmatrix} \\ &\alpha_p \Rightarrow g_1/f_1 = 0.33 \begin{smallmatrix} +0.11 \\ -0.07 \end{smallmatrix} \end{aligned} \tag{40}$$

Oka[27] has recently proposed an interesting possible explanation for the Λ data. He notes that essentially all bounds on right-handed currents (RHC) disappear if the right-handed equivalent of $\cos\theta$ vanishes. (The remaining bounds from μ decay are not violated by his idea.) In this case RHC only effect $\Delta S=1$ semileptonic decay (if ν_R is light enough). However, they affect the two determinations differently, as the Dalitz plot is a parity conserving quantity, while the asymmetries are parity violating. He suggests right-handed currents in the form

$$H = \frac{G}{\sqrt{2}} \cos\theta_1 \sin\theta_1 \cos\theta_3\{(\bar{e}\nu)_L(\bar{u}s)_L + a(\bar{e}\nu)_R(\bar{u}s)_R\} \ . \qquad 41)$$

The data favors $a \neq 0$, along with a reduced $\sin\theta_1 \cos\theta_3$. The value $a = 0.29 \pm 0.06$ nicely explains the inconsistencies. The asymmetries should be extracted soon with better statistics, and therefore also better control of possible systematic effects, and perhaps this will eliminate the need for Oka's hypothesis. It is also testable in other places. The polarization of the μ in $K \to \mu\nu$ is predicted[27] to be $P_\mu = 0.85 \pm 0.06$. Experiment ($P_\mu = 0.97 \pm 0.07$) does not yet rule this out. In addition neutrinos from π decay (purely LH) and from K decay (both LH and RH) produce strangeness with different strengths

$$R = \frac{\sigma(\pi \to \mu\nu \to \nu + p \to \mu + \Lambda)}{\sigma(K \to \mu\nu \to \nu + p \to \mu + \Lambda)} = \frac{1}{1+a^2} = .9 \ . \qquad 42)$$

These neutrinos are separable in certain experimental situations. In addition RHC should be visible in μ decay at level of 10^{-3} or greater.[27]

VII. Nonleptonic Decays and the Nonleptonic Hamiltonian

The dominant decay of strange particles is always into purely hadronic final states. However, these nonleptonic decays are more difficult to understand theoretically because they involve the product of two hadronic weak currents instead of just one as in semileptonic processes. The issues[10] here are: 1) Nonleptonic dominance. The overall magnitude for nonleptonic is generally two orders of magnitude larger than the semileptonic processes.

$$\Gamma(\text{nonleptonic}) \approx 400\ \Gamma\ (\text{semileptonic}) . \qquad 43)$$

However there are no obvious factors, such as Cabibbo angles, which would lead to such an enhancement. 2) The $\Delta I=1/2$ rule. The Hamiltonian contains the product of the $I=1$, $\Delta S=0$ current with the $\Delta S=1$, $I=1/2$ current producing expectations of both $\Delta I=1/2$ and $3/2$ with comparable magnitudes. However, experimentally there is a "$\Delta I=1/2$ rule"

$$\text{Amp}(\Delta I=1/2) \simeq 20\ \text{Amp}(\Delta I=3/2) . \qquad 44)$$

These two are the major features which need to be explained.

The most important physics which determines the structure of the effective nonleptonic weak Hamiltonian is QCD renormalization[28,29]. At energies comparable to M_W, the interaction is the familiar current-current form with the standard tree level currents, Fig. 1a. However, at low energies this is dressed by QCD radiative corrections which introduce sizable logarithmic factors of $\ell n(m_W/\mu)$ (where μ is a hadronic scale where the hadronic matrix elements are taken) and additionally modify the standard structure. Typical diagrams are in Fig. 1b,c. The results can be expressed as

$$H_w = \sum_i c_i\, O_i \qquad 45)$$

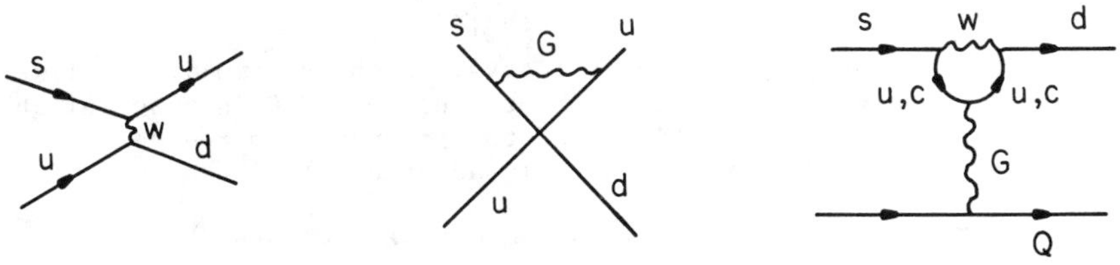

(a) (b) (c)

where c_i are calculable coefficients and O_i are a set of local operators. Rather than deal with the full operator structure here, let us consider just the most important contributions[29]

$$H_w = \frac{G_F}{2\sqrt{2}} \cos\theta_1 \sin\theta_1 \sin\theta_3 \{c_1 O_1 + c_4 O_4 + c_5 O_5\} \qquad 46)$$

with

$$O_1 = \{(\bar{d}u)_{V-A}(\bar{u}s)_{V-A} - (\bar{u}u)_{V-A}(\bar{d}s)_{V-A}\}$$

$$O_4 = \{(\bar{d}u)_{V-A}(\bar{u}s)_{V-a} + (\bar{u}u)_{V-A}(\bar{d}s)_{V-A} - (\bar{d}d)_{V-A}(\bar{d}s)_{V-A}\} \qquad 47)$$

$$O_5 = \sum_{i=u,d,s} \{\bar{d}\lambda^A s)_{V-A}(\bar{Q}_i\lambda^A Q_i)_{V+A}\}$$

and at $\mu = 1$ GeV

$$c_1 = 2.5 \ ; \ c_4 = 0.4 \ ; \ c_5 = 0.06 \ . \qquad 48)$$

The operator O_1 is purely $\Delta I = 1/2$ and has the largest coefficient. The villian in the field is O_4 which is the only $\Delta I = 3/2$ operator. Notice that its coefficient is smaller than c_1. However this by itself is not enough to explain the $\Delta I = 1/2$ rule. Finally O_5 is the famous "penguin" operator[29], about which more will be said later.

VIII. PCAC

The charged currents have a definite chiral structure. This is expressed in the form

$$[F_5^{\,i}, H_w] = + [F^i, H_w] \qquad i = 1,2,3 \qquad 49)$$

where F^i and $F_5^{\,i}$ are the vector and axial vector charges of chiral SU(2). This has been successfully tested via PCAC. The use of soft pion techniques can be used to relate $K \to 3\pi$ to $K \to 2\pi$. The results[30] are accurate to within 10% for both the magnitudes and slope parameters and both $\Delta I = 1/2$ and $\Delta I = 3/2$. In addition to confirming the validity of PCAC, this severely restricts possible admixture of interactions with other chiralities such as RHC.

In addition PCAC is useful for a theorist because it can simplify the necessary calculation. Since it can relate $B \to B'\pi$ to $B \to B'$ and the kaon decays to $K \to \pi$, it implies that we need only calculate

$$<B'|H_w|B> \qquad \text{and} \qquad <\pi|H_w|K>$$

in order to understand nonleptonic decays. Although amplitudes like $B \to B'\pi$ can be calculated directly , the use of PCAC is more reliable than any quark model calculation, and the procedure to reduce the amplitudes to $B \to B'$ and $K \to \pi$ is generally adopted.

IX. Quark Model Calculations of Baryon Matrix Elements

To actually obtain the weak amplitudes one must directly calculate them in some model. In this section I describe this work, neglecting for the moment the penguin diagram.

The method for doing a quark model calculation is reasonably simple[31,32]. One decomposes the weak Hamiltonian by using the hadronic wavefunctions (for example, Eq. 4)

$$\int d^3x\, H_w(x) = \frac{G_F}{\sqrt{2}} \cos\theta_1 \sin\theta_1 \cos\theta_3 \int d^3x(u^2+\ell^2)^2 \left[(d^+u)(u^+s) - (d^+\vec{\sigma}u)(u^+\vec{\sigma}s)\right] + \ldots \qquad 50)$$

This separates out the spatial overlap from the spin and color portion. When a matrix element is taken using the usual spin states, the factor in square brackets becomes a Clebsch Gordon coefficient.

$$A = <N|\int d^3x\, H_w(x)|\Lambda> = \frac{G_F}{\sqrt{2}} \cos\theta_1 \sin\theta_1 \cos\theta_3 \int d^3x(u^2+\ell^2)^2\sqrt{6}\ . \qquad 51)$$

This yields the desired amplitude. Note that since the quark wavefunctions are normalized

$$\int d^3x(u^2+\ell^2) = 1 \qquad 52)$$

the weak amplitudes are scaled by $1/R^3$

$$\int d^3x(u^2+\ell^2)^2 \sim c/R^3 \qquad 53)$$

Thus the magnitude of nonleptonic matrix elements is determined by the hadronic size.

In calculating the baryon matrix elements it is seen that all $\Delta I = 3/2$ effects vanish. This was found by several authors[33], but has come to be called the Pati Woo theorem. It comes about due to the color symmetry of the Hamiltonian. There is a Fierz identity for the Dirac γ matrices

$$[\gamma_\mu(1+\gamma_5)]_{\alpha\beta}[\gamma^\mu(1+\gamma_5)]_{\gamma\delta} = [\gamma_\mu(1+\gamma_5)]_{\alpha\delta}[\gamma^\mu(1+\gamma_5)]_{\gamma\beta} \qquad 54)$$

which allows the $\Delta I = 3/2$ operator O_4 to be written as

$$O_4 = (\delta_{ij}\delta_{k\ell} + \delta_{i\ell}\delta_{kj})[(\bar{d}_i u_j)_L(\bar{u}_k s_\ell)_L - \tfrac{1}{2}(\bar{d}_i d_j)_L(\bar{d}_k d_\ell)_L] \qquad 55)$$

where i,j,k,ℓ are colors. Note that it is symmetric under the interchange of $j \leftrightarrow \ell$ or $i \leftrightarrow k$. The external states are antisymmetric under color exchange of any two colors

$$|\Lambda> \sim \varepsilon^{j\ell m}\, u_j^+\, s_\ell^+\, d_m^+|0>\ . \qquad 56)$$

This feature of symmetric Hamiltonian and antisymmetric states forces the matrix elements to vanish

$$\langle B'|O_4|B\rangle = 0 \ . \qquad 57)$$

The result of these quark model calculations are then[31,32]

1) A $\Delta I = 1/2$ is obtained, as described in the preceding paragraph.
2) The magnitude works out well, without any adjustment of parameters. Nonleptonic dominance in hyperon decay emerges naturally from the quark model. This is true in both the bag model and harmonic oscillator models.
3) The SU(3) structure leaves something to be desired. When parameterized by SU(3) D and F coefficients experiment favors D/F = -.4, while theory requires D/F = -1. Perhaps we should be happy that this is not further off, but given how well the SU(3) behavior of g_1 and f_2 are predicted by the quark model, one could hope for better. (Penguin may help in this regard; see below.)

X. Nonleptonic Amplitudes for Mesons

Here we wish to calculate

$$\langle \pi|H_w|K\rangle$$

and relate it to $K \to 2\pi$, again with the temporary neglect of penguins. In this case, PCAC and SU(3) tells us that the $K \to 2\pi$ amplitudes have a very specific form, linear in the momentum squared, and this is used to relate $K \to \pi$ and $K \to 2\pi$. The results here are[31,32]:

1) There is no $\Delta I = 1/2$ rule. Color counting factors alone predict that

$$\frac{A(\Delta I=3/2)}{A(\Delta I=1/2)} = \frac{4C_4}{C_1} = .6 \qquad 58)$$

in a normalization where the experimental value of this ratio is 0.072 ± 0.002. We see that theory is far from correct. This result is very model independent, depending only on the construction of the mesons from $q\bar{q}$. The operators O_1 and O_4 have a common spin and space factor and differ only in their color quantum numbers. Arguments similar to those leading to the Pati Woo theorem then give the above result.
2) The resulting amplitudes are generally too small. The size of the $\Delta I = 3/2$ piece is roughly correct, but the $\Delta I = 1/2$ term is far too small. When combined with point 1), this suggests that we have correctly obtained the $\Delta I = 3/2$ matrix element, but are missing something in the $\Delta I = 1/2$ sector (penguin?).
3) The calculations are generally not reliable. For example, in the bag model, the matrix element involves large cancellations between the effects of the upper and lower components of the wavefunctions. Reasonably small changes in the parameters lead to sizable changes in the matrix elements. This feature is related to the "helicity suppression" mechanism mentioned earlier in that $q\bar{q}$ coupling to the axial vector current is suppressed. Even in models where the stability under parameter change is less, the reliability is doubtful because of this feature.

We see that our understanding of kaon decay (neglecting penguin) is poor.

XI. An Aside on Vacuum Insertion and Quark Masses

Another standard way to evaluate matrix elements which is widely employed in the literature is "vacuum insertion". For example, one would evaluate

$$\begin{aligned} &<\pi^+|\bar{d}\gamma_\mu(1+\gamma_5)u\ \bar{u}\gamma^\mu(1+\gamma_5)s|K^+> \\ &= <\pi^+|\bar{d}\gamma_\mu\gamma_5 u|0><0|\bar{u}\gamma^\mu\gamma_5 s|K^+> \\ &= f_\pi f_k p\cdot k \end{aligned} \tag{59}$$

by keeping only the vacuum state. This method is not as dissimilar from the quark model calculations as it might seem. Both always yield the same relative rates (i.e. the Clebsch Gordon coefficient is the same). Likewise the rough magnitude is similar. In fact in nonrelativistic models, the two methods are identical in theory. They differ in result because of an inability to calculate f_π. The methods are distinct for relativistic quarks.

However vacuum insertion also shares a drawback with quark model calculations for (V-A)(V-A) products - both are unreliable. Again the helicity suppression enters, through f_π and f_K. This says that corrections should be large, as indeed they are found to be.[34] I know of no reliable method for calculation of (V-A)(V-A) matrix elements. The best one can do is to take their value from experiment[35].

In the case of scalar and pseudoscalar densities (which are relevant in the next section) there is no helicity suppression. Here the vacuum insertion method uses the quark equations of motion to get[29]

$$\begin{aligned} &<\pi^+|\bar{d}(1+\gamma_5)u\ \bar{u}(1-\gamma_5)s|K^+> \\ &= -<\pi^+|\bar{d}\gamma_5 d|0><0|\bar{u}\gamma_5 s|K^+> \\ &= -f_\pi f_k \frac{m_\pi^2}{m_u+m_d}\frac{m_k^2}{m_s+m_u}\ . \end{aligned} \tag{60}$$

Use of current algebra masses leads to a sizable matrix element. Although it is common to refer to this as a large matrix element, it is actually rather standard in size. Rather it is the (V-A)(V-A) amplitude which is small. This is born out in direct quark model calculations. The overlaps have no cancellations, and a result is obtained which roughly agrees in magnitude with vacuum insertion, within the uncertainty of size of the quark masses.

The question of the appropriate quark mass is a subtle one. There are many ways to define a mass, and many different scales to evaluate it at. We are interested in one which is valid at hadronic scales in matrix elements such as above. I will argue that this requires a modification of the usual estimate $m_s = 150$ MeV and m_u, $m_d \sim 7$ MeV. To see this consider Weinberg's arguments[36] which lead to $m_s = 150$ MeV. He notes that mass splittings are due to the mass terms in the Lagrangian

$$L_m = m_s \bar{s}s + m_u \bar{u}u + m_d \bar{d}d \ . \tag{61}$$

Since the u and d masses are small, $\Delta S=1$ mass differences are dominated by the strange quark mass, and to the extent that nucleons have no strange quarks

$$M_\Lambda - M_N \approx \langle\Lambda|m_s \bar{s}s|\Lambda\rangle \ . \tag{62}$$

The physical quantity depends both on the mass and the scalar matrix element. Defining

$$\langle\Lambda|\bar{s}s|\Lambda\rangle \equiv Z \tag{63}$$

and introducing a <u>different</u> mass $m_s^* \equiv m_s Z$, Weinberg estimates

$$m_s^* \approx 150 \text{ MeV} \ . \tag{64}$$

However it is not m_s^* which enters into the vacuum insertion matrix element. To obtain that mass at the hadronic scale one must know the scalar matrix element Z

$$m_s = \frac{m_s^*}{Z} \ . \tag{65}$$

This was first calculated by Adler et al.[37] in the bag model, with the result

$$Z \approx 1/2 \ . \tag{66}$$

Therefore the appropriate mass for hadronic matrix elements is

$$m_s \approx 300 \text{ MeV} \ . \tag{67}$$

Note that this prescription reduces the PP matrix elements, Eq. 60, by a factor of Z^2 over the usual Z=1 prescription.

I would also like to note a more direct measure of the average up and down masses which, unlike the standard method (yielding $m^*_{u,d} \approx 7$ MeV, $m_{u,d} = \frac{m^*_{u,d}}{Z}$ 14 MeV) does not rely on chiral SU(3) x SU(3) but only on SU(2) x SU(2). This is the πN sigma term, defined by

$$[F_i^5, \partial_\mu A_j^\mu] = \delta_{ij}\sigma \ . \tag{68}$$

In QCD

$$\begin{aligned}\sigma &= m_u \bar{u}u + m_d \bar{d}d \\ &= m_q(\bar{u}u + \bar{d}d) \ .\end{aligned} \tag{69}$$

For the matrix element of σ one obtains[11]

$$\langle p|\sigma|p\rangle = 3m_q Z = 3m_q^* \ . \tag{70}$$

Measurements of $\langle\sigma\rangle$ from πN scattering indicate

$$\langle\sigma\rangle = 51 \pm 12 \text{ MeV} \tag{71}$$

which yields

$$m_q^* \approx 17 \text{ MeV} \qquad 72)$$

and if Z = 1/2

$$m_q \approx 34 \text{ MeV} . \qquad 73)$$

This is somewhat higher than the "standard" value, but may be more reliable because it uses chiral SU(2).

Above I have been trying to extract the current algebra masses at the hadronic scale. As G. Ross reminded me, one can sometimes use the running mass to reduce the dependence of a calculation on the scale parameter.[38]

XII. Penguins

The most important addition to the nonleptonic interactions which we have been discussing thus far is the "penguin" interaction, first brought to light by Shifman Vainshtein and Zakharov[29]. The lowest order diagram is depicted in Fig. 1c of Section VII. If calculated directly this yields a local operator

$$H_p = \frac{G_F}{\sqrt{2}} \cos\theta_1 \sin\theta_1 \cos\theta_3 \frac{\alpha_s}{6\pi} \ell n\, m^2/\mu^2\, \bar{d}_L \gamma_\mu \lambda^A s_L \bar{Q}\gamma^\mu \lambda^A Q . \qquad 74)$$

Use of the renormalization group leads to the form previously given in Eq. 47 with $c_5 = .06$ at $\mu = 1$ GeV. This effect only turns on at scales below the charm quark mass, where the charm-up cancellation in the loop from the GIM mechanism breaks down. However, this leads to a coefficient that grows rapidly with decreasing scale, and at scales below 1 GeV (approx.) we would expect the local nature of the operator to change.

The effect of penguins have been studied in weak processes[29,31,32,38]. The consenses seems to be: 1) If the coefficient c_5 is trusted at a believable scale ($\mu = 1$ GeV), then the effect of the penguins is too small to explain the $\Delta I = 1/2$ rule in kaons. The matrix element of O_5 is reasonably large and purely $\Delta I = 1/2$, but c_5 is just too small. 2) If c_5 is treated as a free parameter (to compensate for the low momentum uncertainties), the theory works well for $c_5 \approx .3$. In kaons the overall magnitude and the $\Delta I = 1/2$ rule can be made to work. In baryons, the inclusion of penguins fixes the problem with the SU(3) structure.

At this point, the reader is left to choose among these two results.

XIII. "Galić's Complaint"

H. Galić[39] has pointed out a feature of the QCD renormalization procedure which bears on the use of quark models in calculating matrix elements. He notes that in heavy quark systems the use of the short distance and heavy quark expansion would factorize any dependence on soft gluons into the quark wavefunctions, and would leave a local operator to be evaluated using that wavefunction. However, he notes that for light quarks such a factoriction is not possible. Soft gluon processes such as Fig. 2a (which in the soft pion limit goes into Fig. 2b) are not suppressed by factors of heavy quark or W masses and this simple factorization is spoiled. Certainly such soft gluon processes have not been taken into account. In the next section, I propose that it is feasible to do so.

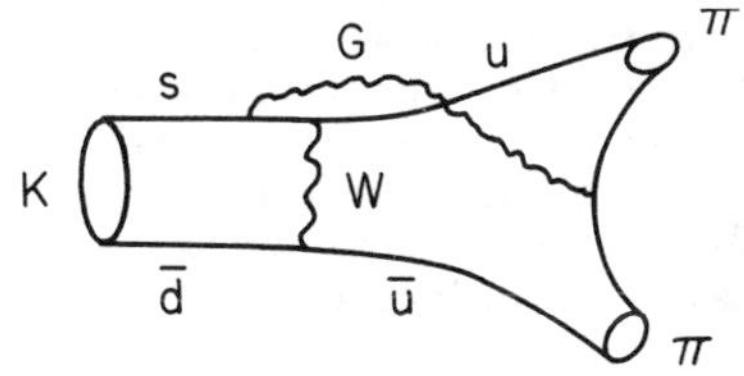

(a)

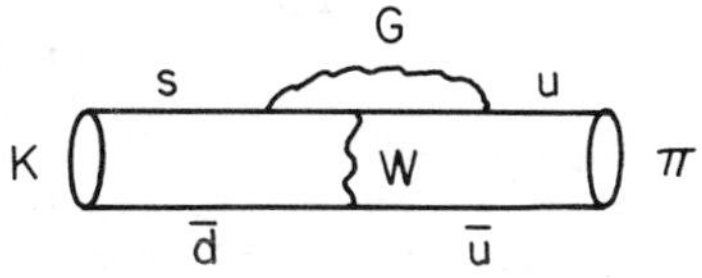

(b)

XIV. A Possible Resolution and Future Direction

Both the troubles with the penguin operator and the comments of Galić point to the importance of low energy effects of gluons. Not all gluonic effects have been taken into account by the renormalization group. I feel that the way to proceed in light of this is to:

1) Use the renormalization group to provide H_W at some scale $\mu = \mu_o$ where μ_o is $1 \to 2$ GeV and is chosen to be high enough that soft gluonic effects are not too important. Then
2) Include in the matrix elements, all intermediate states up to $p \sim \mu_o$.

This procedure means that we cannot just calculate the hadronic matrix elements by using just quark wavefunctions as given in simple quark models. Rather one must include the effects of interactions, such as Fig. 1c or 2b, in the matrix element also. This requires the use of bound state perturbation theory, which, in the bag model at least, has been developed to a point where it is possible to actually carry out this program.

I think that I know what to expect from the result, and have done portions of the calculations. For the renormalization of the usual type of four-fermion vertex, Fig. 2b, the soft gluons will somewhat modify the numerical results of previous efforts. However, the results as I presented them in Sec. X above were general enough that they are unlikely to be modified. We will still have a $\Delta I = 1/2$ rule and D/F = -1 in baryons and no $\Delta I = 1/2$ rule in kaons. It is in the application to the penguin diagram, Fig. 1c, which should prove the most interesting. Since perturbatively this is strongest at low momentum the "low energy penguin" evaluation should be large. In particular there is no small coefficient to worry about because in this approach the diagram is generated from the operator O_1 which has coefficient $c_1 \approx 2.5$. In the days before SVZ and penguins, E. Golowich and I calculated what is essentially this diagram under the phrase "quark sea" contribution[40]. We did find a large result, large enough to reproduce the $\Delta I = 1/2$ amplitude in kaons and also explain the D/F ratio in baryons. Work is in progress to attempt to do the full $O(\alpha_s)$ corrections needed to carry out this program in the bag model.

XV. Parity Violation in Nuclear Physics

Another low energy application of the SU(2) x U(1) weak interaction theory is in the study of parity violation in nuclear physics. This is a field with a long history and a considerable amount of experimental activity. In the early days of the subject, the motivation was to use nuclear parity violation to uncover the structure of the weak interaction, such as neutral currents. Now, however, the direction of information flow is reversed. We know the neutral currents and want to study $\Delta S=0$ processes as a test of our understanding of non-leptonic interactions.

The parity violating nucleon-nucleon force is described by the exchange of mesons, as in Fig. 3, where one vertex is strong and the other is weak and violates parity. To describe this one needs the $NN\pi$, $NN\rho$, $NN\omega$, etc. couplings. These are governed by similar physics as hyperon decay such as $\Lambda \to N\pi$, but differ in that the weak neutral enters into the $\Delta S=0$ interactions. Those couplings with vector mesons also bring in new physics.

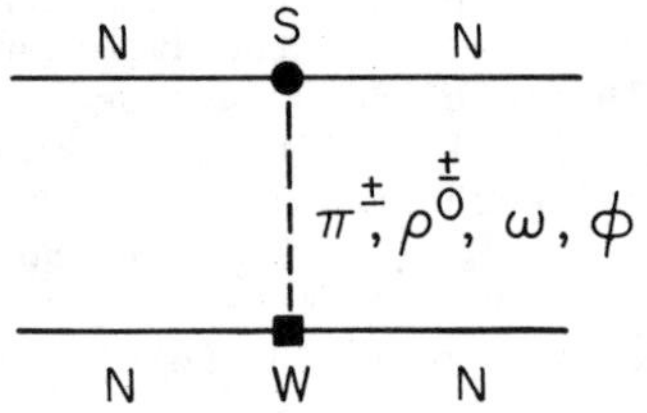

There has been a good deal of theoretical work on these couplings, using SU(3), SU(6) and direct quark model calculations[41-47]. The results have been summarized in ref. 47 (DDH) and the uncertainties studied. A reasonable range of values were given along with a "best" set which were formulated using the present theoretical prejudices. This "best" set has served as a benchmark for comparison of theory and experiment and has been fairly successful.

There have been many fine experiments in this field. One should be aware that most of the effects measured are expected to be of the size of 10^{-5} in order to appreciate the job which has been done. Unfortunately, for many of the systems which have been studied, the nuclear physics aspects of the calculation cannot be done reliably, and the comparison between theory and experiment is rather uncertain. However there has recently been some nice and believable work[48], both experimentally and theoretically, on systems near mass 20 and some other systems. These then form a significant test of the theory. The results are

System	Experiment	"Best value" Prediction
^{18}F	$P_\gamma = (-0.7 \pm 2.0) \times 10^{-3}$	$P_\gamma = -2.1 \times 10^{-3}$

^{19}F	$A_\gamma = -(8.5 \pm 2.6) \times 10^{-5}$	$A_\gamma = -13 \times 10^{-5}$	
$^{21}N_o$	$P_\gamma = (0.9 \pm 5.1) \times 10^{-3}$	$P_\gamma = 9.9 \times 10^{-3}$	75)
pp(15 MeV)	$A = -(1.7 \pm .85) \times 10^{-7}$	$A = -1.5 \times 10^{-7}$	

The values are in rough agreement. This is a more stringent test than it seems, since such agreement cannot be obtained for much of the "allowable range of the parameters in Ref. 47.

One system where theory and experiment seem not to agree is the asymmetry in p - H_2O scattering at 6 GeV for which the experimental value is[49]

$$A = 3 \times 10^{-6} . \qquad 76)$$

All calculations based on meson exchange[50] seem to obtain $A \sim$ few x 10^{-7}. Nardulli and Preparata[51] claimed to be able to reproduce the asymmetry by a parity violating "wavefunction" effect. However this explanation has been shown to be incorrect because it produces effects in the systems listed above which are one to two orders of magnitude too large[52]. It is plausible that the explanation is that the meson exchange calculations should not be applicable at 6 GeV. Goldman and Preston[53] have explored a direct quark model calculation of the asymmetry, and do find a value of $A \sim 10^{-6}$. However, their most important terms look somewhat similar to the Nardulli-Preparata wavefunction effects, and one wonders if they would also run into trouble with other systems. A safe conclusion about the p - H_2O data is that more work is needed before a good understanding of the theory is obtained.

XVI. Hypernuclear Decay

One would think that, after all these years of studying the weak interactions, that all the possible areas would have been looked at. However, there is a new field in low energy weak interactions which is just opening up - hypernuclear decay. Of course there have been many studies of hypernuclei. However, they have been primarily aimed at uncovering the ΛN force, and generally overlook the $\Delta S=1$ processes which destroy the hypernucleus. New experiments should now be able to look at these effects, and will learn about new features of non-leptonic processes.

There are two main processes which modify the Λ lifetime when one puts it in a nucleus. It can still decay in the usual way, $\Lambda \to p\pi$, but the proton comes out with very little energy (KE $\sim$ 5 MeV), which is below the Fermi level in most nuclei. Therefore this transition will be very highly suppressed, a phenomena referred to as "Pauli blocking", resulting in a much longer lifetime. However, there is also the possibility of a "nonmesonic" transition

$$\Lambda + N \to N + N .$$

In this case the nucleon is much more energetic (KE $\sim$ 90 MeV) such that the nonmesonic process proceeds without Pauli blocking. This increases the rate and lowers the lifetime.

These features, and the general framework for studying them, have been spelled out by Dalitz and his collaborators.[54] The nonmesonic transitions can be described via meson exchange as in the figure, leading to definite forms for the interaction

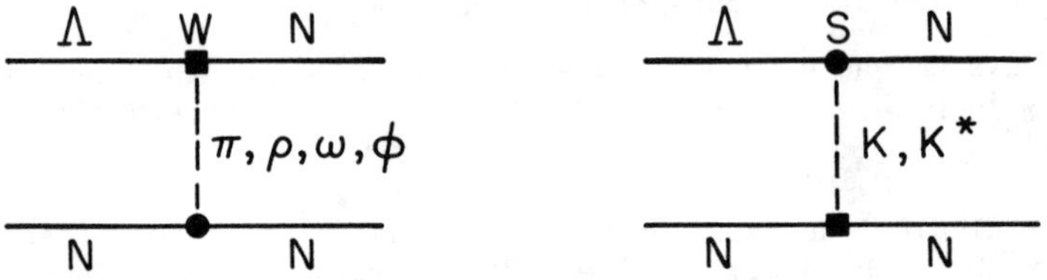

Note that new types of interactions enter, such as a NNK vertex. Earlier work[54] by J. Barkley Adams suggested that the nonmesonic process was unimportant

$$\frac{\Gamma(\Lambda_{\text{NUCLEAR MATTER}})}{\Gamma(\Lambda_{\text{FREE}})} \approx 0.05 \quad , \tag{77}$$

a result that also shows the dramatic effect of Pauli blocking. The study of these questions has been reopened recently, using our improved knowledge of nonleptonic processes. The relevant couplings have been calculated and progress is being made on the nuclear physics aspects of the theory[55]. Our preliminary indications are that Adams was incorrect. A full calculation in nuclear matter gives

$$\frac{\Gamma(\Lambda_{\text{NUCLEAR MATTER}})}{\Gamma(\Lambda_{\text{FREE}})} \gtrsim 1 \ . \tag{78}$$

The nonmesonic process is important. At present the only data is on $^{16}O_\Lambda$

$$\frac{\Gamma(^{16}O_\Lambda)}{\Gamma(\Lambda_{\text{FREE}})} = 3 \pm 1 \tag{79}$$

which also suggests the importance of the nonmesonic transition. Future experiments will be of higher statistics and should allow study of more detailed features.

XVII. Summary

We can see that considerable progress has been made in understanding the structure of the low energy weak interactions of hadrons within the $SU(2)_L \times U(1)$ model. Many of the weak properties can be calculated from the weak currents of quarks through symmetries and the quark model. The techniques thus developed can be, and often have been, extended to try to uncover the effects of new interactions which are being proposed as extensions of the standard model (RHC, GUTS, supersymmetry ...). However, even within the standard model there are features which need to be better understood. Future work will undoubtedly be done on this dual goal: clarifying the known interactions and searching for new effects.

Acknowledgment

I would like to thank my Yugoslav hosts for their hospitality at this meeting. Many of them have played an important role in the studies described above, and almost any member of the local organizing committee would be as qualified as I to give this talk.

References

1] Review of Particle Properties, M. Roos et al., Physics Letters 111B (1982)
2] A. Chodos, R.L. Jaffe, K. Johnson, C. Thorn and V. Weisskopf, Phys. Rev. D9, 3471 (1974)
3] T. DeGrand, R.L. Jaffe, K. Johnson and J. Kiskis, Phys. Rev. D12, 2060 (1975)
4] J.F. Donoghue and K. Johnson, Phys. Rev. D21, 1975 (1980)
5] K. Johnson, Phys. Lett. 78B, 259 (1978)
6] N. Isgur and G. Karl, Phys. Rev. D20, 1191 (1979)
7] J.F. Donoghue and G. Karl, Phys. Rev. D24, 230 (1981)
8] D. Tadić and J. Trampetić, Rudjer Boshovic preprint 1983
9] N. Isgur and C. Hyne, Toronto preprint 1983
10] Theory of Weak Interactions in Particle Physics, R.E. Marshak, Riazuddin and C.P. Ryan (Wiley, New York, 1969)
11] J.F. Donoghue, E. Golowich and B.R. Holstein, Phys. Rev. D12, 2875 (1975)
12] S.L. Adler, Phys. Rev. Lett. 14, 1051 (1965); Phys. Rev. 140, B736 (1965)
W.I. Weisberger, Phys. Rev. Lett. 14, 1047 (1965); Phys. Rev. 143, 1302 (1966)
13] P.N. Bogoliubov, Ann. Inst. Henri Poincare 8, 163 (1968); A. Le Yaouaue, L. Oliver, O. Penè and J.C. Raynal, Phys. Rev. D9, 2636 (1974); A. Chodos, R.L. Jaffe, K. Johnson and C.B. Thorn, Phys. Rev. D10, 2599 (1974); J.F. Donoghue et al., Ref. 11; M. Ruiz, Phys. Rev. D12, 2922 (1975).
14] J.F. Donoghue and D. Wyler, Phys. Rev. D17, 280 (1978); M.B. Gavela, A. Le Yaouane, L. Oliver, O. Penè and J.C. Raynal, Orsay preprint 1982.
15] J.F. Donoghue and B.R. Holstein, Phys. Rev. D25, 206 (1982); A. Halprin, B.W. Lee, and P. Sorba, Phys. Rev. D14, 2343 (1976).
16] B.R. Holstein, Phys. Rev. D26, 698 (1982)
17] R. van Royen, V. Weisskopf, Nuovo Cimento 50, 617 (1967)
18] D. Jensen, private communication
19] A. Garcia and P. Kielanowski, Physics Letters, to be published
20] J. Wise et al., Phys. Lett. 91B, 165 (1980); ibid 98B, 123 (1981)
21] M. Bourquin et al., Proceedings of the 1981 Lisbon Conference, LAL 81/18 and Z. Phys. C12, 307 (1982)

22] J.F. Donoghue and B.R. Holstein, Phys. Rev. D25, 2015 (1982)
23] A. Garcia and P. Kielanowski, Phys. Lett. 110B, 498 (1982)
24] A. Sirlin, Rev. Mod. Phys. 50, 576 (1978)
25] A. Garcia, Phys. Rev. D25, 1348 (1982)
26] P. Keller et al., Phys. Rev. Lett. 48, 971 (1982)
27] T. Oka, Phys. Rev. Lett. 50, 1423 (1983)
28] M.K. Gaillard and B.W. Lee, Phys. Rev. Lett. 33, 108 (1974); G. Altarelli and L. Maiani, Phys. Lett. 52B, 351 (1974)
29] M.A. Shifman, A.I. Vainshtein and V.J. Zakharov, Nucl. Phys. B120, 315 (1977)
30] C. Bouchiat and Ph. Meyer, Phys. Lett. 25B, 282 (1967); Y. Nambu and Y. Hara, Phys. Rev. Lett. 16, 875 (1967); B.R. Holstein, Phys. Rev. 183, 1228 (1969)
31] J.F. Donoghue, E. Golowich, and B.R. Holstein, Ref. 11; J.F. Donoghue and E. Golowich, Phys. Rev. D14, 1326 (1976); J.F. Donoghue, E. Golowich, W. Ponce and B.R. Holstein, Phys. Rev. D21, 186 (1980)
32] H. Galić, D. Tadić and J. Trampetić, Nucl. Phys. B158, 306 (1979); Phys. Lett. 89B, 249 (1980); D. Tadić and J. Trampetić, Nucl. Phys. B171, 471 (1980); Phys. Rev. D23, 144 (1981); M. Mieosevic, D. Tadić and J. Trampetić, Nucl. Phys. B187, 514 (1981); P. Colić, J. Trampetić and D. Tadić, Phys. Rev. D26, 2286 (1982)
33] J. Pati and C. Woo, Phys. Rev. D3, 2920 (1971); K. Muira and T. Minamikawa, Prog. Theor. Phys. 38, 954 (1967); J.G. Körner, Nucl. Phys. B25, 282 (1970)
34] S.B. Treiman and R. Schrock, Phys. Rev. D19, 2148 (1978)
35] J.F. Donoghue, E. Golowich and B.R. Holstein, Phys. Lett. 119B, 412 (1982)
36] S. Weinberg, in I.I. Rabi Festschrift (Academy of Sciences, New York, 1978)
37] S. Adler, E. Colglazer, J. Healy, I. Karlinger, J. Lieberman, Y.J. Ng and H.S. Tsao, Phys. Rev. D11, 3522 (1975)
38] G. Hill and G. Ross, Nucl. Phys. B171, 141 (1980)
39] H. Galić, Stanford Linear Accelerator Center preprint (1982)
40] J.F. Donoghue and E. Golowich, Phys. Lett. 69B, 437 (1977)
41] F.C. Michal, Phys. Rev. B133, 329 (1964); E. Fishchbach and D. Tadić, Phys. Rep. C6, 125 (1973)
42] E. Fischbach, D. Tadić and K. Trabert, Phys. Rev. 186, 1688 (1979)
43] B.H.J. McKellar and P. Peck, Phys. Rev. D6, 2184 (1972)
44] J.F. Donoghue, Phys. Rev. D13, 2064 (1976)
45] H. Galić, B. Guberina and D. Tadić, Phys. Rev. D14, 2327 (1976)
46] B. Desplanques and J. Micheli, Phys. Lett. 68B, 339 (1977)
47] B. Desplanques, J.F. Donoghue and B.R. Holstein, Ann. Phys. 124, 449 (1980)
48] This is reviewed in E. Adelberger et al., Los Alamos preprint LA-UR-83-401
49] N. Lockyer, Phys. Rev. Lett. 44, 699 (1980)
50] A. Barroso, this conference
51] G. Nardulli and G. Preparata, Phys. Lett. 117B, 445 (1982)
52] J.F. Donoghue and B.R. Holstein, Univ. of Mass. preprint UMHEP-180 (to be published in Phys. Lett.)

53] T. Goldman and D. Preston, LA-UR-1285 (1982)
54] K.J. Nield et al., Phys. Rev. C13, 1263 (1976); J. Barkley Adams, Phys. Rev. 156, 1617 (1967)
55] L. De la Torre, J.F. Donoghue, J.F. Dubach and B.R. Holstein (in preparation)

Discussion

J.O. Eeg: When you calculate nonleptonic decays within the bag model, how much of the uncertainties do you think is due to soft pion techniques and how much is due to bag model matrix elements?

Donoghue: Certainly I feel that the use of PCAC is much more reliable than any quark model, especially in the case of kaon decay. The success of PCAC in relating $K \to 3\pi$ to $K \to 2\pi$ in great detail is more than a quark model could hope to do. Quark models are best in cases where the number of particles does not change, such as $\Lambda \to N$ or $K \to \pi$. I advocate using PCAC to turn physical amplitudes into these before applying the quark model.

J.O. Eeg: In connection with the question raised by H. Galić on how reliable the standard techniques are - did I understand you right that, in order to improve the techniques, you would calculate, for instance, the penguin loop diagram inside the bag such that the quarks in the loop feel the confinement?

Donoghue: Yes. Techniques to do this are now available and their use would answer some of the questions about the low energy behavior of these diagrams.

G. Ross: In calculating the penguin coefficient at a scale μ^2 it is important to remember that the operator is also to be calculated at the same scale μ^2. I believe the ratio $C_p(\mu^2)/m_q(\mu^2)$ is relatively insensitive to the scale, so that the overall estimate of the penguin contribution does not depend sensitively on μ^2.

Donoghue: Thank you for reminding me of this and I have included this in Sec. XII. This type of estimate also suggests that the effect of the penguin is small. There still remains the question of the low energy behavior of the penguin diagram, which is not accessible through the perturbative calculation.

G. Senjanović: You have argued in favor of different values of quark masses from the conventionally assumed ones but it appears that the ratio m_d/m_s is not much changed.

Donoghue: That is correct. The ratio is not sensitive to the manipulation which go into determining the absolute value of the masses. To the extent that the values in the text (Eqs. 67,73) differ in ratio from the usual one obtained from the pseudoscalar masses, this could be blamed on the use of SU(3) x SU(3) in the latter case rather than SU(2) x SU(2) in Eq. 73.

E. Fischbach: I would like to comment on your remarks concerning "RAW DATA". In our analysis of the Fermilab data on the $K^o - \bar{K}^o$ system, we studied all the relevant papers describing earlier experiments at low energy. We found that many of these papers were useless because the data presented were too highly "processed". For example, some papers quoted values for the regeneration phase ϕ_{21} for some assumed values of the weak interaction parameters, without telling you how their results would change when the weak parameters changed - which they did. An exception was the very nice paper of Birulev, *et al*. I feel that is important for experimentalists to be encouraged (perhaps by the journals and their editors) to publish their results in the least "processed" manner possible.

PARITY VIOLATION IN PROTON-PROTON SCATTERING

Augusto Barroso *)

CERN
CH - 1211 Geneva 23
Switzerland

ABSTRACT

The present situation regarding the parity violation in p-p scattering is briefly reviewed. Particular attention is paid to the models used in the calculation of the asymmetry at high energies.

In this talk I would like to summarize the present situation regarding parity-violation in p-p scattering. The existing experimental results at low energy[1),2)] are well described in terms of a weak meson exchange potential[3)] which also explains other nuclear physics parity violating experiments [see Ref. 4) for a review]. Furthermore, the so-called Desplanques-Donoghue-Holstein (DDH)[3)] best values of the effective nucleon-meson weak couplings are in reasonable agreement with theoretical calculations based on the standard weak model including QCD corrections [e.g., Ref. 5)].

If $\sigma_\pm$ denote the total cross-section associated with each helicity state of the polarized incoming proton, the information about the weak interaction is contained in the asymmetry,

$$A = \frac{\sigma_+ - \sigma_-}{\sigma_+ + \sigma_-} \; . \tag{1}$$

At low energies, i.e., below the inelastic threshold, one can either solve the two-body scattering problem exactly or one can use a distorted wave Born approximation. As I said before, the calculations are in good agreement with the data [e.g., Ref. 6)].

Let me describe briefly a naive model which despite its simplicity does remarkably well. Consider the strong helicity amplitude $\phi_1 = \langle ++|T_S|++\rangle$. Adding to ϕ_1 the weak Born contribution ψ_1 derived[6),7)] from an effective meson-nucleon Lagrangian, it is easy to see[6)] that the elastic asymmetry A_{el} is

$$A_{el} = \frac{1}{2\sigma_{el}} \frac{\pi}{\bar{k}^2} \,\mathrm{Re}[\phi_1(t=0)] \int_{-4\bar{k}^2}^{0} dt\, \psi_1(t)\exp[\tfrac{1}{2}\gamma t], \tag{2}$$

where $\bar{k}$ is the c.m. momentum and γ is the slope parameter of the differential cross-section $d\sigma/dt$. By a dispersion relation analysis of the scattering data the values of ϕ_1 at $t = 0$ can be obtained[8)]. Using these and $\gamma = 1$ GeV^{-2}, one obtains A_{el}, as a function of the proton

---

*) Permanent address: CFN, Universidade de Lisboa, Portugal.

lab. kinetic energy T_L. This is shown in Fig. 1. Besides the reasonable agreement with the data, notice that the results do not depend crucially on the value of γ. On the contrary, for γ in the range $0.5\ GeV^{-2} \leq \gamma \leq 1.5\ GeV^{-2}$ the variation of A_{el} is less than 2%.

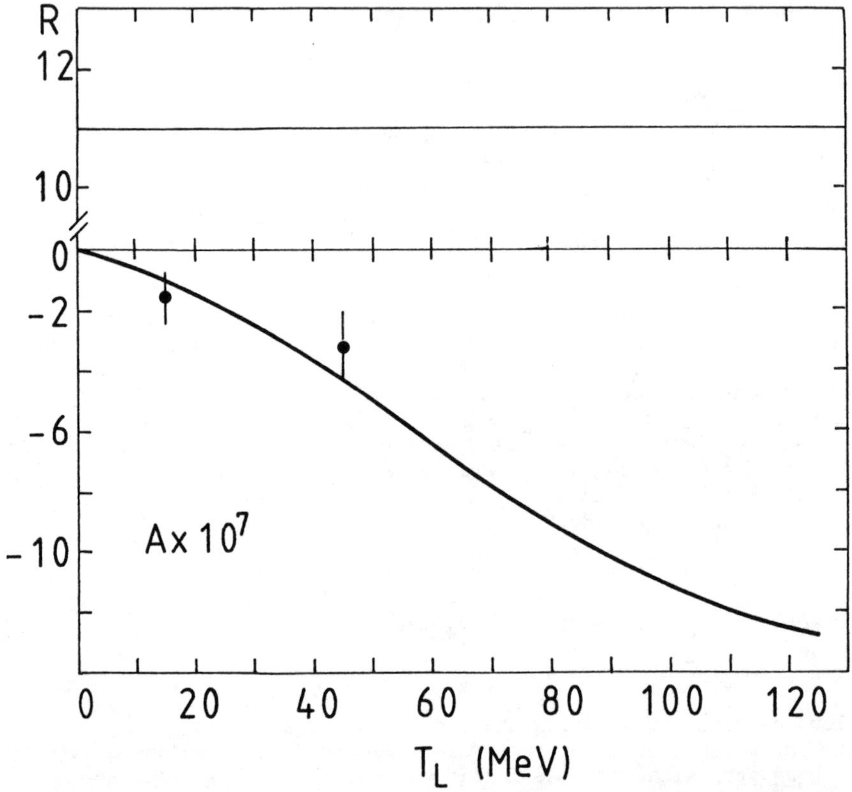

Fig. 1 : Elastic asymmetry in p-p as a function of the proton lab. kinetic energy.

Let me now turn to the high energy region where a recent measurement[9] of A using a water target prompted several calculations[7),10)-13] of this effect. In the pioneer work of Henley and Krejs[10], as well as in some of the recent ones[7),11], the starting point is the calculation of the weak Born helicity amplitudes. The strong distortion is included using two basic approaches. In the first one, for each partial wave, one makes the S matrix unitary. In the second approach, the partial wave series is converted into an integral over the impact parameter b and the Born amplitudes are multiplied by $\exp[i\chi(b)]$ where $\chi(b)$ is the eikonal phase shift. The comparison between these two techniques was made before[6] and so there is no need to be repeated here. I just want to point out that both methods predict, at $p_L = 6$ GeV/c, values of A at least an order of magnitude smaller than the experimental result[9]. Notice also that in the work of Tadić and myself[7], the neutron contribution was calculated and the two-pion exchange diagram was included. Adding coherently the proton and neutron contributions our revised[6] result for water is $A = 3 \times 10^{-8}$ where at the same energy the Argonne experiment[9] gives $(3.66 \pm 0.64) \times 10^{-6}$.

In the work of Nardulli and Preparata[12], the scattering amplitude f which describes the high energy elastic scattering of a polarized nucleon off an unpolarized one is written

$$f = \bar{u}(p') A(s,t)\gamma^{\mu}(1 + \varepsilon\gamma_5) (p + p')_{\mu} u(p). \tag{3}$$

A(s,t) is the pomeron amplitude and the ε parameter is a measure of the parity impurity in the nucleon wave function. From Eq. (3) it is straightforward to obtain

$$A = \frac{|\bar{p}_L|}{E_L} \varepsilon . \tag{4}$$

With their calculated value of ε they[12] predicted $A = 2.13 \times 10^{-6}$ at $p_L = 6$ GeV/c.

It is easy to see that, given an effective parity conserving meson-nucleon Lagrangian, the introduction of a parity admixture into the nucleon field N amounts to the transformation

$$N \to N' = (1 + \varepsilon\gamma_5)N.$$

This, in turn, generates an effective parity violating Lagrangian, $\mathcal{L}^{PV}$. Then, using this $\mathcal{L}^{PV}$ and the model that I described previously I calculated the asymmetry in the low energy region. In the upper part of Fig. 1, I show the ratio R between the asymmetry A_{el} calculated in this way and the one predicted on the basis of DDH[3] weak couplings. R is within 1% constant and equal to 11 which means that the calculation of Nardulli and Preparata[12] overestimates A_{el} by an order of magnitude. Recently, Donoghue and Holstein[14] have also used the same model to re-analyze some well established cases of parity-violation in nuclear physics. They[14] concluded that the values of ε predicted by Nardulli and Preparata[12] always overestimate the experimental results by, at least, an order of magnitude. For instance, in ^{21}Ne the polarization P_γ of the 2.789 MeV γ-ray turned out to be $P_\gamma = 0.18$ whereas the experiment[15] gives $(0.9 \pm 5.1) \times 10^{-3}$.

Since we now have another scattering experiment[16] done at p_L = 1.5 GeV/c and using the same target, one can test this model in a different way. From Eq. (4), one obtains A(1.5 GeV/c)/A(6 GeV/c) = 0.86. On the other hand, the experiments[9],[16] give $R \leq 0.55$ at 90% C.L.

It is fair to say that another calculation[17)] of A(15 MeV) using the Nardulli-Preparata model only overestimates the experimental value by a factor of three and not 11 as I have shown. The reason for this lies in their[17)] use of a very large value for the weak pion-nucleon coupling constant f_π. Their[17)] value $f_\pi = 13.5 \times 10^{-6}$ causes that the two pion contribution cancels partially the ρ and ω exchange terms. However, it is known, both from semi-empirical analysis of nuclear physics data and from theoretical calculations that the value of f_π must be a factor of 20 smaller than the number quoted above. I do not have time to go into a detailed discussion of this point[*)] but let me just mention that a recent calculation[18)] in the framework of the standard weak model including QCD corrections gives $f_\pi = 0.3 \times 10^{-6}$ in very good agreement with the SU(6) analyses[3)].

Finally, let me refer to the work of Goldman and Preston[13)]. They attempted to calculate A using a quark model, i.e., the weak amplitude was given by W and Z exchange between quarks and the strong interaction amplitude was described by one gluon exchange. Besides the tree diagrams they also include one loop corrections. At the Argonne energy they predicted $A \approx -10^{-7}$ which has even the wrong sign. Perhaps not surprisingly, given the drastic assumption in the description of the strong amplitude. Only calling upon the same mechanism of nucleon wave function admixture could they[13)] claim agreement with the data.

In conclusion, I would say that the only model[12)] that claims to explain the Argonne result[**)9)] is in serious difficulty to accommodate all experimental data on low energy parity non-conservation. On the other hand, the Los Alamos result[16)] can be understood on the basis of the conventional calculations[6),12)]. Clearly further experimental and theoretical work is needed to clarify this situation.

---

*) See B.H.J. McKellar, University of Melbourne preprint, May 1983.

**) A large A can result from the decay of longitudinally polarized hyperons. However, in Ref. 9) it is claimed that this effect was eliminated.

REFERENCES

1) J.M. Potter et al., Phys. Rev. Lett. 33 (1974) 1307.

2) R. Balzer et al., Phys. Rev. Lett. 44 (1980) 699.

3) B. Desplanques, J.F. Donoghue and B.R. Holstein, Ann. Phys. (N.Y.) 124 (1980) 445.

4) B. Desplanques in Proc. 8th Int. Workshop on Weak Interactions and Neutrinos, ed. A. Morales, World Sci. Publ. Co. (1983).

5) H. Galić, B. Guberina and D. Tadić, Forts. der Physik 29 (1981) 261.

6) A. Barroso in Proc. 8th Int. Workshop on Weak Interactions and Neutrinos, ed. A. Morales, World Sci. Publ. Co. (1983).

7) A. Barroso and D. Tadić, Nucl. Phys. B364 (1981) 194.

8) W. Grein and P. Kroll, Nucl. Phys. B377 (1982) 505.

9) M. Lockyer et al., Phys. Rev. Lett. 45 (1980) 1821.

10) E.M. Henley and F.R. Krejs, Phys. Rev. D11 (1975) 605.

11) T. Oka, Prog. Theor. Phys. 66 (1981) 977.

12) G. Nardulli and G. Preparata, Phys. Lett. 117B (1982) 445.

13) T. Goldman and D. Preston, Los Alamos preprint, LA-UR82-2777 (1982).

14) J.F. Donoghue and B.R. Holstein, University of Massachusetts preprint UMHEP-180 (1983).

15) K.A. Snover et al., Phys. Rev. Lett. 41 (1978) 145.

16) D.E. Nagle et al., in Proc. 8th Int. Workshop on Weak Interactions and Neutrinos, ed. A. Morales, World Sci. Publ. Co. (1983).

17) G. Nardulli et al., University of Bari preprint BA/GT-82/22 (1982).

18) A. Barroso, D. Tadić and J. Trampetić, Max Planck Institute preprint, MPI-PAE/PTh 18/83 (1983).

FERMI MOTIONS AND STATIC PROPERTIES OF BARYONS

J. Trampetić*

Max-Planck-Institut für Physik und Astrophysik
Werner-Heisenberg-Institut für Physik
Munich, Fed. Rep. Germany

ABSTRACT

Baryonic form factors for nucleons have been investigated. General formulas for calculating the current form factors show explicitly the presence of terms which contain internal quark momenta dependence. It was important to find whether one set of model parameters can fix simultaneously the charge radius, magnetic moment and the axial-vector coupling constant. The excellent agreement with experiment was achieved due to the inclusion of Fermi motions of quarks inside the hadron.

First, a few words about quark models[1,2] are perhaps necessary. All simple quark models fail in some respect in the description of the momentum-dependent and/or relativistic hadronic features.

The harmonic oscillator (HO) quark model,[2] with two body forces acting among quarks, is the model by which it is possible to include the internal quark motions (Fermi motions) in the most simple way (this is the RCHO model in Ref. 3). Namely, in the HO model the center of mass motion of the hadron can be treated exactly in the nonrelativistic limit. The full relativistic treatment, which has not been so far fully carried out, would require tremendous sophistication of the model. However, it is possible to include relativistic corrections to all orders p/m for the internal quark motion.

It is very well known that only a properly relativistic internal quark motion can explain simultaneously the experimental axial-vector nucleon coupling constant g_A, magnetic moment μ_P and charge radius $\langle r^2 \rangle_P$.[4] As the full relativistic treatment of the two-body potential is a complex and thorny problem,[4] we will show that our nonrelativistic HO quark model, which takes into account Fermi motions (RCHO) of quarks produces excellent agreement with experiments for all three quantities.

---

*A. von Humboldt fellow, on leave of absence from the Rudjer Bosković Institute, Zagreb, Croatia, Yugoslavia.

In this paper we have adapted a uniform approach by which all quantities in question are connected to the appropriate form factors. These form factors are always found by calculating the matrix element of the particular current between the baryon states. This approach is quite natural for the HO model.

One has to calculate matrix elements of two quark operators of the type

$$J_\mu^{ij}(\vec{k}_1,\vec{k}_2) = \bar{\psi}^i(\vec{k}_1)\,\Gamma_\mu\,\psi^j(\vec{k}_2), \tag{1}$$

i,j = spin, flavor, color. The quark field ψ_f^c of flavor f and color c can be decomposed as follows:

$$\psi_f^c(\vec{k}) = \left(\frac{m}{E}\right)_f^{1/2} \sum_r \left[u_{f,r}^c(\vec{k})\, b_{f,r}^c(\vec{k}) + v_{f,r}^c(\vec{k})\, d_{f,r}^{c\dagger}(\vec{k}) \right], \tag{2a}$$

$$u_{f,r}^c(\vec{k}) = \left(\frac{E+m}{2m}\right)_f^{1/2} \begin{pmatrix} 1 \\ \dfrac{\vec{\sigma}\vec{k}}{(E+m)_f} \end{pmatrix} \chi_r^c . \tag{2b}$$

The operator (1) is sandwiched between baryon states. The proton state, for example, is according to the SU(6) x $SU(3)_c$ x O(3) group in the momentum space expressed by the following equation:

$$|P(\vec{K},\vec{p}_\rho,\vec{p}_\lambda)\uparrow\rangle = N_P \frac{1}{6} \sum_{\substack{\mathrm{Per.}\,\vec{p}_i \\ (i=1,2,3)}} G_P(p_\rho,p_\lambda)\times$$

$$\frac{\epsilon^{abc}}{\sqrt{18}}\left[\left(b_{u\uparrow}^{a\dagger}(\vec{p}_1)\, b_{d\downarrow}^{b\dagger}(\vec{p}_2) - b_{u\downarrow}^{a\dagger}(\vec{p}_1)\, b_{d\uparrow}^{b\dagger}(\vec{p}_2)\right) b_{u\uparrow}^{c\dagger}(\vec{p}_3)\right]|0\rangle, \tag{3a}$$

$$\vec{p}_1 = \frac{1}{3}\vec{K} + \frac{1}{\sqrt{2}}\vec{p}_\rho + \frac{1}{\sqrt{6}}\vec{p}_\lambda, \qquad \vec{p}_3 = \frac{1}{3}\vec{K} - \sqrt{\frac{2}{3}}\,\vec{p}_\lambda .$$
$$\vec{p}_2 = \frac{1}{3}\vec{K} - \frac{1}{\sqrt{2}}\vec{p}_\rho + \frac{1}{\sqrt{6}}\vec{p}_\lambda, \tag{3b}$$

The norm N_P will be defined later. The function G_P is a solution of the HO model[2] (in momentum space) for the octet baryons (nucleons)

$$G_p(p_\rho, p_\lambda) = (\sqrt{\pi}\alpha)^{-3} \exp\left[\frac{-1}{2\alpha^2}(p_\rho^2 + p_\lambda^2)\right]. \tag{4}$$

In the above formula we have neglected the difference among quark masses. This leads to considerable simplification with possible error being less than 10%.[5)] A general matrix element is

$$M_\mu^{ij}\left(B_1(\vec{k}), B_2(\vec{k}')\right) =$$

$$= \int d^3k_1\, d^3k_2\, d^3p_\rho\, d^3p_\lambda\, d^3p'_\rho\, d^3p'_\lambda \times \tag{5}$$

$$\langle B_1(\vec{k}, \vec{p}_\rho, \vec{p}_\lambda) | \bar{\psi}^i(\vec{k}_1) \Gamma_\mu \psi^j(\vec{k}_2) | B_2(\vec{k}', \vec{p}'_\rho, \vec{p}'_\lambda) \rangle .$$

The quark creation and annihilation operators appearing in (2) and in baryon states (3) can be contracted in various ways. As long as quark masses are equal everything is so symmetric that only one of the possible contributions ought to be calculated. Nevertheless, it might be useful for future use to outline a general procedure. For a typical combination

$$\left(M_{m,n}^{p-n}\right)^1 = \langle p | b_{rm}^{u+}(\vec{k}_1)\, b_{rn}^{d}(\vec{k}_2) | n \rangle , \tag{6}$$

possible contractions are illustrated in Fig. 1 and formulas (2.6) of Ref. 3). There are 3! permutations of impulses in any baryon state, but only 18 different diagrams. Note that in the total matrix element M_μ^{ij} (5) we have 3! x 3! x 4 diagrams (18 independent). They appear in such a mixture of combinations that it is necessary to recount and calculate all of these 144 diagrams. Namely, every one of these 18 independent diagrams appears in the calculation 8 times (8 x 18 = 144), but always in different combinations with other diagrams. So, the symmetry with respect to quark permutations reduces (5) to

$$M_\mu^{\alpha\beta} = \sum_{i=1}^{3} \int d^3p_\rho\, d^3p_\lambda\, \rho_0^i(\vec{p}_\lambda, \vec{Q}^2)\, \rho_1^i(\vec{p}_\lambda, \vec{Q}^2)_\mu^{\alpha\beta}\, G_{B_1} G_{B_2} , \tag{7}$$

$$\rho_1^i(\vec{p}_\lambda, \vec{Q}^2)_\mu^{\alpha\beta} = N_{B_1} N_{B_2} \frac{1}{3} \sum_{m,n} \left(M_{m,n}^{B_1 B_2} \right)^0 \times$$

$$\left(\frac{m_\alpha m_\beta}{E_\alpha E'_\beta} \right)_i^{1/2} \bar{u}_m^\alpha (\vec{p}_i) \Gamma_\mu u_n^\beta (\vec{p}_i') , \tag{7a}$$

$$\rho_0^i(\vec{p}_\lambda, \vec{Q}^2) = \exp\left[\frac{-1}{\alpha^2} (\vec{p}_i - \tfrac{1}{3}\vec{\kappa}) \vec{Q} \right],$$

$$E_i^2 = \vec{p}_{i,\alpha}^{\,2} + m_\alpha^2 \quad , \quad \alpha,\beta = u, d, \cdots \quad ,$$

$$\vec{p}_i' = \vec{p}_i + \vec{\kappa}' - \vec{\kappa} \equiv \vec{p}_i + \vec{Q} . \tag{7b}$$

This is the most general expression for the current matrix element calculated in the HO quark model which includes interanl quark momenta (RCHO). Note that the extra exponential term (in (7) denoted by $\rho_o(\vec{p}_\lambda, \vec{Q}^2)$ is a consequence of the transformation properties of the Gaussian and the spinors, $\bar{u}, u$ under the transformation $\vec{p}_i' \rightarrow \vec{p}_i$.

One can use (7) in order to extract form factors (for example $G_M(\vec{Q}^2)$, $\vec{K}' = -\vec{K} = -\vec{Q}/2$) and then one can switch to the $\vec{K} = \vec{K}' = 0$ case in order to calculate their zero momentum transfer value (for example $G_M(o) = e^{-1}\mu_p$).

Specifying $\Gamma_\mu = \gamma_o, \vec{\gamma}\gamma_5$ it is easy to find:

$$g_V^{pn} = N_p^2 = 1 \quad , \quad E_3^2 = \frac{2}{3}\vec{p}_\lambda^{\,2} + m^2 ,$$

$$g_A^{pn} = \frac{5}{3} \int d^3p_\rho \, d^3p_\lambda \, G_p^2 \left(\frac{E_3 + m}{2E_3} - \frac{1}{3} \frac{E_3 - m}{2E_3} \right). \tag{8}$$

By using the decomposition of the electromagnetic current matrix element (7) in the Breit frame of reference one can easily calculate the electric and magnetic form factors $G_E(\vec{Q}^2)$ and $G_M(\vec{Q}^2)$ (charge radius and magnetic moment, respectively) of the proton:

$$\langle r^2\rangle_p = \left[-6 \frac{\partial}{\partial \vec{Q}^2} G_E(\vec{Q}^2)\right]^p_{\vec{Q}^2=0} = \langle r^2\rangle^0_p + \langle r^2\rangle^1_p + \cdots$$

$$= \alpha^{-2} + \int d^3p_\rho\, d^3p_\lambda\, G_p^2 \frac{4E_3^3 + E_3 m^2 + m^3}{4E_3^4(E_3+m)} + \cdots, \tag{9}$$

$$\mu_p = \frac{e}{2}\int d^3p_\rho\, d^3p_\lambda \frac{G_p^2}{E_3}, \;(e/2M_p). \tag{10}$$

All the detailed explanations about the expressions (7-10) and relevant parameters are done in Ref. 3).

The interesting numerics for the charge radii, magnetic moment and g_A/g_V are summarized in Table 1:

α (GeV) (m = 0.22 GeV)	$\langle r^2\rangle^0_p$	$\langle r^2\rangle^1_p$	$\langle r^2\rangle_p$	$\mu_p(e/2M_p)$	(g_A/g_V)
0.27	0.53	0.28	0.81	2.91	1.31
0.30	0.43	0.26	0.69	2.76	1.27
0.32	0.38	0.24	0.62	2.66	1.25
α = 0.25 GeV, m = 0.33 GeV	0.62	0.18	0.80	2.77	1.47
Exp		0.81 (fm^2)		2.79	1.25

The overall success of the harmonic oscillator quark model is quite good. There is no doubt that the RCHO model offers distinct advantages in both cases, i.e., when dealing with quantities which do not depend on the recoil, such as g_A and when dealing with recoil, or better momentum transfer, dependent quantities such as magnetic moment and charge radii. Unfortunately, although the procedure concerning charge radii is straightforward and clear, the situation is not quite clear with the most interesting quantity, the magnetic moment. Special physical interest lies here in the fact that through this quantity eventually the internal structure of the quarks might show up.

Here the careful study of Table 1 is very instructional. In the framework of the RCHO model g_A, $\mu(P)$ and $\langle r^2 \rangle_P$ can all be fitted with the same parameters with the accuracy of 5% or better. The parameters are somewhat different from the ones used in the baryon spectroscopy[2,6] and in the analysis of the nonleptonic decays.[5,7,8] But the differences are not too large. It certainly seems that nonleptonic decays could be fitted with the parameters used in Table 1. Notice here also that the inclusion of the Fermi motion of quarks in the calculations of the 4-quark mesonic matrix elements[7,9,10] produces extreme stability in $\langle \pi | O^1_{LL} | K \rangle$, $\langle \bar{K}^o | O^2_{LL} | K^o \rangle$ in spite of the variations of the harmonic oscillator strength parameter $\varkappa$ ($\alpha = (3m_u \varkappa)^{1/4}$).

Finally we may conclude that the effects of Fermi motions inside hadrons are extremely important and on the basis of the two-body harmonic oscillator potential (HO quark model) are calculable. They produce significant agreement with experiment for baryonic static properties and better understanding of the weak mesonic matrix elements.

Acknowledgement

I would like to acknowledge the support of the Max-Planck-Institut für Physik und Astrophysik, Munich, Fed. Rep. Germany and the Rudjer Boskovič Institut, Zagreb, Croatia, Yugoslavia.

References

1) A. Chodos, R.L. Jaffe, K. Johnson and C.B. Thorn, Phys. Rev. D10 (1974) 2599;
T. de Grand, R.L. Jaffe, K. Johnson and I. Kiskis, Phys. Rev. D12 (1975) 2060;
A.J.G. Hey, Topics in Quantum Field Theories, Salamanca 1977, ed. J.A. de Azcarraga (Springer 1978) p. 156, and references therein.

2) N. Isgur, G. Karl and R. Koniuk, Phys. Rev. Lett. 41 (1978) 126;
N. Isgur and G. Karl, Phys. Rev. D19 (1979) 2653, D20 (1979) 1191.

3) D. Tadič and J. Trampetič, "Harmonic Oscillator Quark Model for Baryons and the Momentum-Dependent Effects", MPI-PAE/PTh 12/83.

4) R.P. Feynman, M. Kislinger and F. Ravandal, Phys. Rev. D3 (1971) 2706;
P.N. Bogoliubov, Ann. Inst. Henri Poincaré VIII (1967) 163;
F.E. Close, An Introduction to Quarks and Partons (Academic Press, London, 1979).

5) D. Tadič and J. Trampetič, Phys. Rev. D23 (1981) 144.

6) A.J.G. Hey and R.L. Kelly, "Baryon Sepctroscopy", CALT-68-830 (July 1, 1982).

7) P. Colič, J. Trampetič and D. Tadič, Phys. Rev. D26 (1982) 2286.

8) M. Miloševič, D. Tadič and J. Trampetič, Nucl. Phys. B207 (1982) 461.

9) P. Colič, B. Guberina, D. Tadič and J. Trampetič, Nucl. Phys. B221 (1983) 141.

10) J. Trampetič, Phys. Rev. D27 (1983) 1565.

RELICS OF SHORT DISTANCE EFFECTS FOR THE NEUTRON ELECTRIC DIPOLE MOMENT

by [*)]

J.O.Eeg,

Institute of Physics,Univ. of Oslo

Even if the neutron electric dipole moment(NEDM) is a very small quantity,its value is important because it could indicate the mechanism for CP-violation chosen by nature[2].The present experimental upper bound for the NEDM is[3]

$$|D_n|_{exp.} < 6x10^{-25} \text{ e}\cdot\text{cm} \quad . \tag{1}$$

The mechanisms for CP-violation currently discussed in the litterature are: a)Spontanous CP-violation with enlarged Higgs sector, which gives[4] $|D_n| \sim 10^{-25}$ to 10^{-24} e·cm.(This is possibly in conflict with (1).) b)Strong CP-violation,where an upper bound for the well known θ-angle can be deduced[5,6] from (1). c)The Kobayashi-Maskawa(KM) model,where estimates $|D_n| \sim 10^{-34}$ to 10^{-30} e·cm are obtained[6-10]. d)More exotic CP-violating models including horizontal interactions seem to give[11] electric dipole moments of fermions of the order 10^{-27} to 10^{-31} e·cm. In our work[1] we have performed calculations of the NEDM within the KM-model.

NEDM in the KM-model

The intrisic electric dipole moment of a single quark is small, giving $|D_n| \sim 10^{-34}$ e·cm for the NEDM[7].However,a NEDM can also be obtained by taking into account the interplay of two or more quarks inside the neutron.The biggest effect is obtained if a penguin interaction is followed by ordinary W-boson exchange[9,10],as in Fig.1a.CP-violation occurs when heavy quarks (c,t) are entering the penguin loop for d→sG (G=gluon).Intepreting the diagram 1a in terms of baryon poles as in Fig.1b, Gavela et al.[9] obtains

$$|D_n| \sim 10^{-30} \text{ e}\cdot\text{cm} \tag{2}$$

---

*) This work is done in collaboration with I.Picek; see Ref.1

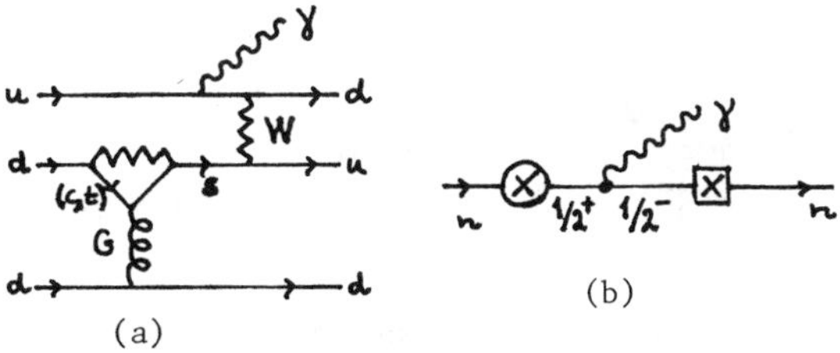

Fig.1.Diagrams for NEDM due to interplay of three quarks in the neutron.(a)On quark level.(b)Intepreted as a pole diagram on baryon level.The cross within the circle(square) represents the penguin interaction(ordinary W exchange)

The estimate (2),which is the biggest obtained within the KM-model,is cruically dependent on long distance effects and therefore very model dependent.To our opinion (2) is overestimated by roughly two orders of magnitude[1].(This conclusion is also in agreement with Ref.6) This has motivated us to look for and to calculate short distance contributions for the NEDM.

Two loop diagrams for ud → duγ

If both the W-boson and the penguin gluon G are attached to the same quark line,we obtain a two loop Feynman diagram(see Fig.2a) for ud → duγ which could apriori contain short distance effects.In addition to diagrams like Fig.2a(with vertices permuted in all possible ways),we must also consider diagrams with γ emitted inside the penguin loop,like in Fig.2b.We will call the loop for s → dGγ a photopenguin loop.To take into account and to calculate all two loop diagrams is a

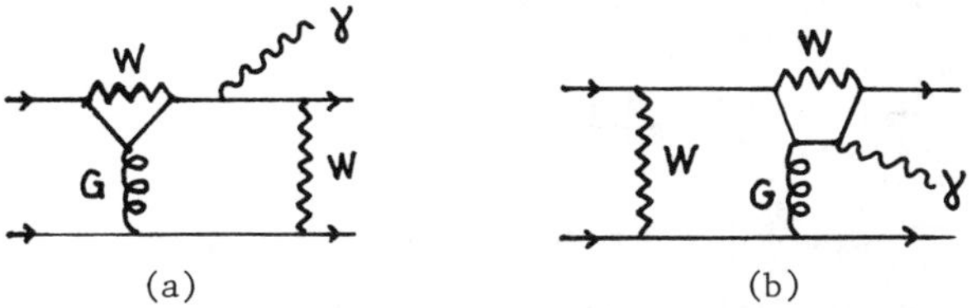

Fig.2.Two loop Feynman diagrams for NEDM due to interplay of two quarks in the neutron.(a)Containing an ordinary penguin loop.(b)Containing a photopenguin loop.Note that also (s,b) quarks can enter the (photo)penguin loop and (c,t) quarks the upper part of the box loop.

rather technical task. Therefore only some main points from the calculations will be given.

The two loop diagram in Fig.2a could also(-as Fig.1a) be intepreted as a pole diagram on baryon level(see Fig.1b) for low quark momenta $\mu \sim 1\text{GeV}$ in the box loop. However, we find that the part of diagram 2a, corresponding to a local four quark penguin interaction, is zero. Thus we clearly avoid double counting if our "short distance" result and the "long distance" result of Ref.9 are added. In this sense our result is complementary to that of Ref.9.

For all diagrams a two-fold GIM-mechanism is operative, first within the (photo)penguin loop and then within the box loop. The total contribution therefore has the formal structure

$$A_{tot.} = A(t,b) - A(c,b) - A(t,s) + A(c,s) . \qquad (3)$$

Using (3), we find that (for $m_t^2 >> m_b^2$, $m_b^2 >> m_c^2$,e.t.c.) the leading contributions from penguin and photopenguin generated diagrams are $\sim \ln(m_b^2/m_c^2)$. Thus the logarithmic contributions $\sim \ln(M_W^2)$ corresponding to loop momenta $\sim M_W$ are cancelled by (3), and we are left with "relics of short distance effects"[1] dominated by loop momenta $\sim m_b$. Due to different loop structures, the total photopenguin generated contribution is 20 to 50 times bigger than the total penguin generated contribution.

The sum of all two loop diagrams induce an effective CP-violating Hamiltonian for $ud \to du\gamma$ which can be calculated within the bag model, say, and we obtain for the NEDM

$$D_n^{Loop} \simeq \frac{4i}{3\pi^2} e \frac{\alpha_s}{4\pi} G_F^2 F_{KM} I_{Bag} \ln(m_b^2/m_c^2) , \qquad (4)$$

where $F_{KM} = s_1^2 s_2 s_3 c_1 c_2 c_3 \sin\delta$ is the standard KM-factor contained in all NEDM calculations[6-10]. We use the numerical value[6] $|F_{KM}| \simeq 5\text{x}10^{-5}$. The factor $I_{Bag} \simeq 1.6\text{x}10^{-3} m_N^3$ (m_N=nucleon mass) stems from the bag model calculation of the matrix elements of the effective Hamiltonian for $ud \to du\gamma$ between neutron states.

We conclude that the "long distance" contribution of Ref.9 and our "short distance" contribution are of the same order of magnitude, and that the NEDM calculated within the KM-model does not exceed the following numerical value:

$$|D_n| \lesssim 10^{-32} \ e \cdot cm \ . \qquad (5)$$

Thus one obtains separate regions for the NEDM within the different CP-violating mechanisms a), c), and d).

References

1) J.O.Eeg and I.Picek, Phys. Lett. 130B(1983)308
2) J.Ellis et al., Phys.Lett. 99B(1981)101
3) W.B.Dress et al., Phys.Rev. D15(1977)9
4) S.Weinberg, Phys.Rev.Lett. 37(1976)657
   A.A.Anselm and D.I.Dyakonov, Nucl.Phys. B145(1978)271
5) V.Baluni, Phys.Rev. D19(1979)2227
   R.J.Crewther et al., Phys.Lett. 88B(1979)123
6) E.P.Shabalin, Usph.Sov.Nauk. 139(1983)561
7) E.P.Shabalin, Yad.Fiz. 31(1980)1665 (Sov.J.Nucl.Phys.31(1980)864)
8) D.V.Nanopoulos et al., Phys.Lett. 87B(1979)53
   E.P.Shabalin, Yad.Fiz. 32(1980)443 (Sov.J.Nucl.Phys.32(1980)228)
   M.B.Gavela et al., Phys.Lett. 109B(1982)83
9) M.B.Gavela et al., Phys Lett. 109B(1982)215
10) I.B.Kriplovich and A.R.Zhitnitsky, Phys.Lett.109B(1982)490
    E.Golowich and B.R.Holstein, Phys.Rev. D26(1982)182
11) O.Shanker, Nucl.Phys. B185(1981)382
    A.S.Joshipura and I.Montvay, Nucl.Phys. B196(1982)147

ELECTRON-POSITRON SCATTERING AND GAUGE THEORIES*

Michel DAVIER

Laboratoire de l'Accélérateur Linéaire
Université Paris-Sud, 91405 Orsay (France)

ABSTRACT

Recent results from high-energy e^+e^- colliding facilities are reviewed in the context of gauge theories. First QCD analyses are discussed and difficulties are seen to arise from the interplay between perturbative QCD and non-perturbative fragmentation processes. Many results have been recently obtained on weak electromagnetic interference, strengthening our faith in the standard SU(2) × U(1) theory : however some pieces are still missing and looked for. Finally, vigourous searches are pursued to find clues for physics beyond the SU(3) × SU(2) × U(1) framework : among those, supersymmetric particles are being actively hunted in a large variety of situations.

I. INTRODUCTION

Electron-positron collisions have traditionally provided a good testing ground for gauge theories. Results were first compared to QED and are now being used in the broader scope of the electroweak gauge theory. Strong support for the gauge theory of the strong interaction (QCD) came with the discovery of the gluon at PETRA, with the required properties of a vector boson.

In this talk, our purpose is to highlight recent results obtained at high energy e^+e^- machines in the context of modern gauge theories. Table I gives an overview of the present activities and emphasis of the experimental programs at the different operating e^+e^- facilities. Since b-quark studies at Cornell are reviewed by Lipari at this meeting, I shall concentrate on the results from the PETRA and PEP machines.

Table I

Overview of experimental activity at e^+e^- colliders (1983)

Collider	Operating CM energy	Detectors in operation	Emphasis of experimental program
DCI	1.4 - 3.8	DM2	low-energy spectroscopy ψ decays ; glueballs
SPEAR	3 - 5	Mark III	ψ,ψ',ψ'' decays ; D,F studies
DORIS	$\sim$ 10	Crystal Ball ARGUS	Υ,Υ' decays ; radiative transitions
CESR	$\sim$ 10	CLEO CUSB	Υ(1S→4S) decays, radiative transitions B decays
PETRA	14-43(46)	CELLO JADE Mark J TASSO	more energy : - new thresholds - electro-weak interferences
PEP	29	Mark II TPC MAC HRS DELCO	more luminosity : - detailed studies - rare processes

II. TESTS OF PERTURBATIVE QCD

In principle the process $e^+e^- \to$ hadrons is a very good place to test QCD. The final state provides us with a good visual demonstration of perturbative QCD through the observation of hadronic jets. Higher energies have revealed higher orders, taking advantage of the easier jet separation : evidence for $(q\bar{q})$ production shows up above $\sqrt{s} \sim 6$ GeV[1], 1 st QCD order $(q\bar{q}g)$ is obvious at $\sqrt{s} \sim 30$ GeV[2], and some indications exist for 2nd order QCD ($q\bar{q}$ gg, $q\bar{q}$ $q\bar{q}$) at the highest PETRA energies[3].

We shall be concerned here with only the latest developments on the subject.

1. Total cross-section measurements

Theoretically the energy dependence of $e^+e^- \to$ hadrons is described by QCD in a well-defined way, independent of the fragmentation schemes. Second order calculations have been performed[4], also taking into account the perturbing effect of electro-weak interference[5] :

$$R_h = \frac{\sigma(e^+e^- \to \text{hadrons})}{\sigma_{point}}$$

$$= \left(3 \sum_i Q_i^2 + \Delta R_{EW}\right) \left[1 + \frac{\alpha_s(s)}{\pi} + C_2 \left(\frac{\alpha_s(s)}{\pi}\right)^2\right] .$$

A good convergence is obtained : $C_2 \sim 1.5$ in the $\overline{MS}$ renormalization scheme, while $C_2 \sim 5$ in the MS scheme.

If the situation is clear-cut theoretically (except perhaps, for the fact that weak and QCD effects have to be disentangled), the problem is mostly experimental, because the predicted energy variation is so small that systematic effects play a dominant role. Normalisation uncertainties (luminosity measurement) and necessary corrections (acceptance, radiative effects, background subtraction) result into a systematic error which is at the 3-5 % level, at best. Recent results[6] are shown in Fig. 1. As an illustration, JADE obtains

$$R_h = 3.93 \pm .03 \text{ (stat)} \pm .09 \text{ (syst)} \quad \text{at} \quad \sqrt{s} \sim 35 \text{ GeV}$$

to be compared with the expected numbers :

$$R_{QPM} = 3 \sum_i Q_i^2 = 3.67$$

$$\Delta R_{EW} = .12 \qquad (\text{GWS model} + \sin^2\theta_W = .23)$$

$$\Delta R_{QCD} = .19 \qquad \text{for } \alpha_s = .15 .$$

Unfolding the electro-weak interference, the s dependence yields a value of α_s which is rather safe, but unfortunately imprecise (as expected) :

$$\alpha_s = .16 \pm .07 \qquad \text{at} \qquad Q^2 \sim (35 \text{ GeV})^2$$

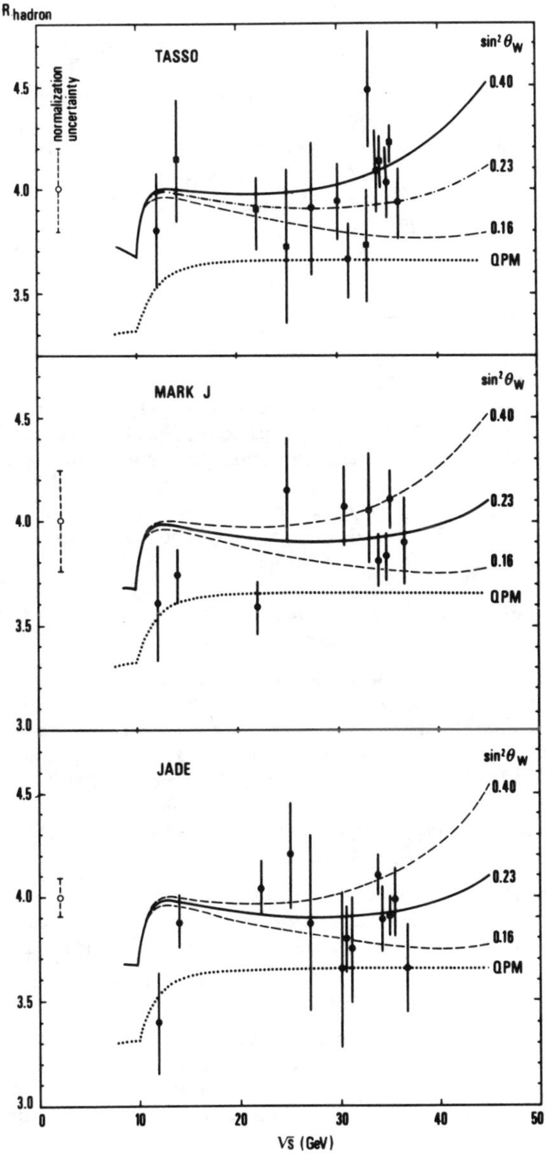

Fig. 1 - Total hadronic cross sections from PETRA experiments with predictions of the quark parton model (QPM) and the QCD-electroweak theory with $\alpha_s = 0.17$ and different values of $\sin^2\theta_W$

2. Inclusive hadron production

Scaling violations have been observed[7] in the inclusive process $e^+e^- \to h^\pm X$, where $h^\pm$ is an unidentified charged hadron. This is corroborated, but not conclusively, by recent results from CELLO[8] on the better-defined process $e^+e^- \to \pi^\circ X$. These scaling violations are qualitatively consistent with QCD with a Λ value of typically 200 MeV[9]. The analysis is unfortunately sensitive to the different fragmentation processes of the different quarks.

3. Rate of 3-jet production

The observation of 3-jet events led to the possibility of directly measuring the strength of the QCD interaction. This method has been used extensively in the past and usually involved the use of quantities such as thrust, oblateness, cluster multiplicity, all sensitive to the jet multiplicity in the final state. However the fact that partons fragment into hadron jets obscures the picture and some knowledge of the fragmentation process must be injected into Monte-Carlo simulation programs to properly describe the data and understand the significance of the "jet" observables.

Unfortunately, no unique model of fragmentation is favoured by experimental results. It was hoped previously that the measured α_s (proportional to the fraction of 3-jet (however defined) events) would be insensitive to the details of fragmentation. It was pointed out by the CELLO collaboration[10] that at least 2 fragmentation models, which are supported by the data and thus essentially indistinguishable for the moment, could lead to quite different α_s values. The 2 schemes considered are

- independent fragmentation of the different partons (Feynman-Field) yielding $\alpha_s \sim .15 - .20$ in 1st QCD order

- fragmentation along colour strings stretching between the separating quarks (Lund) : this model tends to have 3-jet events look more 2-jet like and the deduced α_s value is correspondingly larger, $\alpha_s \sim .23 - .28$ in 1st order.

These conclusions have been confirmed by analyses performed by the Mark II, MAC, Mark J and TASSO collaborations. Clearly, the rate of 3-jet production is not, for the moment, a reliable way to deduce α_s, given the state-of-the-art (mis)understanding of the fragmentation process.

4. Energy-weighted angular correlations

The angular correlation of energy flow E_i, E_j along 2 directions i, j separated by an angle χ is defined as :

$$F(\chi) = \frac{1}{\sigma}\frac{d\sigma}{d\chi}$$

$$= \frac{4}{\sigma}\sum_{ij}\int \frac{E_i E_j}{s}\left(\frac{d\sigma}{dE_i\, dE_j\, d\chi}\right) dE_i\, dE_j \quad .$$

Such a quantity is well-behaved theoretically (not IR-divergent) and should be rather insensitive to fragmentation.

In 1st order, at the parton level, we have

$$F_1(\chi) = a\,[\delta(\chi) + \delta(\chi-\pi)] + \alpha_s\, G_1(\chi)$$

where $G_1(\chi)$ is calculable. Now, fragmentation must be folded in, but in order to cancel most of the q, $\bar{q}$ fragmentation, it is more convenient to compute the asymmetry of $F(\chi)$:

$$A(\chi) = F(\pi-\chi) - F(\chi)$$

which should be proportional to α_s. The asymmetry is however still dependent on the fragmentation scheme (mostly through the gluon hadronization) as was first pointed out[10] by the CELLO collaboration (Fig. 2).

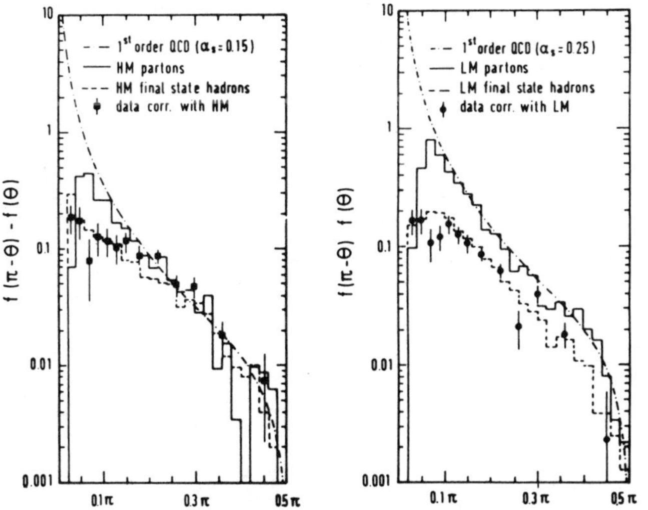

Fig. 2 - Asymmetry of the energy-weighted angular correlation from CELLO analysis (10) in 1st QCD order.

Left : independent fragmentation (HM), Right : string fragmentation (LM)

5. α_s determinations in 2nd QCD order

Most of the recent results are now focused on implementing 2nd order QCD amplitudes in the various Monte-Carlo simulators of $e^+e^- \to$ hadrons. The interest was recently stirred by the results of an analysis by the Mark J collaboration[11]) claiming that the fragmentation dependence observed in 1st order (using energy-weighted angular correlation) was strongly reduced in the 2nd order analysis. This unforeseen result is unfortunately not confirmed by a recent study done by CELLO where a large difference is still found between the string and the independent fragmentation models[12]). The latter conclusion is also reached by the TASSO collaboration[13]) using event shape and cluster analyses.

For the moment, the experimental situation is therefore not settled, with however a clear indication that uncertainties in the fragmentation process can produce large shifts in the deduced α_s values, whether the analyses are done at the 1st or 2nd order (Table II).

Table II

α_s determinations from the final state
in the process $e^+e^- \to$ hadrons (updated July 83)

Ref	Group	Method*	order	α_s values: independent fragmentation	α_s values: string fragmentation
10	CELLO	CT	α_s	.155 ± .015	.235 ± .025
10		EWAC	α_s	.15 ± .02	.25 ± .04
12		EWAC	α_s^2	.12 ± .02	.19 ± .02
14	JADE	CT	α_s	.20 ± .015 ± .03	.20 ± .015 ± .03
14		CT	α_s^2	.16 ± .015 ± .03	.16 ± .015 ± .03
11	Mark J	EWAC	α_s	.15 ± .01	.20 ± .01
11		EWAC	α_s^2	.12 ± .01	.14 ± .01
13	TASSO	CT	α_s	.19 ± .02	.26 ± .03
13		CT	α_s^2	.16 ± .01	.21 ± .01

* CT cluster thrust ; event shape
EWAC energy-weighted angular correlations

6. The photon structure functions

The deep inelastic scattering of electrons on a quasi real photon yields the dominant structure function of the photon, $F_2(x, Q^2)$:

$$\gamma(Q^2)\ \gamma \rightarrow \text{hadrons}$$

The F_2 function is calculable : in the naive quark-parton model, it already does not scale (unlike for the nucleon case) and this behaviour is expected to hold for QCD calculations as well. In general, one expects :

$$F_2(x, Q^2) \sim \ell n \frac{Q^2}{\Lambda^2} .$$

First results have been obtained on this process by PLUTO[15), CELLO[16) and JADE[17). We summarize here the conclusions which can be drawn at the present time :

(i) there is a clear evidence for point-like behaviour

(ii) it is not possible at this stage to discriminate between the quark-parton model and QCD predictions

(iii) although the data are not inconsistent with the prediction, it is not yet possible to determine the $\ell n\ Q^2$ increase. (Fig. 3).

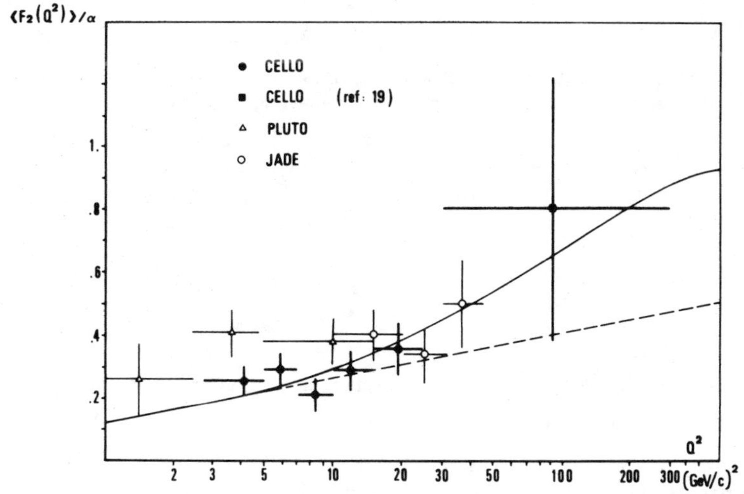

Fig. 3 - $\frac{1}{\alpha} < F_2(x, Q^2) >$ as a function of Q^2. Solid curve : lowest order QCD for u,d,s and c quarks, with Λ = 0.3 GeV. Dashed curve : same without c quark contribution. References in Ref. 16

III. ELECTRO-WEAK NEUTRAL CURRENTS

1. Situation prior to PETRA measurements

Neutral currents can be parametrized in a model-independent way[18] which is useful to test the basic properties of the transitions. Assuming factorization (a single Z° pole), currents can be parametrized by axial and vector couplings to fermions : a_f, v_f.

In the simplest gauge group, SU(2) × U(1), the couplings are determined by the weak isospin assignments of the left and right-handed fermions :

$$a_f = 2\,[I_{3L}(f) - I_{3R}(f)]$$

$$v_f = 2\,[I_{3L}(f) + I_{3R}(f)] - 4\,Q_f \sin^2\theta_w \,.$$

Charged-current phenomenology put f_L in doublets, while the isospin representation of f_R is not specified and must be determined experimentally.

In the minimal SU(2) × U(1)[19], f_R are weak-isospin singlets and the spontaneous symmetry breaking is achieved with a Higgs doublet, giving a single neutral Higgs boson, H°. Nothing much is known about H°, except that its coupling to any fermion f will be proportional to m_f, hence emphasizing decay into the heaviest quarks or leptons.

Before PETRA electro-weak measurements, a unique solution was found[20] for the e, ν_μ, u and d neutral couplings, deduced from cross-section measurements of neutrinos on nucleons and electrons, and the asymmetry of polarized electrons scattered on deuterium. This solution agrees with the GWS model, i.e., all I_{3R}(e,u,d) are consistent with 0 (± .06). If all I_{3R} are taken to be 0, all data are reproduced with a unique $\sin^2\theta_w$ value :

$$\sin^2\theta_w = .234 \pm .013 \,.$$

Such a value for $\sin^2\theta_w$ is unfortunate for e^+e^- experimenters, because v_e (and any v_ℓ) turns out to be essentially zero ($\sin^2\theta_w \sim \frac{1}{4}$) : therefore weak-electromagnetic interference will be a very small effect indeed in total cross-section measurements.

2. Results on e^+e^- annihilation into lepton pairs

For μ and τ pairs, which proceed by s-channel γ and Z° exchange, the total cross-section has the form[21)]

$$R_\ell = \frac{\sigma_\ell}{\sigma_{point}} = 1 + 2\, v_e v_\ell \chi + (a_e^2 + v_e^2)(a_\ell^2 + v_\ell^2)\chi^2$$

$$\text{with } \chi = \frac{g\, s\, M_Z^2}{s - M_Z^2} \quad \text{and} \quad g = \frac{G_F}{8\pi\alpha\sqrt{2}} \; .$$

At $\sqrt{s} \sim 34$ GeV, $\chi \sim -0.06$ and therefore $\chi^2 \ll |\chi|$. As mentioned before, v_e, $v_\ell \sim 0$, so that both the interference term and the purely weak term are negligible, and $R_\ell = 1$ as observed experimentally. A consequence of $v_e \sim 0$ is that no independent experimental information on v_ℓ can be extracted from cross-section data.

The angular distribution shows a well-known forward-backward asymmetry $\langle A_\ell \rangle$:

$$\frac{d\sigma}{d\Omega_\ell} = \frac{\alpha^2}{4s}\left[R_\ell\ (1 + \cos^2\theta) + b_\ell\ \cos\theta\right]$$

$$\langle A_\ell \rangle = \frac{F - B}{F + B} = \frac{3}{8}\, b_\ell = \frac{3}{2}\, a_e a_\ell \chi < 0 \; .$$

The experimental asymmetries, after correction for α^3 QED effects, yield a clear interference (see Fig. 4, 5, 6 for a compilation of PETRA data, as of Summer 82[22)]).

The latest lepton-pair asymmetries from PETRA are shown in Table III.

Contrary to μ- and τ- pair production, Bhabha scattering is dominated by t-channel γ exchange and shows altogether little interference. It can be used to deduce v_e and a_e, and verify that v_e is small (resolution of ν-e V-A ambiguity within the leptonic sector).

3. Leptonic axial couplings

The μ and τ asymmetries are direct measurements of the axial couplings. Assuming $M_Z = 90$ GeV, they yield :

$$a_\mu = -1.26 \pm .14$$
$$a_\tau = -\ .92 \pm .26$$

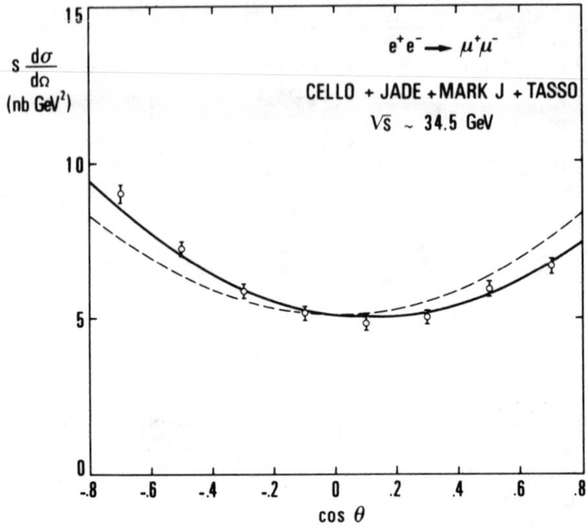

Fig. 4 - Compilation of PETRA high-energy data for the angular distribution of $e^+e^- \to \mu^+\mu^-$

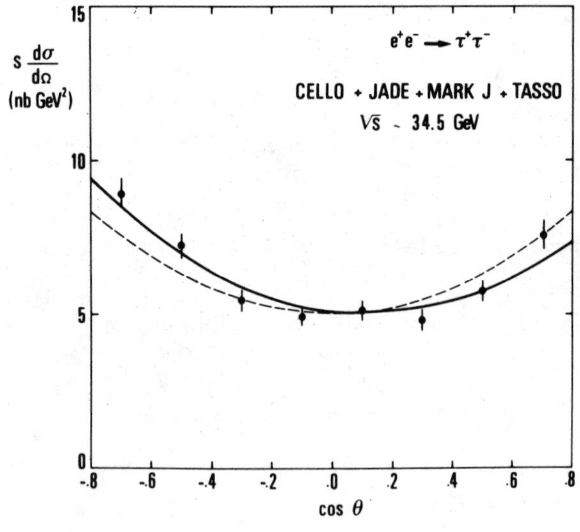

Fig. 5 - Compilation of PETRA high-energy data for the angular distribution of $e^+e^- \to \tau^+\tau^-$

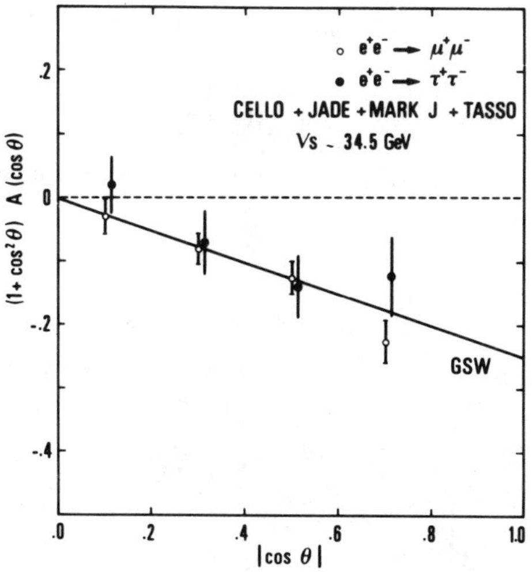

Fig. 6 - Compilation of PETRA asymmetries for $e^+e^- \to \mu^+\mu^-$ and $\tau^+\tau^-$

<u>Table III</u>

Lepton-pair forward-backward asymmetries at PETRA (updated July 83[23])

	$A_{\mu\mu}$	
JADE		$-.110 \pm .018 \pm .010$
Mark J		$-.117 \pm .017$
TASSO		$-.098 \pm .023 \pm .005$
	Average :	$-.110 \pm .012$
	$A_{\tau\tau}$	
CELLO		$-.103 \pm .052$
JADE		$-.079 \pm .039$
Mark J		$-.074 \pm .046$ $\lvert\cos\theta\rvert < .8$
TASSO		$-.054 \pm .045$
	Average :	$-.080 \pm .023$

GWS theory : $-.087$

(after radiative corrections)

Therefore μ_R^- and τ_R^- are weak isospin singlets, like e_R^-.

An overall fit of v, a leptonic couplings, assuming e-μ-τ universality, can be performed on all the data on $e^+e^- \to \ell^+\ell^-$. The resulting couplings, shown in Fig. 7, clearly discriminate between the 2 solutions found in νe scattering. Also, they are now of comparable accuracy.

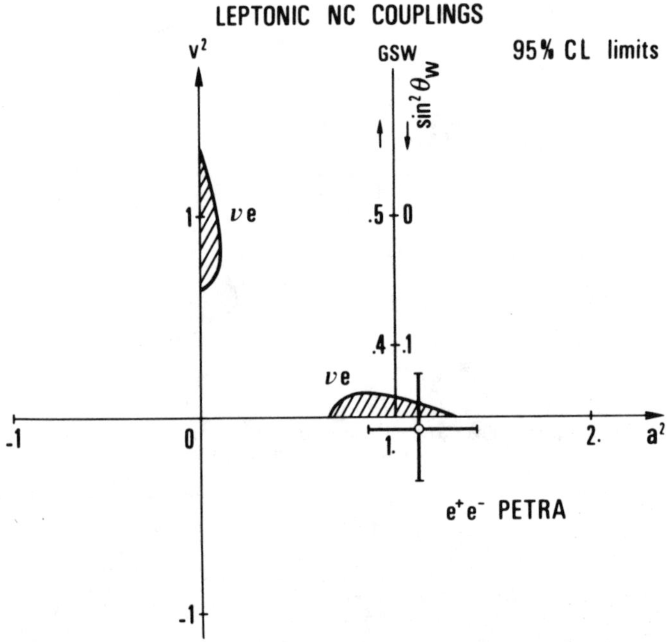

Fig. 7 - Determination of leptonic couplings, v^2 and a^2, from PETRA data and comparison with the 2 solutions found in νe analyses (hatched areas)

Since, at the highest PETRA energy, s cannot be neglected in front of M_Z^2, one can consider the possibility to extract information on M_Z from the data. Fig. 8 shows that it is difficult to achieve this in a model-independent way : the precision is not yet good enough to really measure the curvature of $\langle A(s)\rangle$, thereby extracting the Z° propagator effect. On the other hand, if one assumes the couplings are known (either taking the axial e coupling and making use of universality, or using the GWS value which is independent of $\sin^2\theta_W$), the deviation of

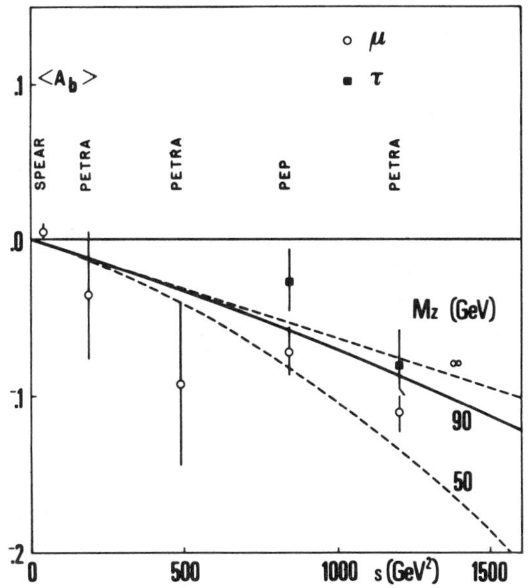

Fig. 8 - Energy dependence of μ and τ asymmetries with updated PEP results (36). The different curves correspond to different assumed Z° masses.

the <A> values at the highest energy with respect to "local" values can be examined :

$$\langle A \rangle = \frac{\langle A \rangle_{M_Z \infty}}{1 - \frac{s}{M_Z^2}}$$

and they deliver :

$$M_Z = (60 \begin{smallmatrix} +33 \\ -7 \end{smallmatrix}) \text{ GeV} \qquad 95 \text{ \% CL} .$$

This is a delicate exercise for large M_Z values as can be seen in Fig. 9 : however, there is a clear evidence for a non-local neutral current interaction (3σ deviation from an infinitely heavy Z°) - a fact which is brilliantly confirmed by collider experiments at CERN[24].

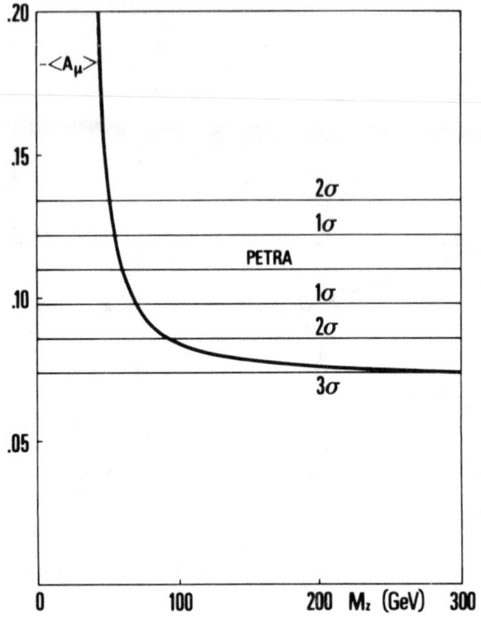

Fig. 9 - Sensitivity of <Aμ> on the M_Z mass at the highest PETRA energy.

4. Leptonic vector couplings

As already mentioned, the vector couplings are not easily measured in e^+e^- experiments because $v_e \sim 0$. One possibility is the measurement of a parity-violating quantity : in the absence of longitudinally polarized beams, such a possibility exists with the measurement of the τ polarization through the semi-leptonic decays

$$\tau^- \to e^- \bar{\nu}_e \nu_\tau$$
$$\qquad \mu^- \bar{\nu}_\mu \nu_\tau$$

and the 2-body hadronic decays

$$\tau^- \to \pi^- \nu_\tau$$
$$\qquad \rho^- \nu_\tau$$

all four channels have been recently analyzed by the CELLO collaboration[25]. With the limited statistics available, only an upper limit for τ polarization can be obtained (Fig. 10). More interestingly, the forward-backward polarization asymmetry can yield information on v_τ, since

$$\langle P_\tau \rangle \sim v_e \, a_\tau$$

$$A(P) = \frac{1}{2}(\langle P_{F\tau} \rangle - \langle P_{B\tau} \rangle) \sim v_\tau \, a_e \, .$$

The result is :

$$v_\tau = -.1 \pm 2.8$$

to be compared with

$$v_\mu = -.24 \pm .32 \qquad \text{(from } \mu \text{ scattering}^{26)} \text{ and ee} \to \mu\mu)$$

$$v_e = -.04 \pm .06 \; .$$

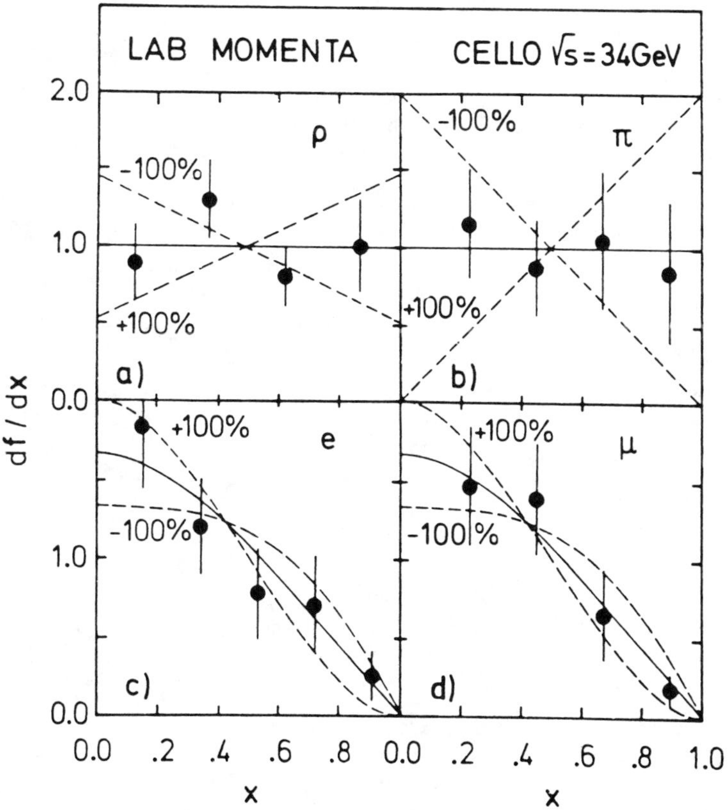

Fig. 10 - Laboratory momentum spectra in τ decays and expected distributions as a function of τ polarization, from CELLO analysis(25).

5. Quark couplings

In the quark-parton model, the total hadronic cross-section, when scaled to the QED point-like value, assumes the form

$$R_h^{QPM} = 3 \sum_i Q_i^2 + 6\chi\, v_e \sum_i Q_i\, v_i + 3(a_e^2 + v_e^2)\, \chi^2 \sum_i (a_i^2 + v_i^2)$$

where i runs over all produced quark types (u,d,s,c,b). Since $v_e \sim 0$, no bound can be obtained on the quantity $\sum_i Q_i v_i$. Some very limited information can be obtained[22] for the term $\sum_i (a_i^2+v_i^2)$, but it is not yet very constraining. Also one must take QCD effects into account, with each of the above 3 terms being multiplied by $(1 + \frac{\alpha_s}{\pi})$ in 1st order. The present data on R_h can yield $\sin^2\theta_W$ values, but this is mostly a measure of the smallness of the interference term ($\sin^2\theta_W \sim \frac{1}{4} \rightarrow v_e \sim 0$), and not of much else.

The most promising method to obtain (axial) quark couplings is the measurement of asymmetries, using a well-defined quark tag.

(i) $e^+e^- \rightarrow c\bar{c}$ is cleanest experimentally, through the fragmentation of c into a leading D^* which can be neatly identified via the low-Q decay

$$D^{*+} \rightarrow D^\circ \pi^+$$
$$\hookrightarrow K^- \pi^+$$

This process is background-free, but so far limited by statistics. The latest result from TASSO[27] is :

$$\langle A_c \rangle = -\,.28 \pm .13$$

$$a_c = +\,1.8 \pm .9$$

to be compared with the GWS values of -.14 and + 1. respectively.

(ii) $e^+e^- \rightarrow b\bar{b}$ can be reached through semi-leptonic decays giving large P_T leptons with respect to the jet axis. This is difficult because of : (a) b,c contributions giving opposite lepton asymmetries ($b \rightarrow \ell^-$, but $c \rightarrow \ell^+$), (b) cascade decays ($b \rightarrow c \rightarrow \ell^+$) and (c) misidentification of hadrons within a jet. As a result, the raw observed asymmetry is strongly diluted and requires large corrections.

As an example, Fig. 11 displays the latest results from MAC on μ inclusive production. Large p_T muons are mostly from direct b decays yielding[28]

$a_b = - .7 \pm 1.2$

in broad agreement with the GWS prediction ($a_b = - 1.$)

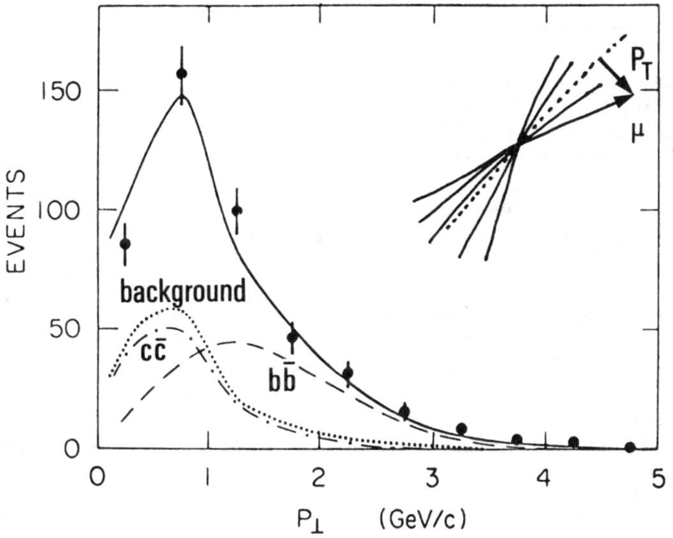

Fig. 11 - Transverse momentum distribution of muons with respect to the jet axis from MAC experiment(28)

IV. TOWARDS A COMPLETE TEST OF THE GWS THEORY

It is our purpose now to quickly review where we stand with respect to the standard electro-weak model, to delineate the areas which are well tested and to focus on still unchecked important features.

1. Factorization of neutral-current transitions

Only 3 tests are experimentally possible so far : 2 involve experiments on parity violation in atoms[22)], while the last one relates leptonic couplings as probed in e^+e^- and νe data. In Hung-Sakurai[18)] notation, it reads

$$\frac{h_{VV}}{h_{AA}} = \frac{g_V}{g_A}$$

Both ratios are experimentally consistent with zero within, respectively, .20 and .13 at 95 % CL.

There is no evidence for a breakdown of factorization, but it is not very well tested.

2. Symmetry breaking and Higgs boson

The well-known ρ parameter is measured to be 1 from ν data : this is consistent with only Higgs doublets. If only one doublet is active, then we have only one neutral Higgs boson (H°). In case of more than one doublet, several physical Higgs bosons are allowed (H°, $H^\pm$...).

A search for H° is very clean in e^+e^- annihilation through the coupling to heavy quarks[29], best used in a quarkonium decay

$$V(Q\bar{Q}) \rightarrow H^\circ \gamma$$

The rate is very small in ψ and γ decays, even for a very light H° (BR < 10^{-4}). On the other hand, a toponium of mass > 40 GeV would be quite suitable for a H° search up to > 30 GeV (BR > 10^{-2}).

If H° is difficult to look for (before toponium is discovered), a search for $H^\pm$ is more straightforward, as it would be pair-produced :

$$e^+e^- \rightarrow H^+H^-$$

in e^+e^- annihilations. Many analyses have been done along these lines with the result[22] that no such boson exists in the 2-13 GeV mass range, for a wide range of possible decay modes. This mass range is particularly relevant in extended technicolor models and these models are therefore in trouble.

3. Fermion multiplets

(i) f_L are in doublets.

This is well established from charged-current phenomenology and b transitions[30]. Of particular interest, we now know that the τ lepton has it own neutrino, from the τ direct lifetime measurements and the absence of $\nu_e \rightarrow \tau$ and $\nu_\mu \rightarrow \tau$ interactions in ν beams[31]. Also, with the measurement of the τ lifetime[32], tests of universality of charged currents have now been extended to the τ, with the result :

$$\frac{g_\tau}{g_e} = .92 \pm .09 \pm .09 .$$

Completion of the 3rd quark doublet awaits the discovery of the t quark. The search is being actively conducted at PETRA in a

direct scan for a toponium resonance : R_h values are measured every 30 MeV in the CM energy, consistent with the energy resolution. A toponium signal would correspond to a value for $\Gamma_{ee} B_h$ of $\sim$ 3.5 keV in the standard phenomenology. Typical results between 33 and 37 GeV are shown in Fig. 12 with the expected signal size. Of course, at the open top threshold, one would observe a step ($\Delta R \sim 1.4$), more isotropic events and a significant increase in the semi-leptonic rate.
As of July 83, the scan has been extended to 43 GeV with no evidence for a toponium signal : typically $\Gamma_{ee} B_h < 2$ keV at 95 % CL in every one of the 4 experiments. The scan will continue up to $\sim$ 46 GeV in the 2nd part of the year.

(ii) f_R are singlets.

This was previously known for e_R, u_R and d_R and has now been extended to μ_R and τ_R. The check for c_R and b_R is within reach.

(iii) how many generations ?

Pair-production of a new charged heavy lepton L^- is excluded for $m_L < 18$ GeV. The domain of sensitivity is soon going to be extended to $\sim$ 22 GeV.

A powerful way to probe the multiplicity of generations is neutrino counting. Besides the celebrated cosmological limit ($N_\nu < 4$ for low mass, stable neutrinos), no good direct limit exists : $N_\nu < 10^4$ from $K \to \pi\nu\bar{\nu}$. However, new information can be derived from recent experimental data sensitive to the total Z° width :

- $N_\nu < 280$ (95 % CL) for $m_\nu < 15$ GeV, from the μ, τ asymmetry at PETRA. Indeed, for a large number of neutrinos, the Z° width could enter significantly in the propagator and the expected asymmetry would be reduced.

- $N_\nu < 50$ from the preliminary observation of a few Z° events at the SPS $p\bar{p}$ collider in UA1[24]. This limit will be improved in the future and could probably reach < 10.

Direct measurements (PEP, PETRA) of the process $e^+e^- \to \gamma$ + nothing detected can also put a limit $\sim$ 10 in the next 1-2 years, through the reaction $e^+e^- \to \gamma\, \nu\bar{\nu}$. Finally experiments at SLC and LEP will eventually measure N_ν precisely and settle the issue at least for neutrinos with $m_\nu < 40$ GeV.

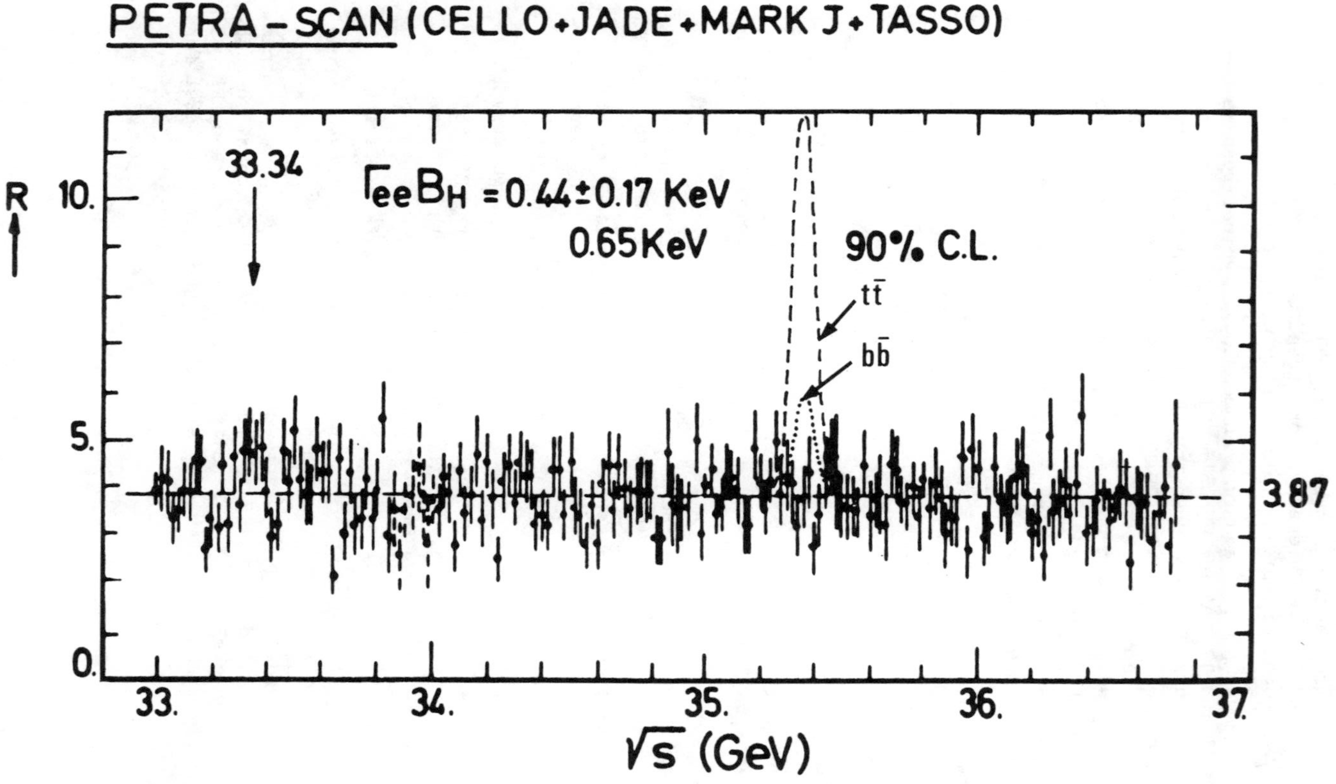

Fig. 12 - Toponium scan from the combined PETRA experiments from 33 to 37 GeV, with the expected size of a $t\bar{t}$ or a $b\bar{b}$ resonance folded with the energy resolution of the beams.

V. BEYOND THE STANDARD GAUGE THEORIES : SUPERSYMMETRY ?

1. Introduction

Supersymmetry is an interesting, plausible and elegant possibility for new physics beyond the "current" $SU(3) \times SU(2) \times U(1)$. In this scheme, Higgs bosons find a natural home and a link to gravity is probably possible. However many new particle states are expected and have to be found, among those :

$J = 0$ scalar leptons and quarks (s_ℓ, s_q), Higgs bosons

$J = \frac{1}{2}$ photino (λ_γ), new leptons (wino, zino)

$J = \frac{3}{2}$ gravitino (λ_g) .

2. Search for charged scalar leptons

They can be pair-produced

$$e^+e^- \rightarrow s_\ell \ \bar{s}_\ell$$

with a fast decay (if the photino is lighter)

$$s_\ell \rightarrow \ell \ \lambda_\gamma \ .$$

The experimental signature is therefore 2 acolinear, acoplanar leptons. The current mass limits are given in Table IV.

Table IV

Mass limits (in GeV) for scalar leptons

	s_e	s_μ	s_τ
CELLO	16.8	16	15.3
JADE	16		14
Mark J		15	14
TASSO	16.6	16.4	
$(g-2)_\mu$		13	

Higher masses can be probed, looking for single scalar electron production[33) :

$$e^+e^- \rightarrow e^{\pm} s_e^{\mp} \lambda_\gamma$$

Such a search in currently in progress at PEP and PETRA, with no result as yet.

3. Search for unstable photinos

The lifetime of unstable photino is clearly model-dependent. If the gravitino is light, the photino could decay through

$$\lambda_\gamma \rightarrow \lambda_g \gamma$$

with a lifetime[34)

$$\tau_{\lambda_\gamma} = \frac{8\pi d^2}{m_{\lambda_\gamma}^5}$$

where $\sqrt{d}$ is the energy scale for supersymmetry breaking.

The process of Fig. 13 has a cross-section which depends on the scalar electron mass and leads to a 2-photon final state with missing energy and momentum. The observable rate is determined by m_{s_e} and m_{λ_γ} (production) and the ratio $\tau_{\lambda_\gamma}/m_{\lambda_\gamma}$ (decay inside detector) with

$$\sigma \sim \frac{s}{m_{s_e}^4} \beta_{\lambda_\gamma}^3$$

where β_{λ_γ} is the photino velocity in the CM.

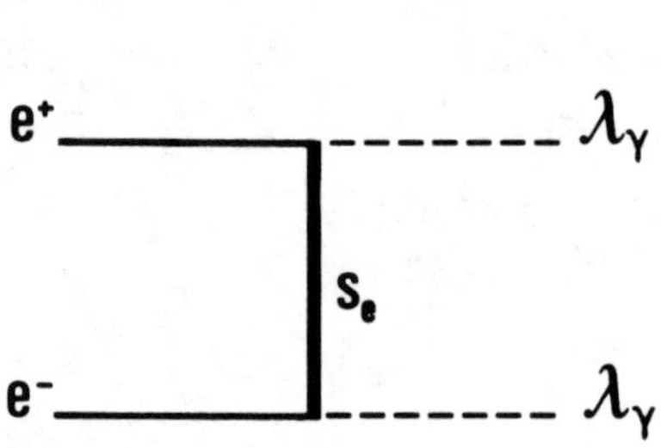

Fig. 13 - Pair production of photinos in e^+e^- annihilation via scalar electron exchange.

Such a study has been conducted by CELLO[35] and excludes (see Fig. 14) a large domain in the (m_{λ_γ}, d) plane for a wide range of scalar electron masses (m_{s_e} < 80 GeV) : for $\sqrt{d} \sim 100$ GeV ($\sim M_{W,Z}$, a plausible choice) the photino must be lighter than $\sim$ 100 MeV or heavier than $\sim$ 10 GeV.

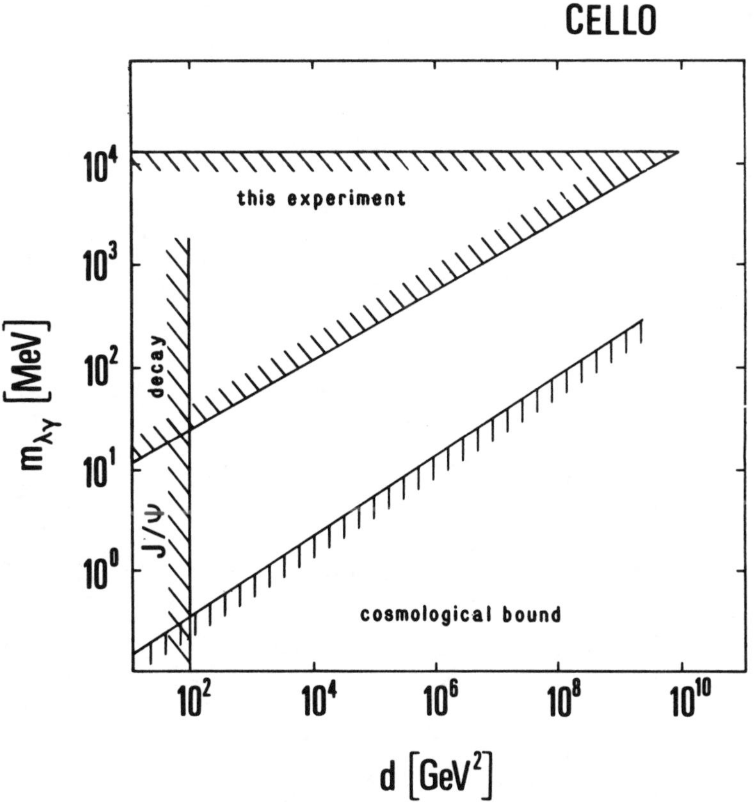

Fig. 14 - Domain excluded at 95 % CL by the CELLO experiment[35] on the photino mass vs. the scale parameter d, assuming photino decay into a light gravitino.

4. Search for stable photinos

Not-too-heavy stable photinos can be produced through the graph of Fig. 15, the radiative version of Fig. 13. Such a process is highly unconstrained, but a rate larger than the expected (?) neutrino rate $e^+e^- \to \gamma\nu\bar{\nu}$, for all ν types, would be a signature for something new, and possibly photino production.

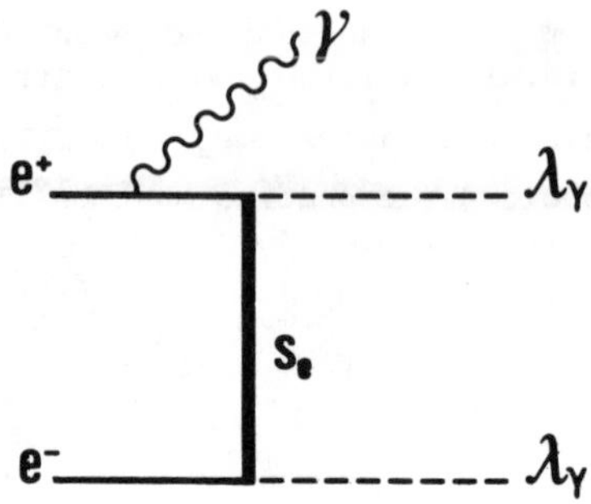

Fig. 15 - Radiative production of photinos, as a means to detect stable photinos.

Fig. 16 gives a measure of the expected cross-section for typical conditions, as a function of the mass of the exchanged scalar electron. The absence of any conspicuous signal would set a limit of $\sim$ 60 GeV for the s_e mass.

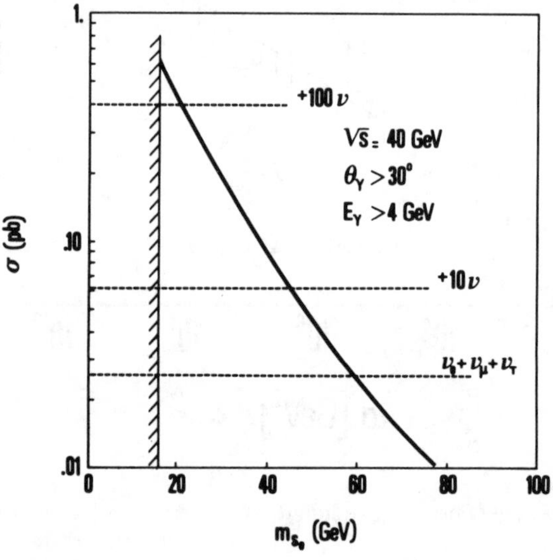

Fig. 16 - Cross-section for radiative photino-pair production as a function of the scalar electron-mass, under the specified experimental conditions. The horizontal lines correspond to the similar process of radiative ν-pair through Z^o s-channel exchange, with different assumed numbers of ν types.

A search is now in progress, both at PEP and PETRA. Experimental problems are tough : QED events, like ee → γ(ee) and γ(γγ), must be efficiently vetoed, together with cosmic ray interactions simulating single photons. At any rate, searching for an unexpected source of single photons is a good signature for new non-interacting stable particles.

In conclusion so far, we do not have, a hint of a clue for any new physics beyond the standard gauge theories : no new lepton type, no experimental sign of the rich (too rich ?) supersymmetric particle spectrum. In the next 1-2 years, much more data are going to be collected and analyzed in an effort to have the broadest possible attack on this problem.

Acknowledgements

It is a pleasure for me to thank the organizers of this very interesting meeting at Dubrovnik, for the enjoyable and stimulating atmosphere they have succeeded to create.

References

[1] R. Schwitters et al., Phys. Rev. Lett. 35 (1975) 1320
G. Hanson et al., Phys. Rev. Lett. 35 (1975) 1609

[2] D. Barber et al. Phys. Rev. Lett. 43 (1979) 830
R. Brandelik et al. Phys. Lett. 86B (1979) 243
C. Berger et al., Phys. Lett. 86B (1979) 418
W. Bartel et al., Phys. Lett. 91B (1980) 142
H.J. Behrend et al. Phys. Lett. 110B (1982) 329

[3] W. Bartel et al., Phys. Lett. 115B (1982) 338

[4] M. Dine and J. Sapirstein, Phys. Rev. Lett. 43, (1979) 668
K.G. Chetyrkin et al. Phys. Lett. 85B (1979) 277
W. Celmaster and R. Gonsalves, Phys. Rev. Lett. 44 (1979) 560

[5] J. Jersak et al., Phys. Lett. 98B (1981) 363

[6] JADE Collaboration, in preparation, see also Ref. 22

[7] R. Hollebeek, Rapporteur talk at the 1981 Intern. Sympos. on Lepton and Photon Interactions at High Energy, Bonn (1981) ; and SLAC-Pub 2989 (Oct. 1982)

[8] CELLO Collaboration, in print

[9] C. Peterson et al., SLAC-Pub 1912 (1982)

[10] H.J. Behrend et al., Nucl. Phys. 218B (1983) 269

[11] B. Adeva et al., Phys. Rev. Lett. 50 (1983) 2051

[12] CELLO Collaboration, in print

[13] TASSO Collaboration, seminar by G. Rudolph, DESY (July 1983)

[14] W. Bartel et al., DESY 82-060 (Sept. 1982)

[15] Ch. Berger et al., Phys. Lett. 107B (1981) 168

[16] H.J. Behrend et al., Phys. Lett. 126B, (1983) 391

[17] W. Bartel et al., DESY 82-064 (1982)

[18] P.Q. Hung and J.J. Sakurai, Ann. Rev. Nucl. and Part. Sci. 31 (1981) 375

[19] S.L. Glashow, Nucl. Phys. 22, (1961) 579
S. Weinberg, Phys. Rev. Lett. 19 (1967) 1264
A. Salam, Proceedings of the 8th Nobel Symposium, Almvist and Wisksell, Stockholm (1968)

[20] J.E. Kim et al., Rev. Mod. Phys., Vol.53 (1981) 211

[21] M. Davier, in Fundamental Interactions, Cargese 1981, NATO Advanced Study Institutes Series, Plenum Press (1982)

[22] M. Davier, Rapporteur talk at the 21st International Conference on High Energy Physics, Paris 1982, Les éditions de Physique(1982)

[23] Results from PETRA experiments, seminars at DESY, July 1983

[24] D. Denegri, invited talk at this meeting
G. Arnison et al. Phys. Lett. 126B (1983) 398

[25] H.J. Behrend et al., Phys. Lett. 127B (1983) 270

[26] A. Argento et al., Phys. Lett. 120B (1983) 245

[27] M. Althoff et al., Phys. Lett. 126B (1983) 493

[28] Private communication from MAC Collaboration and
E. Fernandez et al., Phys. Rev. Lett. 50 (1983) 2054

[29] F. Wilczek, Phys. Rev. Lett. 39, 1304 (1977)

[30] P. Lipari, invited talk at this meeting

[31] see, for example, K. Kleinknecht, 10th Intern. Conf. on Neutrino Physics and Astrophysics, Balatonfured (June 1982)

[32] G.J. Feldman, Phys. Rev. Lett. 48 (1982) 66
J. Jaros, communication at the 21st Intern. Conf. on High Energy Physics, see also SLAC-Pub 2989 (Oct. 1982)

[33] M.K. Gaillard et al., Phys. Lett. 116B (1982) 279

[34] N. Cabibbo et al., Phys. Lett. 105B (1981) 155

[35] H.J. Behrend et al. Phys. Lett. 123B (1983) 127

[36] Private communications from MAC and MARK II Collaborations, and E. Fernandez et al. Phys. Rev. Lett. 50 (1983) 1238.

HADRONIC ENERGY-ENERGY CORRELATIONS IN HIGH ENERGY e^+e^- ANNIHILATION

F.Csikor

Institute for Theoretical Physics, Eötvös University
Budapest, HUNGARY

Hadronic energy-energy correlations in e^+e^- annihilation have been suggested as a promising tool to test QCD[1]. In fact experiments - carried out by five independent groups[2] - compare reasonably well with the QCD prediction. The fitted value of the strong coupling constant α_s /at total center of mass energy $W \approx 30$GeV/ is 0.14-0.16 . It does however depend on the fragmentation model assumed. The above values are true for Feynman-Field type fragmentation, while the Lund model yields $\alpha_s \approx 0.25$. Since fragmentation is expected to decrease relative to the perturbative QCD contribution with increasing energy W, higher energy experiments promise a better test of QCD. In this note I report on a study[3] for energies comparable to the /standard model/ $Z°$ mass.

To define the energy-energy correlation, assume that a large number of hadron production events in e^+e^- collision is observed. The individual events are labelled with A=1,...,N. In each event one measures the energies dE_A, dE'_A carried by the hadrons into the solid angles $d\Omega$, $d\Omega'$ that lie in the directions $\hat{r}$ and $\hat{r}'$ relative to the collision point. /$\hat{r}$, /$\hat{r}'$/ are characterized by the polar and azimuthal angles ϑ, φ /ϑ', φ'/ and the angle between $\hat{r}$ and $\hat{r}'$ is denoted by χ ./ The normalized energy-energy correlation is then defined by[1]

$$\frac{1}{\sigma_{tot}} \frac{d\Sigma}{d\Omega d\Omega'} = \frac{1}{N} \sum_{A=1}^{N} \left(\frac{dE_A}{W d\Omega}\right) \left(\frac{dE'_A}{W d\Omega'}\right) . \qquad /1/$$

Alternatively, one may define it expressed with the exclusive k particle cross sections /see Ref.1./.

At low energies the e^+ and e^- annihilate into a virtual photon, which produces the hadrons. The hadronic part of the cross section is determined by

$$\sum_f \langle 0| J_\gamma^i |f\rangle\langle f| J_\gamma^k |0\rangle , \qquad /2/$$

where J_γ^i is the hadronic electromagnetic current. After summation over all possible final states and polarizations /and multiplication by the appropriate energy factors/

a symmetric tensor V^{ik} is obtained. V^{ik} has a decomposition:

$$\begin{aligned} V^{ik} = {} & \mathcal{A}(\chi)(2\delta_{ik} - \hat{r}_i\hat{r}_k - \hat{r}'_i\hat{r}'_k) \\ & + \mathcal{B}(\chi)(\delta_{ik}\,\hat{r}\cdot\hat{r}' - \tfrac{1}{2}\hat{r}_i\hat{r}'_k - \tfrac{1}{2}\hat{r}'_i\hat{r}_k) \\ & + \mathcal{C}(\chi)\,\delta_{ik}\,, \end{aligned} \qquad /3/$$

where the functions $\mathcal{A}, \mathcal{B}, \mathcal{C}$ do depend also on W. The energy-energy correlation /for unpolarized initial state/ is expressed in terms of $\mathcal{A}, \mathcal{B}, \mathcal{C}$ as

$$\frac{d\Sigma}{d\Omega\, d\Omega'} = \frac{\alpha^2}{2W^2}\sum_f Q_f^2 \left\{ \mathcal{A}(\chi)\frac{2+\cos^2\vartheta+\cos^2\vartheta'}{2} + \mathcal{B}(\chi)\frac{\cos\chi+\cos\vartheta\cos\vartheta'}{2} + \mathcal{C}(\chi)\right\}, \qquad /4/$$

where Q_f is the charge of the quark with flavour f. The functions $\mathcal{A}, \mathcal{B}, \mathcal{C}$ may be calculated in lowest order QCD[1]. In a simple treatment[1] fragmentation gives additive corrections to the perturbative expressions. The lowest order result should be reliable for angles $\chi \neq 0°$, $\chi \neq 180°$ and - as mentioned above - in fact compares reasonably well with experiment.

For high energies annihilation of e^+ and e^- through both virtual photon and Z^0 should be taken into account. This has been done on the Z^0 resonance peak in Ref. 4 and for arbitrary energies in Ref. 3. Both calculations have been performed for arbitrary initial state polarizations.

The hadronic part of the process is determined by

$$\begin{aligned} & \sum_f \langle 0 | J_\gamma | f \rangle \langle f | J_\gamma | 0 \rangle\,, \\ & \sum_f \langle 0 | J_\gamma | f \rangle \langle f | J_{Weak} | 0 \rangle\,, \\ & \sum_f \langle 0 | J_{Weak} | f \rangle \langle f | J_{Weak} | 0 \rangle\,, \end{aligned} \qquad /5/$$

where J_{Weak} is the neutral weak current. For massless quarks, using TCP and the effective charge conjugation invariance of the final state one gets

$$\begin{aligned} & \sum_f \langle 0 | V | f \rangle \langle f | V | 0 \rangle = \sum_f \langle 0 | A | f \rangle \langle f | A | 0 \rangle\,, \\ & \sum_f \langle 0 | V | f \rangle \langle f | A | 0 \rangle = 0\,, \end{aligned} \qquad /6/$$

where V /A/ is a vector /axial-vector/ current. This means that the functions $\mathcal{A}, \mathcal{B}, \mathcal{C}$ determine the energy-energy correlation at high energies, too.

The result for the fully differential energy-energy correlation is complicated /see Ref.3./. On the other hand, the results for the normalized, angle integrated energy-energy correlations

$$\frac{1}{\sigma_{tot}} \frac{d^3\Sigma}{d\cos\chi\, d\cos\vartheta\, d\cos\vartheta'} , \frac{1}{\sigma_{tot}} \frac{d^2\Sigma}{d\cos\chi\, d\cos\vartheta} , \frac{1}{\sigma_{tot}} \frac{d\Sigma}{d\cos\chi} \qquad /7/$$

are simple. They are independent of

a., initial state polarizations

b., weak interaction parameters /Z° mass and width as well as coupling constants./

Assuming the existence of many Z°'s , weak interaction parameters still drop out from the quantities in Eq. /7/ . The result for the experimentally known correlation reads as

$$\frac{1}{\sigma_{tot}} \frac{d\Sigma}{d\cos\chi} = 3\pi \left\{ \frac{4}{3} \mathcal{A} + \frac{2}{3} \cos\chi\, \mathcal{B} + \mathcal{C} \right\} . \qquad /8/$$

Note, that Eq. /8/ is valid for both the perturbative and nonperturbative contributions. It expresses the fact that initial state polarization dependence as well as weak interaction parameter dependence factorizes and is cancelled by similar dependences in σ_{tot} .

This simple factorization properties are obviously spoiled by radiative corrections. Electromagnetic corrections have been studied for the low energy case in Ref.5. Assuming no experimental cuts - the dominant O /$\alpha \ln(W^2/m_e^2)$/ correction has been shown to be less or equal to 15% of the perturbative contribution. For the high energy case electromagnetic corrections have been studied in Ref.6. The energy dependence is shown on Fig.1. Near the Z° pole the correction becomes very small.

In conclusion, the study of energy-energy correlations at energies comparable to the Z° mass seems to be a very promising possibility to test QCD. Both fragmentation and electromagnetic corrections are suppressed near the Z° peak.

References

1. C.L.Basham, L.S.Brown, S.D.Ellis and S.T.Love, Phys.Rev. Lett. 41, 1585 /1978/; Phys.Rev. D19, 2018 /1979/; L.S.Brown and S.D.Ellis, Phys.Rev. D24, 2383 /1981/
2. Ch.Berger et al., Phys.Lett. 99B, 292 /1981/
   H.J.Behrend et al., Z.Physik 14C, 95 /1982/
   D.Schlatter et al., Phys.Rev.Lett. 49, 521 /1982/
   D.M.Rittson, in Proc. of the 21st Int.Conf. on High Energy Physics, Paris 1982, p.52
   J.D.Burger, ibid. p.63
3. F.Csikor, G.Pócsik and A.Tóth, Phys.Rev. D in press
4. L.S.Brown and S.P.Li, Phys.Rev. D26, 570 /1982/
5. S.M.Barr and L.S.Brown, Phys.Rev. D25, 1229 /1982/
6. F.Csikor, G.Pócsik and A.Tóth, Phys.Rev. D in press and ITP Budapest Rep. No. 419 /1983/

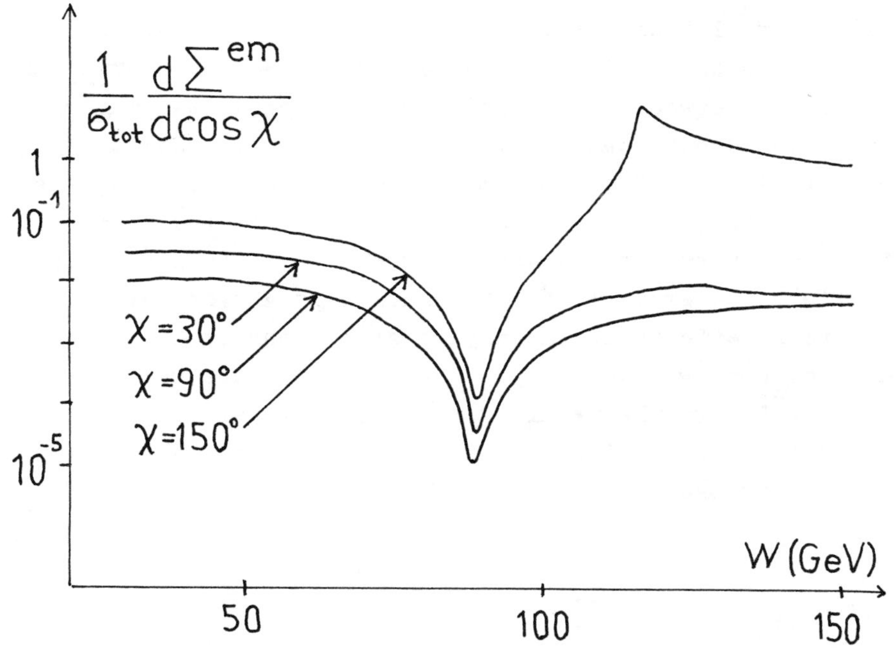

Fig.1. Energy dependence of the electromagnetic correction to the normalized energy-energy correlation at various χ values.

SPIN EFFECTS IN $e^+e^- \to \tau^+\tau^-(\gamma)$

Z. Wąs
Institute of Physics, Jagellonian University,
Reymonta 4, 30-059 Kraków, Poland

The purpose of this talk is to present some results of the work [1]. In this work the cross section for the process $e^+e^- \to \tau^+\tau^-(\gamma)$ was calculated to order α^3 QED including final state spin and mass effects. Radiative corrections include vacuum polarization (leptonic and hadronic), vertex corrections, contribution from box diagrams, soft and hard bremsstrahlung.

Although up to the order α^3 single tau is not polarized (except some numerically negligible effects) there exist correlations between spins of two taus. The spin of tau manifests itself through weak decay so we observe correlations between momenta of tau decay products. The correlations depend substantially on the kinematical cuts used to isolate the experimental sample of the tau pairs.

It is of great importance to control all the effects: i.e. radiative corrections, spin effects, final mass corrections and experimental kinematics in a systematic way. All these effects are hardly separable one from another and the best way to analyze them is the Monte Carlo simulation. Before the results from the M.C. calculations are presented let us give some formulae on which the M.C. algorithm is based

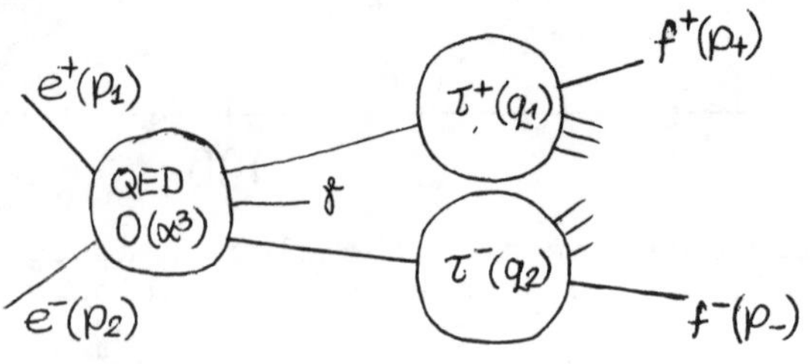

The differential cross section for production and decay process is given by the formula

$$d\sigma = \left[1 + \sum_{i,j/1}^{3} \sigma_{ik}(q_1, q_2)\, g_i(p_+)\, g'_k(p_-)\right] d\sigma_{np}\, dp_+ dp_- \qquad (2)$$

here the matrix $\sigma_{ik}(q_1, q_2)$ is the spin correlation matrix for two final leptons and $dp_\pm$ denotes the differential probability distribution for the decay of unpolarized tau into one charged particle and neutrals:

$$dp_\pm = a(x)\, dx\, d\Omega / 4\pi \ . \qquad (1)$$

The function $\vec{g}(p_\pm)$ in the tau rest frame is equal to $g(x) \frac{\vec{p}_\pm}{|\vec{p}_\pm|}$. $d\sigma_{np}$ is the spin summed differential cross section for $\tau^+\tau^-(\gamma)$ production process.

We limit ourselves to only two decay modes:

DECAY MODE	$g(x)$	$a(x)$	BRANCHING RATIO
$\tau^\pm \to \nu_\tau + \pi^\pm$	1	$\delta(1-x)$	10%
$\tau^{+-} \to \nu_\tau + \rho^\pm$	.48	$\delta(1.186-x)$	23%

In the simple case of α^2 order one can easily calculate the correlation matrix σ_{ik} . It has the following form in the high energy limit $\sqrt{s} \gg 2m_\tau$, and near the threshold $\sqrt{s} \approx 2m_\tau$, respectively.

$$\{r_{ik}\} = \begin{cases} \dfrac{1}{1+\cos^2\Theta}\begin{bmatrix} 1+\cos^2\Theta & 0 & 0 & 0 \\ 0 & -\sin^2\Theta & 0 & 0 \\ 0 & 0 & \sin^2\Theta & 0 \\ 0 & 0 & 0 & 1+\cos^2\Theta \end{bmatrix}; \sqrt{s} \gg 2m_\tau \\[2ex] \begin{bmatrix} 1 & 0 & 0 & 0 \\ 0 & 0 & 0 & 0 \\ 0 & 0 & \sin^2\Theta & .5\sin 2\Theta \\ 0 & 0 & .5\sin 2\Theta & \sin^2\Theta \end{bmatrix}; \sqrt{s} \approx 2m_\tau . \end{cases}$$

Obviously final mass cannot be neglected near the threshold. The tau rest systems used to define correlation matrix and decay products momenta in formulae (2), (3) were chosen as follows:

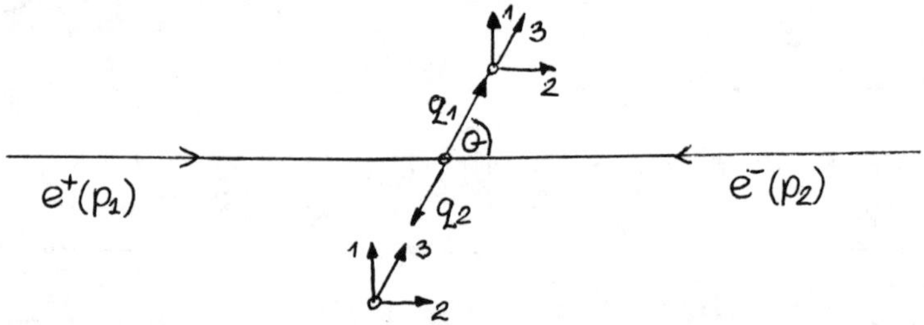

The calculation up to the order α^2, α^3 were done using Monte Carlo method. We have calculated the longitudinal asymmetry

$$A_{lon} = \left[\int_0^{1/2}\int_0^{1/2} + \int_{1/2}^{1}\int_{1/2}^{1} - \int_0^{1/2}\int_{1/2}^{1} - \int_{1/2}^{1}\int_0^{1/2}\right] dy_1 dy_2 \Big/ \int_0^1\int_0^1 dy_1 dy_2 \qquad (4)$$

and the transverse asymmetry

$$A_{tr} = \left[\int_0^{\pi/2} - \int_0^{\pi/4}\right] d\varphi \Big/ \int_0^{\pi/2} d\varphi \qquad (5)$$

where y_1, y_2 denote pions (ρ's) energies in the units of beam energy and φ is an angle between the reaction plane (p_1, p_+) and the plane of decay products (p_+, p_-). These asymmetries show the strength of spin correlations in the direction of the tau momentum and in the perpendicular plane. We can see that there is overpopulation of fast-fast, and slow-slow pairs of pions (or ρ's) as compared to number of slow-fast pairs, which is caused by spin effects. Similarly, the plane of decay products tends to be perpendicular to the reaction plane. These data and relation between spin and radiative corrections is visible from the table

Decay mode		α^2		α^3	
	SPIN	OFF	ON	OFF	ON
π	A_{LON}	0%	24%	3%	25%
	A_{tr} *)	0%	25%	-9%	6%
π, ρ	A_{Lon}	2%	12%	4%	13%
	A_{tr} *)	0%	14%	-13%	-8%

For some details we refer the reader to[1].

*To calculate A_{tr} the cut-off link $[y_i - 0.5] < 0.2$ was used.

Conclusions

Spin effects, radiative corrections and mass effects are hardly separable one from another and thus the best way to analyze them and impose the experimental cuts is the Monte Carlo approach. Generally, spin effects are of the same order as QED $O(\alpha^3)$ corrections (10%).

References

[1] S. Jadach, Z. Wąs, QED $O(\alpha^3)$ Radiative Corrections to the Tau-Pair Production Process Including Spin and Mass Effects, Cracow preprint TPJU 14/83.
[2] F.A. Berends, R. Kleiss, S. Jadach, Z. Wąs, Acta Phys. Pol. B14, 413 (1983).

SEARCH FOR THE INTERMEDIATE VECTOR BOSONS AT THE SPS $\bar{p}p$ COLLIDER

UA1 Collaboration *
presented by D. Denegri

DPhPE, CEN SACLAY
91191 Gif-sur-Yvette Cedex
FRANCE

Abstract

We present the results of a search performed by the UA1 Collaboration for W and Z bosons in the $W^{\pm} \rightarrow e^{\pm}\nu$ and $Z^0 \rightarrow e^+e^-$ or $\mu^+\mu^-$ decay channels. The present search yields 52 $W \rightarrow e\nu$ events, 4 $Z^0 \rightarrow e^+e^-$ and 2 $Z^0 \rightarrow \mu^+\mu^-$ events. The masses of the vector bosons are $M_W = 80.9 \pm 1.5$ GeV and $M_Z = 95.6 \pm 1.4$ GeV . The production and decay features of the W and Z are consistent with expectations from the standard electro-weak model and QCD; in particular, the $W^{\pm} \rightarrow e^{\pm}\nu$ and $Z^0 \rightarrow e^+e^-$ production cross sections are 0.53 ± 0.13 nb and 50 ± 22 pb respectively and the W decay exhibits the asymmetry expected from a V–A coupling.

1. Introduction

We present here the status of our search for the Intermediate Vector Bosons as it stands in the summer of 1983. First evidence for W was obtained in January 1983 [1] from an exposure of $\simeq 18\ nb^{-1}$ sensitivity. With the just terminated 1983 exposure, combining data from 1982 and 1983 and after correction for apparatus efficiency, dead times, losses, our experimental sensitivity is now 136 events/nb. The channels investigated until now are $W^{\pm} \rightarrow e^{\pm}\nu$ and $Z^0 \rightarrow e^+e^-$ or $Z^0 \rightarrow \mu^+\mu^-$, the latter two providing the first evidence for Z^0 production [2]. While the $W \rightarrow e\nu$ and $Z^0 \rightarrow e^+e^-$ samples discussed here are essentially complete and most of the results already published [1,2,3], the $Z^0 \rightarrow \mu^+\mu^-$ results are partial and the $W \rightarrow \mu\nu$ mode, presently under study, is not discussed.

The talk is organized as follows. We first briefly discuss the apparatus and mention the performance of the parts which are essential in the W and Z searches; we then briefly mention the running conditions and event processing in 1983. Next we discuss the extraction of the $W \longrightarrow e\,\nu$ sample and the properties of the W at production and decay. Finally, we discuss the selection of $Z^0 \rightarrow e^+e^-$ and $Z^0 \rightarrow \mu^+\mu^-$ events and compare the features of the W and Z.

2. The apparatus

The UA1 detector, sketched in figs. 1ab, is an essentially 4π solid angle magnetic detector [4]. The interaction region is surrounded by a cylindrical central detector (fig.2), which is a large volume (5.8 m long and 2.3 m in diameter) imaging drift chamber assembly. It is used to "visualize" charged particle tracks and measure their momenta by curvature in the uniform 0.6 Tesla dipole field.

Surrounding the central detector are lead-scintillator sandwich electromagnetic calorimeters to detect e, γ, π^0's. They are of two different geometries. In the central (barrel) part covering $25° \leq \theta \leq 155°$ they have the shape of two cylindrical half-shells subdivided into 48 modules (called gondolas) transverse to the beam direction (fig.3a).In the end-cap regions, covering $5° \leq|\theta|< 25°$, the electromagnetic calorimeters (called bouchons) are subdivided into 32 modules per end-cap in the shape of petals (fig.3b).

Hadron calorimeters, made of an iron -scintillator stack, are used to measure and contain hadrons and surround electromagnetic calorimeters. The central (barrel) part (fig.4), used also as a magnetic flux return, is made of 8 modules (C's) on each side of the beam, while the end-caps are made of 6 pillar-like modules (I's)) per end-cap.

A set of large drift chambers, covering an area of $\simeq$ 500 m^2, fully surrounds the calorimeters to detect and measure muons leaking through the calorimeters and shielding.

The calorimeter assembly described, covering almost full azimuth, extends down to 5° from the beam line; it is complemented by a further set of electromagnetic and hadronic calorimeters down to 0.2°(fig.1b). This $\simeq$ 4π calorimetric coverage is an essential feature of the UA1 apparatus. It ensures transverse energy containement and allows the detection of large transverse energy neutrinos through an apparent transverse energy (momentum) imbalance within individual events.

3. Performances

3.1 Central detector

Momentum measurement precision in the central detector is limited by the localisation error in the drift direction; this error is $\simeq$ 100 μm close to the anode wire and $\simeq$ 350 μm at the maximum drift length of 22 cm. A 1m long track of p = 40 GeV/c in a plane normal to the B field has $\Delta p/p \simeq 20\%$. The error on the coordinate measured by current division is $\simeq$ 3 cm. The multiple ionisation measurement allows the track ionisation to be measured with an accuracy of typically 10%.

3.2 Electromagnetic calorimeters

We discuss in more detail the central electromagnetic calorimeters and their performances, as they are crucial for the detection of the W and Z decay electrons. The gondolas (fig.3a) are made as a lead-scintillator sandwich (1.2 mm lead, 1.5 mm scintillator foil thickness). Each module covers $\simeq 180°$ in azimuth, is 22.5 cm long in the beam direction, about 4m long transverse to the beam and is $\simeq$ 27 radiation lengths (X_0) deep. Each gondola is subdivided in 4 samplings in depth ($3.3X_0$, $6.6X_0$, $9.9X_0$, $6.6X_0$), to follow the longitudinal shower developement shape. Each sampling is read out through wavelength shifter plates by four photomultipliers (PM's), on the top left and right and bottom left and right(fig.3a). Using light attenuation in the wavelength shifter plates, the ratio of top to bottom PM signals can be used to obtain the azimuthal angle for localized energy depositions, with a resolution of $\Delta\phi_{rms}$ (rad) = $0.3/\sqrt{E(\mathrm{GeV})}$. Similarly, using light attenuation in the scintillator, the ratio of left to right PM signals gives the localisation along the beam direction (X axis) with a resolution of $\Delta X_{rms}(\mathrm{cm}) = 6.3/\sqrt{E(\mathrm{GeV})}$. The energy resolution obtained for electrons using all PM's' is $\Delta E_{rms}(\mathrm{GeV}) = 0.15\sqrt{E(\mathrm{GeV})}$. The energy response of the calorimeters to electrons also shows excellent linearity ($\leq$ 1% deviation) in the full range of energies of interest.

The end-cap electromagnetic calorimeters (fig. 3b) are of similar construction and have also a four-fold segmentation in depth. The location of showers is however measured directly by a position detector (fig. 3b) located inside the calorimeter stack, at a depth of $\simeq 11X_0$. The position detector is made of two planes of orthogonal proportional tubes of 2 X 2 cm² cross section. The position accuracy for high energy electrons is ± 2 mm.

3.3 Hadron calorimeter

The structure of a hadron calorimeter module (C), made as an iron-scintillator stack (5 cm Fe, 1 cm scintillator), is shown in fig. 4. It is subdivided into 12 azimuthal segments and is read out in two samplings in depth. The total thickness of the calorimeters in the barrel region at normal incidence is about 5.5 collision lengths.

The use of the hadron calorimeter to detect high energy electrons is essentially as a veto. An energetic electron shower is practically fully contained in our electromagnetic calorimeter; more specifically , for 98% of electrons of 40 GeV, less than 1% of the shower energy should leak to the hadron calorimeter, as measured in test beams.

The pion to electron rejection of the electromagnetic + hadron calorimeter assembly can be estimated from fig.5a which gives the probability for a pion of incident momentum p to deposit an energy below a threshold value E_C^{thr} in the hadronic calorimeter. This is a rapidly decreasing function of p and decreasing E_c^{thr} . A 40 GeV pion has an $\simeq$ 0.3% probability to deposit $E_c^{thr} \leq$ 200 MeV, while 98% of electrons satisfy this.

The electron to pion rejection can be further improved by applying cuts on the response of the first and fourth samplings of the electromagnetic calorimeter.

3.4 Calorimeter calibration

A collimated cobalt source is used for a detailed surface mapping of the electromagnetic calorimeter response (as seen by each individual PM), and to obtain periodically an absolute energy scale calibration of all the calorimeter modules at the site of the experiment. This is done after a cross- calibration of the response of identical spare modules to this same Co source and to an electron test beam. At present the detailed analysis of the systematics of the calibration is not yet finished; we estimate the uncertainty on the absolute energy scale, and therefore on the W and Z masses, to about 3%.

3.5 Missing transverse energy detection

An essential feature of the apparatus is its ability to detect high p_t neutrinos through a missing transverse energy. A vector sum of calorimetric energy depositions over the full solid angle can be performed event by event. It should result in no hadro-electromagnetic energy leakage in the directions transverse to the beams (a substantial amount of longitudinal energy due to beam fragments leaks however through the beam pipe), except for losses due to cracks in the apparatus and dead regions. The observed resolution in the missing transverse energy is ΔE_t^M (GeV) $\simeq 0.6 \sqrt{E_T}$(GeV), where E_T is the scalar sum of transverse energy depositions per event. It has been estimated from minimum bias and jetty events in which no substantial losses due to muons or neutrinos are expected (fig. 5b).

3.6 Muon chambers

The muon detector surrounding the whole apparatus is made up of two layers of proportional drift tubes (45 x 150 mm² cross section, $\simeq$ 4 m long), separated by 60 cm in depth to provide a lever arm. Each layer is made of two orthogonal sets of staggered drift tubes (fig. 6) to measure the two space coordinates, lift the left-right ambiguity and minimize dead spaces. The spatial and angular resolutions achieved are $\simeq$ 300 μm and $\simeq$ 1 mrad respectively, which is comparable to the multiple scattering expected for high energy muons traversing the magnet and shielding (60 cm thick iron walls in the side and top barrel regions).

The signature for a high energy isolated muon is a track penetrating calorimeters and the iron shielding, with energy depositions in the calorimeters consistent with a minimum ionising particle, and with space and angular coordinates measured in the muon chambers consistent with central detector measurements, within the deviations expected from multiple scattering.

4. Running conditions, triggers and data taking

The effective integrated luminosity for the 1982 run was 18 nb^{-1} and for the present 1983 run , it is 118 nb^{-1}; this corresponds to $\simeq 8*10^9$ $\bar{p}p$ collisions taking place in the apparatus. The operating conditions in the 1983 run were: 3 $\bar{p}$ bunches against 3 p-bunches, with typically $\simeq 10^{10}$ $\bar{p}$/bunch and $\simeq 10^{11}$ p/bunch; the top luminosity achieved was $\simeq 1.6 * 10^{29}$ cm^{-2} sec^{-1} , while the typical luminosity at injection was $\simeq 1.1 * 10^{29}$ cm^{-2} sec^{-1}, with an average luminosity lifetime of $\simeq$ 13 hours.

For each $\bar{p}p$ collision detected by front scintillator hodoscopes (the pretrigger), the main trigger operates and takes the decision within the time interval between two successive beam crossings (3.8 μsec). It is made of fast trigger processors which work with the energy depositions in calorimetric cells or the pattern of muon chamber cells hit, looking for the presence of (localised) transverse energy depositions, or for one (or two) muon candidates roughly pointing (within $\simeq$ 150 mrad) to the interaction region. Several trigger conditions are operated simultaneously: electron or jet triggers in the central or end-cap regions, global E_t , one or two muons etc. Fig. 7 shows the pattern of localised E_t depositions defining either an electron trigger or a jet trigger. Typical trigger thresholds were: for electrons either two adjacent gondolas or petals with E_t above 10 GeV, and for jets either 8 adjacent gondolas with two C's in projection, or a whole quadrant of the end-cap, with an E_t above 20 GeV.

The data taking rate was $\simeq$ 1.5 events/sec typically and the total number of recorded events in 1983 is $\simeq 2.2 * 10^6$, with $\simeq$ 40 % of electron triggers. Electron triggers with $E_t > 15$ GeV (fully corrected by response attenuation maps) and di-muon triggers were selected on-line by a set of 168E processors and written on special tapes. These events were fully reconstructed off-line, filtered and analysed by physicists within $\simeq$ 48 hours.

5. Data Analysis

5.1 Selection of $W \to e\nu$ events

We now describe one of the two methods used to extract $W \to e\nu$ events. This selection procedure is based on the missing transverse energy i.e. the emission of a high p_t neutrino. We require :

i) a cluster of two adjacent electromagnetic calorimeter cells with $E_t > 15$ GeV ;

ii) a hard track in the central detector, pointing to the calorimetric cluster within 5σ, with $p_t > 7$ GeV/c ;

iii) a missing transverse energy $E_t^M > 15$ GeV ; this missing energy has to be validated, i.e. not overestimated for obvious instrumental reasons; (for example, events having a jet within ± 10° of the vertical plane are rejected, to avoid energy leakage through the central cut of the apparatus) ;

iv) isolation of the hard track and electromagnetic cluster ; more specifically, less than 4 GeV of E_t in the sum of the four calorimetric cells, two on each side of the cluster, and no other track of $p_t > 1.5$ GeV within a 20° cone around the track ;

v) no jet in the event coplanar (back-to-back) with the electromagnetic cluster within ± 30°.

Notice that we do not require a priori the hard track to behave as an electron, in particular, there is no cut on the energy deposited in the hadronic calorimeter (E_{had}) behind, but rather we control a posteriori that events so selected are consistent with $W \to e\nu$. Also, we do not exclude jetty events, but only remove configurations where the "e" candidate and jet are roughly back-to-back, to avoid contamination from $Q\bar{Q}$ production followed by a semileptonic $Q \to e\ \nu\ Q'$ decay (Q=c,b).

Indeed this selection yields an almost pure sample of electron events. After a detailed scanning of so selected candidates on the interactive graphic facility Megatek to check for possible apparatus malfunctioning and reject backgrounds from cosmics and beam halo, we obtain 52 events where the hard isolated track is consistent with an $e^{\pm}$, and a few events with a hard isolated hadron ($E_{had}/E_{tot} > 3\%$). The latter events are being studied to check consistency with $W \to \tau\nu$ ($\tau^{\pm} \to \pi^{\pm}\pi^{0}$'s) decays for example.

The electron candidates have a very clean instrumental signature. They have $\lesssim 1\%$ of their energy leaking to the hadron calorimeter E_{had} and are well inside the post-selection cuts imposed (fig.8a) ; the longitudinal shower development shape in the four segments of the electromagnetic calorimeter is consistent with expectations for electrons (fig.8b for example). The momentum measurement in the central detector and the calorimetric energy measurement are consistent (fig.9a) and behave as expected for high energy electrons, taking into account radiative losses (fig. 9b).The longitudinal (x) and azimuthal (ϕ) coordinates of electron tracks at the calorimeter surface, as measured independently by the central detector and calorimeter, are also fully consistent within the expected errors (fig.10a,b).

The missing E_t spectrum for the overall sample of 52 $W \to e\nu$ events is shown in fig.11; it already exhibits a clear Jacobian peak behaviour, the tell-tale signature of $W \to e\ \nu$ events. In the subsequent analysis we keep however only events where the electrons are not within ± 15° from the vertical plane through the beam pipe. This fiducial volume cut reduces the sample to 43 $W \to e\nu$ events. It is introduced to avoid biases (systematic underestimate of E_t^e and E_t^ν) due to electrons hitting the gondolas near their ends i.e. close to the junction between wavelength-shifter plates and light guides. Within this sample we estimate the background from $W \to \tau\nu$ ($\tau \to e\ \nu\nu$) at $\simeq 2$ events, and from $W \to \tau\nu$ ($\tau^{\pm} \to \pi^{\pm}\pi^{0}$) at < 0.5 event.

A typical $W \rightarrow e\nu$ event is shown in figs.12. Fig.12a shows the central detector digitizings, fig.12b all the reconstructed tracks and calorimetric E_t depositions (with symbols logarithmically proportionnal to E_t) and fig.12c only tracks with $P_t > 2$ GeV/c and calorimetric cells with $E_t > 2$ GeV. The kinematical configuration of the event is very simple. Also shown is the reconstructed missing transverse energy vector labelled ν.

5.2 Consistency with the $W \rightarrow e\nu$ hypothesis and W mass

We discuss now in more detail the sample of $W \rightarrow e\nu$ candidates. Fig.13a is the scatter plot of the missing transverse momentum components perpendicular and parallel to the electron direction in the transverse plane; fig.13 b is the scatter plot of the electron transverse energy vs the missing transverse energy antiparallel to the electron. The strong Jacobian peak behaviour [5] in both E_t^e and E_t^ν in fig.13b and the pronounced tendency of the electron and missing E_t to be back-to-back (fig.13a) strongly suggest a two-body decay $W \rightarrow e\nu$. The E_t^e projection (on which the resolution is better than on E_t^ν) is shown in fig.14a, and compared to the predictions for a two-body decay $W \rightarrow e\nu$ (with $M_W = 80$ GeV) or a three-body decay $X \rightarrow e\nu\nu$ ($M_X = 80$ GeV). The p_t^W distribution expected from QCD [6], which is in agreement with data, has been folded in. The $W \rightarrow e\nu$ interpretation is clearly favored.

From the inclusive electron transverse energy spectrum in fig.14a a first estimate of the W mass can be obtained : $M_W = (80.5 \pm 0.5)$GeV ; this determination is however sensitive to the p_t^W distribution folded in. An estimate less sensitive to the W production mechanism is provided by the e-ν "transverse mass" (effective mass in the transverse plane) : $M_t^2(e\nu) = 2\, E_t^e E_t^\nu (1 - \cos\phi^{e\nu})$. This quantity is bounded by $M_t(e\nu) \leq M_{eff}(e\nu) \equiv M_W$. The distribution in $M_t^{e\nu}$ is shown in fig.14b and a fit to this distribution gives : $M_W = (80.3 \pm ^{0.4}_{1.3})$GeV. To avoid the possible contamination from τ decays at lower E_t^e, E_t^ν, and to minimize sensitivity to the W production mechanism, we also selected only events where the W decay is largely transverse, requiring E_t^e, $E_t^\nu > 30$ GeV. The resulting $M_t^{e\nu}$ distribution is shown in fig.14c ; a fit to the W mass then yields $M_W = (80.9 \pm 1.5)$GeV. We consider this last value as our most reliable estimate, as it is least affected by systematics. (Note that all these mass estimates are still affected by an overall energy scale uncertainty of $\simeq 3$ %). The fit to this distribution also gives an upper limit to the W width : $\Gamma_W \leq 7$ GeV, at a 90% C.L. These values of M_W and Γ_W can be compared to expectations from the standard model : $M_W = 83.0 \pm 2.4$ GeV (including radiative corrections [8,9], and most of the quoted uncertainty is due to the experimental error on $\sin^2\theta_W$) and $\Gamma_W \simeq 3.0$ GeV, assuming three generations of fundamental fermions.

5.3 W production mechanism and cross section

Fig.15a shows the transverse momentum distribution of the W obtained from the electron and missing transverse momentum vectors. The average value in $< p_t^W > = 6.3$ GeV/c. The curve in fig.15a is the QCD prediction of ref.[6]. Among events with $p_t^W > 10$ GeV/c, 5 events (shaded in fig.15a), i.e. $\simeq$ 10% of the total sample, have a clearly recognizable jet balancing the W transverse momentum. They are interpreted as being due to a hard non collinear gluon bremstrahlung in the initial state [6].

Fig.15b is the (folded) distribution of the W longitudinal momentum, expressed as a fraction of the incident beam momentum $|X_W| = |p_\ell^W| / p_{inc}$. The determination of the longitudinal motion of the $e\nu$ system, assuming it results from the $W \to e\nu$ decay, gives two solutions per event due to the unmeasured longitudinal neutrino component. However, the overall longitudinal energy flow within each event, as determined in particular by our forward angle systems, can be used to kinematically constrain the event. This lifts the ambiguity in $\simeq$ 70% of cases. For the remaining cases, corresponding to W's which are rather slow in the c.m., the two solutions are close and the X_W distribution is little affected by this kinematical ambiguity. The curve in fig.15b is the parton (Drell-Yan) model prediction for W production by $q\bar{q}$ annihilation [5]. From the observed X_W distribution and the parton model relations $X_W = X_q - X_{\bar{q}}$, $X_q \cdot X_{\bar{q}} = M_W^2/s$, we can unfold the distributions of the partons annihilating within the proton (q) and antiproton ($\bar{q}$) , figs.16a,b. Separating now W^+ and W^- production, as $u\bar{d} \to W^+$ and $\bar{u}d \to W^-$, we can also determine separately the $u(\bar{u})$ and $d(\bar{d})$ quark distributions sampled by the W (fig.16c,d). The curves in figs.16 are the parton model (leading log approximation) predictions [5]; they are in qualitative agreement with the data.

Finally, from our experimental sensitivity (integrated luminosity), which is known within ± 15%, and the observed number of $W \to e\nu$ events, after correction for acceptance losses (geometry, E_t^e , E_t^ν cuts, no jet back-to-back, electron isolation cuts), we obtain a cross section:

$$\sigma_{W^\pm} \cdot BR(W^\pm \to e^\pm \nu) = 0.53 \pm 0.8\ (\pm 0.9)\ \text{nb} \quad \text{(statistics + systematics).}$$

This can be compared to the 0.39 nb expected from the standard model, assuming again that only three generations of fermions are kinematically allowed in the W decay.

5.4 W decay

Fig.17 is the scatter plot of the $e^\pm$ transverse energy versus the $e^\pm$ production angles ($\theta^\pm$) in the $p\bar{p}$ center of mass. Notice that the e^+ and e^- distributions have been folded, with the e^+ emission angle (θ^+) measured from the incident $\bar{p}$ line-of-flight and conversely the e^- angle (θ^-) from the incident proton direction. We use here only the 29 $W^\pm \to e^\pm \nu$ events within the fiducial volume for which there is no ambiguity on the charge assignement (cf. fig.9a). The equal probability contour-lines in fig.17 give the relative population probabilities for the different regions of the plot. They are obtained from a parton model calculation assuming a pure V-A coupling at W production and decay, with $M_W \simeq 81$ GeV and $< p_t^W > = 7$ GeV; a sea $q\bar{q}$ annihilation term is also included. The experimentally observed population is in good agreement with expectations, thus providing evidence for the V-A coupling, which is responsible for the forward-backward decay asymmetry, and is the signature of the parity violating weak W decay.

This evidence is however somewhat dependent on the W production mechanism. We can get rid of this dependence by looking at the $e^{\pm}$ emission angles ($\theta^*_{\pm}$), with respect to incident $\bar{p}$ and p directions and folded as above, but in the W rest frame. Now, however, only events which have no kinematical ambiguity on the W longitudinal motion (p^W_{ℓ}) can be used, implying a further reduction of the sample. The two-fold kinematical ambiguity in p^W_{ℓ} corresponds to two symmetrical solutions in $\theta^*_{\pm}$. It is however possible to correct the observed $\cos\theta^*_{\pm}$ angular distribution bin-by-bin. The corrected and folded $\cos\theta^*_{\pm}$ angular distribution in the W rest frame is shown in fig.18. For a pure V-A coupling (and no sea $q\bar{q}$ annihilation contribution), the expected distribution is $(1+\cos\theta^*_{\pm})$, in very good agreement with the data.

5.5 Selection of di-electron events and evidence for $Z^0 \rightarrow e^+e^-$

The selection procedure for di-electron events is the following. We require:

i) two clusters of two adjacent electromagnetic calorimeter cells with $E_t > 25$ GeV;

ii) a hard-track compatible with $p_t > 7$ GeV pointing to each cluster and isolated both in the central detector and calorimetrically, similarly to the $W \rightarrow e\nu$ search;

iii) a transverse energy deposition of not more than 600 MeV in the hadron calorimeter behind the electromagnetic clusters.

This first selection, aiming at electron pairs of mass ≥ 50 GeV, yields directly only 4 events, clustered around 95 GeV in mass. (One of these events turns out to have a well isolated e candidate track within ≃15° from the $\vec{B}$ field making its momentum practically unmeasurable). Fig.19 shows how these 4 events emerge from the sequence of successive cuts indicated.

The events have been carefully scanned to check for possible apparatus malfunctioning. The electron signatures for these 4 events are very clean and consistent with those observed for $W^{\pm} \rightarrow e^{\pm}\nu$ electrons. The two samples of $e^{\pm}$, from $W \rightarrow e\nu$ and from $Z^0 \rightarrow ee$ candidates are compared in figs.8 to 10.Figs.8c,d show the longitudinal shower depositions, fig.9c the momentum versus energy measurements for $Z^0 \rightarrow e^+e^-$ candidates and figs.10c,d compare the longitudinal $(x)e^{\pm}$ coordinates and the azimuthal $(\phi)e^{\pm}$ coordinates. From fig.9c we see that the e^+e^- charge assignement is unambiguous for 3 dielectron events, the fourth event having a track of undetermined charge (unmeasurable momentum). For one of the $Z^0 \rightarrow e^+e^-$ candidates in fig.9c there is also a big mismatch between the momentum measurement (9 GeV/c) and the corresponding calorimetric energy measurement (48 GeV). This event is thought to represent an electron which has radiated $\simeq$ 80% of its energy by either internal or external bremsstrahlung; the probability for this to occur is estimated at $\simeq$ 3% per electron [7].

If in our selection procedure the thresholds in i) and ii) are lowered to clusters with $E_t > 15$ GeV and tracks with $p_t > 7$ GeV, all other criteria remaining the same, only one additional e^+e^- pair is found, at a mass of $\simeq$ 35 GeV. This event (fig.24) is near our present experimental e^+e^- mass threshold and is close to the upper limit in mass of our expected sensitivity to Drell-Yan e^+e^- pairs. The absence of any di-electron signal at $M \gtrsim 35$ GeV shows how well separated from any background the four di-electron events clustering around 95 GeV are. This observation, and the very low estimates, $O(10^{-3})$ or less, for the various possible sources of background, as from bi-jet or possible e-jet events [2],(probably $Q\bar{Q}$ followed by $Q \to e\nu Q'$), suggests as the most plausible interpretation of these 4 di-electron events that they are $Z^0 \to e^+e^-$ decays.

One of our $Z^0 \to e^+e^-$ events, as seen in the central detector and calorimeters is shown in figs.20. Again the event is very simple if only a moderate threshold is imposed on track or calorimetric cell E_t values. Fig.21 shows the total event calorimetric E_t depositions for the four $Z^0 \to e^+e^-$ events, on a two-dimensional rapidity vs ϕ plot. The two large and localised electromagnetic E_t depositions per event are outstanding; one of the events has also a clear jet in addition.

5.6 Z^0 mass and width

An estimate of the Z^0 mass and width can now be obtained from these four e^+e^- events. The raw calorimetric data have to be corrected (track-by-track) for charged and neutral parasitic track pile-up on gondolas, the detailed differences between experimental and fitted gondola response maps vs. $e^{\pm}$ point and angle of incidence, and for the ageing of gondolas due to radiation. The observed dispersion of points is consistent with the estimated resolution. A fit to a gaussian resolution smeared Breit-Wigner form yields :

$$M_{Z^0} = 95.6 \pm 1.4 \text{ GeV} \quad (\pm 3\% \text{ for energy scale uncertainty})$$

$$\Gamma_{Z^0} = 1.8 \pm {}^{5.5}_{1.1} \text{ GeV} .$$

The Z^0 width is < 8.5 GeV at a 90% confidence level and < 11.5 GeV at a 95% confidence level. These values can again be compared with expectations from the standard model which are $M_{Z^0} = 93.8 \pm 2.0$ GeV (including radiative corrections [8,9]) and $\Gamma_{Z^0} \simeq 3.0$ GeV, if there are only three generations of kinematically accessible fermions (if $m_t \gtrsim 40$ GeV then $\Gamma_{Z^0} \simeq 2.84$ GeV). If there are more generations of which only neutrinos are kinematically allowed in Z^0 decay, as each (light) neutrino species contributes to a Z^0 partial decay rate with $\Delta\Gamma_{Z^0} \simeq 0.18$ GeV, our present measured value of Γ_{Z^0} limits the number of neutrino species to $N_\nu \leq 31$ at a 90% confidence level.

5.7 Selection of di-muon events and evidence for $Z^0 \to \mu^+\mu^-$

As mentioned previously, events with a "dimuon" trigger were preselected on-line ($\simeq$ 10 000 events), and only these events have been fully analysed until now. The off-line selection of di-muons requires a hard track in the central detector with $p_t > 5$ GeV and projected length ≥ 40 cm, matching approximately the muon chamber measurements.

The selection procedure and a detailed scan of the candidates yields 7 di-muon pairs altogether; 5 events are close to our experimental $\mu^+\mu^-$ mass lower limit (10 GeV), while 2 events are at large masses. Only these 2 events are further discussed. To ascertain that these are muons, after a careful study of central detector digitizings to reject possible kinks, the energy depositions in the four electromagnetic calorimeter and two hadronic calorimeter samplings traversed are checked for consistency with a minimum ionizing particle (figs.22a,b). The consistency between the central detector and muon chamber measurements in position and angle is shown in fig.22c by comparison with the corresponding distributions observed for vertical cosmic rays used for calibration. (For only 2 of the 4 muon tracks have appropriate cosmic ray calibration data been already analysed). A detailed investigation of these events validates them as $\mu^+\mu^-$ pairs. Their mass values are 95 ± 8 GeV and $88 \pm^{36}_{19}$ GeV respectively. Fig.23 is a display of the first of these events ; this event is particularly interesting as the $\mu^+\mu^-$ pair recoils against a rather hard jet of $E_t \simeq 23$ GeV.

Our overall di-lepton mass spectrum is shown in fig.24. The events observed at $M_{\mu\mu} < 20$ GeV are consistent with expectations for Drell-Yan pair production, taking into account our experimental efficiency. As no events are observed at $M_{\mu\mu} \gtrsim 20$ GeV, it is again most plausible to interpret the 2 high-mass $\mu^+\mu^-$ pairs as $Z^0 \to \mu^+\mu^-$ events. Estimates of background from bi-jet (heavy flavored) events indicate a negligible contribution [2].

5.8 Z° production mechanism, comparison with the W and the Standard Model

In figs.15 c,d are shown the transverse ($p_t^{Z^0}$) and longitudinal (X_{Z^0}) production distributions for our 6 Z° events. They are entirely consistent with W production features shown in figs.15 a,b.

From our integrated luminosity and experimental acceptances, we obtain for the $Z^0 \to e^+e^-$ cross section :

$$\sigma_{Z^0} \cdot BR(Z^0 \to e^+e^-) = (50 \pm 20 \pm 9)\text{pb} \quad \text{(statistics + systematics)}.$$

This is about 1/10 of the $\sigma_{W^\pm} \cdot BR(W^\pm \to e^\pm\nu)$ production cross section, in qualitative agreement with the three generations standard model and QCD [5].

In preceeding sections we compared our observed values of $M_{W,Z}$, $\Gamma_{W,Z}$ and $\sigma \cdot B$ to expectations from the standard model (plus QCD). Conversely, we can now use our measured values of $M_{W,Z}$ to determine the values of the parameters of the model [8]. Using for the relation between Weinberg's singlet-triplet mixing angle θ_W ,(at $Q^2 = M_W^2$) and the W mass the radiatively corrected expression [9]:

$$\sin^2\theta_W = (38.5 \text{ GeV}/M_W)^2$$

we obtain from the measured M_W value: $\sin^2\theta_W = 0.226 \pm 0.016$. This can be compared to the value of $\sin^2\theta_W$ determined from low energy νN scattering and evolved to $Q^2 = M_W^2$: 0.215±0.014 [10].

For the paramater $\rho \equiv G_Z/G_F$ measuring the relative strength of weak neutral to charged current interactions and given in the standard model by the ratio of W and Z masses :

$$\rho \equiv \frac{G_Z}{G_F} = \frac{M_W^2}{M_Z^2 \cos^2\theta_W}$$

using measured values of M_W ,M_Z and the above value of $\sin^2\theta_W$, we obtain $\rho = 0.926 \pm 0.041$, to be compared to the value $\rho = 1$ expected in the (minimal) standard model. The values of $\sin^2\theta_W$ and ρ ,as determined by our experiment, with corresponding confidence levels, are shown in fig.25.

6. Conclusions

In conclusion, we may say that, within the present experimental errors, the observed properties of the W and Z^0 are entirely consistent with the standard model, and their production features consistent with QCD expectations. As the radiative corrections to lowest order standard model W, Z masses generate an upward shift of masses by $\simeq$ 4 GeV, the consistency of our measured values with these predictions test the model at the level of its quantum corrections. Precision measurements of the W, Z masses and widths would provide tight tests of the model and information on further generations of fermions. Such measurements may be possible in not too distant a future even at the $\bar{p}p$ collider.

Acknowledgments

It is a pleasure for me to thank the organizers for their efforts in arranging such an interesting and enjoyable meeting in Dubrovnik.

References

* UA1 Collaboration :
Aachen - Annecy(LAPP) - Birmingham - CERN - Helsinki - Queen Mary College, London - Paris (College de France) - Riverside - Rome - Rutherford Lab. - Saclay (CEN) - Vienna .

[1] G. ARNISON et al., Phys. Letters 122B (1983) 103; see also UA2 results in : M. BANNER et al., Phys. Letters 122B (1983)476.

[2] G. ARNISON et al., Phys. Letters 126B (1983) 398.

[3] G. ARNISON et al., "Further evidence for charged intermediate vector bosons at the SPS collider", to be published in Phys. Letters.

[4] UA1 proposal CERN/SPSC 78-06; see also : M. CALVETTI et al., Nucl. Instr. Methods 176 (1980) 255.

[5] E.F. PAIGE and S. PROTOPOPESCU, ISAJET program, BNL 29777 (1981); see also : L.B. OKUN and M.B. VOLOSHIN, Nucl. Phys. B120 (1977)459, C. QUIGG, Rev. Mod. Phys. 49 (1977) 297, R.F. PEIERLS, T. TRUEMAN, L.L. WANG, Phys. Rev. D16 (1977) 1397; R. HORGAN and M. JACOB, Proc. CERN School of Physics (Malente), CERN 81-04, p.65.

[6] P. AURENCHE and R. KINNUNEN, Annecy preprint LAPP-TH-78 (1983); see also : F. HALZEN and W. SCOTT, Phys. Letters 78B (1978) 318, and Phys. Rev. D25 (1982) 754.

[7] F. BERENDS et al., Nucl. Phys. B202 (1982) 63 and private communication.

[8] S.L. GLASHOW, Nucl. Phys. 22 (1961) 579, S. WEINBERG, Phys. Rev. Letters 19 (1967) 1264, A. SALAM, Proc. 8th Nobel Symposium, Aspenasgarden, 1968 (Almquist and Wiksell, Stockholm, 1968) p.367; see also J. ELLIS et al., Ann. Rev. Nuc. Sci. 32 (1982) 443.

[9] W.J. MARCIANO, A. SIRLIN, Phys. Rev. Letters 46 (1981) 163 and references therein, see also M. CAPDEQUI-PEYRANERE, F.M. RENARD, M. TALON, Z. fur Phys C, 5 (1980) 337.

[10] W.J. MARCIANO and Z. PARSA, Proc. Particle and Fields Summer Study on Elementary Particle Physics and Future Facilities, Snowmass, CO, 1982, p.155.

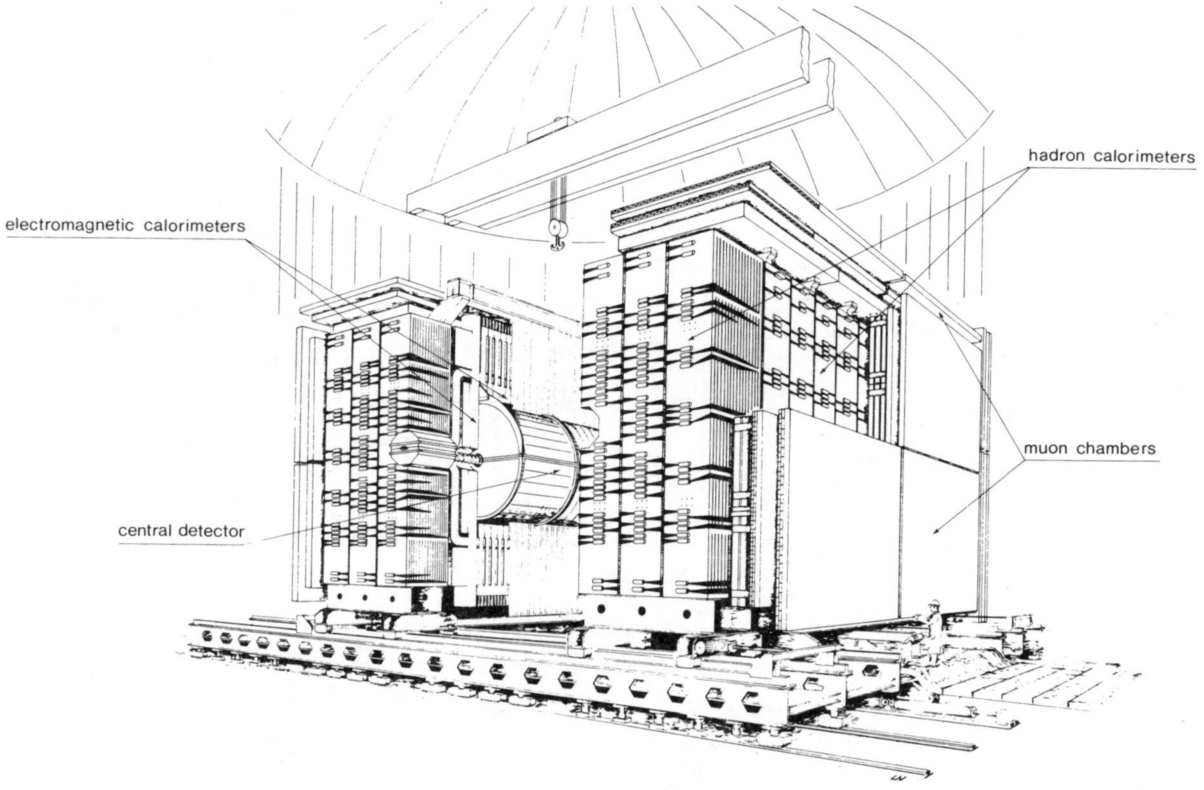

Fig.1 - a) The UA1 detector.

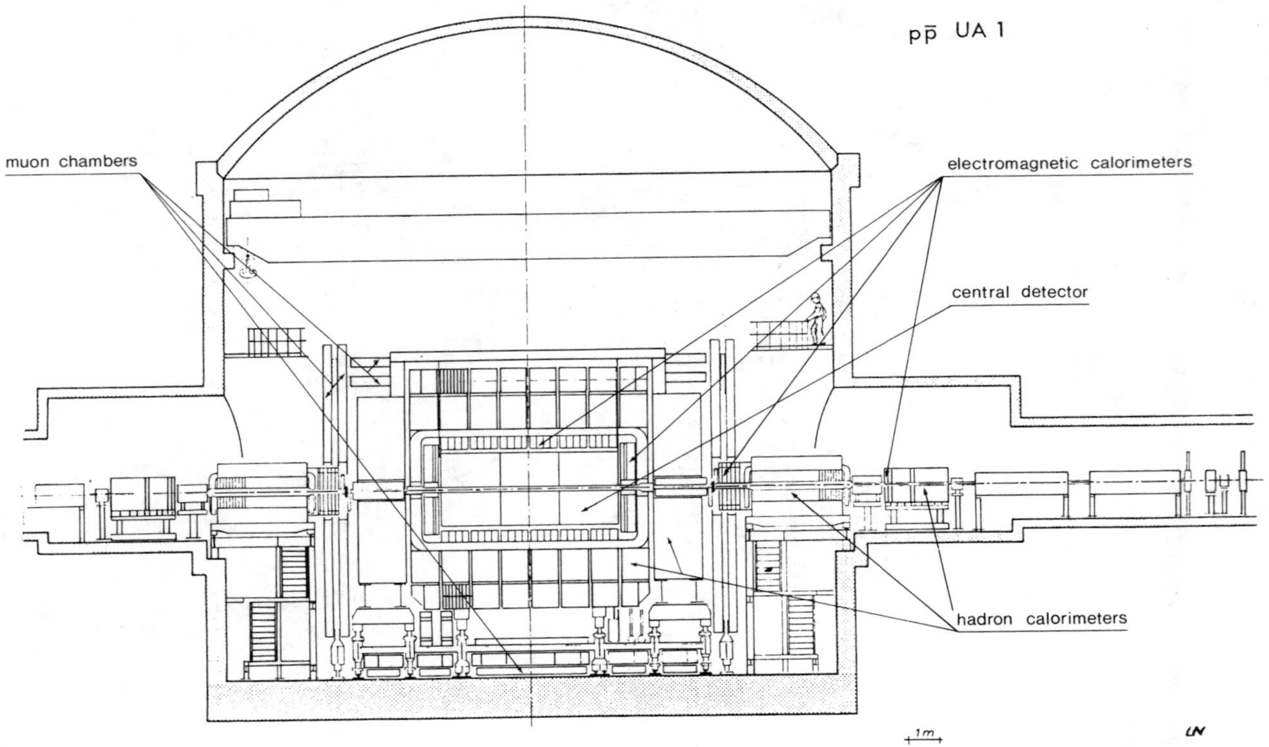

Fig.1 - b) The UA1 detector, vertical section through the beam pipe.

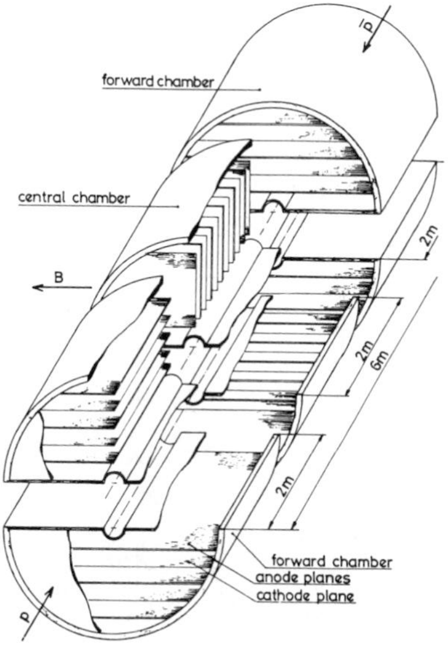

Fig.2 - Diagram of the central detector showing the orientations of the wire planes in the central and forward chambers.

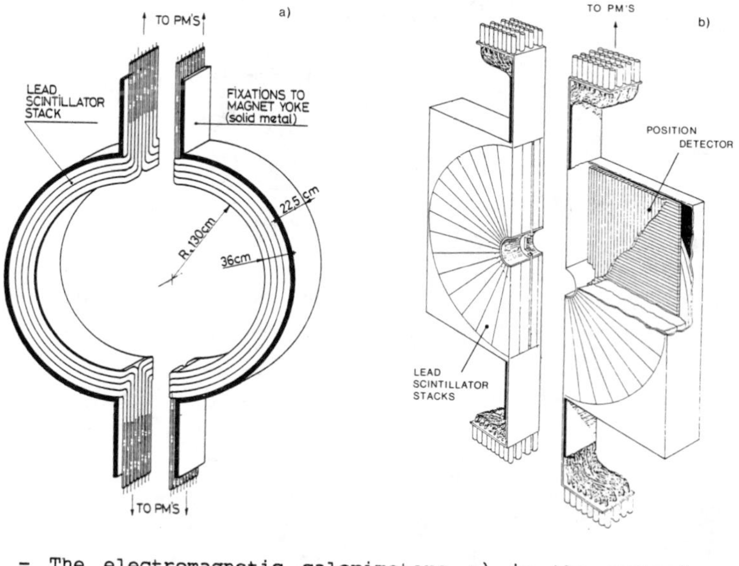

Fig.3 - The electromagnetic calorimeters a) in the central region (gondolas) b) in the end-cap region.

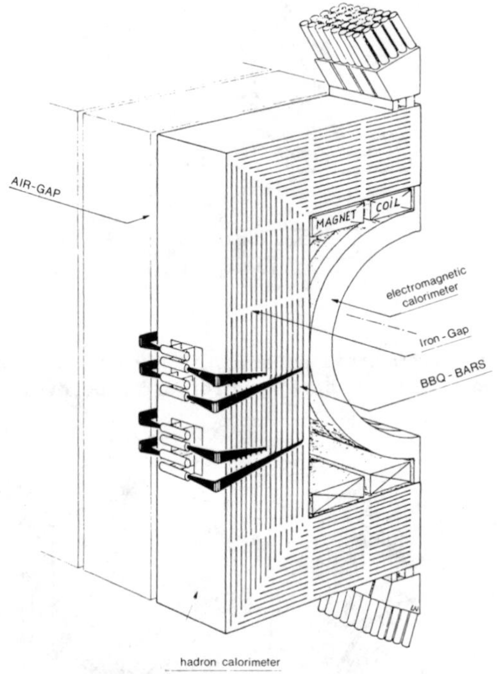

Fig.4 - Element (C) of the hadron calorimeter, with attached electromagnetic calorimeter cells.

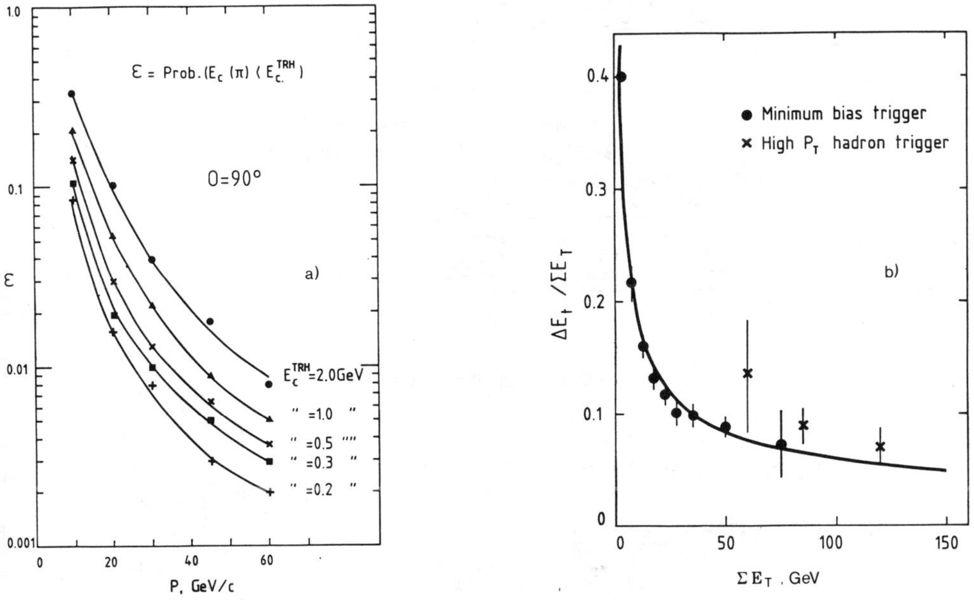

Fig.5 - a)Probability for a pion of incident momentum p to deposit less than E_c^{thr} in the hadron calorimeter behind the electromagnetic one, at normal incidence;
b) Missing transverse energy resolution vs scalar E_t

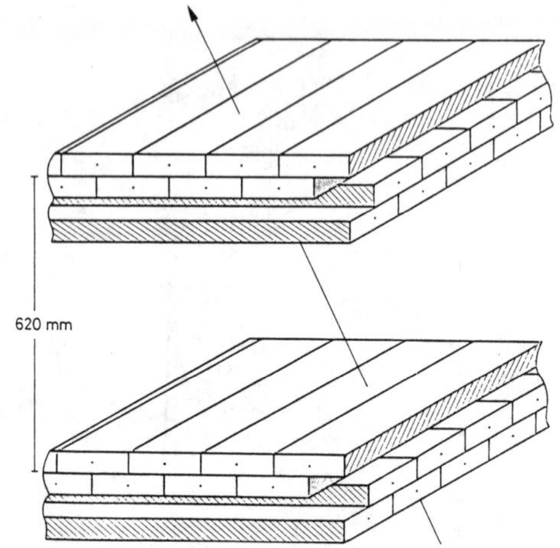

Fig.6 - The muon chambers.

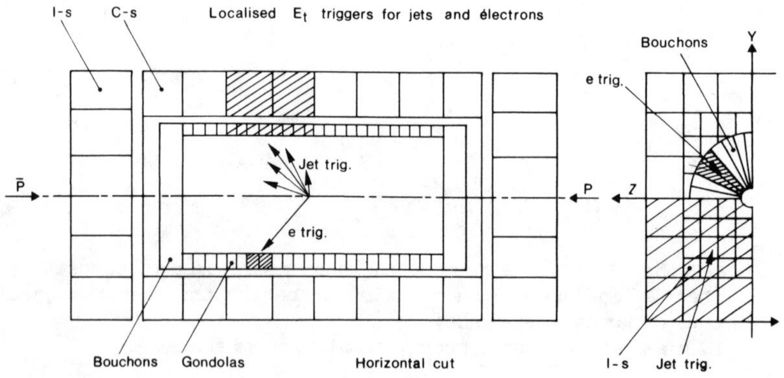

Fig.7 - Patterns of localised transverse energy depositions defining "jet" and "electron" triggers, in the central and end-cap regions.

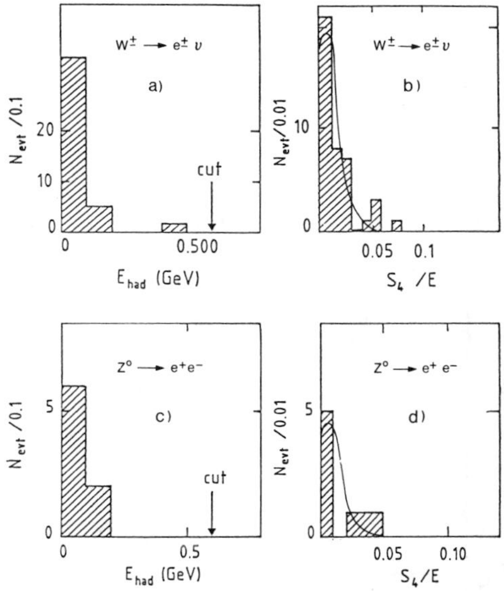

Fig.8 - a) Energy deposition in the hadron calorimeter cells behind the electromagnetic calorimeter (27 X_0 deep), for the sample of $W^\pm \to e^\pm \nu$ electron candidates; b) fractional energy deposition in the fourth segment of the electromagnetic calorimeter, compared to expectations, for same electron sample;
c) and d) same as a),b) but for the sample of $Z^0 \to e^+e^-$ candidates.

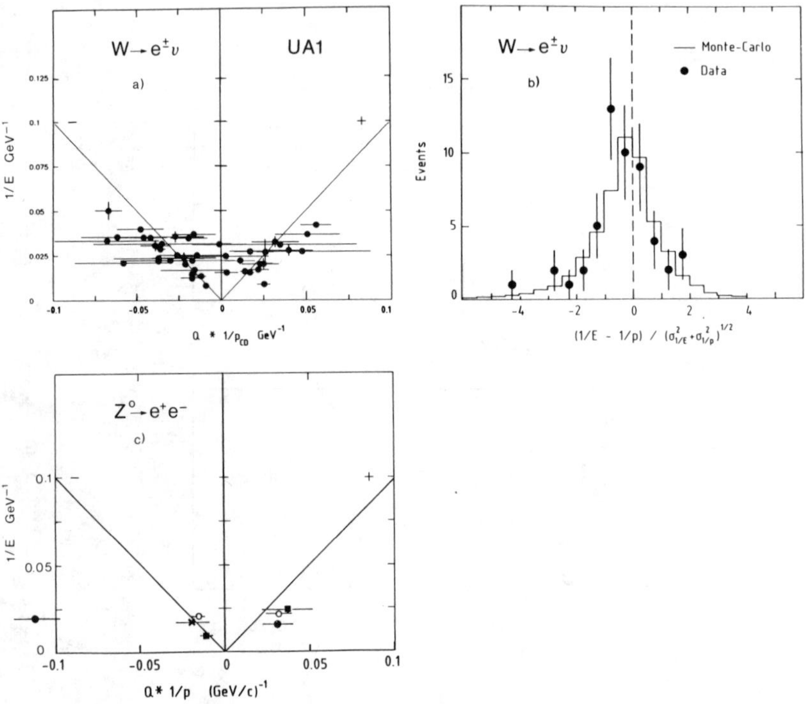

Fig.9 - a) $1/E$ vs $Q.1/p_{CD}$ where E is the electron energy measured in the calorimeter and p_{CD} the momentum measured in the central detector by curvature, for $W^{\pm} \to e^{\pm}\nu$ events (electrons within ± 15° from the vertical plane through the beam pipe are excluded); b) $(1/E - 1/p)$ normalized by its error for $W \to e\nu$ electrons, compared to a Monte-Carlo calculation including the resolution and electron radiative losses; c) same as a), but for electrons from $Z^0 \to e^+e^-$ candidates ; each event is shown separately.

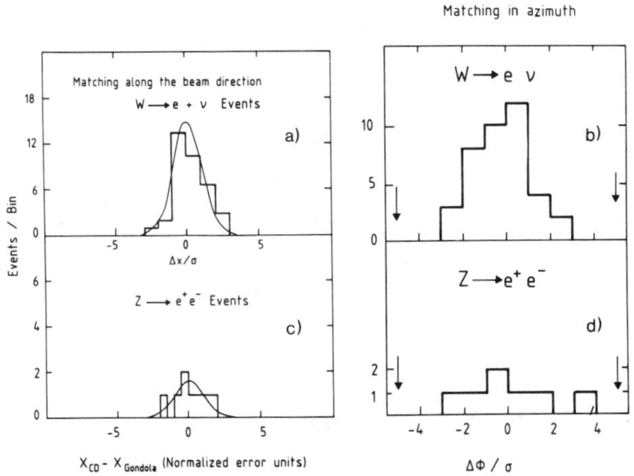

Fig.10 - For electrons from $W \to e\nu$ events, consistency in the x coordinate a) and azimuth b), as determined by the independent measurements in the central detector (track) and calorimetric shower axis; c) and d) same as a) and b) respectively, but for the sample of $Z^0 \to e^+e^-$ events.

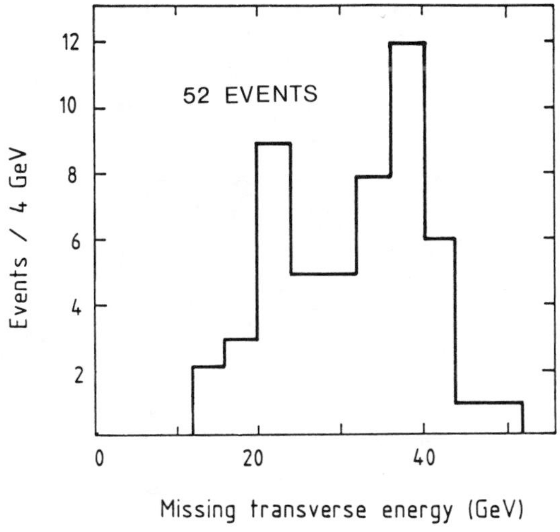

Fig.11 - Missing transverse energy distribution for $W \to e\nu$ candidates.

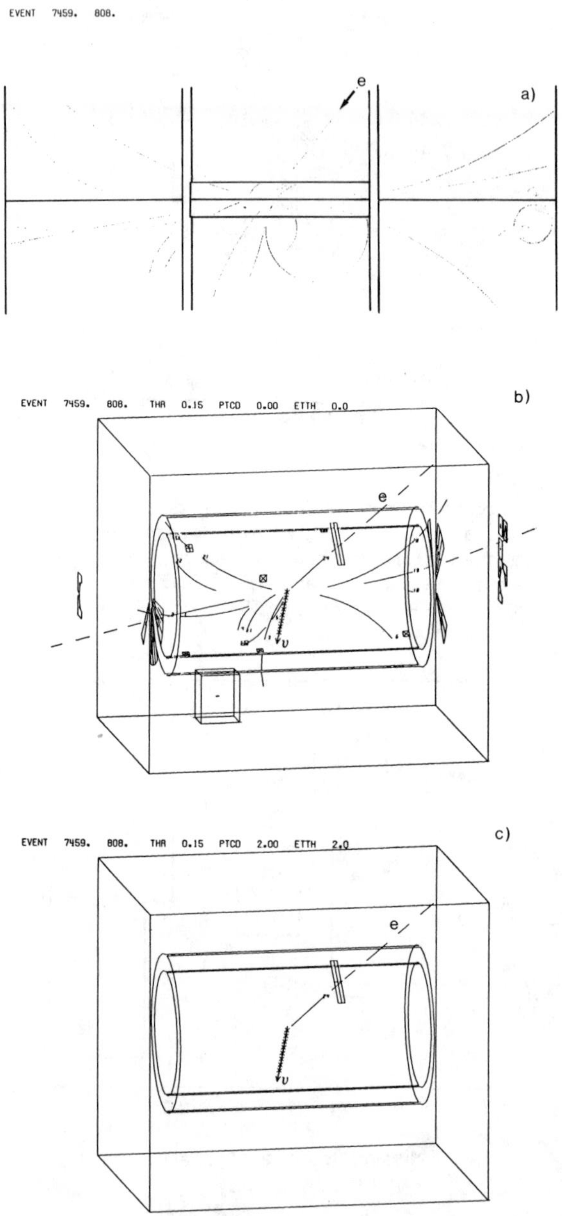

Fig.12 - Display of a $W \to e\nu$ event: a) central detector digitizings; b) all tracks and calorimetric cells; c) only tracks with $p_t > 2$ GeV/c and cells with $E_t > 2$ GeV are displayed; the reconstructed transverse neutrino momentum is also shown.

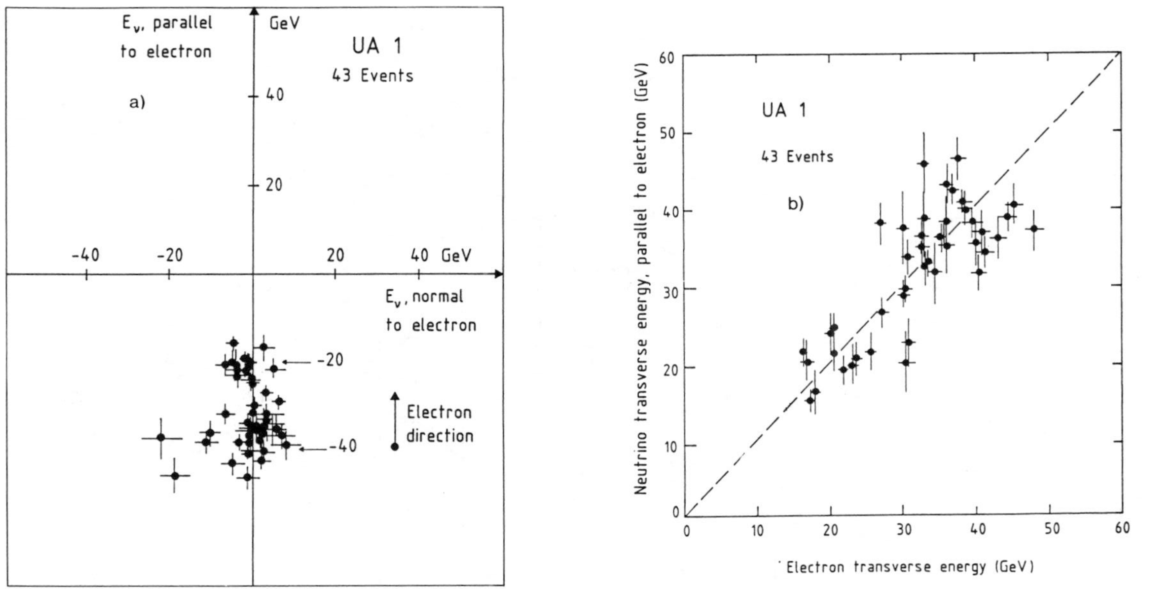

Fig.13 - a) and b) angular and energy correlations between the neutrino and the electron in the transverse plane.

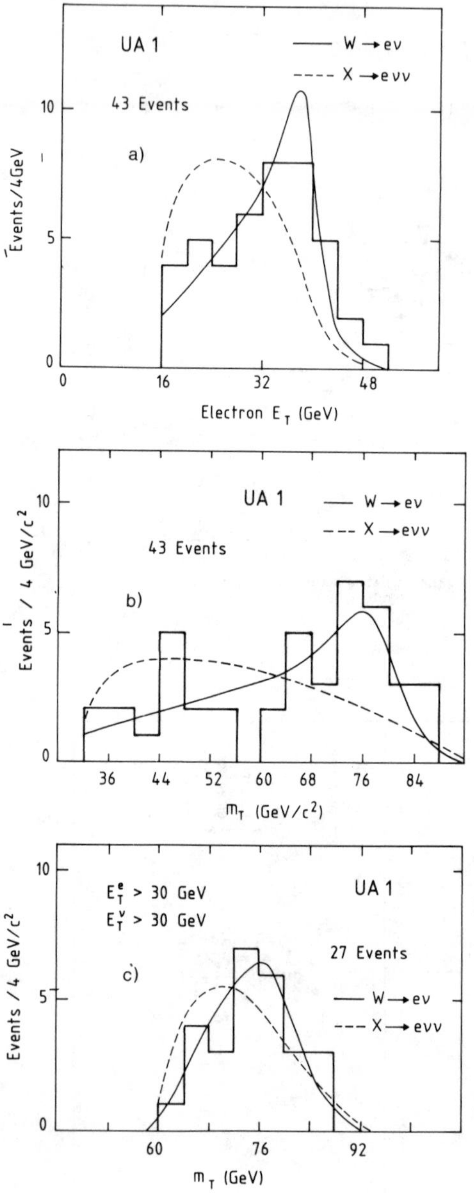

Fig.14 - a) Electron transverse energy distribution; b) and c) electron-neutrino transverse mass distributions; curves are comparisons to a two or three-body decay hypothesis (see text for details).

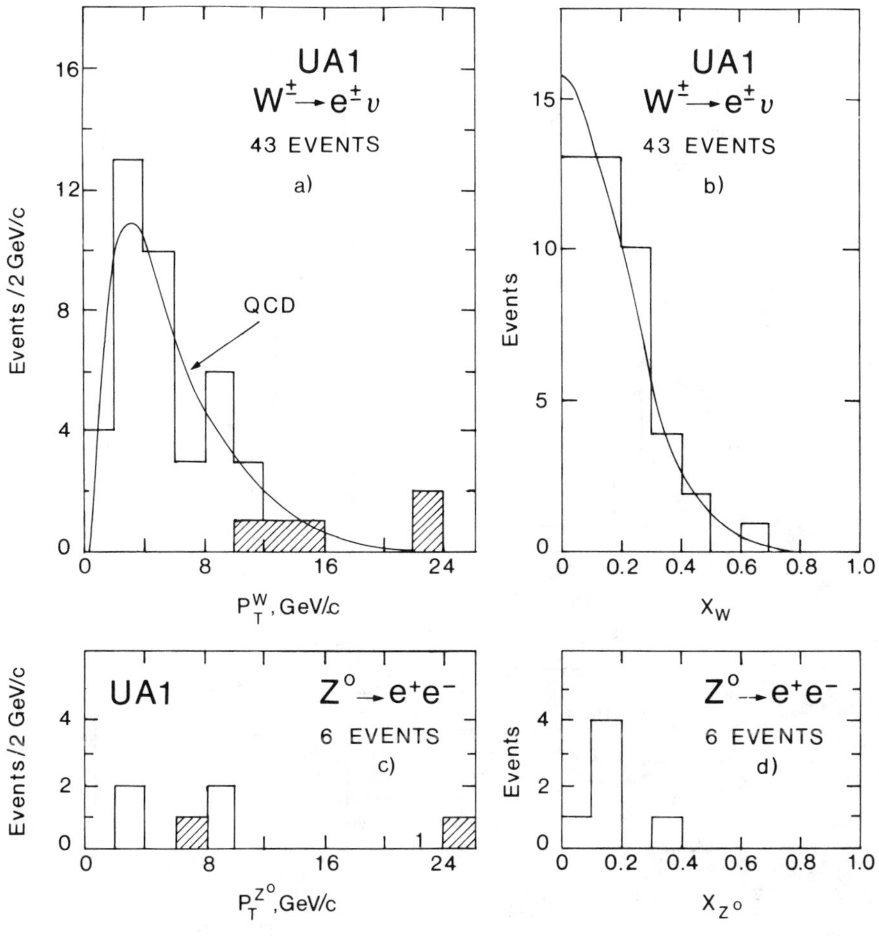

Fig.15 - a) Transverse momentum distribution for $W \to e\nu$ events; events with an accompanying jet of $E_t > 10$ GeV are shaded; the curve is the QCD prediction of ref[6]; b) the fractional longitudinal momentum of the W (folded); the curve is the parton model prediction; c) and d) same as a) and b) respectively, but for the sample of $Z^0 \to e^+e^-$ and $\mu^+\mu^-$ events.

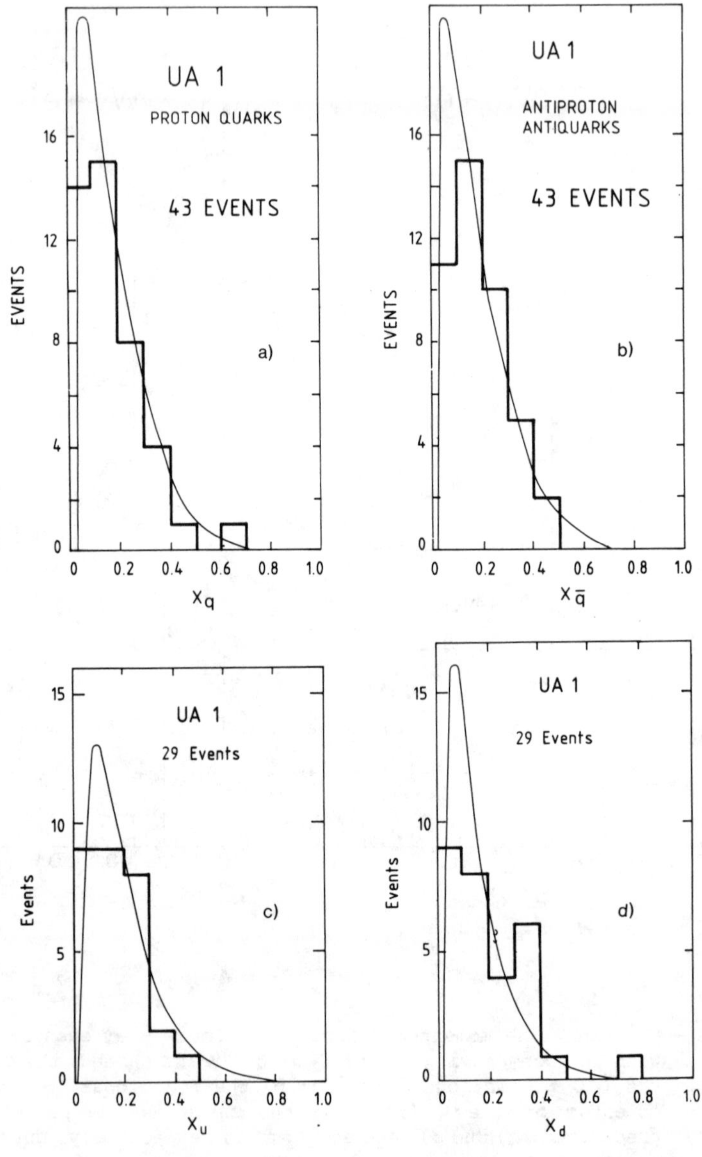

Fig.16 - a), b) the x distribution of the (proton) quarks and (antiproton) antiquarks annihilating into W; c) distribution of u (or $\bar{u}$) quarks (antiquarks) from the proton (antiproton), and d) of d (or $\bar{d}$) quarks (antiquarks) separately (see text for details).

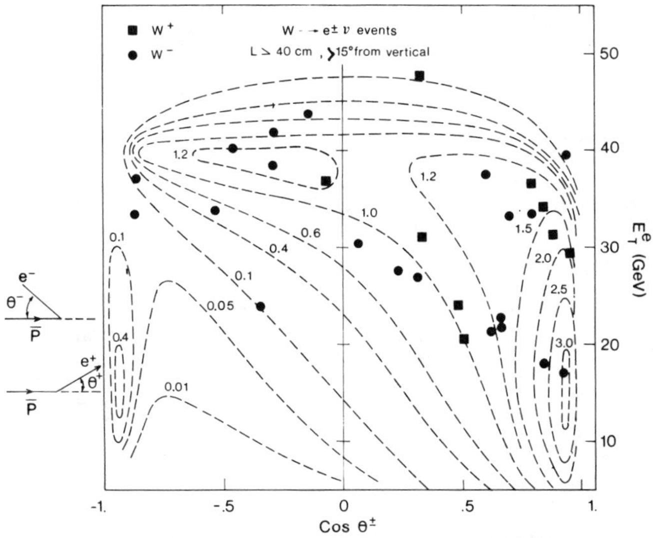

Fig.17 - Electron transverse energy vs emission angle in the lab. frame; e^+ and e^- distributions are folded as indicated; equal probability contour lines are shown.

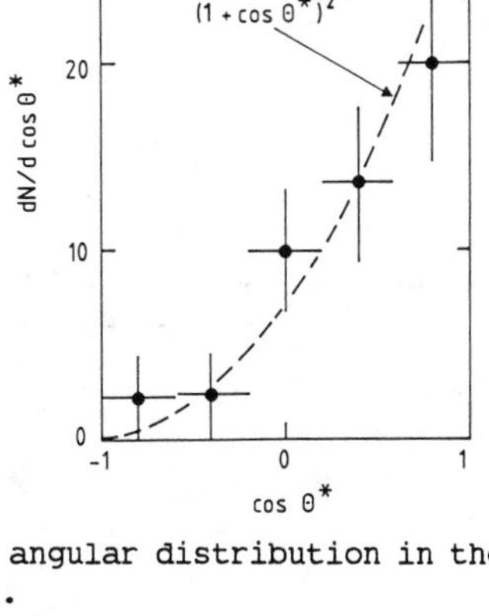

Fig.18 - Electron angular distribution in the W rest frame (see text for details).

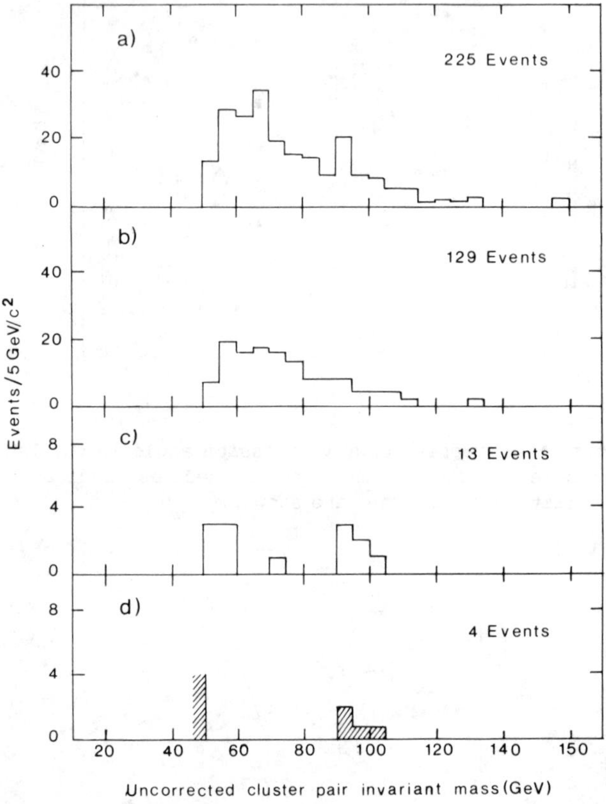

Fig.19 - Uncorrected invariant mass of a pair of electromagnetic clusters of $E_T > 25$ GeV: a) for all clusters; b) at least one cluster with a hard track ($\geq$ 7 GeV/c); c) at least one cluster "electron-like" (hard track isolated and $E_{had} \leq 600$ MeV); d) both clusters "electron-like".

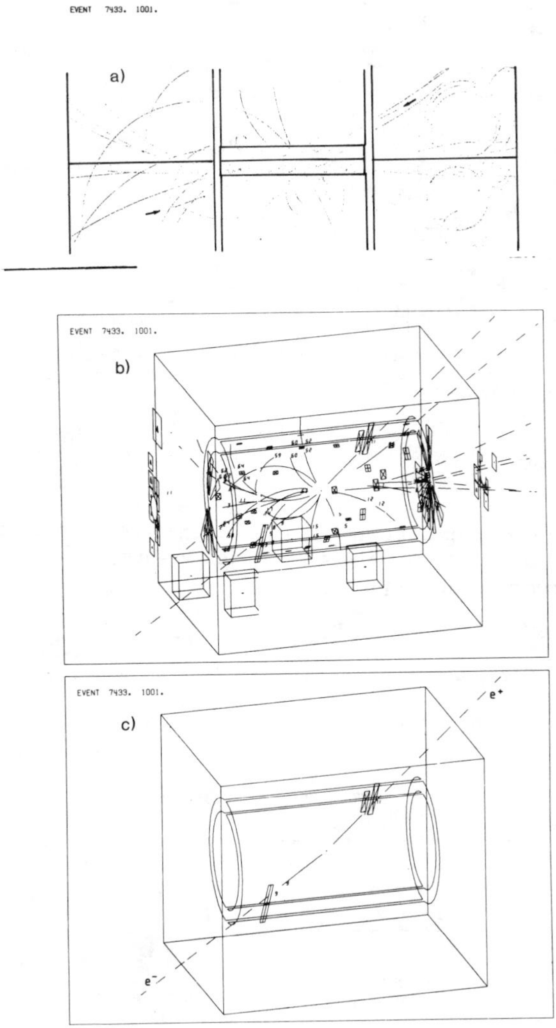

Fig.20 - Display of a $Z^0 \to e^+e^-$ event : a) central detector digitizings; b) all reconstructed tracks and calorimetric cells; c) only tracks with $p_t > 2$ GeV/c and cells with $E_t > 2$ GeV are displayed. The symbols indicating the energy depositions are logarithmically proportional to E_t.

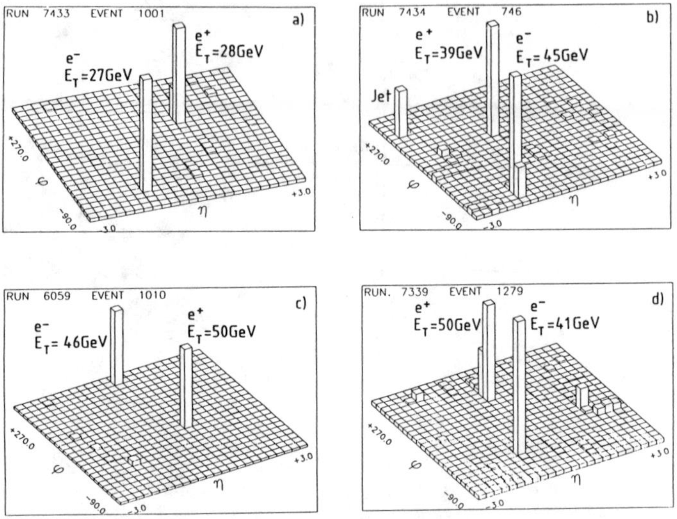

Fig.21 - Energy depositions in the electromagnetic calorimeters (for angles > 5°) for the 4 $Z^0 \rightarrow e^+e^-$ events, on a pseudorapidity vs azimuthal angle plot.

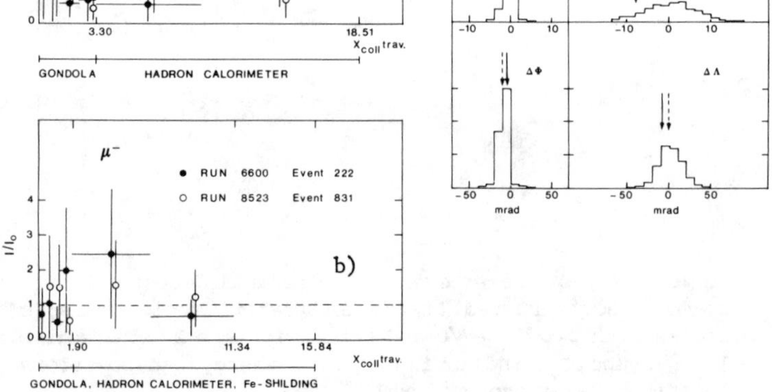

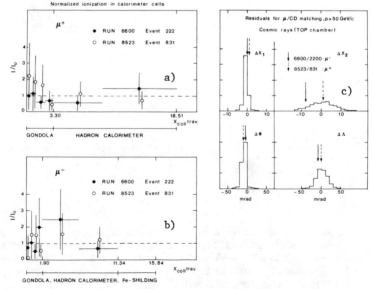

Fig.22 - a) and b) Normalised energy losses in calorimeter cells traversed by the muon tracks for the two $Z^0 \rightarrow \mu^+\mu^-$ candidates; c) coordinate and angular matching (residuals) between central detector and muon chamber measurements, for two muon tracks (see text).

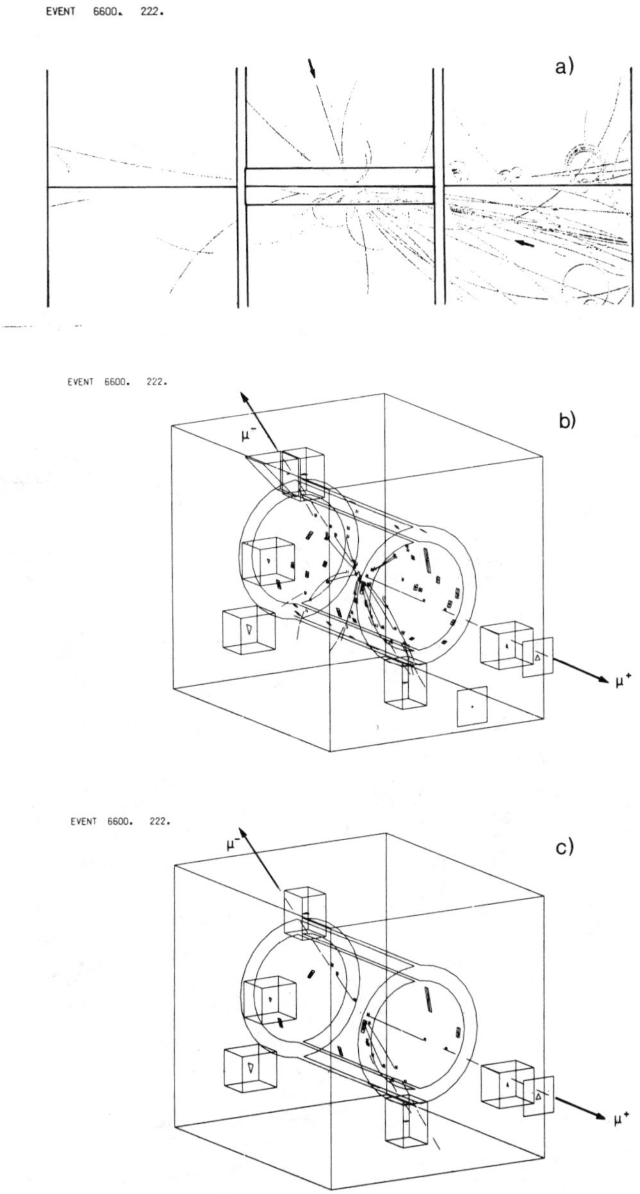

Fig.23 - Display of a $Z^0 \rightarrow \mu^+\mu^-$ event: a) central detector digitizings; b) all reconstructed tracks and calorimeter cells; c) only tracks with $p_t > 1$ GeV/c and cells with $E_t > 0.5$ GeV are displayed.

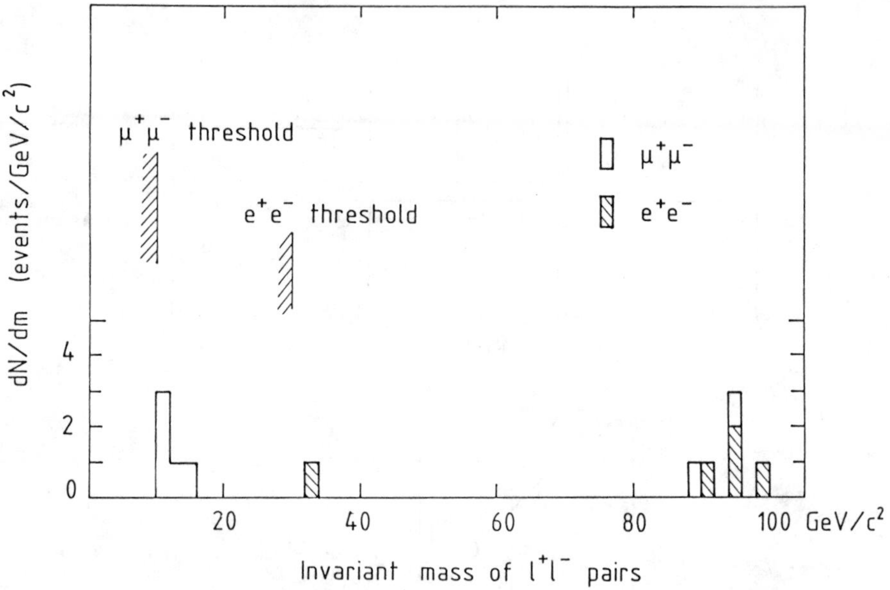

Fig.24 - Invariant mass of lepton pairs.

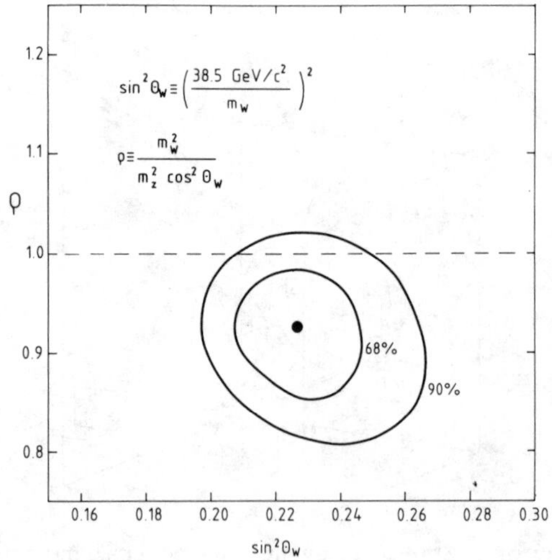

Fig.25 - Confidence levels on the values of $\sin^2\theta_w$ and ρ resulting from our measurements of M_w and M_z.

EXPERIMENTAL RESULTS ON b QUARK DECAY FROM CLEO

Paolo Lipari Syracuse University, Syracuse N.Y.

INTRODUCTION

CLEO [1] is one of the two detectors operating at the Cornell Electron Storage Ring (CESR). The designers of CESR have been very lucky, finding the threshold for a new quark flavour in the energy range of their machine. The hadronic visible cross section for the process $e^+ e^- \to$ hadrons as obtained by CLEO is displayed in Fig 1. Clearly visible are four resonances [2], that are commonly interpreted as the first 4 radial excitations of the $^3S_1$ bound states of a quark-antiquark pair with a new flavour 'b'. The first three resonances $\Upsilon(1S)$, $\Upsilon(2S)$ and $\Upsilon(3S)$ are "narrow", their observed widths are dominated by the c.m. energy resolution of CESR, 4.1 Mev * (s/100 GeV^2). Their natural widths can be obtained from a measure of the semileptonic branching ratio , and

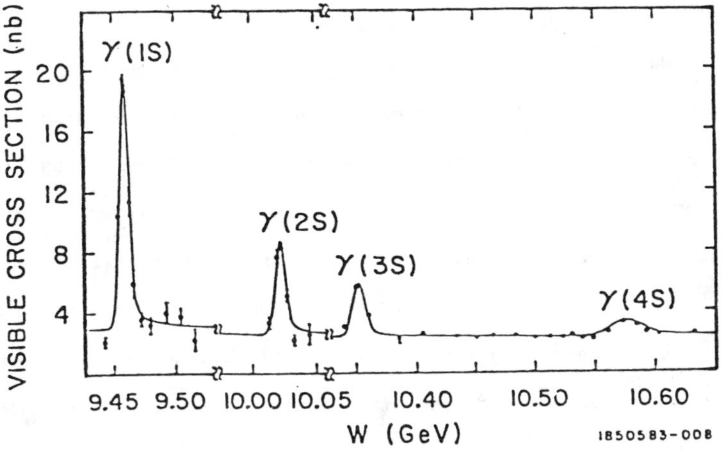

Fig. 1. The visible hadronic cross section as a function of the c.m. energy in the Υ region.

of the area of the resonant peak obtaining : 42 ± 6 KeV for the Υ(1S), 29 ± 5 KeV for Υ(2S) and 24 ± 3 KeV for the Υ(3S). The fourth resonance Υ(4S) is considerably broader, with a measurable natural width of about 20 Mev. This indicates that while the decay of Υ(1S), Υ(2S) and Υ(3S) are suppressed by the OZI rule , the Υ(4S) lies above the threshold for an uninhibited strong decay into a pair of B mesons. The B meson is the ground state of the b-flavoured mesons, and therefore has to decay weakly. This makes the Υ(4S) the ideal laboratory for studying the decay properties of b-flavoured mesons.

In this talk I shall discuss some results obtained by CLEO about B decay. These results are obtained from a data sample that includes 165,000 hadronic events taken at the Υ(4S) (40,800 resonance decay mixed with 124,200 continuum events), and an additional 53,000 continuum events, taken at center of mass energies just below the Υ(4S) to measure and subtract the continuum background.

The CLEO detector has been extensively described elsewhere. In the interest of brevity , I will omit a careful description, giving only the most relevant features of the apparatus. Charged particles are detected, and their momenta measured in a 17 layer cylindrical drift chamber coaxial to the beam line. This inner drift chamber is immersed in the 1.0 Tesla magnetic field provided by a superconducting solenoidal coil. The particles emerging from the interaction traverse the drift chamber, and after penetrating the coil encounter a 117 layer proportional chamber for specific ionization measurements, a Time of Flight system and a 12 radiation lengths segmented shower detector. After the shower detector there is an iron absorber between 0.5 to 1.0

meters thick followed by a bidimensional array of planar drift chambers for muon identification. The capability of CLEO to detect neutral particles, like π^0 and γ's, is very limited.

THE b QUARK IN THE STANDARD MODEL

The decay properties of b-flavoured hadrons are predicted in the theoretical framework of the "standard model". According to this model, the weak-electromagnetic interaction is described by a renormalizable gauge theory based on the group SU(2) X U(1); there are 6 leptons and 6 quarks, organized in left-handed doublets and right-handed singlets. For the quark sector we have:

$$\begin{bmatrix} u \\ d' \end{bmatrix}_L \quad \begin{bmatrix} c \\ s' \end{bmatrix}_L \quad \begin{bmatrix} t \\ b' \end{bmatrix}_L . ; \quad u_R \quad d_R \quad c_R \quad s_R \quad t_R \quad b_R$$

where the states d' s' b' are obtained from the mass eigenstates d, s and b via a unitary matrix V, the Kobayashi Maskawa matrix [3].

$$\begin{bmatrix} d' \\ s' \\ b' \end{bmatrix} = V \begin{bmatrix} d \\ s \\ b \end{bmatrix} = \begin{bmatrix} V(ud) & V(us) & V(ub) \\ V(cd) & V(cs) & V(cb) \\ V(td) & V(ts) & V(tb) \end{bmatrix} \begin{bmatrix} d \\ s \\ b \end{bmatrix} .$$

This matrix can be expressed in the most general form in terms of 4 parameters (N^2-2N+1 for N generation) : 3 angles and one phase. These parameters , waiting for a more complete theory, are considered fundamental constants of Nature. A commonly used representation is :

$$V = \begin{bmatrix} c_1 & s_1\ c_3 & s_1\ s_3 \\ -s_1\ c_2 & c_1\ c_2\ c_3 + s_2\ s_3\ e^{i\delta} & c_1\ c_2\ s_3 - s_3\ c_2\ e^{i\delta} \\ s_1\ s_2 & c_1\ s_2\ c_3 + c_2\ s_3\ e^{i\delta} & -c_1\ s_2\ s_3 - c_2\ c_3\ e^{i\delta} \end{bmatrix} .$$

In this model the neutral current is diagonal in flavour, all quark decays are mediated by the weak charged current (as is well established experimentally for the lighter quarks). The b is in a left-handed doublet with the heavier (and yet undetected) top quark, but can still decay via its Cabibbo mixing with d and s, having transitions to the up and charm quarks.

We want to test experimentally if the theoretical expectations for the decay of the b are verified, or if new dynamics is required . On the other hand, if the decay properties of b-flavoured hadrons are conventional, their experimental study can be an important source of information on several aspects of the standard theory, helping in understanding the importance of strong and electromagnetic effects in weak decays, and determining some of the KM parameters.

The measurement of the KM elements V(bu) and V(bc) is one of the pricipal goals of B meson decay studies. These two elements can be directely obtained by measuring the lifetime of the B meson, and its branching ratio into final states containing charmed particles. Information on these elements can be obtained using the constraints of unitarity on the first two lines of the KM matrix. V(ud) can be obtained from data on nuclear beta decay; V(us) from the semileptonic rate of decay for kaons and strange hyperons; V(cd) and V(cs) have been measured from the rate of charm production (dimuon production) in neutrino deep inelastic scattering. This information can be summarized as follows [5]:

$|V(ud)| = 0.9737 \pm 0.0025$ $\qquad |V(us)| = 0.225 \pm 0.005$

$|V(cd)| = 0.24 \pm 03$ $\qquad |V(cs)| = 0.66 - 1$

from unitarity we then obtain for V(bu) and V(bc) :

$|V(ub)| < 0.09$ $\qquad |V(cb)| < 0.75$

B RECONSTRUCTION

The first result I want to report is the explicit reconstruction of a few exclusive decay channels in B decay [6]. This result is important because establishes directly the fact the $\Upsilon(4S)$ indeed decays into a pair of weakly decaying (narrow) objects, as expected, and gives a precise measurement of the mass of these objects.

In the scheme in wich the B decays according to the standard model through the favoured quark decay chain $b \rightarrow c$, the final states of the B are given by:

$$B^- \rightarrow (D)^+ \ (h)^{--}$$
$$B^- \rightarrow (D)^\circ \ (h)^-$$

$$B^\circ \rightarrow (D)^+ \ (h)^-$$
$$B^\circ \rightarrow (D)^\circ \ (h)^\circ$$

Where with (D) we represents a charmed particle of given charge, and (h) represents the remaining hadronic system . We have been looking for the experimentally more accessible of these channels, in particular we looked for the decays :

$$B^- \rightarrow D^\circ \ \pi^-$$
$$B^- \rightarrow D^{*+} \ \pi^- \ \pi^-$$

$$B^\circ \rightarrow D^{*+} \ \pi^-$$
$$B^\circ \rightarrow D^\circ \ \pi^- \ \pi^+$$

The D°s are easily identified through their decay mode $k^- \pi^+$ where, in order to get background rejection , positive identification was required for the charged kaons in the dE/dx or ToF systems. The D^{*+} are detected through their decay into $D^\circ \pi^+$, with the subsequent decay of the D° into $k^- \pi^+$. No particle identification was required for this reaction because the $(D^\circ \pi^+)$ decay of the D^{*+} has such a low Q value that only a very small background is able to mimic it. Signals for the production of D° and D^{*+} in B decay are shown if Fig. (2). All combinations have been submitted to a two-constraints fitting procedure requiring : (a) the total energy of the combination to equal the beam energy, and (b) the correct mass for the D^0 candidate. After a χ^2 cut, optimized using Monte Carlo simulation, the mass plot given in Fig. (3a) was obtained. The contribution of the different final states is labeled in the figure We observe a cluster of 18 combinations in an interval of 20 MeV around a mass of 5275 MeV, with a background estimated by several methods as between 4 and 7 combinations. For the mass determination we have used only the subsample of final states containing a D^* (the D^0 sample is partially contaminated by $B \to D^*$ events where the D^* is incompletely reconstructed). We find :

$$M\ (B^-) = 5270.8 \pm 2.3 \pm 2.0\ \text{MeV}$$

$$M\ (B^0) = 5274.2 \pm 1.9 \pm 2.0\ \text{MeV}$$

$$M\ (\langle B \rangle) = 5272.3 \pm 1.5 \pm 2.0\ \text{MeV}$$

Here as in the rest of this paper the first error is statistical, and the second systematic. The mass scale has been normalised according to the high precision mass determination of the $\Upsilon(1S)$ through polarization measurements at VEPP-4, CESR and DORIS. The difference between the $\Upsilon(4s)$ resonance and twice the average B meson mass is determined to be 32.4 ±3.0 ±4.0 Mev. The mass difference between the neutral and the charged meson is poorly determined ,but agrees with the theoretical prediction of 4.4 Mev. Using this theoretical value for the mass difference, and the experimental measurement of the average mass, the branching ratio of the decays of the $\Upsilon(4s)$ are obtained from phase space:

$$Br\ [\Upsilon(4s) \to B^+\ B^-] = 60 \pm 2\ \%$$

$$Br\ [\Upsilon(4s) \to B^0\ \bar{B}^0] = 40 \pm 2\ \%$$

From this measurement one can obtain also branching fractions for the reconstructed channels. These measurements are limited by very large statistical and systematic errors (estimation of efficiencies, and

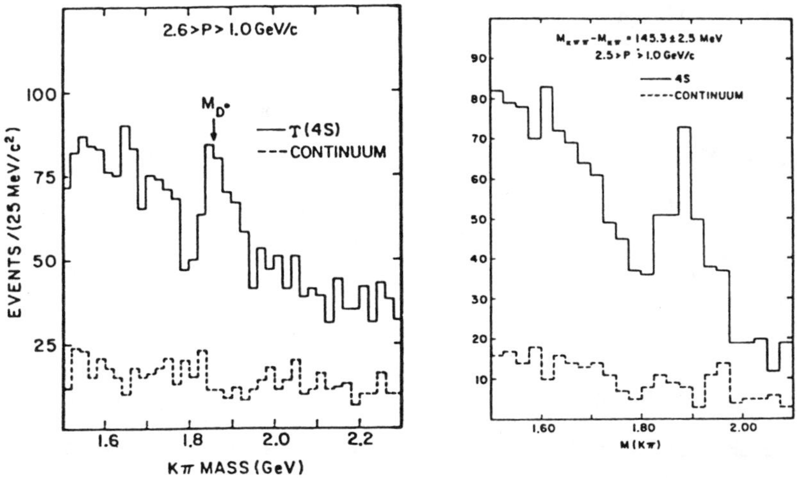

Fig. 2a and 2b. Evidence for D° and D*+ production in B decay.
(a) The $k^- \pi^+$ ($k^+ \pi^-$) spectrum using identified kaons.
(b) The $k^- \pi^+$ ($k^+ \pi^-$) spectrum using the [$k\pi\pi$ - $k\pi\pi$] mass difference to select $D^* \rightarrow D$ candidates.

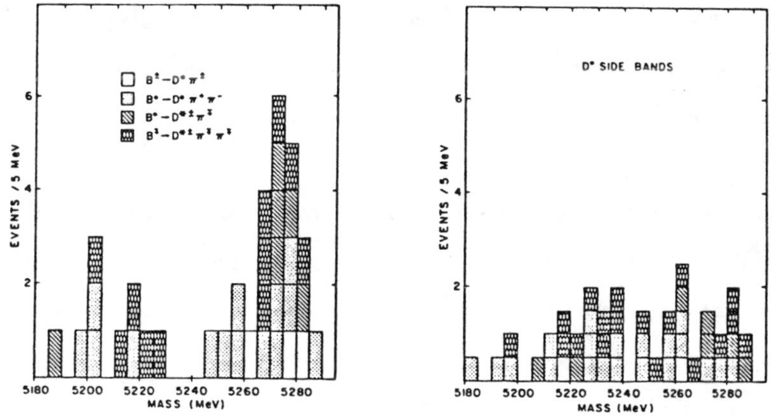

Fig. 3a and 3b. Reconstruction of B mesons.
(a) Mass spectrum for B meson candidates.
(b) Background for B reconstruction estimated using a "D°" mass displaced by ± 200 MeV.

uncertaintes in the charmed mesons branching ratios). They are given below:

Reaction	Branching fraction(%)
$B^- \to D^o \pi^-$	4.2 ± 4.2
$B^o \to D^o \pi^- \pi^+$	13.0 ± 9.0
$B^o \to D^{*+} \pi^-$	4.8 ± 3.0
$B^- \to D^{*+} \pi^- \pi^-$	2.6 ± 1.9

SEMILEPTONIC B MESON DECAY

A study of the inclusive semileptonic decays of the B is particularly important, because these decays are the simplest ones experimentally and theoretically, and allow the least model-dependent comparison of data and theory.

CLEO can identify electrons above 1.0 GeV of momentum, selecting those tracks found in the inner drift chamber that give appropriate electron signals in the specific ionization and shower counters. Muons are also identified by ther capability of penetrating the iron absorber leaving hits on a system of drift chambers.

Correcting for backgrounds and detection efficiencies, the spectra of Fig. (4) are obtained. Estimating by Monte Carlo method the fraction of leptons below the minimum momentum for identification we obtain the branching ratios :

$$Br\ [B \to e^- X] = 11.9 \pm 0.7 \pm 0.4\ \%$$

$$Br\ [B \to \mu^- X] = 10.1 \pm 0.5 \pm 1.0\ \%$$

The two results are consistent with each other within errors. Taking the liberty of averaging the 2 results and combining statistical and systematic errors we have :

$$Br\ [B \to \ell^- X] = 11.15 \pm 0.7\ \%$$

The semileptonic Branching Ratio of the B meson has been predicted by several authors. The naive quark model that approximates the meson decay as the decay of a free quark ignoring all bound state effects and strong interaction corrections, predicts a B_{SL} of about 20 % . Taking into account QCD corrections, that enhance the hadronic modes , and spectator effects, where the B decays via the s- or t- channel exchange of a W boson, the prediction is reduced to the range B_{SL} = 12 - 15 %, in reasonable agreement with the experimental data. The theoretical uncertainty arises from the calculation of the non-leptonic width, and from the quark masses used for the final state phase space [7].

We observe that the semileptonic widths are expected to be equal for neutral and charged B mesons, but the W exchange diagrams should contribute differently to B^0 and B^-. It is then expected that the purely hadronic modes of the B^0 shoud be enhanced with respect to the B^-

$$B_{SL}(B^-) > B_{SL}(B^0) \quad \text{and} \quad \tau(B^-) > \tau(B^0)$$

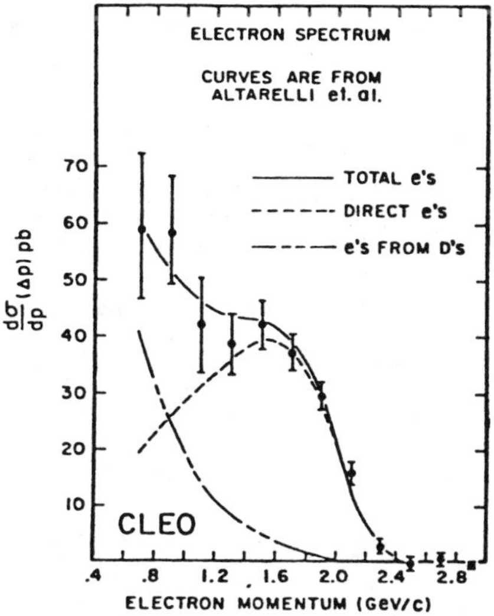

Fig. 4. Electron momentum spectrum. The curves are the contribution from B decay (dashed), D decay (short long dash) and the sum (solid). The shapes are from the model of Altarelli et al. [8].

This effect should be considerably less important than for D mesons, where we have a difference of a factor 2 - 3 between the lifetime of the charged and neutral D mesons, but it could be measurable also for B's. Therefore the results given above should be considered as the average B_{SL} of a mixture of 60% B^- and 40% B°.

The shape of the charged lepton spectrum is very sensitive to the ratio of the KM elements |V(cb)| and |V(bu)|, the analysis of this distribution is in fact the best method, known today, to measure |V(bu)|/|V(bc)|. The spectrum is the sum of two components due to $(b \to u)$ and $(b \to c)$ transitions, with the contribution of each component proportional to the square of the appropriate matrix element. The most sensitive portion of the spectrum is the high momentum tail. We note that the kinematical end point for a $(b \to c)$ transition with a charmed particle in the final state is about 2316 MeV. For a $(b \to u)$ transition the end point is more than 300 MeV higher at 2640 MeV. For this measurement it is therefore crucial to have theoretical control over the high momentum portion of the spectrum where kinematic and hadronization effects can be important. Knowledge of the relative normalisation of the theoretical curves for $(b \to u)$ and $(b \to c)$ is also needed.

We fitted our experimental points to the model of Altarelli et al. [8], finding excellent agreement between data and theory. The result is compatible with a 100 % $(b \to c)$ transition. We can anyway put a limit to the rate of the $(b \to u)$ transition, and using the calculated normalisation, obtain a limit for the ratio of KM elements.

$$\Gamma\ (b \to u\ \ell^-\ \nu)\ /\ \Gamma\ (b \to c\ell^-\ \nu) < .05 \text{ at } 90\ \%\ \text{c.l.}$$

$$|V\ (b \to u)|\ /\ |V\ (b \to c)| < .15 \text{ at } 90\ \%\ \text{c.l.}$$

LIMITS ON THE K-M MATRIX ELEMENTS

Recently two measurements of the B lifetime have been announced (one upper limit had also been published). These results are [9]:

Group	measurement (10^{-12} sec)
JADE	< 1.4 (90 % c.l.)
MAC	1.8 ± 0.6 ± 0.4
MARK II	1.2 (+0.45,-0.36) ± 0.3

It is now possible to combine these measurements with the results obtained in the previous section

$$Br\ [B \to \ell^-\ X] = 11.15 \pm 0.7\ \%$$

$$|V(bu)|\ /\ |V(bc)| < 0.15 \quad 90\ \%\ c.l.$$

to obtain restrictive limits on V(bu) and V(bc).

The semileptonic width for b-flavoured hadrons is calculable with accuracy. For example Altarelli [10] gives :

$$\Gamma_{SL}\ (b \to u) = |V(bu)|^2\ Zu = |V(bu)|^2\ (7.3 - 9.4)\ 10^{13}\ sec$$

$$\Gamma_{SL}\ (b \to c) = |V(bc)|^2\ Zc = |V(bc)|^2\ (3.3 - 4.6)\ 10^{13}\ sec\ .$$

where the theoretical uncertainties arise from lack of knowledge on m_b the mass of the b quark (and the width is proportional to m_b^5), and of bound state effects. The lifetime of the B meson can then be predicted from the theoretical semileptonic width, and the experimental semileptonic branching ratio as :

$$\tau_b = B_{SL}\ /\ \Gamma_{SL}$$

without the uncertainties in the calculation of the hadronic modes width. Combining all the information and taking the liberty of using ($0.6\ 10^{-12}$) and ($1.4\ 10^{-12}$) as lower and upper limits for the B lifetime, V(bu) and V(bc) result severely constrained. They have to be in the region indicated in Fig. (5) , with limiting values :

$$0.0037 < |V(bc)| < 0.0765$$

$$|V(bu)| < 0.0115 .$$

A general discussion of the possible implications of tis result and of the status of the KM parameters measurement is outside the scope of this talk. I want anyhow to comment briefly that it is very interesting to compare the values given above for V(bu) and V(bc) with the constraints on the KM parameters obtained from the analysis of the $k^{o}-\bar{k}^{o}$ system. The mass difference between k_L and k_s, and the CP violating parameter ϵ, can be calculated from the well known box diagrams as a function of the KM parameters and quark masses, obtaining two more constraint equations that involve the KM angles, and the unknown top quark mass. A lower limit on the top quark mass can be extracted using these constraint equations, and the available

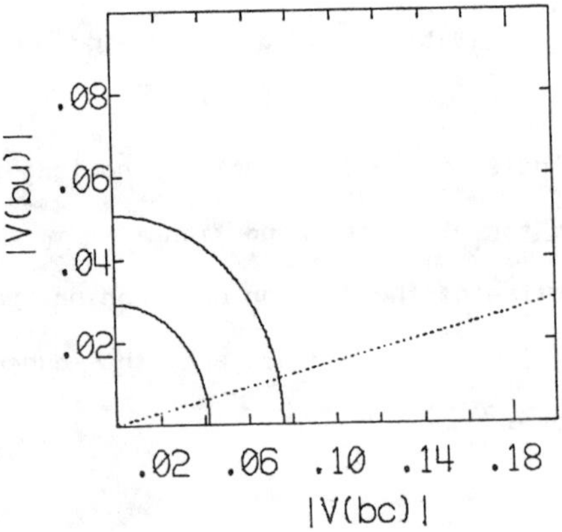

Fig. 5. Allowed region in the |V(bu)|, |V(bc)| space. the dashed curve is the limits coming from the measurement $|V(bu)|/|V(bc)| < 0.15$; the solid curves are the limit coming from the B lifetime measurements.

experimental information can be extracted using these constraint equations, and the available experimental information on KM angles, including the one discussed here. Unfortunately, there is still considerable theoretical contoversy about this analysis. According to the analysis of L.L. Chau et al. [11] these results could push the top quark mass to more than 90 Gev; in the different analysis of Ginsbarg et al. [12] the top quark mass could still be as low as 30 GeV. Alternatively, new physics could be required to describe the k^0-$\bar{k}^0$ system.

In conclusion, we have now a very interesting situation both theoretically and experimentally. It is important to confirm the lifetime measurements, to measure mixing also in systems containing a b quark as [$\bar{b}d$-$b\bar{d}$] or [$\bar{b}s$-$b\bar{s}$] , and of course to find the top quark.

DILEPTONS PRODUCTION

Very intersting information can be obtained from the analysis of those hadronic events that contains 2 charged leptons. There are several sources of dilepton events.

(i) Flavour Changing neutral currents are a source of dileptons in the channels (e^+ e^-) and (μ^+ μ^-) .

(ii) Parallel Decays. This is the expected source of most of the dileptons where each of the two lepton in one event comes from a 'standard' semileptonic decay of a B meson. This source will give opposite sign (e e) or (μ μ) or (e μ) events with equal probability.

(iii) Parallel decays with mixing.. It is well known that the B^0 and the $\bar{B}^0$ can mix through the same box diagrams of the neutral kaon system. The clearest signal for this mixing would be by the production of same sign dileptons (e e) or (μ μ) or (e μ) again with same probabilities. As in the neutral kaon system the amplitude for a B^0 to oscillate into a $\bar{B}^0$ will be in general different from the amplitude for a $\bar{B}^0$ to oscillate into a B^0. This CP violating effect can be detected observing an asymmetry in the number of (ℓ^- ℓ^-) versus (ℓ^+ ℓ^+) events (or observing a charge asymmetry in the inclusive lepton yields).

The most important sources of background are the following:
(i) Serial decays, where one of the leptons is the direct product of a semileptonic B decay, and the other lepton is coming from the semileptonic decay of the charmed meson produced in the same B decay or in the accompanying B particle. This source of background is limited by the fact that the leptons coming from charm decays are much softer than the direct leptons coming from B's. The effect is small but not completely negligible, and it has been calculated and subtracted. In this calculation we have used: Br ($B \rightarrow$ charm) = 100 %, where the charm quantum number is carried by D^* or D with equal probability, and the average semileptonic branching ratio for D^0 and D^+ is taken as 9 % .

(ii) Fakes. The dominant source of background is due to events were one of the candidate leptons is a genuine lepton from B decay, and the other candidate is an hadronic particle that mimics a lepton in the detector. To correct for this background the probability for an hadron to fake an electron or a muon has been estimated as a function of momentum from the yield of dileptons using data taken on the $\Upsilon(1s)$ where it is assumed that all but a neglibly small fraction of the dileptons are due to fakes. It is of course possible with a very small probablity to have 2 fakes in the same events, this effect is also taken into account.

(iii) Contribution from the continuum. (Mainly coming from c c events). This effect is easily eliminated subtracting the dilepton yield obtained from data taken below the $\Upsilon(4S)$ peak.

The largest source of dileptons is expected to be from the parallel decays. It is straightforward to show that the yield of dileptons from parallel decays is predicted from the single lepton yield, with only one uncertainty. The inclusive single lepton yield is given by:

$$N\ (1\ \text{lept}) = N\ (BB) * \epsilon * [\ f^+ * Br(B^+) + f^o * Br(B^o)\ ]$$

$$= N\ (BB) * \epsilon * \langle Br \rangle$$

$$N\ (2\ \text{lept}) = N\ (BB) * \epsilon^2 * [\ f^+ * Br(B^+)^2 + f^o * Br(B^o)^2\ ]$$

$$= N\ (BB) * \epsilon^2 * \langle Br^2 \rangle\ .$$

Where N(BB) is the total number of events analysed, ϵ is the efficiency for identifying a lepton, and f^+ and f^o are the are respectively the fraction of $B^+\ B^-$ and $B^o\ \bar{B}^o$ events in the data sample considered.

Defining :

$$\text{alfa} = \langle Br \rangle^2\ /\ \langle Br^2 \rangle,$$

we obtain :

$$N\ (2\ \text{lept}) = \text{alfa} * N(1\ \text{lept})^2\ /\ (4.*N(BB)\ )$$

Where the detection efficiency dropped out of the formula.

Note that alfa is limited to be :

$$1 < \text{alfa} < \max\ (1/f^+,\ 1/f^o)$$

$$(\ 1 < \text{alfa} < 2 \text{ for } f^+ = f^o = 0.5)\ .$$

So the parameter alfa is always greater or equal to 1, it is minimum if the semileptonic branching ration for the neutral and charged B's are equal, and it is greater than 1 if the semileptonic branching ratios are different. It follows that from the single lepton yield it is possible to predict a minimum number of dilepton events:

$$N(\text{dilelptons minimum}) = N(\text{single leptons})^2 \,/\, (4\ N(BB))$$

For the CLEO data this expected minimum number of dileptons is:

$$N(e\ e) = 22.2, \quad N(\mu\ \mu) = 24.2, \quad N(e\ \mu) = 46.3$$

with negligible errors. An excess over this minimum is indication either of new phenomena, for example Flavour Changing Neutral Currents, or of an asymmetry in the semileptonic branching ratios (and therefore according to orthodoxy an equal asymmetry in lifetime) for the neutral and the charged B.

TABLE I. DILEPTON EVENTS

dilepton	events	background	net	predicted
$\mu^+\mu^-$	37	13.6		
$\mu^+\mu^+$ $\mu^-\mu^-$	10	8.8		
all (μ μ)	46	22.4	24 ± 8	24.2
e^+ e^-	34	9.0		
e^+e^+ e^-e^-	6	6.6		
all (e e)	40	15.6	24 ± 7	22.2
e^+ μ^- e^- μ^+	54	17.9		
e^+ μ^+ e^- μ^-	17	11.4		
all (e μ)	71	29.3	42 ± 10	46.3
all opposite	157	66.3	90 ± 18	93
all same	33	25.8	6 ± 8	
all	71	22.6	49 ± 12	46.4

The data collected is shown in table (1). In the first column is shown the raw number of dilepton events found, before background or continuum subtraction, in the second column there is the calculated background, obtained from the 3 sources listed above, the other 2 columns show the net result and the prediction from the single lepton results. We can interpret the results in the following way:

(i) FCNC limit : the number of (e^+ e^-) and (μ^+ μ^-) events is 49 ± 12, when we expect a mimimum (alfa=1) of 46 from parallel decays. We can then put an upper limit on an additional source of dileptons from FCNC in the form:

$$Br\ (B \rightarrow e^+e^- \text{ or } \mu^+\mu^-) < 0.4\ \%\ \text{at}\ 95\ \%\ \text{c.l.}$$

(ii) Limit of different semileptonic Branching fractions: the total number of dileptons is 90 ± 18, when we expect from parallel decays [N(expected) = alfa * 92.7], we have then measured alfa = 1.0 ± 0.2, or alfa < 1.3 at 90 % c.l., We can the extract a limit on the ratio of the semileptonic branching fraction as:

$$1/3.6 < [Br(B^-)/\ Br(B^o)] < 4.6 \quad \text{at } 90\ \%\ \text{c.l.}$$

Putting a limit on the possible importance of non spectator diagrams in b decay. (the asymmetry in the result is due to the asymmetric composition of B^o B^o and B^+B^- in the data sample)

(iii) Mixing B^o $\bar{B}^o$: the B^o $\bar{B}^o$ constitutes only 40 % of the total number of events, therefore of the 93 expected dilepton events, only 37 are from B^o $\bar{B}^o$ events, for complete mixing we expect 18.5 same sign dileptons. We observe 6 ± 8 same sign dileptons. This result unfortunately is consistent with no mixing, but cannot rule out even very large oscillations. A factor of 10 more data, helped possibly by a better control of the background, could allow a measurement of this very interesting phenomenon.

It is of course impossible to talk of a measurement of CP violation from this very few dilepton events, we observe nonetheless, that from the single lepton measurement we have:

$$[N(\mu^+) - N(\mu^-)]/[N(\mu^+) + N(\mu^-)] = +0.02 \pm 0.04$$

$$[N(e^+) - N(e^-)]/[N(e^+) + N(e^-)] = -0.02 \pm 0.05$$

wich rules out CP violation at a level larger than a few percents.

D° PRODUCTION

From the analysis of the lepton production we have seen that B mesons decay neary 100% of the time in charmed mesons, it is therefore very natural to try to study directly charm production from B decay. CLEO can see a D° signal making invariant mass combinations of all opposite charged tracks, assuming that one is a kaon and the other a pion. It is possible to extract a D° momentum spectrum grouping the $(k\ \pi)$ combinations in different momentum intervals, and fitting each plot to a gaussian D° peak, and a exponentially falling background. It is necessary to do the same work on the continuum taken below the $\Upsilon(4s)$ in order to subtract the contribution from the continuum. The result is given in the following table:

TABLE II. D° PRODUCTION

p (Gev/c)	ϵ (%)	Υ(4s)	continuum	subtracted-corrected
0.0 - 0.5	36±2	12±36	14±18	4 ± 153
0.5 - 1.0	38±2	55±65	-3±31	118 ± 257
1.0 - 1.5	35±2	236±60	3±26	644 ± 244
1.5 - 2.0	35±2	383±61	4±25	1077 ± 243
2.0 - 2.5	29±2	178±40	57±20	156 ± 212
> 2.5	35±5	92±39	36±29	26 ± 171

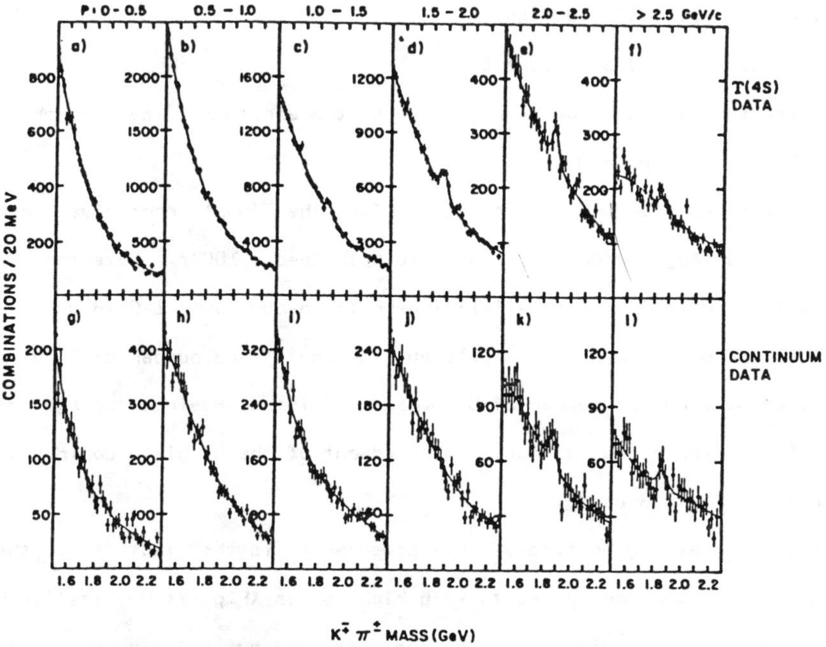

Fig. 6. Mass distribution of all oppositely charged tracks interpreted as $k^- \pi^+$ ($k^+ \pi^-$). The curves are fit of the data with a gaussian signal at the mass of the D^o and an exponentially falling background. Different plots are for different momentum bins for the total momentum of the (k π) combination. ϒ(4S) and continuum data are shown.

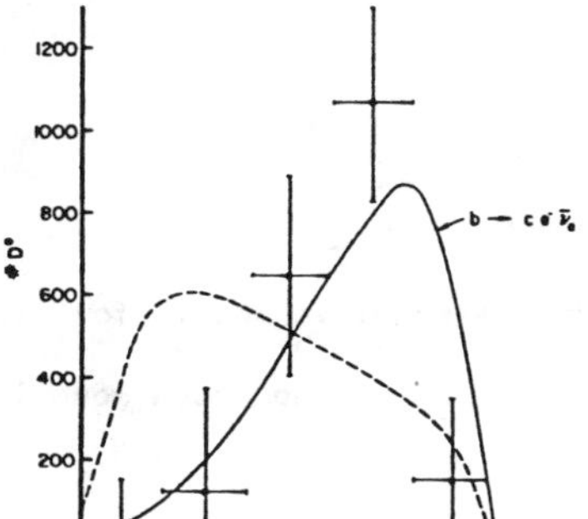

Fig. 7. Momentum spectrum of D^o from B decay. The dashed curve is the result of phase space; the solid curve is spectrum of q in the decay $Q \rightarrow q\ e^-\ \bar{\nu}_e$ with a V-A matrix element, no QCD corrections, when Q has the mass of the B meson and q the mass of the D. The curves are for illustrative purposes.

Summing over all bins we find:

$D^o/(B\ decay) = 0.8 \pm 0.2 \pm 0.2$

Where the systematic error is dominated by the error on the branching ratio $D^o \to k^- \pi^+$ (Br = 3.0 ± 0.6 %).

This result represents direct evidence for the (b→c) mechanism, and within very large errors is compatible with (b→c = 100%). Note that we expect $(D^o + D^+)/$ (B decay) = 1.15 (where the excess over 1.0 is due to the decays $b \to [c\ W^-] \to [c\ \bar{c}\ s]$), but in general the number of D^o wil be different form the number of D^+ because of the asymmetric decays of the D^*'s. Therefore a precise measurement of the D^o yield could give the ratio D^*/D in B decay.

The most interesting feature of this measurement is the fact that the momentum distribution peaks to very high values (Fig. 7) Qualitatively the spectrum is very similar to the one predicted by V-A in a simple spectator model, showing that strong interactions and fragmentation effects are less important than what it could have been naively expected.

CAN THE b QUARK BE NON CONVENTIONAL ?

We want now to discuss alternative models for the b quark decay that have been proposed, and see how much room is left for some new physics in b decay.

(1) Naive topless model [13]. It is perfectly admissible to have both the left- and right-handed b in an SU(2) singlet, with no top quark present. The b can still decay via its mixing with the d and s. As usual the states weakly coupled to the up and charm quarks d' and s' contain a b component

$$d' = V(ud)\, d + V(us)\, s + V(ub)\, b$$

$$s' = V(cd)\, d + V(cs)\, s + V(cb)\, b$$

Because of the absence of the top quark the GIM mechanism does not operate and the neutral current contains non diagonal terms (FCNC) :

$$V(ds)\ [d\ s] = (V(ud)*V(us) + V(cd)*V(cs))\ [d\ s]$$

$$V(db)\ [d\ b] = (V(ud)*V(ub) + V(cd)*V(cb))\ [d\ b]$$

$$V(sb)\ [s\ b] = (V(us)*V(ub) + V(cs)*V(cb))\ [s\ b]$$

with allowed transitions [d s] , [d b] and [s b]. It is possible (but not natural) to choose the V(i,j) in such a way as to cancel the [d s] current in accord to experiment, but then the coefficients for the [s b] and [d b] neutral currents have to remain sizable. Kane and Peskin [14] have shown that the of ratio of partial width for semileptonic decays into neutral and charged current is unambiguosly well constrained to be larger than 0.12 .

$$R = \frac{\Gamma(b \to \ell^+\ell^- X)}{\Gamma(b \to \ell^-\nu X)} = [(1/2-\sin^2(\theta_W))+\sin^2(\theta_W)]\frac{V(bs)^2+V(bd)^2}{V(bu)^2+P*V(bc)^2} > 0.12$$

Where θ_W is the Weinberg angle and P is a phase space factor. The data gives :

$$Br\ (B \to \ell^+\ell^- X) < 0.4\ \%\ (95\ \%\ c.l.)$$

$$Br\ (B \to \ell^- \nu X) = 11.15 \pm 0.7\ \%$$

putting things together we get:

$$R < 0.04 \qquad \text{at } 95\ \%\ c.l.$$

in disagreement with the bound just given. The simplest topless models are therefore ruled out.

(2) The exotic models [15]. It has also been proposed to put again the

b quark in a singlet but to forbid mixing with the d and s quarks giving to the b a new quantum number. B decay are then mediated by some new "exotic" boson outside SU(2). The new quantum number of the b must be shared by some lighter fermion, the only acceptable possibilties being a tau lepton or an antiquark. This leads to quite bizarre final states of the form :

$$[b \rightarrow q\, \ell\, \bar{\ell}] \quad \text{or} \quad [b \rightarrow \bar{q}\, \bar{q}\, \ell].$$

The explicit reconstruction of purely hadronic "traditional" decay channels of the B, completely rules out this class of models, that on the other hand were already giving predictions in contradiction with experiment for some inclusive features of B decay (such as charged energy distribution , leptons and baryons yields) .

(3) The right-handed model [17] One more possibility is a model where the b quark is in a right-handed doublet with the charmed quark:

$$\begin{bmatrix} u \\ d' \end{bmatrix}_L \quad \begin{bmatrix} c \\ s' \end{bmatrix}_L \quad b_L \;;\; u_R \quad d_R \quad s_R \quad \begin{bmatrix} c \\ b \end{bmatrix}_R$$

This model has no FCNC, but predicts short lifetime for the B because the decay has a full strength weak coupling with no Cabibbo suppression. Therefore the observation at PEP of a lifetime of order 10^{-12} sec rules out also this model. (The predicted V+A lepton spectrum is also probably already in contradiction with the existing data).

CONCLUSIONS

(1) All existing experimental information on the properties of B meson decay is well described by the standard model.

(2) Most of the alternative models proposed, are ruled out from the data. In particular most top-less models predict decay rates in flavour changing neutral current in contradiction with the experimental data.

(3) Exclusive decay modes of B meson decay have been reconstructed, and the mass of this new particle has been determined.

(4) From the shape of the charged lepton distribution a limit on the ratio of KM elements |V(bu)|/|V(bc)| is obtained.

(5) Experimental studies of B meson decay are starting to test the strong and electromagnetic corrections to the weak Hamiltonian.

ACKNOWLEDGEMENTS

I would like to express my gratitude to my collaborators in CLEO and in the CESR accelerator group. It is also a pleasure to thank the organisers of the Conference.

REFERENCES

1. "The CLEO Detector" D. Andrews et al., Nucl. Inst. Meth. 211, 47, (1983)

2. D. Andrews et al., Phys. Rev. Lett. 44, 1108 (1980)
T. Bohringer et al. ibid 111 (1980)
D. Andrews et al., Phys. Rev. Lett. 45, 219 (1980),
G. Finocchiaro et al. ibid, 222.

3. R.K. Plunkett, Ph.D. thesis Cornell University(1982) (unpublished).

4. M. Kobayashi and T. Maskawa, Prog. of Theor. Phys. 49 (1973).

5. L. Maiani, "Theoretical ideas in heavy flavour weak decays ". 21st International Conference of High Energy Physics, ed Petieau et Porneuf, Paris (1982).

6. S. Beherends et al., Phys. Rev. Lett. 50, 88 (1983)

7. J. Leveille, University of MIchigan Preprint UMHE81-18.

8. G. Altarelli, N. Cabibbo, G. Corbo', L. Maiani and G. Martinelli, Nucl. Phys. B208, 365 (1982)

9. E. Fernandez et al., Phys. Rev. Lett 51 1022 (1983)
N.W. Reay Proceedings of the International Symposium on Lepton Photon Interactions at High Energies, Ithaca N.Y. (1983) to be published.

10. G. Altarelli, University of Rome preprint 351.

11. J. Green et al., Phys. Rev. Lett. 5, 347 (1983).

12. L.L. Chau, Physics Reports 95, 1 (1983)
L.L. Chau, W.Y. Keung and M.D. Tran, Phys Rev. D27, 2145 (1983)
V. Barger et al., Phys. Rev. Lett. 42, 1585 (1979).
R.E. Shrock et al., Phys Rev. Lett. 42 1589 (1979).

13. P.H. Ginsparg, S.L. Glashow and B.M Wise, Phys. Rev. Lett 50, 415 (1983).

14. V. Barger and S. Paksava, Phys. Rev. Lett. 81B 195 (1979).

15. G.L. Kane and M.E. Peskin, Nucl. Phys. B195 29(1982)

16. E. Derman, Phys. Rev. D19 (1979) 317.
H. Georgi and S.L. Glashow, Nucl Phys. B176 173 (1979)
H. Georgi and M. Machacek, Phys. Rev. Lett. 43 1639 (1979).

17. S. Tye and M.E. Peskin, "Implication of the (c,b) model", Proceedings of the Cornell Z° Workshop (1982)

LEFT-RIGHT SYMMETRY IN WEAK INTERACTIONS: PRESENT STATUS

Goran Senjanović

Physics Department
Brookhaven National Laboratory
Upton, New York, U.S.A.

ABSTRACT

The basic features of the left-right symmetric electroweak theory are reviewed. The experimental situation regarding the scale M_R of the breakdown of parity is summarized. I further discuss in detail the connection with weak and strong CP violation and especially, grand unification. Also coverd are the issues of cosmological domain walls and the compositeness of quarks and leptons.

1. Introduction

In this talk I shall attempt to summarize the present situation, both experimental and theoretical, regarding the possibility that parity is the spontaneously broken symmetry of the underlying theory of weak interactions. This idea was put forward almost a decade ago and a great deal of work has been done since, pursuing its realization. My convinction, which I would like you to share with me, is that the attempt is definitely worthwhile since the understanding of this fundamental space-time symmetry has been completely left out of the standard $SU(2)_L \times U(1)$ electroweak model. This is carried further in the construction of the minimal grand unified theory of electroweak and strong forces, the SU(5) model. Even if these theories are correct in the energy regimes they describe, it is hard to believe that they are not the parts of the more complete and more symmetric theory that provides the understanding of the observed V-A structure of charged weak interaction. The question then is, and this constitutes the main portion of this review: if this is so, at which energies does the parity restoration manifest itself? It is not surprising that I will fail to answer this question. Rather, I will discuss the experimental constraints on this scale, and especially the situation regarding the possibility that it is in the soon reachable region on the order of TeV. This will naturally take us to the issue of whether or not left- right symmetry could be an "oasis" in the grand desert of unified theories and will be discussed below in detail.

An interesting aspect of left-right symmetric theories is that they provide a possible connection between parity and CP violation and also offer a possibility of understanding the smallness of strong CP violation. I will only briefly touch these questions, for more details the reader is recommended the recent review by Mohapatra and myself[1].

Now, parity transformation is a discrete symmetry, so that the left-right symmetric theory runs into the usual difficulty of spontaneously broken discrete symmetries, i.e. the problem of formation of domains in the early universe. The possible ways out are discussed, such as the idea of symmetry nonrestoration at high temperature and even more interesting, in the context of grand unification embedding of the discrete symmetry into the center of the particular gauge group, so that the different vacua can be reached by a continuous symmetry and no domain walls would be formed.

Finally, the connection between left-right symmetry and the idea of compositeness of quarks and leptons is briefly discussed.

The rest of this review can then be summarized with the following table of contents:

2. Left-Right Symmetry: Experimental Situation

Before plunging into the plethora of physical processes that will give useful contraints, let me first say a few words as to what I mean by the L-R electroweak model. Namely some of the constraints follow from the general characteristics of the idea of spontaneous breakdown of parity, but most of them depend on the specific features of the theory. This, although unfortunate, is not surprising, since it is the general property of electroweak gauge theories.

In the absence of any firm criteria, we shall stick, as in the original work, to the ideas of minimality and simplicity, and as I shall explain, the possibility of dynamical symmetry breaking through fermionic condensates. The minimal gauge group which incorporates L-R symmetry[2] is $SU(2)_L \times SU(2)_R \times U(1)_{B-L}$. The theory if assumed invariant under parity conjugation. This results in

(i) $g_L = g_R \equiv g$; g_L and g_R being $SU(2)_L$ and $SU(2)_R$ coupling constants

(ii) the fermionic sector consists of left and right-handed doublets

$$\psi_L = \binom{\nu}{e}_L \,, \quad \psi_R = \binom{\nu}{e}_R \,, \quad Q_L = \binom{u}{d}_L \,, \quad Q_R = \binom{u}{d}_R \qquad (2.1)$$

with xerox copying for more generations;

(iii) from (2.1) electric charge is

$$Q_{em} = I_{3L} + I_{3R} + \frac{B-L}{2} \ . \tag{2.2}$$

Recall that in the standard model B-L is an exact **global** symmetry, anomaly free. Here is the minimal extension that gauges this global symmetry.

(iv) We will demand that the Higgs sector, besides being L-R symmetric, complies with the principles of simplicity and the possibility of dynamical symmetry breaking, i.e. the scalar fields should carry the quantum numbers of fermionic bilinears. As described by Mohapatra and myself[3], the relevant Higgs fields are the following[4]

$$\phi = \begin{pmatrix} \phi_1^0 & \phi_2^+ \\ \phi_1^- & \phi_2^0 \end{pmatrix}$$

$$\Delta_L = \begin{pmatrix} \Delta_L^{++} \\ \Delta_L^{+} \\ \Delta_L^{0} \end{pmatrix} \qquad \Delta_R = \begin{pmatrix} \Delta_R^{++} \\ \Delta_R^{+} \\ \Delta_R^{0} \end{pmatrix} \tag{2.3}$$

where we have shown the composition into the particles with given charge.

One envisions the following pattern of symmetry breaking, making sure that it corresponds to the absolute minimum of the potential

$$\begin{array}{c} SU(2)_L \times SU(2)_R \times U(1)_{B-L} \\ \big\downarrow \ \langle\Delta_R\rangle \simeq M_R \\ SU(2)_L \times U(1) \\ \big\downarrow \ \langle\phi\rangle \simeq M_W, \ \ \langle\Delta_L\rangle \ll \langle\phi\rangle \\ U(1)_{em} \end{array} \tag{2.4}$$

Neutrino Mass. Through the first stage of symmetry breaking $\langle\Delta_R\rangle \simeq M_R$, right-handed neutrino becomes heavy **Majorana** particle[3], with $m_{\nu_R} \simeq fM_R$ (f being a Yukawa coupling) and so decouples at low energies (I shall not go here into the possibility that f is exceedingly small[5]). In turn ν_L picks up a small Majorana mass[6] $\sim M_R^{-1}$, so that the **smallness of neutrino mass is tied to the maximality of parity violation in weak interactions.**

This is to be contrasted to the case of Dirac neutrinos, where it is a major mystery to understand why ν_L is so light[7]. From now on, most of what I will say will be true for Majorana neutrinos, whose nature results from the choice of Higgs sector (2.3).

Quark mass matrices. From the form of Yukawa couplings (H is the coupling matrix in the flavor space)

$$L_Y(\phi) = \bar{Q}_L H\phi Q_R + \bar{Q}_R H^+\phi^+ Q_L \qquad (2.5)$$

L-R symmetry implies, assuming $\phi \to \phi^+$

$$H^+ = H \ . \qquad (2.6)$$

Since in general $\langle\phi\rangle$ is complex, this implies no relation for quark masses, except in two interesting cases

$$\text{(i)} \quad \langle\phi\rangle \in R \Longrightarrow M_q^+ = M_q \quad \text{(manifest L-R symmetry)}^8$$

$$\text{(ii)} \quad H \in R \Longrightarrow M_q^T = M_q \quad \text{(pseudomanifest - 11 -)}^9 \ . \qquad (2.7)$$

We are now equipped to study the burning question of the value of M_R, especially in view of the possible experimental detection of W_R. Since there is no way of predicting it, the best we can do is to study experimental constraints on M_R and see whether this scale could be in an interesting, testable TeV region of energies.

Charged currents. Let us now go through various different processes that have impact on M_R.

(a) **Leptonic and semileptonic decays.** In the **Majorana** case no useful limit can be obtained (unfortunately) from μ and β decays, since ν_R decouple at low energies. This is in contrast to the **Dirac** case, where one gets the limit[8,10] $M_R \gtrsim 380$ for general L-R mixing ξ_{LR}, and $M_R > 450$ GeV for $\xi_{LR} = 0$.

(b) **Nonleptonic decays.** The limits that one gets on M_R are not so stringent[11]: $M_R > 200$-300 GeV, when all uncertainties are taken into account; however, these processes put an excellent limit on the mixing between W_L and W_R: $\xi_{LR} \lesssim 10^{-3}$-$10^{-4}$. Therefore, this additional parameter that could obscure the phenomenological predictions can be safely ignored.

K_L-K_S mass difference. This process has a remarkable property of a conspiracy of enhancements of diagrams which include both W_L and W_R, as opposed to pure W_L exchanges. Of course, the calculability of these diagrams requires the equality of left and right handed quark mixing angles. This restricts us to cases (2.7). Let U_L and U_R be left and right handed Cabibbo rotations, the (2.7) implies

$$M_q = M_q^{+} \quad \text{(manifest L-R)} \Longrightarrow U_L = U_R$$

$$M_q = M_q^{\,T} \quad \text{(pseudomanifest - 11 -)} \Longrightarrow U_L = U_R^{\,*} \,. \qquad (2.8)$$

Assuming either of the cases in (2.8), let us for the moment concentrate on the four quark case as in the original work of Beall, Bender and Soni[12]. The contribution from the box diagrams gives for the effective Hamiltonian

$$H_{eff} = \frac{G_F^2 M_W^2}{4\pi^2} \sin^2\theta_C \cos^2\theta_C \frac{m_C^2}{M_W^2} \{\bar{s}\gamma_\mu Ld \; \bar{s}\gamma^\mu Ld$$

$$+ \left[8\left(1+\ell n \frac{m_C^2}{M_W^2}\right) + 2\ \ell n \frac{M_W^2}{M_R^2}\right] \frac{M_W^2}{M_R^2} \bar{s}Ld\ \bar{s}Rd\} \qquad (2.9)$$

where $L,R \equiv (1+\gamma_5)/2$. The conspiracy is evident: the coefficient of LR instead of being of order 1, becomes ($\ell n\, m_C^{\,2}/M_W^{\,2} \simeq -8$) of order 100, and furthermore, the matrix element of the LR operator is expected to be larger than the one of the LL operator. In the vacuum insertion approximation[12] $\langle LR\rangle/\langle LL\rangle \simeq 8$, and the correct sign of K_L-K_S mass difference gives a rather stringent limit: $M_R \gtrsim 1$-2 TeV (I am not quoting the precise value due to the usual uncertainties the estimation of matrix elements).

How general is the above result? Namely, we could think that the inclusion of t quark effects could relax the conclusion, especially if t quark is not light. Furthermore, in this theory there are necessarily flavor changing neutral currents induced through Higgs exchanges and as such must be included in the effective Hamiltonian. This has prompted us (and others[13]) recently to re-examine carefully the situation including all the possible relevant effects. Not surprisingly, it turned out that the limit on M_R becomes a function of Higgs and t quark masses and at the time we did our work it looked as though it could be as low as 200 GeV or so, with the constraints on the mixing angles much more stringent than in the standard model.

For the sake of illustration, Fig. 1 displays the regions of allowed mixing angles for different values of top quark mass, taken from our paper. In the usual notation, $s_i = \sin\theta_i$; $s_\delta \equiv \sin\delta$, where θ_i are K-M angles and δ is a phase. Notice (and the same is true for other values of m_H and M_R) that in both curves $s_2 < s_3$ and that s_δ is almost vanishingly small.

However, now there are much stricter restrictions on K-M angles coming from the new measured upper limits on $\Gamma(b \to ue\nu)$ compared to $\Gamma(b \to ce\nu)$[14]

$$\frac{\Gamma(b \to ue\nu)}{\Gamma(b \to ce\nu)} \lesssim 0.05 \,.$$

This recently enabled Gilman and Reno[15] to show the inconsistency of our solution. They first show that our results analytically imply as $\delta \simeq -1$, $s_3 > 2\sqrt{m_c/m_t}$; whereas the above limits require $s_2 \lesssim 0.1$, $s_3 \lesssim 0.04$ (private communication from W.-Y. Keung).

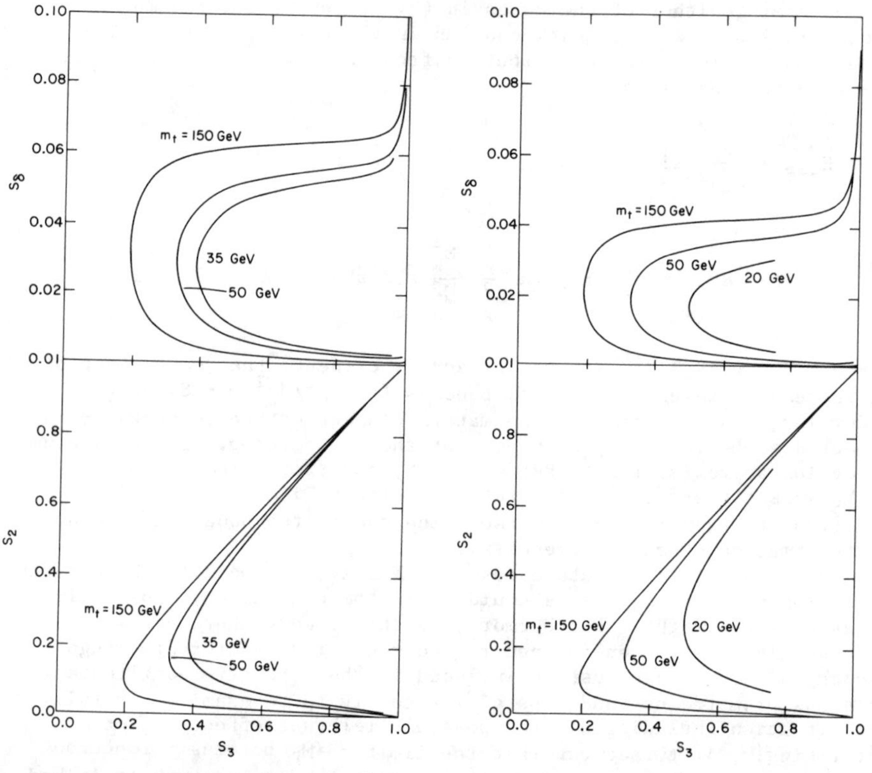

Fig. 1 S_δ **and** s_2 **vs** s_3 **for Higgs mass** m_H **= 100 GeV with**

(a) M_R = 200 GeV (b) M_R = 300 GeV .

In short, for the **same left and right mixing angles,** the scale of parity restoration is pushed into the TeV region

$$M_R \text{ (manifest L-R)} \gtrsim 1\text{-}2 \text{ TeV} . \qquad (2.10)$$

Neutral currents. Since the ratio of neutral and charged gauge boson masses is fixed, albeit in a somewhat model dependent manner, neutral currents can be a useful source of the limit on M_R. For example, in our minimal model[3]

$$M_{Z_1}^2 \simeq \frac{M_W^2}{\cos^2\theta_W} \;, \qquad M_{Z_2}^2 \simeq 2\,\frac{\cos^2\theta_W}{\cos 2\theta_W}\,M_R^2 \tag{2.11}$$

where, as usual, $\sin^2\theta_W \equiv e^2/g^2$. The presence of the additional gauge boson changes the meaning and the value of $\sin^2\theta_W$, compared to the standard model.

Let us illustrate the above point on the case of deep inelastic neutrino-hadron scattering. The effective Hamiltonian is[3]

$$H^{\nu} = \frac{G_F}{\sqrt{2}}\,\bar{\nu}\gamma_{\mu}(1+\gamma_5)\nu\;\bar{q}\gamma^{\mu}(g_v+g_A\gamma_5)q \tag{2.12}$$

with

$$g_v = (1+\eta_R)[T_3 - 2Q\,\sin^2\theta_W]$$

$$g_A = T_3 \tag{2.13}$$

and η_R is defined through

$$\eta_R \equiv \frac{M_{W_L}{}^2/M_{W_R}{}^2}{1 - M_{W_L}{}^2/M_{W_R}{}^2} \;. \tag{2.14}$$

It is easy to see that the presence of the η_R term in (2.13) **increases** the value of $\sin^2\theta_W$ compared to the standard model. As demonstrated by Rizzo and myself[16], one can fit the data even with $\sin^2\theta_W$ as large as 0.27, for W_R sufficiently light: $M_R \sim 200$ GeV or so. However, the recent work of Barger et al. and Deshpande and Johnson[17] which does the best fit analysis of all neutral current data (including the SLAC experiment on polarized electron-hadron scattering) suggests that the value of $\sin^2\theta_W$ should not exceed 0.25 and for light W_R this value would be preferred. This, per se, does not mean much, but as we shall see in the subsequent section has an important impact on the grand unification of the left-right symmetric model.

In short, neutral current data allow M_R to be as low as 150-200 GeV (this is the model independent statement), with simultaneously $\sin^2\theta_W$ as large as 0.25. This issue of light W_R shall soon be cleared by the precise measurements of W and Z gauge bosons. Namely, the value of $\sin^2\theta_W$ determines M_W and M_Z and with $\sin^2\theta_W \simeq 0.25$, W and Z would be substantially lighter (~ 5 GeV) than in the standard model.

Light W_R and its signatures. Light W_R, if it exists, would have rather clear experimental signatures[18]. Imagine you produce W_R^+; it would decay

$$W_R^+ \to \nu_R \, \mu^+$$

$$\nu_R \to \mu^- \, u\bar{d}$$
$$\nu_R \to \mu^+ \, d\bar{u} \qquad (2.15)$$

The existence of the last mode is the consequence of the Majorana nature of ν_R. Therefore, we should expect, with equal probability, two same charge muons in the final state. Unlike in the case of W_L, we have no missing energy in the final state with a unique possibility of the direct test of Majorana nature of neutrinos and the lepton number violation.

Neutrino-less double β decay. This is another manifestation of the lepton number violation due to the Majorana character of ν_R. Through the exchanges of W_R and ν_R, the dimensionless parameter η which measures the strength of the process is[3]

$$\eta \simeq \left(\frac{M_L}{M_R}\right)^4 \frac{E(\ 1\ \mathrm{GeV})}{m_{\nu_R}} \simeq 10^{-4} - 10^{-5} \qquad (2.16)$$

for $M_R \simeq 3M_L$ (or so). Experimentally, $\eta_{exp} \lesssim 10^{-4}$.

Neutrino masses. For light W_R, left-handed neutrinos are expected also in the interesting region of energies[3]

$$m_{\nu_e} \simeq 10\ \mathrm{eV}, \quad m_{\nu_\mu} \simeq 100\ \mathrm{keV}, \quad m_{\nu_\tau} \simeq 100\ \mathrm{MeV} \qquad (2.17)$$

so that ν_e could play an important cosmological role of determining the energy density of the universe. One, of course, has to make sure that ν_μ and ν_τ have decayed by now, again for cosmological reasons; for further discussion see Ref. 19.

It is quite probable that you have been bored by all this and that (hopefully) you just care about the present experimental status of L-R symmetry. This table summarizes the results of the section

L-R Symmetry and M_R

μ and β decays	Dirac neutrinos: $M_R \gtrsim 380$ GeV Majorana neutrinos: no limit
nonleptonic decays	$M_R \gtrsim 200$-300 GeV ξ_{LR} (L-R mixing) $\lesssim 10^{-3}$
K_L-K_S mass difference	$\theta_{iL} = \theta_{iR}$ (Cabibbo angles): $M_R \gtrsim 1$-2 TeV $\theta_{iL} \neq \theta_{iR}$: no limit
Neutral currents	$M_R \gtrsim 150$-200 GeV $\sin^2\theta_W < 0.25$

TABLE 1 - Summary of limits on M_R

3. SO(10) and M_R

In any electroweak scale, the scale of symmetry breaking is a free parameter, determined only by the phenomenology of low energy phenomena. The same is not true when we unify electroweak with strong interactions[20]. The minimal grand unified theory, the SU(5) model of Georgi and Glashow[21], determines not only the scale of grand unification M_X, but also $\sin^2\theta_W$, or in turn M_W and M_Z - the scale of weak interactions; the only input being the measured strength of the strong interaction coupling constant.

The question is whether we can do the same regarding M_R in SO(10) - the minimal L-R symmetric GUT[22]. The answer, of course, is **no.** An extra scale enables us only to give M_R as a function of M_X or $\sin^2\theta_W$. We will choose the latter. The precedure is well known - one follows the renormalization group prescribed dependence of coupling constants with energy[23], the only problem being the usual one: what are the light Higgs scalars that then contribute to $\sin^2\theta_W$ and α_s above their threshold? This immediately makes all the predictions model dependent, although some general statements can still be made if one assumes the so-called survival principle for Higgs scalar masses[24]. **Survival principle** or the **principle of minimal** fine tuning simply means that **besides the original tuning of M_W/M_X ratio, no other parameters (in particular the Higgs masses)** will be **tuned,** but rather allowed to have their natural values. The main consequence of this physically attractive hypothesis is in simplest terms the result that **all Higgs scalars that can become superheavy do in fact become superheavy.**

A few years ago Rizzo and I performed a detailed study[25] of the embedding of the minimal L-R symmetrical model (as discussed in §2) in the SO(10) GUT. Meanwhile, there have been new developments, especially on the phenomenological side, changing some of our conclusions[17]. The rest of this section will be devoted to the summary of the present situation.

In order to be as precise as possible, with Caswell and Milutinovic, we have performed[26] two-loop determination of low energy parameters with the following results. Assume the pattern of symmetry breaking

$$O(10) \underset{M_X}{\rightarrow} SU(2)_L \times SU(2)_R \times U(1)_{B-L} \times SU(3)_C$$

$$\underset{M_R}{\rightarrow} SU(2)_L \times U(1) \times SU(3)_C \underset{M_W}{\rightarrow} U(1)_{em} \times SU(3)_C \,. \qquad (3.1)$$

Our computations give $\sin^2\theta_W$, M_X and τ_p as a function of Λ_{MS} **for light W_R:** $M_R = 200$ GeV

Λ_{MS}	$\sin^2\theta_W(M_W)$	M_X(GeV)	t_p(yr)
100	.273	2×10^{16}	8×10^{35}
200	.271	4×10^{16}	4×10^{37}
300	.269	7×10^{16}	2×10^{38}

Table 2

The calculated value of $\sin^2\theta_W$ tends to be somewhat large: ~ 0.27, which contradicts the new phenomenological estimates[17]. If we accept, on the other hand, $\sin^2\theta_W < 0.25$, then $M_R \gtrsim 10^6$–10^7 GeV, increasing towards M_X for lower value of $\sin^2\theta_W$. In conclusion, **accepting survival principle for Higgs scalar masses appears to rule out SO(10) embedding of weakly broken parity.**

This makes an interesting parallel with SU(5), which, as the minimal GUT of the standard model seems to be ruled out because of the too short estimate of proton lifetime. On the other hand, maybe we should still wait and see.

What happens if we give up survival principle? Recently, in an interesting paper[27], Šokorac has explored the consequences of the possibility that Higgs scalars survive down to lower energies, imagining some unspecified symmetry (supersymmetry?, ...). Assuming to be specific, the opposite from the survival principle, i.e. that only those scalars that must be superheavy do become superheavy, he finds, among other results, a case with $M_R \simeq 200$ GeV and $\sin^2\theta_W \simeq 0.25$ with $M_X \simeq 2 \times 10^{14}$ GeV. A comment is needed regarding proton lifetime, since this result would imply $\tau_p \lesssim 10^{31}$ yr as in SU(5), and now we know[28] that $(\tau_p)_{exp} \gtrsim 7 \times 10^{31}$ yr. However, experimental limit regards the mode $p \to e^+\pi^0(\mu^+\pi^0)$, which is **forbidden**[29] if parity is a good symmetry (at M_X), allowing other modes such as, say $p \to \rho^0 e^+$, for which better limits are needed.

I tend to believe in survival principle, or at least I believe that it should be accepted as a working hypothesis, since only then can we make well defined predictions. On the other hand, many people do not share my feelings and so, until this issue is completely resolved, perhaps low M_R should not be completely ruled out of the context of SO(10). I should also add, that in the limit when Higgs effects are negligible, some interesting general results regarding M_R in SO(10) can be obtained[30].

L-R symmetry and n-n oscillations. I will close this section with a few brief comments on n-n oscillations in connection with L-R symmetry and SO(10). Consistent with our philosophy of Higgs scalars having the quantum numbers of fermionic bilinears, we should expect further states such as diquarks

$$\Delta_L^q \sim Q_L^T C Q_L, \quad \Delta_R^q \sim Q_R^T C Q_R \ . \qquad (3.2)$$

The presence of these particles leads, as pointed out by Marshak and Mohapatra[31], to n-n oscillations. The model they constructed was based on the Pati-Salam $SU(2)_L \times SU(2)_R \times SU(4)_C$ symmetry. Now, observability of this process requires the scale of symmetry breaking M_c to be less than about 10^6 GeV, whereas the $\sin^2\theta_W$ analysis[32] suggests $M_c > 10^{12}$ GeV.

The situation is no better in SO(10). There, one can achieve[33] $M_c \simeq 10^5$ GeV at the expense of pushing M_R at M_X; however, not all the diquarks remain light, but rather some get superheavy mass. In any case, with survival principle operating, the prospects for observable n-n oscillations are hopeless and only by giving it up is there a chance[27].

4. L-R Symmetry and CP Violation

Some number of years ago, at the time when we still had only four quarks, Mohapatra and Pati suggested a rather ingenious possibility of connecting[2] P and CP violation. Assuming **spontaneous breakdown** of P and CP in the minimal L-R model, they were led (see (2.6)) to symmetric quark matrices $M_q^T = M_q$, or in other words

$$U_R = U_L^* K \qquad (4.1)$$

where K is diagonal and unitary:

$$K_{ij} = e^{i\phi_i}\,\delta_{ij}\ .$$

Making U_L real as usual, one gets for the weak Hamiltonian

$$H_{wk} = \frac{g}{\sqrt{2}}\,[\bar{P}_L\gamma^\mu U_L N_L W^+_{\mu_L} + \bar{P}_R\gamma^\mu U_R N_R W^+_{\mu_R}]\ \text{th.c.} \qquad (4.2)$$

with

$$U_L = \begin{pmatrix} \cos\theta & \sin\theta \\ -\sin\theta & \cos\theta \end{pmatrix},\quad U_R = \begin{pmatrix} e^{i\alpha}\cos\theta & e^{i\delta}\sin\theta \\ -e^{-i\delta}\sin\theta & e^{-i\alpha}\cos\theta \end{pmatrix}. \qquad (4.3)$$

One can show then for CP violation in K meson system

$$\eta_{+-}(K) = \eta_{00}(K) \simeq \sin\delta\,\frac{M_L^{\,2}}{M_R^2} \qquad (4.4)$$

providing a **tie between the smallness of CP violatioin and the predominant V-A structure of weak interactions.**

Furthermore, as we pointed out later with Kane, one can get an interesting possibility of large CP violation in semileptonic D meson decays[36] (for light W_R), a distinguishing feature from the Kobayashi-Maskawa and Higgs model. Namely, for an equivalent of $\eta(K)$, one has

$$\eta(D) \simeq \sin\alpha\,\frac{M_L^{\,2}}{M_R^{\,2}} \qquad (4.5)$$

with α arbitrary, so that $\eta(D)$ can be as large as 0.1. On the other hand, we live in the world with at least six (?) quarks. The generalization of the above idea has been performed by Chang[35], who manages to preserve the essence of (4.4). He has utilized the work of Beall et al.[12], which pushes M_R in the TeV region, and has enabled him to arrive at the situation where the usual K-M contribution to CP violation is suppressed compared to the W_R exchange.

Strong CP violation. A somewhat different class of L-R models could play an important role in understanding the smallness of strong CP violation. Recall that the strong CP problem is a problem of understanding why the effective QCD-electroweak CP parameter

$$\bar{\theta} \equiv \theta + \arg\det M_q \qquad (4.6)$$

has to be so small[36] (in order that the electric dipole moment of the neutron is not too large)

$$\bar{\theta} \lesssim 10^{-9} . \qquad (4.7)$$

I will not go into the celebrated Peccei-Quinn mechanism that leads to the existence of the axion. Suffice it to say that, due to cosmological constraints, Peccei-Quinn mass scale must lie in a small range at energies $10^{9}-10^{12}$ GeV, and furthermore it appears hard to solve the domain wall problem which emerges in this solution[37].

The alternative strategy employing L-R symmetry was suggested[38] a few years ago.

(a) Use L-R symmetry $\Longrightarrow \theta = 0$,

(b) have manifest L-R symmetry $\Longrightarrow M_q = M_q^{+} \Longrightarrow \arg \det M_q = 0$,

and so

$$\bar{\theta}^{\,\text{tree}} = 0 \qquad (4.8)$$

The finite, in higher orders induced $\bar{\theta}$ turns out be be small: $\bar{\theta}^{\text{ind}} < 10^{-10}$. Unfortunately, the suggested models were complicated and worse, employed ad hoc discrete symmetries to meet constraint (b). An interesting attempt, which demanded **no** such discrete symmetries enabled Masiero et al. to achieve[38]

$$\bar{\theta} \simeq \frac{M_L^{\,2}}{M_R^{\,2}} \qquad (4.9)$$

which would favor heavy W_R in the range of energies $> 10^5$-10^6 GeV. Again, the price paid lies in the enormous complexity in the Higgs sector. I am personally still somewhat unhappy about the attempts until now.

An amusing possibility exists that maybe the minimal model works[40], but more work is needed before any comments are made.

Spontaneous breakdown of CP and GUTS. Let me close this section with an interesting connection between spontaneous breakdown of CP and intermediate mass scales[41] in GUTS. The simplest way to break CP spontaneously is to enlarge the standard model with an additional Higgs doublet and demand all couplings to be real[42]. We can then achieve

$$\langle\phi_1\rangle = \begin{pmatrix} 0 \\ v_1 \end{pmatrix}, \quad \langle\phi_2\rangle = \begin{pmatrix} 0 \\ e^{i\alpha} v_2 \end{pmatrix} . \qquad (4.10)$$

In the context of GUTS, say e.g. SU(5) the same would be achieved by taking two Higgs $\underline{5}$'s. However, according to survival principle, only one doublet remains light($\sim M_W$), whereas the other becomes superheavy, leading to $\alpha = 0$. In other words, $\alpha \neq 0$ would require further fine-tuning.

On the other hand, in the L-R model no modification is needed since (see(2.4)) Φ contains two $SU(2)_L$ doublets (ϕ_1^+, ϕ_1^0) and (ϕ_2^+, ϕ_2^0), with $SU(2)_R$ acting in the horizonal direction. Therefore the second doublet gets the mass $\mathbf{M_R}$, and **not** $\mathbf{M_X}$. The naturalness of the theory would require (approximately)

$$M_R/M_W \lesssim 100 \tag{4.11}$$

In other words, spontaneous breakdown at CP invariance in GUTS, when tied up to the idea of minimal fine tuning seems to require the existence of the intermediate mass scale, not far from M_W. The scale of parity restoration could very well play that role, if a simple and consistent GUT with low M_R is constructed. Could the right theory be SU(16)?[45]

5. Spontaneous Breakdown of Parity and the Domain Wall Problem

Until now we have completely ignored a serious cosmological problem inherent in all theories that incorporate the spontaneous breakdown of a discrete symmetry, i.e. the infamous domain wall problem[44]. In our case, both V+A and V-A vacua are equally probable; these vacua being physically distinct and not connected by a gauge transformation. By analogy with ferromagnets we know that in the process of cooling down the early universe would have necessarily formed different domains of V-A and V+A vacua, with the energy density in domain walls orders of magnitude above the energy density of the universe. Of course, this is based on the well-known belief that all the systems behave by analogy with ferromagnets or superconductors, i.e. that the symmetries are always restored at high temperature[45].

Symmetry nonrestoration at high T. The subtitle provides an answer: the above is not necessarily true[46]. The main effect at high T is T-dependent mass term for Higgs fields

$$m_H^2(T) = m_H^2(0) + (\Sigma\, C_i \lambda_i)\, T^2 \tag{5.1}$$

where λ_i are Higgs quartic self-couplings, and C_i are positive coefficients (let us ignore gauge and Yukawa couplings).

In the case of a single Higgs field, $\lambda > 0$ and so, at sufficiently high T, $m_H^2(T) > 0$ and the symmetry is restored. In general, however, not all $\lambda_i > 0$. For example, with two Higgs fields one can achieve at high T

$$m_1^{2}(T) > 0, \quad m_2^{T}(T) < 0 \tag{5.2}$$

and so we would have $\langle\phi_2\rangle \neq 0$ at all temperatures for which we can trust our approximations.

Let us now come to the case of our interest: the L-R model. In §2 we have learned that the Higgs sector contains triplets Δ_L and Δ_R and multiplet ϕ. Due to the lack of space I refer to reader to find the details in our original work; the net result is that one can find a solution at high T

$$T > T_c \sim M_R: \quad \begin{array}{c} \langle\Delta_L\rangle = 0; \qquad \langle\Delta_R\rangle \sim T \\ \langle\phi\rangle = 0 \end{array} \tag{5.3}$$

so that parity keeps being broken.

The above solution, although it eliminates the domain wall problem, is not physically very appealing and runs somewhat counter to our intuition. A nicer approach is to embed $SU(2)_L \times SU(2)_R \times U(1)_{B-L}$ into a single group.

SO(10) and the domain wall problem. In SO(10), parity (or better CP) becomes identified with the element at the center of the group[47]. In other words, different vacua can be reached by a continuous gauge transformation and so it costs no energy to go from one vacuum to another. This eliminates the domain wall problem, however, as I stressed before, the problem of the consistency of light W_R and $\sin^2\theta_W$ prediction still remains. In any case, the general idea is rather appealing and should be pursued.

Light W_R and matter-antimatter asymmetry of the universe. Let me now move to a rather interesting cosmological objection to light W_R raised by Kuzmin and Shaposnikov[48]. They have noticed that the amount of baryon asymmetry produced in the early universe is proportional to the strength of the breakdown of parity

$$\frac{n_B}{n_\gamma} = \left(\frac{n_B}{n_\gamma}\right)_0 \frac{\langle\Delta_R\rangle - \langle\Delta_L\rangle}{M_X} \tag{5.4}$$

where $(n_B/n_\gamma)_0 \simeq 10^{-9}$ is what we would get in a broken theory. This, if true, would completely invalidate the idea of light W_R (independently of details of the theory) and would require $\langle\Delta_R\rangle \simeq M_R > 10^{12}$ GeV. The answer to this objection was provided by Masiero and myself[49] at the expense of enlarging the Higgs sector of the model. We have used the idea of symmetry nonrestoration at high T to construct

$$\frac{\langle\Delta_R(T)\rangle - \langle\Delta_L(T)\rangle}{M_X} \simeq \frac{T}{M_X} \simeq 10^{-1} \tag{5.5}$$

at relevant temperatures when the baryon number at the universe was created. Although our answer is completely correct, I am not to crazy about the complexities we were forced to introduce in our model.

Peccei-Quinn mechanisms and L-R symmetry. I have mentioned in §4 that the scale of the breakdown of Pecci-Quinn symmetry, M_{PQ}, which quarantees the absence of strong CP violation is between 10^9 and 10^{12} GeV. It turns out, in the context of SO(10), that M_R could play that role[50]: $M_R = M_{PQ}$, and furthermore such a model can be made free from the cosmological domain wall problem[51]. Of course, this depends on $\sin^2\theta_W$ (and so is testable), which varies[50] between 0.24 and 0.22 for M_R between 10^9 and 10^{12} GeV. In other words, one emerges with the following picture of symmetry breaking

$$
\begin{array}{l}
O(10) \\
\Big\downarrow \; M_X \\
SU(2)_L \times SU(2)_R \times U(1) \times SU(3)_C \\
\Big\downarrow \; M_R = M_{PQ}:\ 10^9\text{–}10^{12}\ \text{GeV} \\
SU(2)_L \times U(1) \times SU(3)_C \\
\Big\downarrow \; M_W \\
U(1)_{em} \times SU(3)_C
\end{array}
\qquad (5.6)
$$

leading to a standard model at low energies. Again, measurement of M_W and M_Z can serve as a check of this idea. The amusing consequence of the above idea is the connection between axion and neutrino masses

$$m_a = m_\pi \frac{f\pi}{M_R}$$

$$m_\nu = \frac{m_q^2}{M_R} \qquad (5.7)$$

or

$$m_\nu = \frac{m_q^2}{m_\pi f\pi}\, m_a \ . \qquad (5.8)$$

6. Preons and L-R Symmetry

This section has been included more for the sake of completeness than any other reason and will lack completely any details and conceptual organization. I just want to mention the fact that many of the composite models of quarks and leptons end up with residual theories being L-R symmetric, as in the examples lprovided by Harari and Seiberg[52], Greenberg and Sucher[53], Barbieri, Masiero and Mohapatra[54], and others[55].

Without any good reason for discrimination, let me say a few words about Harari-Seiberg model[52] (rishon model) as the prototype of ideas at compositeness.

(i) They, as most of the other workers in the field assume the force that binds preons together to be some SU(N) gauge theory (hypercolor), by analogy with QCD. The gauge symmetry operating on the preon level is then $SU(N) \times SU(3)_C \times U(1)_{em}$.

(ii) The choice of preon assignments is

$$T(3,3,1/3)\ ,\quad V(3,\bar{3},0) \tag{6.1}$$

where the numbers in the brackets stand for hypercolor, color and electric charge, respectively.

(iii) Among other (arbitrary) assumptions they need is that the light states are lowest color states, which determine the quantum numbers of light composite fermions, represented in Table 3.

States	Color	B-L	Hypercolor
$TTT(e^+)$	1	1	1
$TTV(u)$	3	1/3	1
$TVV(\bar{d})$	$\bar{3}$	-1/3	1
$VVV(\nu_e)$	1	-1	1

Table 3

where B-L is identified as

$$B=L = 1/3\ (n_T - n_V) \tag{6.2}$$

(iv) For a generation: $e(\bar{T}\bar{T}\bar{T})$, $\nu_e(VVV)$, three up-quarks (TTV), three down-quarks ($\overline{TVV}$), the total preon contact is $6(T+\bar{T}+V+\bar{V})$. The charge vanishes when summed over one generation, even in the T and V charges are not specified.

Since the model is L-R symmetric, it leads naturally to $SU(2)_L \times SU(2)_R \times U(1)_{B-L}$ symmetry at the composite level. Of course, the dynamics of the composite theory is not known. However, **assuming** the effective Lagrangian to be renormalizable, it should be approximately gauge invariant under $SU(2)_L \times SU(2)_R \times U(1)_{B-L}$. The gauge boson states in this model are, unfortunately, rather complicated:

$$W_L^+ = (T_L T_L)\, T_R (V_R V_R)\, V_L; \qquad W_R^+ = (T_R T_R)\, T_L (V_L V_L)\, V_R, \text{ etc.}$$

The lack of space doesn't allow me to go any deeper into many unanswered questions, such as say, chiral symmetry breaking. Preon models are at the stage when many assumptions (often ad hoc) are needed to make sure that the resulting theories make sense. I just wanted to point out that, under some not so unreasonable assumptions, one may be led to L-R symmetry. It is amusing to mention that the analysis of residual weak interactions in their theory, led Harari and Seiberg[56] to exactly the model of Mohapatra and myself, discussed at length in §2.

I should mention, of course, that L-R symmetry is by now no means a necessary feature of composite models. Among many others, an interesting composite model with the scale of symmetry compositeness at M_X and residual SU(5) symmetry has been provided by P. Senjanovic.

7. Summary and Comments

In this review I have tried to go through, what I believe, are the most important features of the ideas that the origin of parity violation in weak interactions is due to spontaneous breakdown of left-right symmetry, incorporated in the gauge theory based on $SU(2)_L \times SU(2)_R \times U(1)_{B-L}$ group. I have paid most attention to the question of the existing experimental constraints on the scale M_R of parity restoration in order for the reader to know where we stand today and what to expect in the near future. In that sense, this review is more a compilation or summary of various aspects of L-R symmetry rather than being a pedagogical expose.

We concluded that low $M_R \sim 200$ GeV (or so) is still perfectly consistent with all the data both in the realm of charged and neutral currents, if $\sin^2\theta_W \simeq 0.25$. The only exception to this is the case of manifest (or pseudomanifest) L-R symmetry, characterized by the same left and right flavor mixing angles, in which case K_L-K_S mass difference leads to a more stringent constraint: $M_R \gtrsim 1$-2 TeV. This unfortunately includes the interesting model of weak and strong CP violations.

If W_R still turned out to be light ($\theta_L \neq \theta_R$), its signature would be clean and interesting, leading among other things to a direct test of lepton number violation through the Majorana nature of neutrinos. Furthermore, it would make neutrino-less double β decay potentially observable, and more than anything, give us a chance to directly observe parity restoration at high energies.

Rather than dwell on various theoretical aspects of L-R symmetry discussed in this review, I would like to summarize my talk with the assessment of the prospects for low lying scale of parity restoration. The only strong motivation for it was its apparent realization within SO(10), which now appears to be ruled out. Furthermore, the recent measurement of W and Z boson masses, being announced as I am writing these last lines, strongly encourages the validity of the standard model at low energies. It should be interesting to see more precisely what these new results imply for the mass of the right handed charged gauge boson. In any case, it appears rather safe to conclude that M_R is pushed up, at least into the TeV region which although not accessible now, will be come reachable in the next generation of accelerators being built or at least planned today. In all honesty, it is perfectly possible (and encouraged by SO(10) results) that M_R is high up in the desert ($\gtrsim 10^7$ GeV), possibly providing the Peccei-Quinn scale between 10^9 and 10^{12} GeV and providing and interesting link between axion and neutrino masses. All we can do now is to wait and see; and, as always, let the experiment decide. What I do hope, however, is that this review persuaded you that, at least on the theoretical side, L-R symmetry offers some interesting issues which are not encountered in the standard model such as neutrino masses, calculable $\bar{\theta}$, link between P and CP violation and the domain wall problem.

Acknowledgments

The work described here has been over the years mostly in collaboration with Rabi Mohapatra, but also Bill Caswell, Gordy Kane, Yee Keung, Antonio Masiero, Janko Milutinovic, Marco Roncadelli, Tom Rizzo, Sasko Sokorac and Minh Tran. I want to thank the organizers of this excellent meeting, especially Hrvoje Galic, Silvio Pallua, and Dubravko Tadic for making my stay in Dubrovnik so enjoyable. More than anything, I am grateful to my brother, Pavle Senjanovic, who has never failed to provide the encouragement when I needed it most, and who played a crucial role in my pursuit of the understanding of the phenomena described here.

References and Footnotes

1. R.N. Mohapatra and G. Senjanovic, Univ. of Maryland preprint (1983); to be published in the Proc. of the Symposium on Intense Medium Energy Sources of Strangeness, March 1983.

2. J.C. Pati and A. Salam, Phys. Rev. D10 (1974) 275;
R.N. Mohapatra and G. Senjanović, Phys. Rev. D11 (1975) 566; 2558;
G. Senjanović and R.N. Mohapatra, Phys. Rev. D12 (1975) 1502;
For a review of the basics of L-R Symmetry, see G. Senjanovic, Nucl. Phys. B153 (1979) 334.

3. R.N. Mohapatra and G. Senjanovic, Phys. Rev. Lett. 44 (1980) 912; Phys. Rev. D23 (1981) 165.

4. I will ignore here the scalars that have quantum numbers of diquarks since they play no role in ordinary weak interactions.

5. See, M. Gronau and S. Nussinov, SLAC preprint (1982) and preprints by M. Gronau (1982).

6. As in the mechanism of M. Gell-Mann, P. Ramond and R. Slansky, unpublished (1979) and T. Yanagida, KEK lecture notes (1979).

7. See, G.C. Branco and G. Senjanović, Phys. Rev. D18 (1978) 1621.

8. M.A.B. Bég, R.V. Budny, R.N. Mohapatra and A. Sirlin. Phys. Rev. Lett. 38 (1977) 1252.

9. R.N. Mohapatra, F.E. Paige and D.P. Sidhu, Phys. Rev. D17 (1978) 2642; R.N. Mohapatra, "New Frontiers in High Energy Physics", eds. A. Perlmutter and L. Scott, Plenum Press (1979).

10. B. Holstein and S. Treiman, Phys. Rev. D16 (1977) 2369. For an early work, see E. Lipmann, Sov. J. Nucl. Phys. 6 (1968) 395. The new limit is due to J. Carr et al., LBL preprint (1983).

11. J. Donoghue and B. Holstein, Phys. Lett. 113B (1982) 282;
I.I. Bigi and J.M. Frére, Phys. Lett. 110B (1982) 255.

12. G. Beall, M. Bender and A. Soni, Phys. Rev. Lett. 48 (1982) 848. See also, J. Trampetic, Phys. Rev. D27 (1983) 1565.

13. R.N. Mohapatra, G. Senjanović, M.D. Tran, Phys. Rev. D28 (1983) 546;
G. Ecker, W. Grimus and H. Nuefeld, Univ. of Vienna preprint (1983).

14. See P. Lipari, talk at this Conference.

15. F. Gilman and M.H. Reno, SLAC-Pub-3123 (1983) to appear in Phys.

Lett. B. There may still be some hope in the pseudomanifest case, see H. Harari and M. Leuver, Fermilab preprint (1983). I thank Fred Gilman for a useful discussion on this and other points.

16. T.G. Rizzo and G. Senjanović, Phys. Rev. Lett. 46 (1981) 1315 and Phys. Rev. D24 (1981) 704.

17. V. Barger, E. Ma and K. Whisnant, Phys. Rev. D26 (1982) 2378; N.G. Deshpande and R.J. Johnson, Phys. Rev. D27 (1983) 1165.

18. W.-Y. Keung and G. Senjanović, Phys. Rev. Lett. 50 (1983) 1427.

19. M. Roncadelli and G. Senjanović, Phys. Lett. 107B (1981) 59; P.B. Pal, Carnegie-Mellon preprint (1982); B. McKellar and S. Pakvasa, Los Alamos preprint (1982).

20. J.C. Pati and A. Salam, Phys. Rev. D10 (1974) 275; H. Georgi and S.L. Glashow, Phys. Rev. Lett. 32 (1974) 438.

21. H. Georgi and S.L. Glashow, Ref. 20.

22. H. Georgi, in Particles and Fields, 1974, ed. C.E. Carlson, (AIP, New York 1975); H. Fritzsch and P. Minkowski, Ann. Phys. (NY) 93 (1975) 193.

23. H. Georgi, H. Quinn and S. Weinberg, Phys. Rev. Lett. 33 (1974) 451.

24. F. del Aguila and L.E. Ibanez, Nucl. Phys. B177 (1981) 60; R.N. Mohapatra and G. Senjanović, Phys. Rev. D27 (1983) 1601. The survival hypothesis was originally introduced for fermions by H. Georgi, Nucl. Phys. B156 (1979) 126.

25. T.G. Rizzo and G. Senjanović, Phys. Rev. D25 (1982) 235.

26. W.E. Caswell, J. Milutinović and G. Senjanović, Phys. Rev. D26 (1982) 161.

27. A. Šokorac, Phys. Rev. D (in press).

28. See, R. Bionta et al., "Search for Proton Decay into $e^+\pi^0$", Phys. Rev. Lett. 51 (1983) 27.

29. G. Karl and P.J. O'Donnell, Nucl. Phys. B204 (1982) 1.

30. Y. Tosa, G.C. Branco and R.E. Marshak, VPI preprint (1983).

31. R.N. Mohapatra and R.E. Marshak, Phys. Rev. Lett. 44 (1980) 1316.

32. For a review and original references, see G. Senjanović, Proc. of

the Harvard Workshop on Neutron Oscillations, 1982, eds. M. Goodman and M. Machecek, 1983.

33. G. Senjanovic and A. Šokorac, Z. für Physik (in press).

34. G. Kane and G. Senjanović, Phys. Rev. D25 (1982) 173.

35. D. Chang, Carnegie-Mellon preprint (1983).

36. V. Balumi, Phys. Rev. D18 (1979) 2227;
R. Crewther, P. Di Vecchia, G. Veneziano and E. Witten, Phys. Lett. 88B (1979) 123.

37. For a review and references, see P. Sikivie, talk at the IV GUT Workshop, Univ. of Pennsylvania, April 1983 (to appear in the proceedings).

38. M.A.B. Bég and H.S. Tsao, Phys. Rev. Lett. 41 (1978) 278;
R.N. Mohapatra and G. Senjanović, Phys. Lett. 79B (1978) 283.
For a review and further references, see G. Senjanovic, Proc. XX Int. Conf. on High Energy Physics, Madison, WI (1980), eds. L. Durand et al., AIP (1981).

39. A. Masiero, R.N. Mohapatra and R. Peccei, Nucl. Phys. B192 (1981) 66.

40. G. Beall, private communication.

41. G. Senjanović, Z. für Physik C18 (1983) 271.

42. T.D. Lee, Phys. Rev. D8 (1973) 1226.

43. J.C. Pati, A. Salam and J. Strathdee, Phys. Lett. 108B (1982) 121;
R.N. Mohapatra and M. Popović, Phys. Rev. D25 (1982) 3012;
A. Raychandhury and U. Sarker, Univ. of Calcutta preprint (1982);
A. Mohanty, Univ. of Maryland preprint (1982).

44. Ya. B. Zeldovich, I. Yu. Kobzanev and L.B. Okun, Sov. Phys. JETP 40 (1975) 1.

45. D.A. Kirzhnitz and A.D. Linde, Phys. Lett. 42B (1972) 471;
S. Weinberg, Phys. Rev. D9 (1974) 3537;
L. Dolan and R. Jackiw, Phys. Rev. D94 (1974) 2904.

46. R.N. Mohapatra and G. Senjanović, Phys. Rev. Lett. 42 (1979); Phys. Rev. D20 (1979) 3390; Phys. Lett. 89B (1979) 57.

47. G. Lazarides and Q. Shafi, Phys. Lett. (1980).

48. V.A. Kuzmin and M. Shaposnikov, Phys. Lett. 92B (1980) 115.

49. A. Masiero and G. Senjanović, Phys. Lett. 108B (1982) 191.

50. R.N. Mohapatra and G. Senjanović, Z. für Physik C17 (1983) 53.

51. R. Holman, G. Lazarides and Q. Shafi, Rockefeller preprint (1983).

52. H. Harari and N. Seiberg, Phys. Lett. 98B (1981) 269; Nucl. Phys. B204 (1982) 141.

53. O.W. Greenberg and J. Sucher, Phys. Lett. 99B (1981) 339.

54. R. Barbieri, A. Masiero and R.N. Mohapatra, Phys. Lett. 105B (1981) 369.

55. For a review of compositeness, see M. Peskin, in Proc. 1981 Int. Symp. on Lepton Photon Interactions at High Energies, Bonn, ed. W. Pfeil (1982).

56. H. Harari and N. Seiberg, Phys. Lett. 100B (1981) 41.

57. P. Senjanović, Fizika 15 (1983) 165.

EXPERIMENTAL CONSTRAINTS ON NEW COSMOLOGICAL FIELDS

Ephraim Fischbach

Physics Department, Purdue University, West Lafayette, IN 47907
USA

ABSTRACT

A recent analysis of Fermilab data on the K^o-$\bar{K}^o$ system suggests that the parameters Δm, τ_S, and η_{+-} have an anomalous energy dependence. We summarize this analysis, and review the arguments which demonstrate that effects of the type suggested by the data cannot arise from any known mechanism. Some mechanisms which can give rise to such effects are also discussed, including the possibility of a breakdown of Lorentz invariance. Various experiments are also discussed to check and extend the existing results.

1. Introduction

Recently my colleagues Sam Aronson, Greg Bock, Hai-Yang Cheng and I presented experimental evidence[1-4] that the numerical values of the fundamental parameters of the K^o-$\bar{K}^o$ system may depend on the energy (or velocity) of the kaons with respect to the laboratory. We also demonstrated theoretically that these effects-if real-could also be the signal for the existence of a new long-range force (or a new medium) permeating space, whose presence had hitherto gone undetected. It is, of course, not clear at the present time whether the data reported in Refs. 1-4 are correct. Nonetheless their existence has led us and others to reopen the question of whether there can exist other so-called "cosmological fields" permeating ostensibly empty space, which influence the outcome of "local" experiments. The object of this talk is to review the body of data which bear on the question of new cosmological fields, and to indicate which possibilities remain viable ones at the present time[5]. Since the only actual evidence for some new field comes from the data of Refs. 1-4, we will pay particular attention to these experiments, and to others presently in progress, which will also study the K^o - $\bar{K}^o$ system. In the course of this discussion it will become clear that the K^o - $\bar{K}^o$ system can be used to derive stringent constraints on various possible cosmological fields.

Before proceeding to a discussion of the technical details of various experiments, it is useful to illustrate by means of an example how cosmological fields show up experimentally. To start with, we will use the term "cosmological field" to generically denote <u>any</u> external influence present in otherwise empty space, which could affect the outcome of some experiment such as kaon regeneration. Examples of cosmological fields would then be the well-known electromagnetic and gravitational fields, the cosmological neutrino sea (presumed to be a relic of the big-bang), and the often-raised possibility of a long-range field which couples to hypercharge. We will also allow for the possibility that the "cosmological field" isn't an actual field (i.e. an influence due to some matter distribution), but represents instead a fundamental breakdown of Lorentz invariance. As we will show, the effects of Lorentz-noninvariance can in principle be distinguished from those of an external field by appropriate experiments. Let us then consider the example of an external field which couples to hypercharge. Such a field has been proposed for a variety of reasons, including as a mechanism for explaining the CP-violating mode $K_L \to 2\pi$.[6] Suppose that such a field emanated from our galaxy. In analogy to the electromagnetic case, the potential $A_o(\vec{x})$ due to such a static distribution of charges seen by a K^o at rest on the Earth would be given by

$$A_o = + f^2 \frac{Y_G}{R_G} \quad , \tag{1.1}$$

where f^2 is an appropriate coupling constant, Y_G is the hypercharge of the galaxy, and R_G is the effective distance between the Earth and the hypercharge sources in the galaxy. If A_o is assumed to be the time component of a 4-vector A_μ, then a K^o moving with velocity β (where c = 1) in the z-direction would see a potential A_o' in its proper frame given by

$$A_o' = \gamma(A_o - \beta A_z) \xrightarrow{A_z = 0} \gamma A_o \ ,$$
$$\gamma = (1 - \beta^2)^{-1/2} = E_K/m \ , \tag{1.2}$$

where E_K is the kaon energy and m is its mass. Hence the effective strength of the coupling of the K^o to the hypercharge field would <u>increase</u> as the energy (or velocity) of the K^o increased. Since K^o and $\bar{K}^o$ would couple to such a field with opposite signs, the effective masses of K^o and $\bar{K}^o$ would become

$$m_{eff}(K^o) = m + \gamma A_o \ ; \quad m_{eff}(\bar{K}^o) = m - \gamma A_o, \tag{1.3}$$

and $[m_{eff}(K^o) - m_{eff}(\bar{K}^o)]$ would increase with increasing kaon energy. It is a straightforward matter to show[4] from Eq. (1.3) that the energy-dependence of the mass difference $\Delta m = m_L - m_S$ between the physical eigenstates K_L and K_S becomes

$$(\Delta m)_u^2 = [(\Delta m)^4 + 4A_o^4\gamma^4]^{1/2} + 2A_o^2\gamma^2 \quad , \tag{1.4}$$

where $(\Delta m)_u$ is the mass difference in the presence of the field, and Δm is the usual low-energy field-free value, $\Delta m = 0.5349(22) \times 10^{10} \hbar s^{-1}$.

We see from Eq. (1.4) that in the presence of a hypercharge field $(\Delta m)_u$ is a monotonically increasing function of γ, whereas the data of Refs. 1-4 indicate just the opposite, that $(\Delta m)_u$ is decreasing with increasing γ. From this and other similar observations one can conclude that effects of the type suggested by the data of Refs. 1-4 cannot be attributed to an external hypercharge field, or more generally to any C-odd field such as electromagnetism.

The preceding example also serves to illustrate how one might distinguish between the γ-dependent effects produced by an external field, and those due to an intrinsic violation of Lorentz invariance. To start with we note that any dependence of the mass difference on γ, such as that given by Eq. (1.4), represents at the very least an apparent Lorentz-noninvariant (LNI) effect. Bearing in mind that Eq. (1.4) gives the K_L - K_S mass difference in the proper frame of the kaons [See Eq. (1.2)], such an effect literally means that two observers comoving with K_L and K_S respectively can measure their common velocity with respect to ostensibly empty space by measuring Δm. If the evacuated beam pipe in which the kaon experiments are carried out were truly empty, meaning that it contained no matter and no fields, then a variation of Δm with γ would represent a manifest violation of Lorentz invariance. The alternative explanation for such an effect is that space isn't really empty due to the presence of a field. Any apparent LNI effects can then be understood physically as arising from the fact that the field and its sources define a preferred frame of reference, with respect to which a kaon's velocity can be detected.

Suppose, then, that a variation of the K_L - K_S mass difference consistent with Eq. (1.4) were to be seen experimentally. How could one distinguish between a genuine LNI effect, and an apparent LNI effect due to an external field? We observe that a field produced by a distribution of ordinary matter would arise in part from the Earth itself, so measuring the spatial variation of $(\Delta m)_u$ in the Earth's field is one way of knowing that a field is present. We will describe below two kinds of experiments (which will call the "EPR" and "mass-gap" experiments respectively) which could be sensitive to a force arising from the Earth, whose range was somewhere between ~ 1m and several km. If the range of the force were much larger than ~ 10^2km, then kaon experiments might no longer be useful in measuring its spatial variation, but analogous experiments involving neutrino oscillations could be effective, should neutrinos eventually be found to oscillate. Forces whose range were on the order of the dimensions of our galaxy could be detected in other ways, such as by the Hughes-Drever experiments described below. If the range of the force were much smaller than 1m, say of order 1 cm, then the dominant influence on the K^o - $\bar{K}^o$ system would not come from the Earth, but rather from the experimental apparatus itself. A force whose range is ~ 1 cm could be detected by means of the impulse that would be imparted by the target in a regeneration experiment. We thus refer to this proposal for detecting such forces as the "target impulse effect" (TIE).

We can then summarize the preceding discussion in the following way: A classical (nongravitational) field defines a preferred frame, so that motion with respect to this field can be detected, for example, by the velocity-dependence of some physical parameter such as the $K_L - K_S$ mass difference. (Gravitational fields must be treated separately, as we discuss in more detail in Refs. 2 and 4.) However, a velocity-dependence of some physical parameter may also arise from a fundamental violation of Lorentz invariance, and these two possibilities can be distinguished by measuring the spatial variation of the relevant parameter over an appropriate distance scale. Detecting such a variation would suggest the presence of a field, and would at the same time allow its strength and range to be determined, as we discuss below.

In Sec. 2 we review the data of Refs. 1-4, and in Sec. III a summary is given of the phenomenological analysis of Refs. 2 and 4. This leads to the conclusion that effects of the type suggested by the data require the introduction of some new field or medium in space. In Sec. 4 some models of this new interaction, generically referred to as the "U-field", are discussed. Sec. 5 considers the possibility that the $K^o - \bar{K}^o$ data actually represent a fundamental breakdown of Lorentz invariance. This can be distinguished from the effects of a physical external field by experiments which we discuss in Sec. 6, where we also present a summary of the constraints that apply to various cosmological fields.

2. Energy-Dependence of the Fundamental Parameters of the K^o-$\bar{K}^o$ System

In this section we briefly summarize the salient features of the data in Refs. 1-4. The data were obtained from a series of regeneration experiments[7] carried out at Fermilab, where the incident kaon energy E_K was in the range $30 \lesssim E_K \lesssim 130$ GeV. As is well known, if an incident kaon beam described by the wavefunction $|\Psi_i\rangle = |K_L\rangle$ passes through a material target, then the emerging beam $|\Psi_f\rangle$ will be a linear combination of $|K_L\rangle$ and $|K_S\rangle$,

$$|\Psi_f\rangle \equiv |\Psi(t = 0)\rangle \cong |K_L\rangle + \rho|K_S\rangle \ , \tag{2.1}$$

where the regeneration parameter ρ ($|\rho|<<1$) is given by

$$\rho = i\pi N\Lambda_S\, \alpha(L/\Lambda_S)\, (f - \bar{f})_o/k \ ,$$

$$\alpha(L/\Lambda_S) = \frac{[1 - \exp(-1/2 + i\Delta m\tau_S)L/\Lambda_S]}{1/2 - i\Delta m\tau_S} \ . \tag{2.2}$$

Here k is the K^o wave number, N = number of scatterers/unit volume, L = length of target, $\Lambda_S = \beta\gamma c\tau_S$, and $(f-\bar{f})_o$ is the difference between the forward scattering amplitudes for K^o and $\bar{K}^o$, respectively, on the target in question. Since both components of $|\Psi_f\rangle$ can decay into $\pi^+\pi^-$, the interesting experimental quantity is the rate of production of $\pi^+\pi^-$ pairs as a function of the proper time t, measured from the instant the beam leaves the target. This is given by[3)]

$$dI^{+-}/dt = \Gamma_S^{+-} N_L\{|\rho|^2 \exp(-t/\tau_S) + |\eta_{+-}|^2 \exp(-t/\tau_L) + 2|\rho||\eta_{+-}| \otimes$$

$$\otimes \exp[(-t/2)(1/\tau_S + 1/\tau_L)]\cos(\Delta m t + \phi_\rho - \phi_{+-})\},$$

$$\eta_{+-} = \frac{A(K_L \to \pi^+\pi^-)}{A(K_S \to \pi^+\pi^-)} = |\eta_{+-}|\, e^{i\phi_{+-}} \quad ; \; \rho = |\rho| e^{i\phi_\rho} \; . \qquad (2.3)$$

In Eq. (2.3) $\tau_{L,S}$ are the lifetimes of $K_{L,S}$, $\Gamma_S^{+-} = \Gamma(K_S \to \pi^+\pi^-)$, N_L is the number of incident K_L's, and $\Delta m = m_L - m_S$ is the $K_L - K_S$ mass difference. A typical value of $|\rho|$ is $|\rho| \cong 0.04$ for 1m of C at $E_K = 75$ GeV, which means that $|\eta_{+-}| \lesssim |\rho| \lesssim 1$ under the conditions of these experiments. The data of Refs. 1-4 come predominantly from H and C targets, with some additional information being provided by a sample of Pb data.

The motivation for undertaking the experiments in Refs. 7 was to measure ρ, and hence $(f-\bar{f})_o$, for a variety of targets in an effort to test Regge theory. For these purposes the expression for dI^{+-}/dt in (2.3) was fitted to the data to determine the best values of $|\rho|$ and ϕ_ρ, assuming that the fundamental kaon parameters $\tau_{L,S}$, Δm, $|\eta_{+-}|$, and ϕ_{+-} had their usual low-energy ($E_K \lesssim 10$ GeV) values as given by the Particle Data Group[8)] (PDG). The starting point in the analysis of Refs. 1-4 was the observation that the regeneration data were sufficiently good that all of the parameters in (2.3) could be extracted simultaneously. This would lead to the first determination of the fundamental kaon parameters at Fermilab energies. [In fact τ_L could not be determined, since $t/\tau_L \simeq 0$ for all accessible t in this experiment.] It should be emphasized at this point that if one were setting out with the specific aim of determining the kaon parameters at Fermilab energies, this would not be the optimum way to proceed. [A discussion of appropriate experiments is given in Ref. 3]. However, these were (and still are) the only data available from which one could extract information about the kaon parameters, and hence the analysis of Refs. 1-4 required a detailed understanding of the regeneration process itself, particularly for ϕ_ρ.

Table I below shows the results of fitting the data to Eq. (2.3) to extract the kaon parameters (assumed to be constant in the energy range $30 \lesssim E_K \lesssim 110$ GeV).

Table I. Results of Refs. 1-4 for the kaon parameters in the energy range $30 \lesssim E_K \lesssim 110$ GeV.

Parameter (units)	Value (Refs. 1-4) ($30 \lesssim E_K \lesssim 110$ GeV)	PDG Value (Ref. 8) ($E_K \simeq 5$ GeV)	Difference
Δm ($10^{10}\hbar$ sec^{-1})	0.482(14)	0.5349(22)	4σ
τ_S (10^{-10} sec)	0.905(7)	0.8923(22)	2σ
$\|\eta_{+-}\|$ (10^{-3})	2.09(2)	2.274(22) post-1971	9σ
		1.95(3) pre-1971	7σ
$\tan\phi_{+-}$	0.709(102)	0.986(55)	3σ

We see immediately that the new results differ from the PDG values by 2-9 (new) standard deviations. Interestingly enough the Fermilab result for $|\eta_{+-}|$ is in excellent agreement with an earlier result due to Birulev et al.[9] in the energy range 14-50 GeV who found $|\eta_{+-}| = 2.15(14) \times 10^{-3}$. As we point out in in Refs. 1-4, the data of Birulev et al. also lend support to the Fermilab value for $\tan \phi_{+-}$.

Since the only difference in principle between the Fermilab results and the earlier results quoted in the PDG is the kaon energy, the discrepancies shown in Table I led us to investigate the possibility that the kaon parameters had an anomalous energy-dependence. To test for this we returned to Eq. (2.3) and this time allowed each of the parameters $x = \Delta m$, τ_S, $|\eta_{+-}|$, and $\tan \phi_{+-}$ to vary with energy as

$$x = x_o[1 + b_x^{(N)}\gamma^N] \ ; \quad N = 1,2$$
$$\gamma = E_K/m = (1 - \beta^2)^{-1/2} \ . \tag{2.4}$$

Bearing in mind again that the x's are being determined in the <u>proper frame</u> of the kaons, we would expect that the $b_x^{(N)}$ should all be zero. Instead we found the results shown in Table II below.

Table II. Results of Refs. 1-4 for the fits $x = x_o[1 + b_x^{(2)}\gamma^2]$.

Parameter (units)	x_o	$10^6 b_x^{(2)}$	Significance of $b_x^{(2)} \neq 0$
Δm ($10^{10}\ \hbar\,\mathrm{sec}^{-1}$)	0.557(36)	-8.48(289)	3σ
τ_S (10^{-10} sec)	0.880(15)	+1.77(90)	2σ
$\lvert\eta_{+-}\rvert$ (10^{-3})	2.14(4)	-2.01(86)	2σ
$\tan\phi_{+-}$	1.276(499)	-33.7(123)	3σ

We note that all of the "slope parameters" $b_x^{(2)}$ differ from zero by 2-3 standard deviations. Since these results are derived using only the high-energy Fermilab data, they are free from any systematic biases that might arise from comparing the high- and low-energy data, as we did in Table I. Note also that the low-energy intercepts x_o agree rather well with the PDG values, as they should. The exception is $|\eta_{+-}|$, which is itself plagued by some uncertainty as to what the correct low-energy value should be. It is not clear at present whether there is any significance to the fact that the low-energy intercept of $|\eta_{+-}|$ happens to fall almost exactly inbetween the pre- and post-1971 averages.

The results of Tables I and II clearly raise the possibility that the fundamental parameters of the $K^o - \bar{K}^o$ system have an anomalous dependence on laboratory energy or velocity. We will show in Sec. III below that if these data are taken at face value, they cannot be explained by any presently-known mechanism, and hence it is crucial to establish whether the energy-variation suggested by the analysis of Refs. 1-4 is a real effect or not. Suffice it to say that an exhaustive series of checks was carried out on the Fermilab data, and nothing found which could have produced these results. Refs. 1-4 describe these checks in detail, and also discuss the support for the present results implied by the data of Birulev, et al.[9] Of course what is urgently needed is a series of high-energy experiments designed to measure each of the kaon parameters in an optimum way, including τ_L which has not as yet been determined. It turns out, however, that an experiment presently under way (E - 617 at Fermilab) will be able to measure the energy-dependence of $|\eta_{+-}|$ (and perhaps τ_S as well) over roughly the same energy range as in Refs. 1-4. We will return to discuss E - 617 and its potential signficance shortly.

3. Theoretical Analysis of the Energy-Dependence of the Kaon Parameters

In Refs. 2 and 4 a detailed phenomenological framework is developed in order to rigorously demonstrate that the experimental data shown in Tables I and II cannot be attributed to any presently known mechanism. As is so often the case, however, the essential content of this formalism can be conveyed by simple arguments. We will thus confine the discussion in the present section to a brief sketch of the phenomenology, followed by a summary of the arguments of Refs. 2 and 4.

In the absence of any external influences on the $K^o - \bar{K}^o$ system, the time evolution of the $K^o - \bar{K}^o$ wavefunction $\Psi(t)$ in its proper frame is given by

$$-\partial\Psi/\partial t = iH_o\Psi = (\Gamma + iM)\Psi = \begin{pmatrix} id & p^2 \\ q^2 & i\bar{d} \end{pmatrix} \Psi \quad . \tag{3.1}$$

To incorporate the effects of an external field we write

$$\begin{aligned} iH_o \rightarrow iH &= \Gamma + iM + iF \quad , \\ F &= u_o\mathbf{I} + u_x\sigma_x + u_y\sigma_y + u_z\sigma_z \quad , \end{aligned} \tag{3.2}$$

where the σ's are the usual Pauli matrices. The u's are complex numbers which are functions of γ and, in principle, of position as well. In practice the experiments in Refs. 1-4,7 were insensitive to the spatial variations of any external fields, and hence any possible dependence of the u's on position can be ignored for present purposes. However, if the results of Refs. 1-4 are confirmed by E-617 and/or other experiments, then the spatial variation (if any) of these effects will be an important clue in unravelling the nature of the external influence(s) on the $K^o - \bar{K}^o$ system. For this reason we have devoted considerable attention recently to the design of experiments to measure $\vec{\nabla}u_a(\vec{x})$ $(a = 0,x,y,z)$, and these will be discussed in greater detail in Sec. 6 below. We can decompose the u_a into their real and imaginary parts, and expand each of these in powers of γ,

$$u_a = [\xi_a^{(0)} + \xi_a^{(1)}\gamma + \xi_a^{(2)}\gamma^2 + \ldots] + i[\zeta_a^{(0)} + \zeta_a^{(1)}\gamma + \zeta_a^{(2)}\gamma^2 + \ldots]. \tag{3.3}$$

$\xi_a^{(N)}$ and $\zeta_a^{(N)}$ are now numbers which can be directly related to the experimentally determined slope parameters b_x. To do this we note that the eigenvalues of H in (3.2) give the masses and widths of $K_{L,S}$ in the presence of the external fields described by the u_a. In particular, it is easy to show that[2,4)]

$$\tfrac{1}{2}(\Gamma_L - \Gamma_S)_u + i(\Delta m)_u = 2pq\{1 + (pq)^{-2}[iu_x(p^2+q^2) - u_y(p^2-q^2) - (u_x^2 + u_y^2 + u_z^2)]\}^{1/2}, \tag{3.4}$$

where the subscript u on $\Gamma_{L,S}$ and Δm denote the corresponding field-dependent quantities. We can then compare the predictions of (3.4) to the results in Table II for various assumptions about the nature of the external field. For example, the hypercharge field described by Eqs. (1.1) - (1.4) evidently corresponds to the case

$$u_z = A_o\gamma \;,$$

$$\xi_z^{(1)} = A_o,\ \xi_z^{(N)} = 0 \text{ for } N \neq 1;\quad \zeta_z^{(N)} = 0, \quad \text{for all } N. \tag{3.5}$$

Combining Eqs. (3.4) and (3.5) we find immediately, (for $|A_o|/\Delta m < 1$),

$$(\Delta m)_u \simeq \Delta m[1 + (A_o/\Delta m)^2\gamma^2] \;, \tag{3.6}$$

and hence $b_\Delta^{(2)}$, the slope parameter for Δm, is necessarily <u>positive</u> for a hypercharge field, whereas the results in Table II show that experimentally $b_\Delta^{(2)}$ is <u>negative</u>. This observation alone is sufficient to rule out a hypercharge field as the source of the observed effects. By extension this argument also rules out any other C-odd mechanism whose effects can be cast in the form of (3.5), including any coupling of the kaons to an electromagnetic field, or an interaction with stray charges. For the case when $|A_o/\Delta m| > 1$ we can use the exact result given in (1.4), which indicates that $(\Delta m)_u$ is a monotonically increasing function of γ for all γ. These and other arguments also rule out scattering from the background neutrino sea: K_S regeneration can occur via the (weak) interactions $K^o(\bar{K}^o) + \nu \to K^o(\bar{K}^o) + \nu$, mediated by Z^o-exchange, in which the neutrino sea behaves as any ordinary material target. Parity arguments restrict the $K^oK^oZ^o$ and $\bar{K}^o\bar{K}^oZ^o$ couplings to be pure vector, which is again odd under C, and hence ruled out by the previous analysis. Moreover, in the standard SU(2) ⊗ U(1) model, the $K^oK^oZ^o$ and $\bar{K}^o\bar{K}^oZ^o$ couplings actually vanish if $(u,d)_L$ and $(c,s)_L$ are assigned to left-handed weak isodoublets. Finally, even in unconventional models where these charges would be nonzero, the density of neutrinos expected in the vicinity of the Earth is too small to produce any observable effects in kaon regeneration. We thus conclude that a comparison of Eqs. (3.6) or (1.4) to experiment is sufficient to rule out a hypercharge field, the electromagnetic field, stray charges or the neutrino sea, as possible explanations of the observed effects. These conclusions are further reinforced by considering the predictions of each of these mechanisms for the energy-variation of $|\eta_{+-}|$ and tan ϕ_{+-}. The details of these and other arguments leading to the same conclusions are given in Refs. 2 and 4, but the point of the present discussion of Δm is to demonstrate how the preceding mechanisms can be ruled out on the basis of fairly simple considerations.

The last remaining mechanism to consider is a gravitational field. In any metric theory of gravity there should be no preferred frame singled out, except possibly for gravitational phenomena themselves. However, as we have already noted in Sec. 1, the energy variation of Δm (or any of the other parameters) does in fact single out a preferred frame, specifically the rest frame (with respect to the field) in which Δm would have the largest possible positive value. It is thus not surprising that such an effect would not arise from any acceptable relativistic theory of gravity. These intuitive arguments can be fleshed out by appealing to a formulation of the Einstein Equivalence Principle (EEP) due to Thorne, Lee, and Lightman[10]: In a local experiment "dimensionless ratios of nongravitational physical constants must be independent of location, time, and velocity." Hence the energy-(or velocity-) dependence of $2\Delta mc^2/\hbar\Gamma_S$, $|\eta_{+-}|$, and tanϕ_{+-} cannot be accounted for by any theory of gravity which incorporates the EEP, which is the case for all known presently viable theories.

We conclude from the above discussion that we can in fact rule out the most common external influences as possible sources of the effects reported in Refs. 1-4. Moreover, we can go even further and use the above analysis to set stringent limits on the very existence of certain types of fields. It can be shown, for example, that not only is a hypercharge field ruled out as a possible explanation of the effects we are seeing, but that its coupling to ordinary matter (if nonzero) must be so small as to preclude the possibility of it being detected in other experiments as well. To see this we examine the slope parameter $b_\eta^{(2)}$ describing the γ-dependence of $|\eta_{+-}|$. It is a straightforward matter to show that this is given by

$$b_\eta^{(2)} = \frac{A_o^2}{|\varepsilon|^2(\Delta m)^2} = \frac{1}{|\varepsilon|^2(\Delta m)^2}\left(\frac{f^2Y_G}{R_G}\right)^2 , \qquad (3.7)$$

where ε = 1-q/p is the usual CP-violating parameter, and we have assumed that A_o originates from the galaxy. At the 3σ level the data exclude $b_\eta^{(2)} \geq +0.57 \times 10^{-6}$, which then implies a limit

$$f^2/Gm_p^2 < 1 \times 10^{-14}, \quad 99.7\% \text{ C.L.}, \tag{3.8}$$

where G is the Newtonian constant of gravitation, and m_p is the proton mass. This limit can be compared to that which we can infer from the Eötvös-Dicke-Braginskii[11] experiments, which measure the difference in acceleration of two test masses to the Earth or to the Sun. If there exists a hypercharge coupling, then the Sun can interact with a mass m by both gravitational and hypercharge forces,

$$F_m = ma_m = -\frac{GMm}{R^2} + \frac{f^2Yy}{R^2}, \tag{3.9}$$

where M, Y (m,y) are the mass and hypercharge of the Sun (test mass). It follows from (3.9) that two different masses m_1 and m_2 will have different accelerations to the Sun, the difference δa being given by

$$\frac{\delta a}{g} = \frac{f^2}{Gm_p^2} \left(\frac{Y}{\mu_S}\right)\left(\frac{y_1}{\mu_1} - \frac{y_2}{\mu_2}\right), \tag{3.10}$$

where $g = -GM/R^2$, and $\mu_1 = m_1/m_p$ etc. Using the result of Roll <u>et al</u>.[11] for Al and Au, $\delta a/g = (1.3 \pm 1.0) \times 10^{-11}$, we find at the 2σ level

$$\frac{f^2}{Gm_p^2} < 6 \times 10^{-8}, \quad 95\% \text{ C.L.} \tag{3.11}$$

We thus see that the limit implied by the energy variation of $|\eta_{+-}|$ (or the lack thereof) is far more stringent than that arising from the EDB experiments. Moreover, this limit stands to be significantly improved at the Fermilab Tevatron, since the availability of higher energy kaons will allow $b_\eta^{(2)}$ to be determined with greater precision.

Having demonstrated that no known field can describe the energy-dependent effects suggested by the data, we turn to ask what sort of mechanism might do the job. Examination of the data indicates that an external field which contributed a term of the form $u_x\sigma_x$ to H could account for the data. Such a term leads to a simple prediction which is consistent with the data, namely,

$$\frac{1}{2} b_\phi^{(N)} - b_\Delta^{(N)} - b_\eta^{(N)} = 0, \tag{3.12}$$

where $b_\phi^{(N)}$ is the slope parameter for tan ϕ_{+-}. $u_x\sigma_x$ is even under C and CP, and this may provide an important clue as to the detailed origin of the anomalous energy-dependent effects. In the next section we present some models of the external coupling to the $K^o - \bar{K}^o$ system which gives rise to the u_a, and which we thus refer to as the "U-field".

4. Models of the U-field

We outline in this section several models of the U-field which are compatible with the phenomenological results discussed in Sec. 3, particularly Eq. (3.12). In simple intuitive terms we can distinguish between "hard" (C-odd) mechanisms which produce nonzero contributions to u_y and /or u_z, and "soft" (C-even) mechanisms which contribute to u_o and/or u_x. This distinction follows from the observation[2,4] that "hard" mechanisms give rise to much larger values of b_η and b_ϕ, than do "soft" mechanisms which, by contrast, lead to the gentler energy variations seen in the data. The net result of the preceding discussion is that the data point strongly in the direction of a "soft" mechanism. If we imagine that the external field arises from the exchange of quanta with spins J = 0, 1, or 2 (which need not be massless), then it is easy to show (following the discussion leading to Eq. (1.2)) that for a J = 0 field, the $K^o - \bar{K}^o$ parameters would be energy-independent. The most likely J = 1 candidates are the electromagnetic and hypercharge fields, and these have already been ruled out as the source of the observed effects. By extension, any C-odd J = 1 field can also be excluded. This leaves open the possibility of a J = 1 axial-vector field, which would be C-even. However, the coupling of such a field to the $K^o - \bar{K}^o$ system must be proportional to the matrix element of the corresponding axial charges $\langle K^o|Q^5|K^o\rangle$ and $\langle \bar{K}^o|Q^5|\bar{K}^o\rangle$, which vanish by parity arguments. The remaining candidate would be a <u>massive</u> spin-2 field, the massless possibility being excluded because such a theory is equivalent[12)] to General Relativity (GR), which we have already ruled out as an explanation of the observed effects. By contrast the predictions of a massive tensor field are quite different from those of GR, an observation which is of paramount importance in the ensuing discussion. We note that the only known quantum numbers through which a macroscopic piece of matter can couple to kaons are hypercharge and mass-energy. Since hypercharge has already been ruled out as the source of the observed effects, we would naturally be led to examine a coupling to mass-energy as a possible mechanism. It is interesting from this point of view that the preceding discussion points in the direction of a massive spin-2 field, whose source would indeed be mass-energy.

Let us briefly describe some of the phenomenological consequences of a theory in which the U-field were a massive tensor field, hereafter called $U_{\mu\nu}$, whose quanta had a mass κ. For $\kappa \neq 0$ the theory has a mass (and hence length) scale, and thus is not invariant under general coordinate transformations as is GR. Moreover, in the limit $\kappa \to 0$ such a theory does not revert to GR, but rather to some scalar-tensor admixture. This is the reason why its predictions differ radically from those of GR, and the means by which we can set a limit on its coupling. Let us assume that $\hbar/\kappa c$ is large compared to the size of the solar system. Then the effective potential V(r) seen by a photon or other particle at a distance r moving in the field of the Sun is

$$V(r) = -\frac{GM_{\odot}(E/c^2)(1+\gamma'\beta^2)}{r} , \tag{4.1}$$

where E is the photon energy, $\beta = v/c$, and G is the Newtonian gravitational constant. γ' (usually called γ by other authors) is one of the so-called parametrized-post-Newtonian (PPN) parameters[13], which distinguish among different relativistic theories of gravity. For GR $\gamma' = 1$, whereas for the massive tensor theory[14] $\gamma' = 1/2$. Hence for light scattering the relative strengths of the massive tensor and GR couplings, for the same overall strength G, are

$$\frac{\text{massive tensor}}{\text{GR}} = \frac{3}{4} \quad . \tag{4.2}$$

It follows from (4.2) that the deflection of light by the Sun (or radar time delay) in a massive tensor theory is predicted to be 3/4 that of the GR value. Since the experimental value of γ', as deduced from radar time delay,[15] is

$$\gamma' = 1.000 \pm 0.002 , \tag{4.3}$$

it follows that the prediction of the massive tensor theory is in violent contradiction with the data, unless the overall strength G is appropriately adjusted. However, we see from (4.1) that this would bring the massive tensor theory into strong disagreement with ordinary Newtonian physics (where $\beta << 1$). Hence there is no escape from the conclusion that a theory of gravity based on a massive tensor field $U_{\mu\nu}$ by itself cannot work, no matter how small κ is.[14] But there is no objection to a 2-tensor theory in which $U_{\mu\nu}$ coexisted along with the usual metric tensor $g_{\mu\nu}$, provided that we adjust their relative strengths appropriately. To this end we replace $g_{\mu\nu}$ in the usual phenomenology by $f_{\mu\nu}$,

$$f_{\mu\nu} = \cos^2\theta_u \, g_{\mu\nu} + \sin^2\theta_u \, U_{\mu\nu}, \tag{4.4}$$

where $g_{\mu\nu}$ is allowed to arise from any massless combination of fields, and so may be characterized by $\gamma' \neq 1$ (even in the absence of $U_{\mu\nu}$). Eq. (4.1) is now modified to

$$V(r) = -\frac{GM_{\odot}(E/c^2)}{r} \{\cos^2\theta_u(1+\gamma'\beta^2) + \sin^2\theta_u \, (1+\tfrac{1}{2}\beta^2)\} , \tag{4.5}$$

which is appropriately normalized to the Newtonian expression for $\beta << 1$. For relativistic particles or photons (4.5) and (4.3) then give

$$|(1-\gamma') + (\gamma' - 1/2)\sin^2\theta_u| \lesssim 4 \times 10^{-3} \quad , \tag{4.6}$$

so that for GR (with $\gamma' = 1$) we find

$$\sin^2\theta_u \lesssim 8 \times 10^{-3} \quad . \tag{4.7}$$

Thus $g_{\mu\nu}$ and $U_{\mu\nu}$ can coexist under these conditions, and all the usual phenomenology would remain valid. However, since $U_{\mu\nu}$ would behave vis a vis the kaon experiments as an ordinary classical field (in contradistinction to $g_{\mu\nu}$ which does not), the arguments leading to Eq. (1.2) would apply to $U_{\mu\nu}$, and motion in such a field would lead to velocity-dependent effects, just as in the hypercharge case. One must be cautious at this stage not to claim too much for such a two-tensor theory, because all of its phenomenological implications have not yet been explored. One particular concern is the compatibility of such a theory with the Hughes-Drever (H-D) experiments[16], which can be interpreted as setting a limit on the strength of $U_{\mu\nu}$ by measuring the spatial anisotropy that would be manifested in a freely falling frame (where $g_{\mu\nu}$ was diagonal) due to $U_{\mu\nu}$. At the moment it appears that such a theory could in fact be compatible with the H-D experiments by an appropriate choice of $\sin^2\theta_u$ and κ, but this question (and others associated with the viability of this theory) are presently being investigated more thoroughly.

Although a massive tensor theory is a natural candiate to explain the energy-variation of the various $K^o - \bar{K}^o$ parameters, including η_{+-}, it does not explain the origin of η_{+-} itself. This is completely consistent with the prevailing view that CP-violation arises, not from some external effect, but rather from an internal mechanism such as a CP-violating phase in the Kobayashi-Maskawa matrix, or a CP-violating Higgs coupling, etc. The energy-variation of η_{+-} then comes about because the ratio p/q, which determines the admixture of K^o and $\bar{K}^o$ in K_L and K_S, is changed by the addition of a term proportional to u_x in an energy-dependent way:

$$\frac{p}{q} \rightarrow \frac{(p^2 + iu_x)^{1/2}}{(q^2 + iu_x)^{1/2}} \equiv \frac{p_u}{q_u} \neq \frac{p}{q} \quad . \tag{4.8}$$

We observe from (4.8) that if there is no intrinsic CP-violation (i.e. $p = q$), then $p_u/q_u = 1$ independent of u_x, and the kaon eigenfunctions are $K_1^o = (K^o - \bar{K}^o)/\sqrt{2}$ and $K_2^o = (K^o + \bar{K}^o)/\sqrt{2}$ independent of energy. The fact that a term proportional to u_x does not by itself give rise to CP-violating effects is what characterizes it as "soft".

One may, however, wish to pursue the notion that the same mechanism which produces the energy-variation of η_{+-} (and the other parameters), should be the origin of η_{+-} itself. At first sight this possibility seems to be ruled out by the large body of phenomenology which militates against the original suggestion[6)] that a hypercharge field was the source of CP-violation. These include particularly the following observations: a) In such a theory $|\eta_{+-}| \propto \gamma$, in violent disagreement with the data; b) The branching ratio for the decay $K^o \to \pi^+\pi^-$"γ", where the hyperphoton "γ" is the (necessarily massive) quantum of the hypercharge field, is unphysically large (the Weinberg[17)] catastrophe"). It is clear that in order to overcome these objections some unconventional theory will be needed, and the following one[18)] may provide a useful guide in formulating such a theory. In the spirit of contemporary unified theories we consider a long-range field which couples to the conserved quantum number (B-L), where B is baryon number and L is lepton number. Since B-L is zero for kaons, there is no analog of the potential A_o in (1.1) and (1.2) for a kaon in the presence of a matter distribution, even though the latter has a non-zero value of B-L. A CP-violating transition in the $K^o - \bar{K}^o$ system can be induced by an external (classical) B-L field through the coupling

$$L = \frac{1}{2} f_B K_1^o K_2^o \, \varepsilon_{\mu\nu\alpha\beta} \, F^{\mu\nu} F^{\alpha\beta} = f_B K_1^o K_2^o \, \vec{E}_b \cdot \vec{B}_b \quad , \tag{4.9}$$

$$F_{\mu\nu} = \partial_\mu b_\nu - \partial_\nu b_\mu \quad ,$$

where b_μ is the B-L field, f_B is an appropriate constant, and $\vec{E}_b(\vec{B}_b)$ is the corresponding electric (magnetic) field. Since $\varepsilon_{\mu\nu\alpha\beta} F^{\mu\nu}F^{\alpha\beta}$ behaves as a Lorentz scalar, the CP-violating $K_1^o - K_2^o$ transition (and hence η_{+-}) is a constant as a function of energy, thus avoiding problem a) in the analogous hypercharge case. Moreover, since -in contrast to the hypercharge case- B-L is <u>conserved</u> (at least up to $O(1/M_X)$ where M_X is the mass of the superheavy gauge boson) the analog of the Weinberg catastrophe is also avoided. There remains, however, a potential problem with the EDB experiments, since b_μ would also give rise to a static force on the test masses due to the Sun. It appears that his difficulty can be surmounted by first fixing f_B to be consistent with (3.11), and then assuming that $\vec{E}_b \cdot \vec{B}_b \neq 0$ arises from the analogs of the solutions described recently by Khare and Pradhan[19)] for the electromagnetic case. It is straightforward to show that these solutions have the property that they exert no net force on a static mass, and thus avoid the EDB problem, even though $\langle \vec{E}_b \cdot \vec{B}_b \rangle \neq 0$. In such a model an energy-dependence of η_{+-} would come about by combining (4.9) with higher-order contributions from b_μ.

5. Lorentz Noninvariance

As noted in the Introduction, the energy-dependence of the kaon parameters can be directly interpreted as a manifest violation of Lorentz invariance. Various authors have recently considered the possibility that Lorentz invariance is in fact violated[20)] under some circumstances, and have set experimental limits on appropriate phenomenological parameters. Among these the limits implied by the previously mentioned Hughes-Drever experiments[16], and the agreement between the values of the magnetic moment of the electron (or g_e-2) as determined at different energies[21], appear to be quite restrictive. Hence any attempt to explain the kaon data as a manifestation of a Lorentz noninvariant (LNI) effect, must grapple with the question of why LNI effects show up there and apparently nowhere else. (We hasten to add that the same question applies to whatever explanation is advanced to describe the kaon data, including the massive tensor field which we discussed previously.) Of course, the $K^o - \bar{K}^o$ system is special in a number of ways, including the fact that the small $K_L - K_S$ mass difference makes the $K^o - \bar{K}^o$ system particularly sensitive to the effects of small perturbations. We note, for example, that if the observed energy variations arise from a term of the form $u_x\sigma_x$, then the slope parameter $b_\Delta^{(2)}$ is given by,

$$b_\Delta^{(2)} = (-8.5 \pm 2.9) \times 10^{-6} = \frac{2\xi^{(2)}}{\Delta m} \qquad (5.1)$$

and hence

$$\xi^{(2)} = \frac{1}{2} b_\Delta^{(2)} \Delta m = -1.5 \times 10^{-11} \text{ eV}. \qquad (5.2)$$

Thus in the regeneration experiments the $K^o - \bar{K}^o$ system is sensitive to the presence of an additional interaction term which contributes an energy as small as $\sim 10^{-11}$ eV. This clearly is too small an effect to be detected by most other experiments, and may be part of the reason why energy-dependent effects show up more clearly in the $K^o - \bar{K}^o$ system than elsewhere. It is almost certainly the case, however, that this is not the complete explanation of why we are seeing what we are in the kaon experiments, since the H-D and $g_\mu-2$ experiments are at least as sensitive. This is clearly one of the most pressing problems that we confront at the present time.

In Ref. 4 we discuss in more detail specific models for introducing LNI effects. In broad terms these generally arise from some combination of the following mechanisms: a) The existence of a fundamental unit of length, b) the existence of a preferred frame (an example being a physical lattice in space or space-time), c) the assumed noncausal behavior of some propagator (such as the X-boson of grand unified theories), d) the spontaneous breakdown of Lorentz invariance due to the formation of some condensate in the vacuum. A detailed analysis of one interesting model has been given by Nielsen and Picek[20] (NP), who also give an excellent discussion of various experimental constraints on possible LNI effects. In the NP model one adds to the usual metric tensor $g_{\mu\nu}$ a constant tensor $\chi_{\mu\nu}$, which is symmetric, traceless and Hermitian. In the simplest version of their model $\chi_{\mu\nu}$ has the form

$$\chi_{\mu\nu} = \alpha(i)\begin{pmatrix} 1 & & & \\ & 1/3 & & \\ & & 1/3 & \\ & & & 1/3 \end{pmatrix}, \tag{5.3}$$

where $\alpha(i)$ is a constant, which may be different for each interaction i. The effects of $\chi_{\mu\nu}$ are manifested via the changes that are induced in the massless electron propagator, due to the exchange of a massive gauge boson. NP find for the inverse propagator,

$$\not{p} = g_{\mu\nu}\gamma^{\mu}p^{\nu} \rightarrow g^{full}_{\mu\nu}\gamma^{\mu}p^{\nu} ,$$

$$g^{full}_{\mu\nu} = g_{\mu\nu} + a_{L,R}\chi_{\mu\nu}; \quad a_{L,R} = \begin{cases} -8.15 \times 10^{-4} & \text{for } e_L \\ -0.80 \times 10^{-4} & \text{for } e_R \end{cases} . \tag{5.4}$$

The modification of $\not{p}$ due to $\chi_{\mu\nu}$ leads to a variety of effects which are described in detail by NP. For present purposes, the point to notice is that since $\chi_{\mu\nu}$ is <u>spatially constant</u> it makes no contribution to $\vec{\nabla}u_a(\vec{x})$. Hence if we measure $\vec{\nabla}u_a(\vec{x})$ in the Earth's field, by means of experiments similar to those discussed in the following section, we expect no contribution if the observed energy-dependences arise from a LNI source such as $\chi_{\mu\nu}$. By contrast, if they arise from a genuine field, part of which arises from the Earth itself, then by an appropriate series of experiments we should be able to measure $\vec{\nabla}u_a(\vec{x}) \neq 0$.

6. The Crucial Experiments

In the discussion thus far we have raised a large number of as yet unanswered questions, ranging from whether the experimental results of Refs. 1-4 are correct in the first place, to what the origin of these effects would be if they turn out to be real. In this section we discuss various crucial experiments in light of Refs. 1-4.

Evidently the first question that must be settled is whether the experimental results reported in Refs. 1-4, as summarized in Tables I and II, are correct. A program to do this was outlined in Ref. 3. Fortunately several experiments which were proposed for other reasons, and which are either in progress or about to get under way, will be able to measure various $K^o - \bar{K}^o$ parameters at high energies. The first new results should come from E-617 at Fermilab early in 1984. This experiment was designed to measure $|\eta_{+-}|/|\eta_{oo}|$, where η_{oo} is defined as in (2.3) for the $\pi^o\pi^o$ final state, but will also be able to measure $|\eta_{+-}|$ and $|\eta_{oo}|$ separately. In this experiment there are two side-by-side K_L beams, one of which passes through a C regenerator to produce K_S. The numbers of $K_L \to \pi^+\pi^-$ and $K_S \to \pi^+\pi^-$ decays are measured, which then determines $|\eta_{+-}|^2/|\rho|^2$. An important feature of this experiment is a carefully designed lead-glass array for detecting the $\pi^o\pi^o$ mode, which then leads to a determination of $|\eta_{oo}|^2/|\rho|^2$ using the two-beam method. $|\eta_{+-}|^2/|\eta_{oo}|^2$ is then obtained by taking the ratio

$$\frac{|\eta_{+-}|^2}{|\eta_{oo}|^2} = \frac{|\eta_{+-}|^2/|\rho|^2}{|\eta_{oo}|^2/|\rho|^2} \quad , \tag{6.1}$$

in which $|\rho|^2$ cancels out. The nice feature of this method is that it is relatively insensitive to differences in efficiences for detecting $\pi^+\pi^-$ and $\pi^o\pi^o$. E-617 should also be capable, at least in principle, of measuring τ_S by using the K_S's which decay behind the regenerator.

In the absence of external influences acting on the $K^o - \bar{K}^o$ system, we would naturally expect the same results from Refs. 1-4 and E-617. However, the design of these experiments is not the same, so that in the presence of a field they could in principle obtain different results. Among the pertinent differences are the following:

a) In Refs. 1-4 η_{+-} is determined from K_L decays which occur after the K_L beam has passed through a regenerator, whereas in E-617 the $K_L \to \pi^+\pi^-$ decays are from the beam which has <u>not</u> passed through the regenerator. Bearing in mind that we have no way of determining at present the range of the field responsible for the effects of Refs. 1-4, suppose that the range were on the order of ~ 1 cm - 20m. Then the target itself could be the dominant source of the observed effects, and this could lead to different results for $|\eta_{+-}|$ in E-617 as compared to Refs. 1-4. Indeed one can even give some arguments as to why such a force might exist. To start with, there is some evidence for deviations from Newtonian gravity which has been emerging in recent years from geophysical determinations of G. If $V_N(r)$ denotes the usual Newtonian gravitational potential, then there is a suggestion that the actual potential V(r) has the form[22]

$$V(r) = V_N(r)[1 - 0.01 \exp(-r/20m)] \ , \tag{6.2}$$

where the [ ] differs from 1 by perhaps 2σ. Such a non-Newtonian contribution from V(r) could conceivably manifest itself on distance scales $\lesssim$ 20 m, which just happens to be the characteristic scale of the experiments in Refs. 1-4, 7. A second heuristic argument for such an intermediate-range force can be formulated by arguing (in the spirit of Dirac's large-number hypothesis) that there might exist a force whose range was the geometric mean between the longest-and shortest-range forces known. For the longest range force we use gravity, whose range R_G is in principle infinite. In practice R_G can be taken to be the radius of the universe, $R_G = c/H \cong 1.8 \times 10^{28}$cm, where $H \cong 50$ kms^{-1} Mpc^{-1} is the Hubble constant. For the shortest range we take the Compton wavelength of the X-boson of grand unified theories, with $M_X = 2.7 \times 10^{14}$ GeV, which gives $R_X = 7.3 \times 10^{-29}$ cm. Hence if this new force has a range R_u we find

$$R_u = \sqrt{R_G R_X} = 1.2 \text{ cm} \quad . \qquad (6.3)$$

It follows that if such a field were actually realized in nature, it could mediate a force between a regenerator (when present) and the $K^o - \bar{K}^o$ system.

b) Another difference which may be significant in light of Stacey's results[22] is that E-617 iy situated above ground, whereas the earlier Fermilab experiments took place in a tunnel several meters below the surface.

c) A third difference between E-617 and the earlier Fermilab experiments, is that in the latter the observed $\pi^+\pi^-$ events arise from a coherent superposition of $K_L \to \pi^+\pi^-$ and $K_S \to \pi^+\pi^-$ amplitudes. This is not the case for E-617, and hence if there were a breakdown of the usual quantum mechanics in the $K^o - \bar{K}^o$ system at high energies[4,23], it could show up in the earlier regeneration experiments, but not necessarily in E-617.

d) In Ref. 3 we note that neither E-617 nor the earlier experiments actually measures the full energy-dependence of $|\eta_{+-}|$. This has to do with the fact that in order to measure $|\eta_{+-}|^2 = \Gamma(K_L \to \pi^+\pi^-)/\Gamma(K_S \to \pi^+\pi^-)$ directly one would need both a K_L and K_S beam simultaneously, and the latter is not available. Hence an indirect method is used, in which the quantity actually measured in Refs. 1-4, 7 is $\Gamma(K_L \to \pi^+\pi^-)/\Gamma(K_L \to \pi\mu\nu)$. As we note in Ref. 3, if $\Gamma(K_L \to \pi^+\pi^-)$ is compared to some (CP-conserving) mode(s) other than $K_L \to \pi\mu\nu$, then the result could well be that $|\eta_{+-}|$ would have a different energy-dependence from that reported in Refs.1-4. Given the differences in a)-d) above (and perhaps others as well), any lack of agreement between the results in Refs. 1-4 and E-617 could (optimistically!) be taken as evidence for one of these mechanisms operating. Contrariwise, should E-617 support the earlier results then the fact that these experiments agree, despite the above differences, means that at least some theories on the origin of the u_a can be ruled out or sharply constrained.

One parameter whose energy-variation was not determined in Refs. 1-4 was $\Gamma_L = 1/\tau_L$, and it is extremely important that this be measured in the near future, as we now explain. If we denote the slope parameters for Γ_L, Γ_S and $\Gamma_L - \Gamma_S$ by $b_{\Gamma L}$, $b_{\Gamma S}$, and b_Γ respectively, then it is straightforward to show that

$$b_{\Gamma L}^{(N)} = \frac{\Gamma_S}{\Gamma_L}\,(b_{\Gamma S}^{(N)} - b_\Gamma^{(N)}) \quad . \qquad (6.4)$$

This relation, unlike (3.12), is completely model-independent. $b^{(2)}_{\Gamma S}$ ($\simeq -b^{(2)}_{\tau S}$) is given in Table II, and $b^{(2)}_{\Gamma}$ can be inferred from the other slope parameters if we assume [consistent with (3.12)] that the observed effects arise from a term $u_x\sigma_x$. In that case[4)]

$$b^{(2)}_{\Gamma} = b^{(2)}_{\Delta} - b^{(2)}_{\phi} = (14.1 \pm 7.2) \times 10^{-6} . \tag{6.5}$$

Combining (6.4) and (6.5) we find

$$b^{(2)}_{\Gamma L} = -(9.0 \pm 4.2) \times 10^{-3} , \tag{6.6}$$

with $\Gamma_S/\Gamma_L = 581$. This implies that Γ_L is a much more rapidly varying function of energy than the other parameters in Table II. This evidently arises from the fact that since $b^{(2)}_{\Gamma S}$ and $b^{(2)}_{\Gamma}$ are each $O(10^{-6})$, $b^{(2)}_{\Gamma L}$ will necessarily be $O(10^{-3})$ unless there is an almost exact cancellation between $b^{(2)}_{\Gamma S}$ and $b^{(2)}_{\Gamma}$. Such a possiblity is not excluded by the data, and can occur in some interesting theoretical models. A value of $b^{(2)}_{\Gamma L}$ as large as that given in (6.6) would mean that the various appoximations that weuse in deriving Eqs. (3.12) and (6.4) - (6.6) would break down at Fermilab energies, and so all that we can really infer at present is that $b^{(2)}_{\Gamma}$ could be several orders of magnitude larger than the other slope parameters. Notwithstanding the magnitude of $b^{(2)}_{\Gamma L}$, the existing determinations[8)] of Γ_L cover too small a range of (low) energies, and are too imprecise, to allow (6.6) to be tested. However, since $b^{(2)}_{\Gamma L}$ is likely to be eithervery large or very small (compared to the other slope parameters), a decisive experiment should be possible at Fermilab, Brookhaven, or LAMPF II, and could thereby provide an important constraint on models of the U-field.

Let us suppose that the experiments that we have just discussed do in fact confirm the results o Refs. 1-4, as summarized in Tables I and II. We will then be faced with the question of determining the origin of these effects, and distinguishing between a possible LNI contribution,and that of an actual field or medium. As we have already noted, if the observed effects are due to a field which arises from a matter distribution, then part of this field will presumably arise from the Earth itself, and this can be studied by measuring $\vec{\nabla} u_a(\vec{x})$ in the Earth's field. Depending on the range of the effects, different high energy experiments may be appropriate. If it is on the order of hundreds of km, then experiments utilizing neutrino oscillations will be useful, if neutrinos are in fact found to oscillate. We may consider an experiment of the type proposed by Mann and Primakoff[24)], in which a neutrino beam from Fermilab is passed through the Earth to a detector in Canada. If the observed energy-dependences in the $K^o - \bar{K}^o$ system arise from a field which couples to mass-energy, or if they are due to some LNI effect, then we would expect analogous effects in neutrino oscillations. The Earth's contribution to $\vec{\nabla} u_a(\vec{x})$ could then be studied by the changes that are induced in the neutrino oscillation parameters, as the distance of the beam below the surface of the Earth is varied. If the range of the field is $\lesssim$ 50 m roughly, then kaon experiments of the type we now describe will be useful, and these are called the "EPR" and "mass-gap" experiments respectively.

To describe the EPR experiment[25] consider for illustrative purposes the process

$$e^+e^- \rightarrow \phi(1020) \rightarrow K_L K_S \,, \tag{6.7}$$

where K_L and K_S each subsequently decay to $\pi^+\pi^-$. Because the kaons in the final state arise from the ϕ which has odd parity ($J^{PC} = 1^{--}$), the initial kaon wavefunction $|i\rangle$ in the $K^o - \bar{K}^o$ basis must have the form[26]

$$|i\rangle = (1/\sqrt{2})\,|K^o(+z);\ \bar{K}^o(-z) - K^o(-z);\ \bar{K}^o(+z)\rangle \,, \tag{6.8}$$

where the z-axis is chosen to be along the direction of momentum of the outgoing kaons, with the ϕ located at $z = 0$. It should be understood that (6.8) gives the wavefunction at the moment of production of the kaons ($t = 0$), and that $K^o(\pm z)$ denotes the K^o moving in the $\pm z$ direction, etc. At any subsequent time, the kaon wavefunction can be obtained by reexpressing (6.8) in terms of K_L and K_S which then evolve in time in the usual way. Because we can in fact choose to view the final state as either $K^o\bar{K}^o$ or $K_L K_S$, this system can be used to study the Einstein-Podolsky-Rosen (EPR) effect,[26,27] which is the origin of our name for this experiment. Suppose that we now consider the decay of $|i\rangle$ into 2 $\pi^+\pi^-$ pairs, one each in the $\pm z$ directions. It is straightforward to show that the matrix element for this process is given by[26]

$$\sqrt{2}\, pq \,\langle f(t_1, +z);\ f(t_2, -z)|T|i\rangle = \langle f|T|K_L\rangle\langle f|T|K_S\rangle \times$$
$$\exp[-(\lambda_L + \lambda_S)(t_1 + t_2)/2]\ \sinh[(\lambda_S - \lambda_L)(t_1 - t_2)/2] \,, \tag{6.9}$$
$$\lambda_{L,S} = \frac{1}{2}\Gamma_{L,S} + i\, m_{L,S} \,,$$

where $|f\rangle = |\pi^+\pi^-\rangle$, and the notation $f(t_1, +z)$ denotes the $\pi^+\pi^-$ pair resulting from the decay at t_1 of a kaon moving in the +z direction. It should be emphasized that the amplitude in (6.9) represents the superposition of the two contributions in (6.8) reexpressed in the $K_L - K_S$ basis, so that $|f(t_1, +z)\rangle$ can be produced by the decay of either K_L or K_S moving in the +z direction. Note that the transition amplitude in (6.9) has the property that it vanishes when $t_1 = t_2$, which is a reflection of the fact that $|i\rangle$ is antisymmetric under $z \leftrightarrow -z$.

Suppose now that we examine the same process in the presence of an external field. For illustrative purposes let the e^+e^- beam be in the horizontal direction, and +z be "up" in the Earth's field. We see that now motion in the ±z directions are no longer the same and, because the symmetry of the initial wavefunction is modified by the field, the transition amplitude in (6.9) will no longer vanish when $t_1 = t_2$. Moreover, we see that the extent to which sinh[...] in (6.9) differs from zero depends on how much motion in the +z direction differs from motion in the -z direction, i.e., on the gradient of the field. Thus the EPR experiment is a null experiment, which allows the gradient of the Earth's contribution to $\lambda_{L,S}$ (i.e. $\vec{\nabla}u_a$) to be measured. Complete details on the EPR experiment, including effects of backgrounds, will be given elsewhere.[25)]

Another method for measuring $\vec{\nabla}u_a$ involves adapting the mass-gap method[28)] for measuring Δm, by adjusting the gap and the two regenerators to produce a null for the net $\pi^+\pi^-$ amplitude at the exit face of the second regenerator. As in the case of the EPR experiment, the null is shifted in the presence of a field. Hence by comparing the counting rates when the beam is oriented up or down with respect to the horizontal, one can again measure $\vec{\nabla}u_a(\vec{x})$. The EPR and mass-gap experiments complement each other in various ways, as we discuss in more detail in Ref. 25.

We conclude our discussion by summarizing in Table III some of the constraints that apply to various cosmological fields from existing data. A more complete version of this Table will be presented in Ref. 5.

7. Acknowledgements

The results and ideas presented here are the outgrowth of a long collaboration with Sam Aronson, Greg Bock, and Hai-Yang Cheng, to whom I am enormously indebted. I would also like to thank Dubravko Tadić for organizing this conference and for the invitation to speak here. On July 25, 1983 I learned with deep sadness that my friend and advisor Henry Primakoff had died that day, after a heroic battle with cancer. He had an enormous influence on me and my career, and I dedicate this talk to him. This work was supported by the U.S. Department of Energy.

REFERENCES

1. S. H. Aronson, G. J. Bock, H. Y. Cheng, and E. Fischbach, Phys. Rev. Lett. 48, 1306 (1982).

2. E. Fischbach, H. Y. Cheng, S. H. Aronson, and G. J. Bock, Phys. Lett. 116B, 73 (1982).

3. S. H. Aronson, G. J. Bock, H. Y. Cheng, and E. Fischbach, Phys. Rev. D28, 476 (1983).

4. S. H. Aronson, G. J. Bock, H. Y. Cheng, and E. Fischbach, Phys. Rev. D28, 495 (1983).

5. A detailed review of the experimental and theoretical status of cosmological fields and Lorentz invariance is presently under way. See H. Y. Cheng, E. Fischbach, and M. Haugan, (in preparation).

6. J. Bernstein, N. Cabibbo, and T. D. Lee, Phys. Lett. 12, 146 (1964); J. S. Bell and J. K. Perring, Phys. Rev. Lett. 13, 348 (1964); O. Nachtmann, in Particle Physics, ed. by P. Urban (Springer, Berlin, 1969) [Acta Phys. Austriaca Suppl. 6, 485 (1969)].

7. G. J. Bock et al., Phys. Rev. Lett. 42, 350 (1979); J. Roehrig et al., Phys. Rev. Lett. 38, 1116 (1977), and 39, 674(E) (1977); W. R. Molzon et al., Phys. Rev. Lett. 41, 1213 (1978).

8. M. Roos et al., Phys. Lett. 111B, 1 (1982); R. L. Kelly et al., Rev. Mod. Phys. 52, S1 (1980); C. Bricman et al., Phys. Lett. 75B, 1 (1978).

9. V. K. Birulev et al., Nucl. Phys. B115, 249 (1976).

10. K. S. Thorne, D. L. Lee, and A. P. Lightman, Phys. Rev. D7, 3563 (1973).

11. R. v. Eötvös, D. Pekár, and E. Fekete, Ann. Phys. (Leipzig) 68, 11 (1922); P. G. Roll, R. Krotkov, and R. H. Dicke, Ann. Phys. (N.Y.) 26, 442 (1964); V. B. Braginskii and V. I. Panov, Sov. Phys. - JETP 34, 463 (1972).

12. S. Weinberg, Phys. Lett. 9, 357 (1964) and Phys. Rev. 135, B1049 (1964); D. G. Boulware and S. Deser, Ann. Phys. (N.Y.) 89, 193 (1975).

13. C. M. Will in Experimental Gravitation, ed. by B. Bertotti (Academic, New York, 1974), p. 1.

14. H. van Dam and M. Veltman, Nucl. Phys. B22, 397 (1970); Gen. Relativ. Gravit. 3, 215 (1972); D. G. Boulware and S. Deser, Phys. Rev. D6, 3368 (1972); V. I. Zakharov, JETP Lett. 12, 312 (1970).

15. R. D. Reasenberg et al. Astrophys. J. 234, L219 (1979).

16. V. W. Hughes, H. G. Robinson, and V. Beltran-Lopez, Phys. Rev. Lett. 4, 342 (1960); R. W. P. Drever, Philos. Mag. 6, 683 (1961); R. H. Dicke, The Theoretical Significance of Experimental Relativity (Gordon and Breach, New York, 1964), pp. 14-22.

17. S. Weinberg, Phys. Rev. Lett. 13, 495 (1964).

18. H. Y. Cheng and E. Fischbach (in preparation).

19. A. Khare and T. Pradhan, Phys. Rev. Lett. 49, 1227 and 1594(E) (1982); 51, 1108(E) (1983).

20. For a list of references see Ref. 4 and H. B. Nielsen and I. Picek, Nucl. Phys. B211, 269 (1983).

21. D. Newman, G. W. Ford, A. Rich, and E. Sweetman, Phys. Rev. Lett. 40, 1355 (1978).

22. F. D. Stacey in Science Underground: Los Alamos 1982, edited by M. M. Nieto *et al*. (AIP Proceedings #96), p. 285.

23. W. C. Carithers *et al.*, Phys. Rev. D14, 290 (1976); B. Laurent and M. Roos, Phys. Lett. 13, 269 (1964).

24. A. K. Mann and H. Primakoff, Phys. Rev. D15, 655 (1977).

25. S. H. Aronson, H. Y. Cheng, and E. Fischbach (in preparation).

26. H. J. Lipkin, Phys. Rev. 176, 1715 (1968).

27. A. Einstein, B. Podolsky, and N. Rosen, Phys. Rev. 47, 777 (1935).

28. J. H. Christenson *et al.*, Phys. Rev. 140, B74 (1965); S. H. Aronson *et al*., Phys. Rev. Lett. 25, 1057 (1970).

DISCUSSION

Rubinstein: Milgrom, and Bekenstein and Milgrom, have a modified model of gravitation that might avoid the need for the "missing-mass" hypothesis. Could this be related to your work?

Fischbach: Milgrom's work [since published in Astrophysical Journal 270, 365-389 (1983)] proposes a modification of Newtonian mechanics for systems with accelerations $\lesssim 2 \times 10^{-8}$ cm s^{-2}. Accelerations in typical terrestrial experiments are much larger than this, and so it is difficult to imagine such an effect being important in the $K^o - \bar{K}^o$ system. Nonetheless, one is tempted to look for a common thread in his work and ours, but Milgrom, Bekenstein, and I have exchanged some letters on this question, and none of us has found an obvious connection.

Peccei: Why should your new field care particularly about kaons?

Fischbach: Our phenomenology suggests that the U-field cares equally about all particles, but the K^o-$\bar{K}^o$ system is more sensitive than most others.

Table III. Limits on various cosmological fields

SCALAR FIELD

Source	Limits	Experiments [parameter]
mass-energy	scalar/tensor = 0 ± 0.001 $\gamma' = 1.000 \pm 0.002$ ω(Brans-Dicke) $\gtrsim 500$	radar time delay (Ref. 15) $[\frac{1}{2}(1+\gamma')]$

VECTOR FIELD

hypercharge	$f^2/Gm_p^2 \lesssim 6 \times 10^{-8}$ (95% C.L.)	EDB (Ref. 11) $[\delta a/g]$
	$f^2/Gm_p^2 \lesssim 1 \times 10^{-14}$ (99.7 C.L.)	$K^o - \bar{K}^o$ (Ref. 4) $[b_\eta^{(2)}]$
mass-energy	$\lvert\tilde{\gamma}\rvert \lesssim 5 \times 10^{-5}$ $\frac{\text{(rate of clock moving with respect to cosmos)}}{\text{(stationary clock)}} = 1 + \tilde{\gamma}\beta^2$	Turner-Hill (PR <u>134</u>, B252 (1964) $[\delta(\Delta\nu/\nu]$

TENSOR FIELD

mass-energy	Gravity mediated by a tensor field with finite range is ruled out	radar time delay light deflection
	$f_{\mu\nu} = \cos^2\theta_u g_{\mu\nu} + \sin^2\theta_u U_{\mu\nu}$ $\sin^2\theta_u \lesssim 8 \times 10^{-3}$	radar time delay
	$f'_{\mu\nu} = g_{\mu\nu} + X_{\mu\nu}$ (locally anisotropic) $\lvert X_{\mu\nu}T^{\mu\nu}\rvert / \lvert g_{\mu\nu}T^{\mu\nu}\rvert \lesssim 10^{-22}$	Hughes-Drever (Ref. 16) $[\Delta\nu/\nu]$

LORENTZ NON-INVARIANCE AT THE WEAK INTERACTION SCALE

Ivica Picek

Rudjer Bošković Institute
41001 Zagreb, P.O.B. 1016
Croatia, YUGOSLAVIA

Here I report briefly on part of the work[1,2] done in collaboration with H.B. Nielsen in Copenhagen. Our approach, heretical in a sense, is based on symmetries in the infrared (IR), as opposed to symmetries in the ultraviolet (UV), which are the main topic of this meeting. Thus, let us first try to look at a possible explanation of Lorentz invariance observed in the IR and then try to construct an explicit model for Lorentz invariance breaking. I will restrict myself to the main lines of the approach and to some philosophical background.

1. Symmetries in the UV; Symmetries in the IR

The standard unification programme rests upon symmetries in the UV. This means that a certain internal (local) symmetry is realized at some high-energy scale where gauge couplings join together. In this way, the known physics at low energies is extrapolated in order to achieve the electro-weak unification at 10^2 GeV, the electro-weak and -strong unification at 10^{14} GeV and the super-unification (which also includes gravity) at 10^{19} GeV:

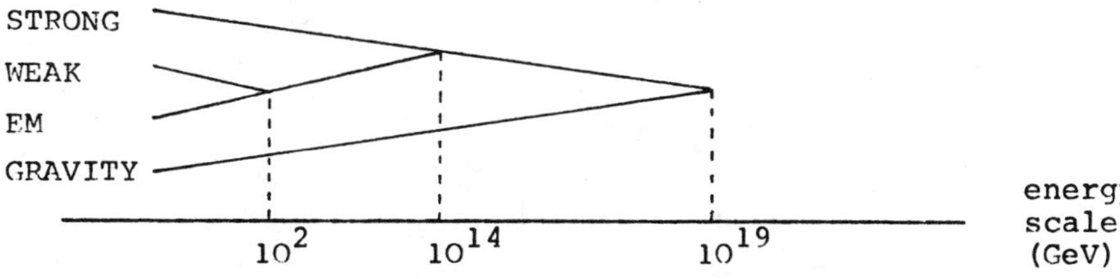

On the other hand, global symmetries show a tendency to increase in the IR. For example, in the standard unification schemes, the conservation of baryon number is no longer regarded as a fundamental symmetry and it appears as an "automatic" consequence[3] of the physics at low energy. Similarly, it is expected that CP violation is more effective at high than at low energies; symmetry in the IR is due to some CP-violating terms being decoupled at low energies[4]. A study of the behaviour of Yukawa couplings and scalar quartic couplings in gauge theories also shows that global symmetry has a tendency to increase in the IR[5]. Another study[6], performed by using one-loop β functions, shows the IR stability for small orthogonal groups and for simple supersymmetric models.

In an approach[7] developed by H.B. Nielsen and collaborators, various symmetries observed in nature are proposed to be "IR attractive fixed points" of a large class of theories which are not endowed with these symmetries a priori. The most important symmetries treated in this way are Lorentz and gauge invariance. The former is a subject of this discussion.

2. Lorentz Invariance as a Low-Energy Phenomenon

The introduction of Lorentz symmetry (the principle of special relativity) marked the beginning of an era of symmetries in physics. Specifically, the whole of the particle physics building rests upon Lorentz symmetry. Yet, one would like to understand the possible deeper origin of such a mighty principle. A first step toward such an understanding might be some kind of explanation of a high degree of Lorentz symmetry experienced in fundamental interactions of elementary particles. Such an "explanation" for non-covariant electrodynamics with fermions has been offered in a paper of Chadha and Nielsen[8] as a pure renormalization-group effect. The same type of argument has been shown to work when applied to a pure Yang-Mills theory[9]. Starting from a very general lagrangian density in which gauge fields realize Lorentz non-invariant couplings and calculating the pertinent renormalization-group β functions, it has turned out that the theory becomes Lorentz invariant with higher and higher accuracy as it is studied in the longer and longer wavelength regime. Thus, the observed Lorentz invariance may be due to the fact that our experiments are performed at very low energy relative to the fundamental energy scale at which the breaking of Lorentz invariance might be of the order of unity.

3. Empirical Evidence for Deviations from Lorentz Symmetry

According to the philosophy presented above, one should approach a very high-energy (short-distance) scale in order to have the best chance for observation of deviations from Lorentz invariance. The universe in its past was sufficiently hot to provide a really high-energy laboratory. By observing the relics from the first 10^{-35} sec of the universe, such as the baryon number and magnetic monopoles, we have a chance to probe the short-distance physics predicted by grand unified theories. As considered recently by Zee[10], proton decay, which probes the same scale, might exhibit LNI. LNI in proton decay still turns out to be experimentally unaccessible, unless some bizarre decay modes appear providing the breaking of rotational symmetry.

There are also remains of the radiation produced at a time close to the big bang, known as a 3K microwave background. Modern technology, unattailable to Michelson and Morley, led to the discovery of this type of "ether" which defined an absolute zero of velocity[11]. Such an apparent conflict with the principle of special relativity is not yet a real test of Lorentz non-invariance in particle physics. While the 3K radiation represents photons which (after 10^5 yr of the existence of the universe, when the electromagnetic interaction is frozen out)[12] propagate freely, we would like to check Lorentz symmetry in the interactions of elementary particles.

Actually, there are two groups of measurements probing the weak interaction (10^{-16} cm) scale which exhibit three-standard deviations from Lorentz invariance.

The first group of data refer to the velocity dependence of weak decaying particle lifetimes, tested for the following processes[1,2]:

	Decay	Mode (fraction)	Relativistic $\gamma=(1-\beta)^{-1/2}$	Effect (in S.D.)	
(i)	$\pi^+ \to \mu^+ + \nu_\mu$	(100%)	~ 2.5	3	
(ii)	$K^+ \to \mu^+ + \nu_\mu$	(65.5%)	~ 4	3	
	$\to \pi^+ + \pi^0$	(21%)			(1)
(iii)	$\mu^+ \to e^+ + \nu_e + \bar{\nu}_\mu$	(100%)	~ 30	No effect .	

The first two processes show up the velocity-dependent effect. The lifetime of the moving meson deviates from the proper lifetime when transformed to the rest frame by Lorentz transformation. In contrast to this, there is no LNI effect observed in muon decay. Since this decay was measured at considerably higher relativistic γ, it was considered as the best test of Lorentz invariance.

The second group of data refer to the energy-dependent parameters of the K^0-$\bar{K}^0$ system:

$$\begin{aligned}
&(j)\quad \Delta m = m_{K_L} - m_{K_S} , \\
&(jj)\quad \tau_S \sim |A(K_S^o \to \pi^+\pi^-)|^2 , \\
&\left.\begin{aligned}&(jjj)\quad |\eta_{+-}| \\ &(iv)\quad \tan \Phi_{+-}\end{aligned}\right\} \eta_{+-} = \frac{A(K_L^o \to \pi^+\pi^-)}{A(K_S^o \to \pi^+\pi^-)} ,
\end{aligned} \tag{2}$$

as reported by Fischbach et al.[13]. The advantages of these data are ascribed to the fact that they refer to a wide range of high values of $\gamma \in (60,260)$.

To the best of our knowledge, the quantities described in (1) and (2) provide a list of known direct measurements which support deviations from Lorentz symmetry. Thus, they should be incorporated in an explicit model of LNI.

4. A Simple Model of LNI

Given the "explanation" of Lorentz invariance as a low-energy phenomenon, followed by empirical evidence for deviations from Lorentz symmetry, we would like to take on a more ambitious task - the construction of an explicit model of LNI.

In order to have a realistic model, we want to incorporate LNI into existing unified models, keeping Lorentz invariance in the IR. LNI may be attributed to the pure gauge sector of the standard (GSW) model:

$$- \frac{1}{4} F^a_{\mu\nu} F^{a\mu\nu} - \frac{1}{4} B_{\mu\nu} B^{\mu\nu} \tag{3}$$

extended à la Chadha, Nielsen and Ninomiya[8,9] to the following form which is Lorentz non-invariant:

$$- \frac{1}{4} \eta^{\mu\nu\rho\sigma} (F^a_{\mu\nu} F^a_{\rho\sigma} + B_{\mu\nu} B_{\rho\sigma}) . \tag{3'}$$

Still, as shown by Ellis et al.[14], for such couplings, the goodness of Lorentz invariance at low energies guarantees that Lorentz invariance will also be good at the proton decay scale. Thus, some additional couplings have to be invoked in order to produce any experimentally accessible LNI effect. The couplings originating from the Higgs sector, which is not yet well understood, have a chance of being most Lorentz invariance breaking. Accordingly, we generalize the Higgs term

$$g^{\mu\nu} (D_\mu \phi)^\dagger (D_\nu \phi) \tag{4}$$

into a slightly modified form, but still gauge invariant,

$$h^{\mu\nu}(D_\mu\phi)^\dagger(D_\nu\phi) . \qquad (4')$$

Although (4´) has a formally covariant appearance, the coupling constants $h^{\mu\nu}$ are not to be transformed under Lorentz transformation. In order to have a small deviation from Lorentz symmetry, we introduce the notation

$$h^{\mu\nu} = g^{\mu\nu} - \chi^{\mu\nu} . \qquad (5)$$

Expression (5) denotes a perturbation expansion in the deviation from Lorentz invariance. Then, at the low-energy limit, LNI is dominated by the inverse of the Higgs-coupling term[1,2)]

$$\frac{1}{h^{\mu\nu}\langle\phi\rangle^2} \simeq \frac{1}{M_W^2}(g_{\mu\nu} + \chi_{\mu\nu}) . \qquad (6)$$

It manifests itself in the LNI propagation of a massive gauge boson, described at the low-energy limit by

$$D_{\mu\nu}(x - y) = \frac{1}{M_W^2}(g_{\mu\nu} + \chi_{\mu\nu})\delta^4(x - y) . \qquad (7)$$

This results in an effective local current-current interaction of the form

$$H_{eff} = \frac{G_F}{\sqrt{2}}(g_{\mu\nu} + \chi_{\mu\nu})J^{\mu\dagger}(x)J^\nu(x) . \qquad (8)$$

By imposing a chain of conditions on the LNI metric $\chi_{\mu\nu}$,

$$\chi_{\mu\nu}\text{(16 components)} \xrightarrow{\text{symmetry}} \text{(10 components)} \xrightarrow{\text{traceless}} \text{(9 components)} \xrightarrow[\text{preferred frame}]{\text{rotational invariant}} \text{(3 components)}, \qquad (9)$$

we obtain a very simple model where LNI is parametrized by a single number α. The meaning of the last step in (9) is to bring $\chi_{\mu\nu}$ to the principal axes by choosing the rotational invariant $\chi_{\mu\nu}$, say in a frame at rest with the ancient matter which has emitted the 3K background radiation. One of the principal axis is the time axis, the location of the other three space axes of a rotational invariant tensor being arbitrary, and the four principal values are related by

$$\chi_{00} = \alpha \ ; \quad \chi_{11} = \chi_{22} = \chi_{33} = \alpha/3 . \qquad (10)$$

It has been shown that such a simple model accounts easily for the first group of data, displayed in (1). The decay widths of the first two processes in (1) exhibit a "Rédei-like" behaviour of the decay rates:

$$\Gamma_{LNI}^{(\pi,K)} = \gamma^{-1}\,\Gamma_{o}^{(\pi,K)}\left[1 + \frac{4}{3}\,\alpha(\gamma^{2} - \frac{1}{4})\right] . \tag{11}$$

Matching the "Rédei-like" behaviour with the measured behaviour for $\pi^{\pm}$ and $K^{\pm}$ gives

$$\alpha(\pi^{+}) = (-3.79 \pm 1.37)\times 10^{-3} , \tag{12a}$$

$$\alpha(K^{+}) = (0.61 \pm 0.17)\times 10^{-3} , \tag{12b}$$

and a weighted total average

$$\langle\alpha\rangle = (0.54 \pm 0.17)\times 10^{-3} . \tag{12c}$$

The absence of such a "Rédei-like" behaviour for a muon-decay experiment, which pretended to set the best upper limit to LNI, was found to be a consequence of the selection rule; no LNI effect could be detected by performing the total-rate measurement in muon decay[1]. This was the starting-point of a recent investigation[15] of the Michel parameter for the angular distribution of polarized muon decay. From the measured value $\rho = 0.7518 \pm 0.0026$ the authors of ref. 15 find that

$$\alpha = (-3.6 \pm 5.2)\times 10^{-3} . \tag{13a}$$

Still, they do not state explicitly that for another Michel parameter, $\delta = 0.755 \pm 0.009$, the value of α is

$$\alpha = (1 \pm 1.8)\times 10^{-2} . \tag{13b}$$

(Note that this value of α is of the opposite sign.)

In an attempt to explain the second group of data, we encountered difficulties associated with calculations of non-leptonic processes[2]. Thus, at best, we were able to give a very crude prediction of the LNI behaviour for the quantities in (2). For example, the calculation of the first quantity in (2) in the vacuum-insertion approximation can be related to the $K^{+} \to \mu^{+}\nu_{\mu}$ decay width represented by (11):

$$(m_{K_L} - m_{K_S})_{LNI} \simeq \frac{4}{3\pi}\left(\frac{m_c}{m_\mu}\right)^{2} \cos^{2}\Theta_C\,\Gamma_{LNI}(K^{+} \to \mu^{+}\nu_{\mu}) . \tag{14}$$

Since α on the RHS is 0.61×10^{-3} (eq. (12b)), in contrast to the value of α of -0.85×10^{-5} given by Fischbach et al.[13] for the LHS, our model does not fit together the two groups of three-standard-deviation data, (1) and (2). However, the relation (14) is strongly model-dependent and highly accidental. Theoretical uncertainties in non-leptonic physics prevent us from drawing a completely firm conclusion that decay lifetimes and K^0-$\bar{K}^0$ parameters disagree with each other in our model.

5. Conclusion

Apart from the good agreement (a selection rule) between our model and a muon-decay experiment performed at moderate γ, there is a rather inconclusive situation in non-leptonic physics. The apparent disagreement is not reliable. On the one hand, there is an experimental disadvantage that meson decays are performed at a very small γ. On the other hand, the relativistic K^0-$\bar{K}^0$ system faces the shortcomings of theoretical calculations. In view of that, additional indirect tests of our model are highly desirable. An attempt in this direction was given in ref. 2, but it is out of the scope of the present report.

Still, the indication[13)] of a C-even "cosmological field" coupled to the K^0-$\bar{K}^0$ system agrees with our model. However, our C-even LNI interaction is due to the perturbation in a metric for Higgs bosons. In such a picture, LNI should manifest itself in all heavy-gauge-boson propagations (and not only in superheavy-gauge-boson propagations, as auggested by Zee[10)]).

At the end, let me recall that new, subtle interactions of elementary particles, were always recovered owing to the breakdown of some symmetry which governed a set of conventional, known interactions. In view of this historical wisdom, let us hope that LNI will provide a small window into a large world of technicolour-like physics.

This work was supported in part by the SIZ I of SR Croatia and the US National Science Foundation under grant No YOR 82/051.

References

1) H.B. Nielsen and I. Picek, Phys. Lett. 114B (1982) 141
2) H.B. Nielsen and I. Picek, Nucl. Phys. B211 (1983) 269
3) S. Weinberg, Phys. Rev. D26 (1982) 287
4) J. Ellis, M.K. Gaillard and D.V. Nanopoulos, Phys. Lett. 88B (1979) 320
5) D.I. Kazakov, Dubna preprint E2-82-880 (1982)
6) S. Midorikawa and K. Yamamoto, Nucl. Phys. B219 (1983) 376

7) H.B. Nielsen, Fundamentals of quark models, ed. J.M. Barbour and A.T. Davies (Univ. of Glasgow, 1977) p. 528. H.B. Nielsen, Particle physics 1980, ed. I. Andrić, I. Dadić and N. Zovko (North-Holland, 1981) p. 125.
8) S. Chadha and H.B. Nielsen, Niels Bohr Institute report (1977) and Nucl. Phys. B217 (1983) 125
9) H.B. Nielsen and M. Ninomiya, Nucl. Phys. B141 (1978) 153
10) A. Zee, Phys. Rev. D25 (1982) 1864
11) P.A.M. Dirac, Symmetries in Science, ed. B. Gruber and R.S. Millman (Plenum Press, 1980) p. 1
12) D.N. Schramm, Phys. Today, April 1983, p. 27
13) E. Fischbach, these proceedings, and S.H. Aronson, G.J. Bock, H-Y. Cheng and E. Fischbach, Phys. Rev. Lett. 48 (1982) 1306 E. Fischbach, H-Y. Cheng, S.H. Aronson and G.J. Bock, Phys. Lett. 116B (1982) 73
14) J. Ellis, M.K. Gaillard, D.V. Nanopoulos and S. Rudaz, Nucl. Phys. B176 (1980) 61
15) R. Huerta-Quintanilla and J.L. Lucio M., Phys. Lett. 124B (1983) 369

QCD SPECTROSCOPY AND COUPLINGS WITH SUM RULES: AN OVERVIEW*)

L.J. Reinders, H.R. Rubinstein+) and S. Yazaki++)

CERN -- Geneva

ABSTRACT

An overview is presented of the results for masses and couplings of resonances obtained in recent years with QCD sum rules.

---

*) Lecture presented by HRR.

+) On leave of absence from the Weizmann Institute, Rehovot, Israel.

++) On leave of absence from the University of Tokyo, Japan.

In this paper we will review the status of the QCD sum rule approach to hadronic physics. Details of the calculations can be found in the original papers referred to below, in review papers already in the literature or in a Physics Reports which is at present in preparation.

We will discuss many topics and will try to give a coherent view of the present situation. We will answer criticism and discuss outstanding questions and problems.

THE SVZ EXPANSION

Several years ago Shifman, Vainshtein, and Zakharov[1] showed how to generalize the short-distance expansion for theories with a non-trivial vacuum. Although the method is very appealing physically, it is not clear that the prescription suggested by the ITEP people is indeed correct. Phenomenologically, as can be seen in the accompanying tables, the success is impressive. Theoretically there is considerable resistance to this approach. There are some situations of solvable models in which the prescription works, e.g. expansion in an external instanton field[2]. Also, contrary to initial claims[3] the solution of ϕ^4 in the perturbative vacuum in the presence of condensates agrees with the SVZ prescription[4] (the answer is the same before and after shifting). There are studies in other models by David[5] which raise other difficulties. Essentially, it is claimed that condensates which are not protected by a symmetry are necessarily ill-defined. We believe that the question is not settled.

SPECTROSCOPY

The calculation of masses works schematically as follows. In the Euclidean region one calculates the polarization function for a current with a well defined set of quantum numbers that single out a particular partial wave. For example, the current $\bar{u}\gamma_\mu \bar{u} - \bar{d}\gamma_\mu d$ for light quark vector states like the ρ meson $(I = 1,\ J^{PC} = 1^{--})$, while the current $\bar{c}\gamma_\mu c$ would select vector states made of charmed quarks. The momentum Q^2 flowing through the current is chosen in the asymptotically free region. While in the examples given above the current is physical and measured in e^+e^- annihilation, other currents will be unphysical.

Applying the SVZ expansion to the polarization function, one obtains an expression of the form

$$T_{\mu\nu\ldots}\Pi^j(Q^2) = i\int d^4x\, e^{iqx} \langle 0|T(j_1(x)j_2(0))|0\rangle = \sum_i a_i \langle 0|O_i|0\rangle, \quad Q^2 = -q^2 \qquad (1)$$

$\Pi^j(Q^2)$ is a scalar function of Q^2; $T_{\mu\nu}\cdots$ a tensor depending on the current in question, the O_i are local operators constructed of quark and gluon fields, and the a_i the corresponding Wilson coefficients. Equation (1) represents the theoretical side of the sum rules and is calculated in terms of the fundamental parameters of QCD (α_s, quark masses) and of condensates (vacuum matrix elements of the operators O_i). The dynamics of QCD is buried in the Wilson coefficients a_i. These can be calculated in perturbation theory and their magnitude determines the validity region of the expression, which is only applicable if the neglected terms are indeed small. The first operator in (1) is the identity operator. Its coefficient a_o contains the ordinary perturbative contributions and in most cases is calculated to first order in α_s. Therefore, one has to make sure that higher corrections are small. For dimensional reasons the coefficients of the higher dimensional operators in (1) fall off by corresponding powers of Q^2. These power corrections measure the breakdown of asymptotic freedom and grow fast with distance. The theory makes sense if the power corrections are big enough for quarks to resonate and small enough so that contributions from higher dimensional operators can be neglected. The balancing of the various corrections is a tricky path and people keep falling into the precipice[6]. In most cases the errors can be calculated and although the method cannot solve all problems its range of validity can always be tested.

The phenomenological side that matches the theoretical expression has the following simple form in the physical region

$$\sum_i \frac{g_i^2}{m_i^2 - q^2} + \text{continuum} \qquad (2)$$

where the (g_i, m_i) are the parameters of the resonances. The continuum in (2) contains the parameter s_o which is the threshold at which the smooth background starts.

After analytic continuation to the Euclidean region via the moment or Borel method[1] the two sides hopefully overlap. Using one or the other method depends on whether the problem has a natural scale (like a heavy quark) or not. Nothing basic is involved in the choice of method. For massless quarks it is just inconvenient to use a reference momentum as a scale. The crucial question is whether one is gaining physical insight and information, or is just trading masses and couplings for new parameters like condensates and thresholds.

The spectroscopy can be divided in a number of sections:

1. light quark mesons with L = 0[1)]
2. light quark mesons with L = 1[7),8)]
3. charmonium[1),9)]
4. bottonium[9),10)]
5. mesons made of light and heavy quarks[11),12)]
6. light quark baryons[13-17)]
7. baryons with one heavy quark[18)]
8. QCD non-quark model states[19-20)].

We will briefly give a status report for each case with emphasis on parameter dependences.

1. <u>Light quark mesons with L = 0[1)]</u>

The operator expansion series (1) for the polarization operator can be cut off at dimension $d = 6$ for the operators O_i. Consequently, the operators which give important contributions to these mesons are (apart from the identity operator)

$$\begin{aligned} &\langle 0|\tfrac{\alpha_s}{\pi} G^a_{\mu\nu} G^a_{\mu\nu}|0\rangle && \text{the gluon condensate,} \quad d = 4 \\ &\langle 0|m\bar{q}q|0\rangle && \text{the quark condensate,} \quad d = 4 \\ &\langle 0|\bar{q}\Gamma_1 q\bar{q}\Gamma_2 q|0\rangle && \text{four-fermion condensate,} \quad d = 6 \end{aligned} \tag{3}$$

Assuming dominance of the vacuum intermediate state[1)] the last operator in (3) can be expressed in terms of $\langle 0|\bar{q}\, q|0\rangle$. This is claimed to be accurate within about 10%[21)]. However, due to uncertainties in the light quark mass values, $\langle 0|\bar{q}\, q|0\rangle$ is only known up to a factor of two (from PCAC).

Consider as an example the resulting expression for the polarization function of the ρ-meson current (after Borel transforming)

$$\int e^{-s/M^2} \mathrm{Im}\,\Pi(s)\,ds = \frac{1}{8\pi^2} M^2 \Big[1 + \frac{\alpha_s(M)}{\pi} + \frac{8\pi^2}{M^4}\langle 0|m\bar{q}q|0\rangle + + \frac{\pi^2}{3M^4}\langle 0|\frac{\alpha_s}{\pi} G^a_{\mu\nu} G^a_{\mu\nu}|0\rangle - \frac{448}{81}\cdot\frac{\pi^3\alpha_s}{M^6}\langle 0|\bar{q}q|0\rangle^2 \Big]. \tag{4}$$

A second sum rule can be derived by differentiating with respect to M^2. An expression for the ρ-meson mass can be obtained by substituting

$$\mathrm{Im}\,\Pi(s) = \frac{\pi m_\rho^2}{g_\rho^2}\,\delta(s - m_\rho^2) + \frac{1}{8\pi}\left(1 + \frac{\alpha_s}{\pi}\right)\theta(s - s_0) \tag{5}$$

into (4) and into the derivative sum rule, transferring the continuum contribution to the right-hand side and taking the ratio

$$m_\rho^2 = M^2 \frac{(1+\frac{\alpha_s}{\pi})\left[1-(1+\frac{s_0}{M^2})e^{-s_0/M^2}\right] - \frac{\pi^2}{3M^4}\langle\frac{\alpha_s}{\pi}G^2\rangle + \frac{896}{81}\cdot\frac{\pi^3\alpha_s}{M^6}\langle\bar{q}q\rangle^2}{(1+\frac{\alpha_s}{\pi})\left[1-e^{-s_0/M^2}\right] + \frac{\pi^2}{3M^4}\langle\frac{\alpha_s}{\pi}G^2\rangle - \frac{448}{81}\cdot\frac{\pi^3\alpha_s}{M^6}\langle\bar{q}q\rangle^2} \quad (6)$$

where we have neglected the contribution from $m\bar{q}q$ which is small compared to the gluon condensate. It can be seen from (6) that the perturbative corrections $(1+\frac{\alpha_s}{\pi})$ do not play a role as they can be divided out at the expense of introducing a 20% error in the values for the condensates.

In (6) the mass m_ρ^2 is controlled by the gluon and quark condensates on an equal footing, and although the ρ' is far away at 1.6 GeV it still contributes about 30% to the sum rule at $M^2 \simeq m_\rho^2$. This contribution is controlled by s_o. Due to the uncertainties in s_o and $\langle\bar{q}q\rangle$ it is not possible to determine the gluon condensate $\langle\frac{\alpha_s}{\pi}G^2\rangle$ from (6) better than within a factor of two. The sum rule can also be analyzed without ρ dominance using the e^+e^- annihilation data. This analysis[22)] confirms the values of the matrix elements to this accuracy. One can use the sum rule (6) to determine the parameters of the ρ meson. For $s_o = 1.5\ \text{GeV}^2$ which is suggested by the data, one gets

$$m_\rho = 770\ \text{MeV} \pm 10\%$$

$$g_\rho^2/4\pi \simeq 2.5\ .$$

Similar sum rules can be derived for all other vector mesons. Their masses and couplings can be calculated with the same accuracy. The pattern of SU(3) breaking comes out correctly. The mass of the strange quark is not accurately fixed by these sum rules. In Table I the results have been summarized.

The pseudoscalars are too light for the method to be able to determine their masses. Moreover, direct instanton contributions to the pseudoscalar sum rules not included in the matrix elements $\langle O_i\rangle$ of Eq. (1) have to be accounted for[23)]. Using axial vector sum rules at $M^2 \simeq m_\rho^2$ where on one hand the power corrections are small and on the other hand the pseudoscalars saturate the sum rule, one can obtain the couplings in good agreement with experiment. Also, the consistency of the axial sum rules for the A_1 demands the pion pole at zero.

2. The L = 1 states[7),8)]

The L = 1 states with massless quarks give about 15 new predictions with the same operators and parameters. Although these states are more sensitive to the continuum, reasonable variations in s_o do not change the results by more than 10%. As can be seen in Ref. 7), the power corrections are always important and a gluon condensate which is a factor two bigger than the standard value would completely ruin the nice agreement for spin 2 mesons. This is indirect evidence for the standard value. Also, these states require m_s to be small (about 100 MeV). The results are collected in Table II.

3. Charmonium[1),9)]

This system isolates the gluon condensate. Moreover, for kinematical reasons everything conspires to give maximal accuracy. This is achieved by allowing the reference momentum Q^2 to vary in the region where asymptotic freedom is valid. Besides getting a better stability region the results are stable for a wide range of Q^2 [Ref. 9] which is strong support for the theory. Using moment sum rules one can make sure that the continuum contribution is unimportant, which can be verified from the measured cross-section in the vector current case. The mass of the charmed quark is accurately fixed and the gluon condensate is pinned down with about 30% accuracy and at the same value as in light quark spectroscopy. The masses come out naturally and accurately. The results are collected in Table III. Corrections due to higher operators are very small for dimension six operators and although large for dimension eight operators at $Q^2 = 0$,[24)] their contribution is expected to go down when Q^2 is shifted away from zero where the stability is best[9)]. This calculation has to be performed and if our expectation is confirmed, this will corroborate the results in a strong way.

4. Bottonium[9),10)]

This system is unfortunately on the limit of being Coulombic and therefore very different from charmonium. Since the gluon condensate coefficient is down by the ratio of the quark masses to the fourth power, it is clear that low moments are dominated by perturbative corrections. To feel the resonances one has to go to large distances, but then higher order perturbative corrections are also not negligible. It is only when the quark mass is about 20 GeV that the system becomes tractable again[25),26)]. A few things can nevertheless be said (see Table III) and with further assumptions one can make predictions (but at a risk)[10)].

5. Heavy-light quark bound states[11),12)]

Unfortunately, moment sum rules cannot be used to obtain the masses of open charm states. As stated in the Introduction, conditions on the size of the various contributions must be met for the polarization operator formula to be valid. Using the reference momentum in a range where asymptotic freedom is valid one can tune these contributions. At the same time, however, one increases the contribution from the continuum to such an extent that the lowest lying resonance cannot be disentangled from the background.

For open bottom the situation is better and the results show quite interesting physics. The quark mass is fixed from the sum rules for bottonium and the only parameter is the continuum threshold s_o. A stable set of states which depend on s_o is obtained[11)]. The most interesting result is that the P-wave mesons are higher than in potential models because of the appearance of terms of the form $m_Q \langle\bar{q}q\rangle$ where m_Q is the heavy quark mass.

Recently[12)] Borel transformed sum rules for open charm and beauty have been analyzed in order to obtain the couplings f_D and f_B which within errors are equal to f_π. In this case the experimental mass values were used as input. Although there is a large uncertainty in the values obtained, these results and those of Ref. 11) rule out the large value for f_D that has been conjectured in the charm case to explain the $D^+ - D^o$ lifetime[33)].

6. Baryons

Light quark baryons are nicely understood in this language, although it is very difficult to obtain high accuracy. For the $J = 1/2$ baryons there are two structure functions $A(q^2)$ and $B(q^2)$, which have odd and even numbers of dimensions respectively. Consequently, the expansion for the odd dimensional function $A(q^2)$ is dominated by $\langle 0|\bar{q}q|0\rangle$ which appears without the mass of the light quark. Approximating one sum rule (from $A(q^2)$) by the quark condensate contribution only, the other (from $B(q^2)$) by the bare loop, and taking the ratio one finds the celebrated formula of Joffe[13)]

$$M_N^3 = -2(2\pi)^2 \langle 0|\bar{q}q|0\rangle . \qquad (7)$$

Using the PCAC value of $\langle 0|\bar{q}q|0\rangle$ one obtains $M_N \cong 1$ GeV (very sensitive to the value of $\langle 0|\bar{q}q|0\rangle$). This result can be improved by including higher dimensional operators and the continuum contribution but results at the 10% accuracy level or better, which are necessary to reproduce the splittings within the octet must wait some further calculations and a more accurate determination of $\langle 0|\bar{q}q|0\rangle$ which has a rather large uncertainty[27].

Nevertheless, there is considerable qualitative agreement with experiment and with theoretical prejudice. The nucleon mass vanishes with the condensate. The lowest lying states fit into a positive parity 56 representation while negative parity states come out higher[16]. It turns out that the octet baryons provide an effective way to establish the value of

$$\gamma = -1 + \langle 0|\bar{s}s|0\rangle / \langle 0|\bar{u}u|0\rangle$$

irrespective of the values of the other parameters[17]. Provided the strange quark mass is between 100 and 150 MeV, one finds $\gamma = -0.18 \pm 0.06$. The sign does not agree with extrapolations from chiral perturbation theory which, however, is not surprising since the quark mass is of order Λ_{QCD}[23].

The decuplet masses are marginally within reach of the method since the non-perturbative contributions are significantly larger in this case. Qualitatively, however, the agreement is satisfactory.

In general the baryon spectrum is dense which implies that s_o is low and that the baryons saturate less than 50% of the sum rule. It will take more detailed calculations to reach 10% or better accuracy. In particular, the perturbative gluon exchange contributions have not yet been taken into account. Finally, the dimension five operator $\bar{q}\sigma_{\mu\nu}q\, G_{\mu\nu}$ gives an important contribution to the octet-decuplet splitting. Its matrix element is not well known and no hard prediction is possible here.

Finally, the coupling λ_N of the proton to the current which measures the strength of the proton transition into three quarks has been used[34] to calculate the proton lifetime in the SU(5) model of grand unification.

7. Heavy-light baryons

The situation here is quite open. There are some calculations in the literature[18] based on rough approximations. We do not believe that these test the theory, but it is reassuring that with the known mass of the charmed quark the charmed baryon appears at the expected mass.

8. Exotic states

It is rather distressing that the gluonic degrees of freedom of QCD are not seen. Some calculations of glueballs and of matter with glue have been performed with QCD sum rules.

The ITEP group[23] has made a semiquantitative sum rule analysis for glueballs and concludes that they should be relatively high in mass and that the spin 2 glueball lies lowest. Experimentally the situation is still confused, but it is important to emphasize that bag models give different results.

For mesons with glue there exist two calculations in the literature[19],[20]. They disagree and therefore must be checked. One of them[20] makes unnecessary assumptions on subtractions but claims that the Wilson coefficients in Ref. 19) are not correct. Both predict a low mass for the exotic $\bar{q}qG$ state with $J^{PC} = 1^{-+}$ which is worrying. We believe that experiments searching for these states are as interesting as glueballs and should be pursued.

Similar calculations for baryons with glue are in progress but experimentally there seems to be little room for more states below 2 GeV as predicted by QCD like models and bags[28]. If the sum rules give similar results, it is important to understand the reasons.

9. Three-point functions

The use of these methods for three-point functions was pioneered by the ITEP group in 1978[29] and developed to new realms since.

One application is to electromagnetic processes like $\eta_c \to 2\gamma$[30] and $\psi' \to \eta_c\gamma$[31]. The anomaly diagram is used here in a different domain. By making a moment expansion (or a double moment expansion for $\psi' \to \eta_c\gamma$) one looks for a region in which the relevant states dominate. Combining the results with couplings determined from two-point function analyses one can extract the transition rates. Unfortunately, the perturbative piece in the case of $\psi' \to \eta_c\gamma$ cannot be calculated. However, it is quite remarkable that the non-perturbative gluon condensate contribution substantially reduces these rates, bringing them in better agreement with experiment.

Another interesting application is the calculation of strong interaction coupling constants like $g_{\pi NN}$ and $g_{\omega\rho\pi}$[32]. These calculations have been performed by applying the Wilson expansion to the product of three currents and can be checked by considering two-point functions sandwiched between the vacuum and a pion state. The procedure followed for three-point functions is to isolate the pion pole term and analytically continue the residue. This procedure is consistent with chiral invariance and the relations obtained are equivalent to the Goldberger-Treiman relation or current algebra results. We obtain for example:

$$g_{\pi NN} \simeq 2(2\pi)^2 \sqrt{2}\, \frac{f_\pi}{M_N}$$
$$g_{\omega\rho\pi} \simeq \sqrt{2}\,(2\pi)^2 \frac{f_\pi}{m_\rho^2} \tag{8}$$

The numerical values of these and other couplings are tabulated in Table IV.

Finally we have to mention the applications of the three-point function technique to the calculation of form factors[35),36)] and an alternative method to calculate coupling constants[37)].

Table I

Light quark mesons with L = 0 (Ref. 1)

State J^{PC}	Mass exp	Mass theor	Coupling exp	Coupling theor	Remarks
π	140	-	f_π=133	125	masses too low direct instantons f_π, f_K well computed.
K	495	-	$f_K \simeq f_\pi$		
0^{--}					
η	550	-			
η'	920	-			
			$g^2/4\pi$		masses and couplings calculated with ∿ 10% acc. ρ-ω interference has also been obtained. Relevant parameters are $\langle G^2\rangle$, $\langle\bar{q}q\rangle$, α_s, s_o, $m_q \equiv 0$, I = 0,1 degeneracy, SU(3) breaking o.k., m_s not well fixed.
ω	780	770	2.4	2.5	
ρ	770	770	2.4	2.5	
1^{--}					
K^*	890	930	1.39	1.4	
ϕ	1020	1070	12.0	14.	

Table II

Light quark mesons with L = 1 (Ref. 7, 8)

J^{PC}	state	mass exp	mass theor	coupling exp	coupling theor	Remarks
2^{++}	A_2	1320	1320	couplings not directly useful; g_f=0.04 calculated with further assumption, agrees with exp.		I = 1,0 degeneracy. m_s low ∿ 120 MeV. Large $1/M^4$ term gives bound on $\langle G^2 \rangle$.
	f	1270	1320			
	K^{**}	1430	-			
	f'	1520	1520			
1^{++}	A_1	1200	1150	$\frac{4\pi}{f^2_{A_1}}$ =.15	.16	two sum rules for A_1; D meson requires m_s ∿ ∿ 100 MeV; for D only one sum rule, since divergence of axial current has U(1) problem in this channel.
	D	1285	1290			
	E	1420	1460			
	Q_1	1270	-			
	Q_2	1414	-			
0^{++}	δ	980	1010			δ, S^* assumed to be pure $\bar{q}q$, no instanton contributions included.
	S^*	980	1010			
	ε	1300	1350			
1^{+-}	B	1240	?			no calculation possible; power corrections vanish at one-loop level
2^{-}	A_3	1680	1630			

Table III

Heavy quark mesons with L = 0 and L = 1

J^{PC}	State	mass exp. (GeV)	mass theor (GeV)	Coupling	Remarks
Charmonium (Ref. 1,9)					
1^{--}	J/ψ	3.10	3.10±0.01	Only for J/ψ:	$m_c(p^2=-m_c^2)=1.28$ GeV
0^{--}	η_c	2.98	3.01±0.02	exp: $\Gamma_{e^+e^-}$ =	very accurate indep. of s_o.
0^{++}	χ_0	3.42	3.40±0.01	4.7 ± .6 keV	Gluon condensate same as in light
1^{++}	χ_1	3.51	3.50±0.01	theor: $\Gamma_{e^+e^-} \simeq$	quark case $\langle \frac{\alpha_s}{\pi} G^2 \rangle$
2^{++}	χ_2	3.56	3.56±0.01	5.34 keV	$\simeq (330\ \text{MeV})^4 \pm 30\%$.
1^{+-}		?	3.51±0.01		Same parameters fit P-waves.
Bottonium (Ref. 9)					
1^{--}	Υ	9.46	$m_\Upsilon - m_{\eta_b} \sim$		$m_b(p^2=-m_b^2) \simeq 4.26$ GeV
0^{--}	η_B	?	~ 60 MeV		moment method fails, no single resonance saturation
Open bottom (Ref. 11,12)					
0^{-+}	$(\bar{u}b)$	5.27	5.31	$f_P \simeq 140\text{-}180$ MeV	continuum very important; splittings cannot be resolved.
1^{--}			5.38	$g_V^2/4\pi \simeq 24$	
0^{++}			6.13	$f_S \simeq 380$ MeV	S-P splitting large because of $m_Q\langle\bar{q}q\rangle$.
1^{++}			6.17	$g_A^2/4\pi \simeq 13$	
0^{-+}	$(\bar{s}b)$		5.42	$f_P \simeq 320$ MeV	
1^{--}			5.46	$g_V^2/4\pi \simeq 17$	
0^{++}			6.29	$f_S \simeq 400$ MeV	
1^{++}			6.34	$g_A^2/4\pi \simeq 12$	

Table IV

Couplings $g^2/4\pi$ of Goldstone bosons to hadrons (Ref. 32)

	exp[38]	theory	
πNN	14.5	12.5	all within 20% of
$\pi\Sigma\Sigma$	13±2	10	exp value
$\eta_8 NN$	~4.5	6.4	$\alpha = D/(F+D) = 7/12$
$K\Sigma N$	~1	1	(compare $\alpha(SU/6)) = 2/3$)
$\pi N\Delta$	~15 GeV^{-2}	18 GeV^{-2}	
$\omega\rho\pi$	~16 GeV^{-1}	13 GeV^{-1}	

References

1. M.A. Shifman, A.I. Vainshtein, and V.I. Zakharov, Nucl. Phys. B 147 (1979) 385.

2. V.A. Novikov, M.A. Shifman, A.I. Vainshtein, and V.I. Zakharov, Nucl. Phys. B 174 (1980) 378.

3. S. Gupta and H.R. Quinn, Phys. Rev. D 26 (1982) 499.

4. C. Taylor and B. McClain, MIT preprint CTP-1069 (Febr. 1983).

5. F. David, Nucl. Phys. B 209 (1982) 433;
F. David, Preprint Saclay (May 1983).

6. K. Zalewski and A. Zalewska, Phys. Lett. 125 (1983) 89.

7. L.J. Reinders, H.R. Rubinstein and S. Yazaki, Nucl. Phys. B 196 (1982) 125.

8. T.M. Aliev and M.A. Shifman, Phys. Lett. 112 B (1982) 401.

9. L.J. Reinders, H.R. Rubinstein and S. Yazaki, Nucl. Phys. B 186 (1981) 109.

10. M.B. Voloshin, Yad. Fiz. 29 (1979) 1368 [Sov. J. Nucl. Phys. 29 (1979) 703].

11. L.J. Reinders, H.R. Rubinstein and S. Yazaki, Phys. Lett. 104 B (1981) 305.

12. T.M. Aliev and V.L. Eletsky, Preprint ITEP-47 (1983).

13. B.L. Joffe, Nucl. Phys. B 188 (1981) 317 [Erratum: B 191 (1981) 591].

14. Y. Chung et al., Phys. Lett. 102 B (1981) 175; Nucl. Phys. B 197 (1982) 55.

15. D. Espriu, P. Pascual and R. Tarrach, Nucl. Phys. B 214 (1983) 285.

16. V.M. Belyaev and B.L. Joffe, Preprints ITEP-59 and ITEP-132 (1982).

17. L.J. Reinders, H.R. Rubinstein and S. Yazaki, Phys. Lett. 120 B (1983) 209.

18. E.V. Shuryak, Nucl. Phys. B 198 (1982) 83.

19. I.I. Balitsky, D.I. Dyakonov and A.V. Yung, Phys. Lett. 112 B (1982) 71;
I.I. Balitsky, D.I. Dyakonov and A.V. Yung, Sov. J. Nucl. Phys. 35 (1982) 761.

20. J. Govaerts, F. de Viron, D. Gusbin, and J. Weyers, Phys. Lett. 128 B (1983) 262.

21. V.A. Novikov, M.A. Shifman, A.I. Vainshtein, M.B. Voloskin and V.I. Zakharov, Preprint ITEP-71 (1983).

22. S.I. Eidelman, L.M. Kurdadze, and A.I. Vainshtein, Phys. Lett. 82 B (1979) 278.

23. V.A. Novikov, M.A. Shifman, A.I. Vainshtein, and V.I. Zakharov, Nucl. Phys. B 191 (1981) 301.

24. S.N. Nikolaev and A.V. Radyushkin, Phys. Lett. 124 B (1983) 242 and JINR preprint R 2-82-914.

25. H. Leutwyler, Phys. Lett. 98 B (1981) 447.

26. M.B. Voloshin, Preprint ITEP-30 (1981).

27. J. Gasser and H. Leutwyler, Phys. Reports 87 (1982) 77.

28. E. Golowich, E. Haqq and G. Karl, Phys. Rev. D 28 (1983) 160.

29. V.A. Novikov, L.B. Okun, M.A. Shifman, A.I. Vainshtein, M.B. Voloshin and V.I. Zakharov, Phys. Reports 41 (1978) 1.

30. L.J. Reinders, H.R. Rubinstein, and S. Yazaki, Phys. Lett. 113 B (1982) 411.

31. A. Yu. Khodjamirian, Erevan Preprint EFI-65 I (4I)(1983).

32. L.J. Reinders, H.R. Rubinstein and S. Yazaki, Nucl. Phys. B 213 (1983) 109.

33. M. Bander, D. Silverman and A. Soni, Phys. Rev. Lett. 44 (1980) 7; H. Fritzsch and P. Minkowski, Phys. Lett. 90 B (1980) 455.

34. V. Berezinsky, B. Ioffe and Ya. Kogan, Phys. Lett. 105 B (1981) 33.

35. B.L. Ioffe and A.V. Smilga, Phys. Lett. 114 B (1982) 353.

36. A.V. Nesterenko and A.V. Radyushkin, Phys. Lett. 115 B (1982) 410.

37. V.I. Eletsky, B.L. Ioffe and Y.I. Kogan, Preprint ITEP-98 (1982).

38. O. Dumbrajs et al., Nucl. Phys. B 216 (1983) 277.

SOME COMMENTS ON QCD SUM RULES*

E.de RAFAEL

CENTRE DE PHYSIQUE THEORIQUE
Section II
C.N.R.S. - LUMINY - CASE 907
F - 13288 MARSEILLE - CEDEX9

These comments are based on talks the author has given at recent workshops in Dubrovnik, Santa-Barbara, DESY and Vienna.

The main subject of my talk at the Dubrovnik Conference and at recent workshops has been Gaussian-like sum rules in QCD and local duality. I have been reporting on work in progress at the time done in collaboration with Reinhold Bertlmann and Guy Launer which has now appeared in preprint form [1].This preprint gives a rather technical description of our work. Therefore, here, I shall limit myself to a few qualitative comments with the hope that they will clarify the perspective on some aspects of the so-called QCD sum rules.

1 Duality of two-point functions.

Formally, the kind of object one is dealing with are two-point functions like:

$$\Pi(q^2) = i \int d^4 x\, e^{iq.x} \langle 0 | T(J(x),\, J(0)^+) | 0 \rangle , \tag{1.1}$$

where $J(x)$ denotes a composite local operator of quark and gluon fields with specified quantum numbers. Ever since the advent of QCD, there has been a lot of effort to find ways of relating the behaviour of two-point functions like (1.1) in the deep euclidean region, where the theory makes firm predictions, to the properties of the resonances and multihadron states which the operator $J(x)$ can extract from the vacuum.

The battle horse of this relationship is the dispersion relation :

$$\Pi(q^2) = \int_0^{\infty} ds \frac{1}{s-q^2-i\epsilon} \frac{1}{\pi} \operatorname{Im} \Pi(s) + \text{substractions}, \tag{1.2}$$

which follows from the analyticity properties of two-point functions like (1.1). This relation can be regarded as a global duality relation[1)] in the sense that the weighted average of the hadronic spectral function $1/\pi \operatorname{Im} \Pi(s)$ in the r.h.s.(which up to kinematical factors is a total cross-section) for sufficiently large space-like q^2-values, must match $\Pi(q^2)$ in the l.h.s. which up to subtractions is a calculable quantity in QCD.

Various forms of duality sum rules which follow more or less directly from eq.(1.2) have been proposed in the literature:

a) Moment Sum Rules [3],[4]: ($Q^2 = q^2 > 0$)

$$(1.3) \qquad (-1)^N \frac{d^N}{(d\,Q^2)^N} \Pi(q^2) = \int_0^{\infty} ds \frac{N!}{(s+Q^2)^{N+1}} \frac{1}{\pi} \mathrm{Im}\,\Pi(s) \;;$$

with N $\gtrsim$ than the number of substractions required in (1.2).

b) Lorentz-type Sum Rules [5]

$$(1.4) \qquad F(\hat{s},\Delta) = \int_0^{\infty} ds \frac{1}{(s-\hat{s})^2 + \Delta^2} \frac{1}{\pi} \mathrm{Im}\,\Pi(s) \;;$$

proposed for the comparison between $e^+ e^- \to$ Hadrons data and QCD;

c) Finite Energy Sum Rules [6] :

$$(1.5) \qquad \Sigma(s_0, n) = \int_0^{s_0} ds\; s^n \frac{1}{\pi} \mathrm{Im}\,\Pi(s) \;;$$

d) Laplace transform (Borel transform; exponential moment) Sum Rules [7],[8] :

$$(1.6) \qquad \mathcal{M}(\sigma) = \int_0^{\infty} ds\; e^{-s\sigma} \frac{1}{\pi} \mathrm{Im}\,\Pi(s) \;.$$

In all these sum rules the l.h.s. is evaluated by theory and compared to phenomenological input in the r.h.s.

Following the original ideas developped by Shifman, Vainshtein and Zakharov in the first of the papers quoted in ref.[7], there has been a lot of effort to improve on a purely QCD perturbative evaluation of the l.h.s. of eqs.like (1.3) to (1.6). These authors have proposed to use the Wilson's operator product expansion [9] of the time ordered product in eq.(1.1) to parametrize non-perturbative effects due to the confining nature of the QCD vacuum which at short-distances appear as power corrections to the asymptotic freedom behaviour. More precisely, the coefficients of these power corrections are products of short-distance terms, the Wilson-coefficients, calculable within perturbation theory, times vacuum expectation values (v.e.v.) of local operators like $\bar{\psi}\psi$, the so-called quark vacuum condensate; $\alpha_s\ \vec{G}^{\mu\nu}.\vec{G}_{\mu\nu}$ the so-called gluon condensate; and v.e.v.'s of local operator of higher dimensionality. These vaccum condensates are phenomenological parameters governed by the long distance properties of QCD and their values, which are not known a priori, have to be extracted from some phenomenological input. However, once they are fixed they should be the same -but for questions of renormalization invariance which can be dealt with [10]- in all the sum rules.This semiphenomenological parametrization of non-perturbative corrections to the asymptotic freedom behaviour of two-point functions like (1.1) is now commonly refered to as the SVZ-approach and has been applied to a large variety of two-point functions.

In practice only two or three of these non-perturbative power terms are retained in the evaluation of the sum rules, and the method used to make predictions varies from author to author. The source of the difficulties is twofold: on the one hand there is a problem of choice of an optimal range where to fix the scale which inevitably appears in every sum rule -like Q^2 in eq.(1.3) or σ in eq.(1.6)- so that the theoretical input is sensitive to the calculated power corrections, but not too sensitive to the unknown higher powers. On the other hand, there is the problem of the dependance of the prediction one is trying to make on the particular phenomenological ansatz made for the corresponding spectral function -usually a δ-function at the first resonance position plus an hadronic asymptotic freedom continuum starting at some threshold. In spite of these difficulties SVZ, using their method [2)], found rather impressive results in their early work quoted in ref.[7]; and more recently, another group of authors [3)] even claims to be able to reproduce many of the known masses and couplings of both light and heavy quark systems to an accuracy often better than 10% !

In our work of ref.[1] we propose to use a new type of sum rules which appear to us as a good framework to formulate quantitatively the idea of local duality; and at the same time are useful to check the consistency between phenomenological input and predictions in the SVZ-approach. They are sum rules based on the Gauss-Weierstrass transform of spectral functions :

(1.7)

$$G(\hat{s},\tau) = \frac{1}{\sqrt{4\pi\tau}} \int_0^{\infty} ds \, \exp\left(-\frac{(s-\hat{s})^2}{4\tau}\right) \frac{1}{\pi} \, \mathrm{Im}\, \Pi(s) ,$$

i.e. the convolution of the spectral function with a gaussian centered at an arbitrary value $\hat{s}$ with a finite width $\sqrt{2\tau}$ resolution. Formally, in the limit $\tau = 0$ the gaussian weight becomes a δ-function and $G(\hat{s},0)$ coincides with the spectral function $1/\pi \, \mathrm{Im}\, \Pi(s)$. In QCD the parameter τ which has dimensions of a mass to the fourth power is the short-distance scale analogous to $1/\sigma$ in the Laplace transform (1.6) and Q^2 in the dispersion relation ; i.e., τ has to be kept moderatly large ($\tau \gtrsim 1$ GeV^4) so that $G(\hat{s},\tau)$ can be evaluated within perturbation theory to asymptotic freedom. Non-perturbative corrections à la SVZ can also be incorporated. Here they appear as inverse powers in $2\sqrt{\tau}$ times Hermite polynomial in the variable $s/2\sqrt{\tau}$ times $\exp(-\hat{s}^2/4\tau)$. In ref. [1] we have shown how $G(\hat{s},\tau)$ can be explicitly calculated from the QCD expression for the two-point function $\Pi(q^2)$ in (1.1) and/or the Laplace transform $\mathcal{M}(\sigma)$ in (1.6).

The Gauss-Weierstrass transform $G(\hat{s},\tau)$ is dual to the spectral function $1/\pi \, \mathrm{Im}\, \Pi(s)$ in the sense that the more we know about QCD the sharper we can take our gaussians (i.e., τ smaller) and the more accurately $G(\hat{s},\tau)$ should approximate the physical spectrum. There is also an interesting analogy between hadronic gaussian sum rules and the theory of the heat equation, which has been developped in [1]. The analogy is based on the observation that $G(\hat{s},\tau)$ obeys the differential equation

$$\frac{\partial^2 G(s,\tau)}{(\partial s)^2} = \frac{\partial G(s,\tau)}{\partial \tau} \,, \tag{1.8}$$

which is the one-dimensional heat equation if we re-interpret s as a "position" variable and τ as a "time" variable. In this analogy, the hadronic spectral function $1/\pi \, \mathrm{Im}\, \Pi(s)$ corresponds to the initial heat distribution in a semiinfinite rod $0 \leq s \leq \infty$ and $G(\hat{s},\tau)$ measures the evolution in time τ of the heat distribution in this rod. This provides a good framework to check the consistency between a given phenomenological ansatz for the spectral function and a specific choice of vacuum condensate parameters in QCD : after a time τ ($\tau \gtrsim 1$ Gev^4) the predicted QCD heat distribution $G(\hat{s},\tau)_{QCD}$ should match the evolution of the phenomenological ansatz ; i.e. for $\tau \gtrsim 1$ GeV^4

$$G(\hat{s},\tau)_{QCD} = \frac{1}{\sqrt{4\pi\tau}} \int_0^\infty ds \, \exp\left(-\frac{(s-\hat{s})^2}{4\tau}\right) \frac{1}{\pi} \, \mathrm{Im}\, \Pi(s)_{PHEN}. \tag{1.9}$$

We call this the <u>Heat evolution test</u>.

Several authors have proposed to use the SVZ-approach within the framework of finite energy sum rules [16]. In our heat equation analogy these sum rules follow from the principle of conservation of the total heat :

$$(1.10) \qquad \int_{-\infty}^{+\infty} ds\, G(s,\tau) = \int_{0}^{\infty} ds\, \frac{1}{\pi}\, \mathrm{Im}\, \Pi(s)$$

at all τ-values ; and the property that in QCD, asymptotically in $\hat{s}$ we have that [1] : for finite $\tau \gtrsim 1\ \mathrm{GeV}^4$,

$$(1.11) \qquad \lim_{s \gg \sqrt{\tau}} G(s,\tau) = \frac{1}{\pi}\, \mathrm{Im}\, \Pi(s) \quad .$$

We have been able to rederive in this way finite energy sum rules like (1.5) explicitly showing the way that perturbative corrections modify them. The picture which clearly emerges from these sum rules is that v.e.v.'s of local operators are dual to a <u>mixture</u> of resonance parameters and the hadronic continuum ; and not to the resonance parameters alone.

2 - The SVZ-approach and Quantum Field Theory

Field theorists would like to have a better understanding of the SVZ-approach. Here, the question is whether the factorization of successive power corrections into Wilson coefficients which are calculated perturbatively and non-perturbative vacuum expectation values of local operators is meaningful to all orders of perturbation theory. Gupta and Quinn [17] have analyzed this question within a scalar Φ^4-theory with spontaneous symmetry breaking due to a negative mass term. They calculate the large q^2-behaviour of the propagator from the operator product expansion in two ways : i) around the perturbative vacuum ; ii) around the physical vacuum and claim to obtain different answers, i.e., i) $\neq$ ii). The same analysis has been re-examined by Taylor and McClain [18] who, contrary to the previous claim, find that with a consistent use of the BPHZ substraction procedure one gets i) = ii).

More recently the SVZ-approach has been analyzed in the two-dimensional O(N) non-linear σ-model by David [19]. In his second paper [19b] -which corrects his previous one [19a] - it is claimed that v.e.v.'s of local operators are ambiguous because of poles at $Re\epsilon > o$($d = 4-\epsilon$ regularization). Only operators protected by a symmetry such that they are logarithmically U.V. divergent at most, are free from such ambiguities.

Other papers that I have seen on the SVZ-approach in quantum field theory models with more or less strong claims are listed in refs. [20]. It is not clear what to conclude from all these papers (ref. [17] to ref. [20a]). Obviously one must await further careful work in this direction.My own feeling is that a well-defined prescription should emerge from the analyses of field theory models. This feeling is based on the following naive observations :

i) The explicit calculations done so far in QCD are rather intricate ; yet once a renormalization scheme has been chosen, there are no ambiguities. Several calculations by now have been done by different people in different ways with the same results [4)].

ii) I fail to understand why α_s $\langle G^2 \rangle$ should be ill-defined as claimed by David in ref. [19b]. In the chiral limit $\beta(\alpha_s)/4$ $\langle \vec{G}^{\mu\nu}.\vec{G}_{\mu\nu} \rangle$ is precisely the energy-momentum trace anomaly. I would then conclude that this operator must be protected by dilatation invariance. In another context, Kenneth Johnson has recently derived an interesting sum rule which in principle could be taken as a way to measure α_s $\langle G^2 \rangle$. The sum rule states that [21]

$$(2.1) \qquad \frac{m_\eta^2 F_\eta^2}{6} + \int_0^{m^{*2}} \frac{dm^2}{m^2}\, \sigma(m^2) =$$

$$= \frac{1}{64\pi^2}\, \alpha_s^2(m^{*2})(m^{*2})^2 + \frac{1}{16\,\pi}\, \alpha_s(m^{*2})\, \langle \frac{\alpha}{\pi} G^2 \rangle_{REN.}$$

where m_η is the η-mass ; F_η the η-to-vacuum coupling constant and $\sigma(m^2)$ denotes the spectral function associated to a two-point function like (1.1) with

$$J(x) = \frac{\alpha_s}{8\pi}\, \epsilon^{\mu\nu\rho\sigma} \sum_A G_{\mu\rho}^{(A)}(x)\, G_{\rho\sigma}^{(A)}(x) \quad ,$$

a good renormalization invariant operator.

iii) To a good approximation -good enough for phenomenological purposes - the combination of v.e.v.'s of local operators appearing in the successive $1/Q^2$ - powers in the SVZ-approach can always be defined in terms of finite energy sum rules involving integrals of physical spectral functions. In a way eq.(2.1) is one such example.

This last comment brings me to the next subject that I wish to discuss here : the relation between the SVZ-approach and the old Weinberg sum rules in current algebra.

3 - The Weinberg Sum Rules in the light of the SVZ-approach

The Weinberg sum rules were derived in 1967, [22] prior to the development of QCD. They follow from superconvergence requirements at the chiral limit of the two-point functions [5]

$$W^{\mu\nu}(q) = i\int d^4x\, e^{iq\cdot x}\langle 0 \mid T(L^{\mu}(x), R^{\nu}(0)^{+}) \mid 0 \rangle \quad .$$

where $L^{\mu}(x)$ and $R^{\mu}(x)$ are left and right quark bilinear currents which mix charge 2/3 type quarks with charge - 1/3 type quarks. In terms of vector and axial vector spectral functions $\mathrm{Im}\,\Pi_{V,A}^{(1)}$; $\mathrm{Im}\,\Pi_{V,A}^{(0)}$ with angular momentum J = 1 and 0 they read as follows :

(3.1) 1st rule :

$$\int_0^{\infty} ds(\mathrm{Im}\,\Pi_V^{(1)}(s) + \mathrm{Im}\,\Pi_V^{(0)} - \mathrm{Im}\,\Pi_A^{(1)} - \mathrm{Im}\,\Pi_A^{(0)}) = 0 \quad ;$$

(3.2) 2nd rule : $$\int_0^{\infty} ds\; s(\mathrm{Im}\,\Pi_V^{(1)}(s) - \mathrm{Im}\,\Pi_A^{(1)}(s)) = 0 \quad ;$$

(3.3) 3rd rule : $$\int_0^{\infty} ds\; s(\mathrm{Im}\,\Pi_V^{(0)}(s) - \mathrm{Im}\,\Pi_A^{(0)}(s)) = 0 \quad .$$

In the case of strangeness conserving currents, saturation of (3.1) and (3.2) with the low lying states, always in the chiral limit ($m_\pi^2 \longrightarrow 0$), gives the results

(3.4) 1st rule : $$\frac{M_\rho^2}{2\gamma_\rho^2} - \frac{M_{A_1}^{\;2}}{2\gamma_{A_1}^2} = 2f_\pi^{\;2} \quad ;$$

and

(3.5) 2nd rule : $$M_\rho^2\,\frac{M_\rho^2}{2\gamma_\rho^2} - M_{A_1}^{\;2}\,\frac{M_{A_1}^{\;2}}{2\gamma_{A_1}^2} = 0 \;,$$

where f_π = 92.3 MeV and γ_ρ is the ρ-coupling constant related to its electronic width by the relation

(3.6) $$\Gamma(\rho \rightarrow e^+e^-) = \frac{2}{3}\,\pi\alpha^2\,\frac{M_\rho}{2\gamma_\rho^{\;2}} \quad .$$

Solving for M_A in terms of M_ρ, γ_ρ and f_π and using the Rosenfeld table values we find

$$M_{A_1} \quad 1266 \text{ MeV} \tag{3.7}$$

to be compared to the experimental value

$$(M_{A_1})_{exp} = 1275 \pm 30 \text{ MeV} \tag{3.8}$$

I wish to emphasize that the result in eq.(3.7) can now be viewed as a QCD prediction in the SVZ-approach. I shall explain this briefly to illustrate the compatibility of the SVZ-approach with current algebra [6]).

The idea of a quark-condensate $\langle\bar\psi\psi\rangle$ already appears in the Gell-Mann, Oakes, Renner picture [24] of spontaneous chiral symmetry breaking via the relation

$$(m_u + m_d)\ \langle\bar\psi_u\psi_u + \bar\psi_d\psi_d\rangle \simeq -2f_\pi^{\ 2}\ m_\pi^{\ 2} \quad . \tag{3.9}$$

This relation follows from a current algebra Ward identity relating two two-point functions like (1.1) [one where J(x) $\equiv A^\mu(x) = \bar{u}(x)\gamma_\mu\gamma_5\, d(x)$; the other with $J(x) \equiv \partial_\mu A^\mu(x)$] ; and PCAC. The existence of such a quark-condensate automatically implies power corrections like $m\langle\bar\psi\psi\rangle/Q^4$ at short-distances and the SVZ-appraoch gives a precise recipe to compute them. In the particular case of the 1st-Weinberg sum rule the pattern of short-distance behaviour in increasing powers of $1/Q^2$ is as follows : the leading $1/Q^2$ term is the one induced by explicit breaking of chiral symmetry via quark mass terms in the QCD-Lagrangean. As first pointed out in ref. [6c] this term is quadratic in the quark masses and proportional to α_s . The next-to-leading term in powers of $1/Q^2$ is induced by $m\langle\bar\psi\psi\rangle$ and is also proportional to α_s [23b]. Both these $1/Q^2$ and $1/Q^4$ corrections vanish in the chiral limit $m_q \longrightarrow 0$ and the leading behaviour is then $O(1/Q^6)$ with a coefficient governed by a new type of v.e.v., the condensate of four quarks in the vacuum $\langle\bar\psi\,\Gamma_1\,\psi\,\bar\psi\,\Gamma_2\,\psi\rangle$ which appears naturally in the SVZ-approach [7]. It is precisely due to this $1/Q^6$ behaviour that the Weinberg sum rules at the chiral limit converge well enough to justify the validity of eqs.(3.1) and (3.2) and therefore, to the extent that the up and down quark masses are small, the prediction in eq.(3.7).

4- Light-quark masses

The first serious attempt to estimate the absolute values of the current algebra quark masses was made by Leutwyler [25] in 1974, i.e., at the early stages of the development of QCD. He compared the matrix elements

$$\langle 0 | \partial_\mu A^\mu | \pi \rangle \qquad \text{and} \qquad \langle 0 | V^\mu_{I=1} | \rho \rangle$$

using SU(6)-symmetry to relate the Bethe-Salpeter wave functions of the π and the ρ , and obtained the nice result

$$(4.1) \qquad \frac{1}{2} (m_u + m_d) = \frac{2}{3} f_\pi \frac{m_\pi^2}{M_\rho^2} \gamma_\rho^2 \simeq 5.4 \text{ MeV} ,$$

where γ_ρ has been defined in eq. (3.6). Since then, there has been quite a lot of effort to find phenomenological relations like (4.1) within the framework of QCD. Here again, the SVZ-approach has proved to be useful in deriving quark-mass relations consistent with the standard picture of spontaneous chiral symmetry breaking [23a]. The two-point functions which are sensitive to the absolute size of light-quark masses are those involving current divergences. Laplace transform sum rules associated to the axial-vector current divergences, both strangeness changing and strangeness conserving have been studied in refs. [8a,b] and [26]; and more recently, the Laplace transform sum rules associated to the corresponding vector current divergences which are governed by the differences of quark masses $m_u - m_d$ and $m_u - m_s$ have also been studied in ref. [27]. The calculations in [8a,b] and [27] have been made at the two-loop level in perturbation theory and include the effect of the leading non-perturbative power corrections à la SVZ. The results, for a $\Lambda_{\overline{MS}} \simeq 100$ MeV, and in terms of invariant quark masses [7] are the following

$$(4.2a) \qquad m_{up} = 6.2 \pm 1.5 \text{ MeV}$$

$$(4.2b) \qquad m_{down} = 14.8 \pm 3.6 \text{ MeV}$$

$$(4.2c) \qquad m_{strange} = 266 \pm 64 \text{ MeV}$$

where the source of the quoted errors comes from a generous estimate of the possible effects due to higher order corrections. The consistency of these results has now been checked at the three-loop level [29].

A good determination of the light-quark masses is crucial, among other things, to extract the value of the quark-condensate $\langle\bar{\psi}\psi\rangle$ from the PCAC relation in eq. (3.9). This is an important parameter to determine specially in connection with the application of the SVZ-approach to the baryon sector [30].

5 - Positivity constraints of the Laplace-transform of spectral functions

In this last comment I wish to prove a more or less trivial theorem which may be useful in certain phenomenological applications of QCD sum rules. It concerns the function

$$\mathcal{R}(\sigma) = -\frac{d}{d\sigma} \log \mathcal{M}(\sigma) \quad , \tag{5.1}$$

where $\mathcal{M}(\sigma)$ is the Laplace-transform in eq.(1.6) :

$$\mathcal{M}(\sigma) = \int_0^\infty ds\ e^{-s\sigma}\ \frac{1}{\pi}\ \mathrm{Im}\ \Pi(s) \quad ,$$

and it can be generalized to other types of transforms as well. The function $\mathcal{R}(\sigma)$, in the form given in eq.(5.1), has been introduced by Bell and Bertlmann [8c], who have extensively studied it within the framework of potential models. It corresponds to the ratio of exponential moments

$$\mathcal{R}(\sigma) = \frac{\int ds\ e^{-s\sigma}\ s\ \frac{1}{\pi}\ \mathrm{Im}\ \Pi(s)}{\int ds\ e^{-s\sigma}\ \frac{1}{\pi}\ \mathrm{Im}\ \Pi(s)} \quad . \tag{5.2}$$

which is one of the quantities proposed by SVZ as a potentially sensitive way of exploring the mass of the lowest lying resonance contributing to $1/\pi\ \mathrm{Im}\Pi(s)$. In practice we know how to calculate the asymptotic behaviour of $\mathcal{R}(\sigma)$ for $\sigma \longrightarrow 0$ thanks to the asymptotic freedom property of QCD. It is not difficult to see that in this regime $\mathcal{R}(\sigma)$ has the general behaviour

$$\mathcal{R}(\sigma) \simeq \frac{d+1}{\sigma}\ (1 + \ldots) \quad , \tag{5.3}$$

where d is the asymptotic power behaviour in s, for $s \longrightarrow \infty$, of the corresponding spectral function. (For example d = 0 in the case where J(x) in (1.1) is the vector-isovector current.) This dependence in d is the only reminiscence left from the substractions needed in the dispersion relation for the initial two-point function. The dots in (5.3) correspond to peturbative corrections ; quark mass corrections ; and non-perturbative power corrections. Ideally, we want the behaviour of $\mathcal{R}(\sigma)$ for $\sigma \longrightarrow \infty$, since it is hoped that as $\sigma \longrightarrow \infty$

$$(5.4)\qquad M_R^2 \simeq \lim_{\sigma \to \infty} \mathcal{R}(\sigma)$$

The question is how to extrapolate from the knowledge of the dots in eq. (5.3) to the ground state. It is clear that in this respect any "dot indepent" information on the behaviour of the function $\mathcal{R}(\sigma)$ from the regime $\sigma \to 0$ in (5.3) to the regime $\sigma \to \infty$ should be welcomed. The following theorem is a first step in this direction :

THEOREM : $1/\pi\ \mathrm{Im}\Pi(s) \geqslant 0$ in eq. (5.2) implies that $-\log \mathcal{M}(\sigma)$ must be a concave function in the variable σ i.e., the slope of the curve $\mathcal{R}(\sigma)$ must always be negative or zero.

<u>PROOF</u>

The proof is based on the fact that for a positive spectral function $1/\pi\ \mathrm{Im}\Pi(s) > 0$, the matrix

$$(5.5)\qquad A(\sigma)_{M,N} = \int_0^\infty ds\ e^{-s\sigma}\ s^{M+N}\ \frac{1}{\pi}\ \mathrm{Im}\ \Pi(s) \equiv \mathcal{M}^{(M+N)}(\sigma)$$

of exponential moments ; $M,N = 0,1,2,\ldots$ is a positive definite matrix. Indeed, for arbitrary real numbers ξ_N, we have

$$(5.6)\qquad \sum_{N,M} \xi_N\ \xi_M\ A(\sigma)_{M,N} \geq 0 \quad .$$

It follows then, in particular, that

$$(5.7)\qquad \det \begin{vmatrix} A(\sigma)_{0,0} & A(\sigma)_{0,1} \\ A(\sigma)_{1,0} & A(\sigma)_{1,1} \end{vmatrix} \geq 0\ ;$$

i.e.,

$$(5.8)\qquad \mathcal{M}^{(2)}(\sigma)\ \mathcal{M}(\sigma) - \mathcal{M}^{(1)}(\sigma)\ \mathcal{M}^{(1)}(\sigma) \geq 0\ ;$$

but this is precisely the necessary and sufficient condition for the convexity of $\log \mathfrak{M}(\sigma)$, since

$$(5.9) \qquad \frac{d^2}{(d\sigma)^2} \log \mathfrak{M}(\sigma) = - \frac{d}{d\sigma} \mathfrak{R}(\sigma) =$$

$$= \frac{\mathfrak{M}^{(2)}(\sigma)\, \mathfrak{M}(\sigma) - \mathfrak{M}^{(1)}(\sigma)\, \mathfrak{M}^{(1)}(\sigma)}{(\mathfrak{M}(\sigma))^2} .$$

There is a much simpler proof of this theorem which I found while reading the excellent Einstein biography that Pais has offered to the scientific community (see section 4c of ref. [31]) : equation (5.2) can be viewed as the equilibrium "energy" $\langle s \rangle$ of a system with variable energy s in thermal equilibrium with a second system at "temperature" $1/\sigma$. In this analogy $1/\pi \,\mathrm{Im}\, \Pi(s)$ is the density of states with energy s ; and eq. (5.9) is nothing but the mean square "energy" fluctuation

$$(5.10) \qquad \langle \delta^2 \rangle \equiv \langle (s - \langle s \rangle)^2 \rangle = \langle s^2 \rangle - \langle s \rangle^2 ,$$

obviously a positive definite quantity.

FOOTNOTES

1) For a detailed discussion of duality where many references can be found see e.g. the review of article in ref. [2].

2) Other methods have been recently severely criticized by SVZ and their collaborators in ref. [13]. See however the replies in refs. [14] and [15].

3) See the talk of Hector Rubinstein in these proceedings where many references to the "successful" literature can be found.

4) So far, the most sophisticated calculations in this domain are those made by Nikolaev and Radyushkin [11] who have evaluated the Wilson coefficients of gluonic operators of dimension 6 and 8 appearing in the charmonium two-point function. See also refs. [12].

5) The reader unfamiliar with the Weinberg sum rules may find helpful to look at ref. [6c] where a modern version of these sum rules within the context of perturbative QCD, is discussed.

6) For complementary details to the discussion which follows below see refs. [23].

7) The relation between the invariant mass $\hat{m}$ in the MS-scheme and the running mass $\overline{m}(M^2)$, at the one-loop level is

$$\overline{m}(M^2) = \hat{m}/(\frac{1}{2}\log\frac{M^2}{\Lambda^2})^{2/-\beta_1}\ , \text{ where}$$

$$\beta_1 = -\frac{11}{2} + \frac{1}{3}n_f \quad ,$$

n_f is the number of flavours. For details see e.g. ref. [28].

REFERENCES

[1] R.A. BERTLMANN, G. LAUNER and E. de RAFAEL, Gaussian sum rules in Quantum Chromodynamics, CPT-Preprint P.1586 Marseille, 1984.

[2] R.A. BERTLMANN, Acta Phys.Austriaca 53,305 (1981).

[3a] T.W. APPELQUIST and H.D. POLITZER, Phys. Rev. D12, 1404 (1975).

[3b] F.J. YNDURAIN, Phys. Lett. 66B, 181 (1977).

[4] V.A. NOVIKOV, L.B. OKUN, M.A. SHIFMAN, A.I. VAINSHTEIN, M.B. VOLOSHIN and V.I. ZAKHAROV, Phys. Rep. 41, 1 (1981).

[5] E.C. POGGIO, H.R. QUINN and S. WEINBERG, Phys. Rev. D13, 1958 (1976).

[6a] R. SHANKAR, Phys. Rev. D15, 755 (1977).

[6b] K. CHETYRKIN, N. KRASNIKOV and A. TAVKELIDZE, Phys. Letters 76B, 83 (1978).

[6c] E. FLORATOS, S. NARISON and E. de RAFAEL Nucl. Phys. B155, 115 (1979).

[6d] J.J. SAKURAI, K. SCHILCHER and M.D. TRAN, Phys. Letters 102B, 55 (1981).

[7] M.A. SHIFMAN, A.I. VAINSHTEIN and V.I. ZAKHAROV, Nucl. Phys. B147, 385, 448, 519 (1979).

[8a] S. NARISON and E. de RAFAEL, Phys. Letters 103B,57 (1981)

[8b] E. de RAFAEL, Current Algebra Quark Masses in QCD, Proceedings of the NSF-CNRS Joint Seminar on Recent Developments in QCD, CPT-81/P.1344 (1981).

[8c] J.S. BELL and R.A. BERTLMANN, Nucl. Phys. B177, 218 (1981); B187, 285 (1981).

[9] K.G. WILSON, Phys. Rev. 179, 1499 (1969).

[10a] R. TARRACH, Nucl. Phys. B196, 45 (1982).

[10b] S. NARISON and R. TARRACH, Phys. Letters 125B, 217 (1983)

[11] S.N. NIKOLAEV and A.V.RADYUSHKIN, Phys. Letters 110B, 476 (1982) ; 116B, 469 (1982) ; 124B, 243 (1983) and Nucl. Phys. B213,285 (1983).

[12a] W. HUBSCHMID and S. MALLIK, Nucl. Phys. B207,29 (1982).

[12b] S.C. GENERALIS and D.J. BROADHURST, The Heavy-Quark expansion and QCD Sum Rules for light Quarks; Preprint OUT-4102-10 (1983).

[13] V.A. NOVIKOV, M.A. SHIFMAN, A.I. VAINSHTEIN, M.B. VOLOSHIN and V.I. ZAKHAROV, Use and misuse of QCD Sum Rules, factorization and related topics; ITEP Preprint-71, Moscow 1983.

[14] A. ZALEWSKA and K. ZALEWSKI, On the interpretation of the non-perturbative parameter obtained by applying the SVZ sum rules to heavy quarkonia; TPJU-Preprint 17/83, Kraköw, 1983.

[15] J.S. BELL and R.A. BERTLMANN,SVZ Moments for Charmonium and potential models ; CERN Preprint TH-3769, 1983.

[16a] N.V. KRASNIKOV, A.A. PIVOVAROV and N.N. TAVKHELIDZE, The use of finite energy sum rules for the description of the hadronic properties of QCD, CERN-Preprint TH-3422 (1983).

[16b] T. TRUONG, Phys. Letters 117B, 109 (1982).

[16c] A.L. KATAEV, N.V. KRASNIKOV, A.A. PIVOVAROV, Phys. Letters 123B, 93 (1983).

[17] S. GUPTA and H.R. QUINN, Phys. Rev. D26, 499 (1982) ; D27, 980 (1983).

[18] C. TAYLOR and B. Mc CLAIN, The operator product expansion and the asymptotic behaviour of spontaneously broken scalar field theories, MIT-Preprint-CTP-1069 (1983).

[19a] F. DAVID, Nucl. Phys. B209, 433 (1982).

[19b] F. DAVID, On the ambiguity of composite operators, I.R. re normalons and the status of the operator product expansion Saclay Preprint, SPh-T/83-59 (1983).

[20a] F.V. TKACHOV, Phys. Letters 125, 85 (1983).

[20b] A.I. VAINSHTEIN, V.I. ZAKHAROV, V.A. NOVIKOV and M.A. SHIFMAN, Low energy theorems, operator product expansion and all that in σ-models and QCD (in russian), ITEP-Preprint No 64c,I-56 (1983).

[20c] M. SOLDATE, Operator product expansions in the massless Schwinger model, SLAC-Preprint-PUB-3054 (1983).

[20d] A.A. PIVOVAROV, N.N. TAVKHELIDZE and V.F. TOKAREV, Phys. Letters 132B, 402 (1983).

[21] K. JOHNSON, the M.I.T. bag model in the context of QCD, MIT-Preprint-CTP-1101 (1983).

[22] S. WEINBERG, Phys. Rev. Letters 18, 507 (1967).

[23a] C. BECCHI, S. NARISON, E. de RAFAEL and F.J. YNDURAIN, Z. Phys. C. - Particles and Fields 8, 335 (1981).

[23b] P. PASCUAL and E. de RAFAEL, Z. Phys.C.-Particles and Fields, 12, 127 (1982).

[24] M. GELL-MANN, R.J. OAKES and B. RENNER, Phys. Rev. 175, 2195 (1968).

[25] H. LEUTWYLER, Nucl. Phys. B76, 413 (1974).

[26] J. GASSER and H. LEUTWYLER, Phys. Reports, 87, 77 (1982).

[27] S. NARISON, N. PAVER, E. de RAFAEL and D. TRELEANI, Nucl. Phys. B212, 365 (1983).

[28] E. de RAFAEL, Lectures at the GIFT seminar on Quantum Chromodynamics, Jaca (Spain), June 1979. Lecture Notes in Physics, Vol. 118, J.L. Alonso and R. Tarrach eds. Berlin, Heidelberg, New York : Springer 1980.

[29] S.G. GORISHNY, A.L. KATAEV and S.A. LARIN, Next-Next-to-leading perturbative QCD corrections and light quark Masses. Dubna-Preprint E2-83-533 (1983).

[30a] B.L. IOFFE, Nucl. Phys. B188, 317 (1981) ; (erratum : B191, 591 (1981)).

[30b] Y. CHUNG, H.G. DOSCH, M. KREMER and D. SCHALL, Phys. Letters 102B, 175 (1981) ; Nucl. Phys. B197, 55 (1982).

[30c] D. ESPRIU, P. PASCUAL and R. TARRACH Nucl. Phys. B214, 285 (1983).

[30d] V.M. BELYAEV and B.L. IOFFE, ITEP-Preprints-59 and 132, Moscow 1982.

[31] Abraham PAIS, The Science and the life of Albert Einstein, Clarendon Press-Oxford University Press (1982)

CONSTRAINTS ON K^o-$\overline{K^o}$ MIXING FROM QCD SUM RULES

Branko Guberina

Rudjer Bošković Institute
41001 Zagreb, P.O.B. 1016
Croatia, Yugoslavia

1. K_L-K_S Mass Difference

With the advent of gauge theories, GUTs, SUSY, and composite models, the calculation of the K_L-K_S mass difference has become a crucial test for these theories. In the enlarged version of the standard model, the six-quark Kobayashi-Maskawa (K-M) scheme, CP violation appears to be due to an arbitrary phase in the K-M mixing matrix. Theoretically, the K_L-K_S mass difference is due to K^o-$\bar{K}^o$ mixing and presumably dominated by the contributions of the box diagram[1]. This contribution essentially picks up the short distance part because of the large masses of the two W's which squeeze not only the W propagators, but also the q u a r k propagators to a point. Assuming this is the case, it is possible to calculate QCD corrections in a perturbative way[2,3]. Unfortunately, the box diagram contains the whole physics only in the limit $m_W \to \infty$ and since the W's have a finite, although large mass, the K^o-$\bar{K}^o$ mixing could be influenced by long-distance effects[4].

The expression for the m_L-m_S difference takes the form[3,5]

$$m_L - m_S = \left(\frac{G_F^2}{16\pi^2}\right) \mathcal{M} \; \Phi(\theta_i, \delta, m_j, m_{Higgs}, \eta_k) \;, \tag{1}$$

where Φ is a function of K-M angles and phase, θ_i and δ, quark masses m_j, Higgs mass m_H, and QCD coefficients η_k.

$$\mathcal{M} = \langle \bar{K}^o | O_{\Delta S=2} | K^o \rangle \tag{2}$$

with $O_{\Delta S=2}$ being the local operator of the form

$$O_{\Delta S=2} = (\bar{s}^i_L \gamma_\mu d^i_L)(\bar{s}^j_L \gamma^\mu d^j_L) \equiv J_\mu J^\mu \quad . \tag{3}$$

Here i and j are color indices, and $q_L \equiv \frac{1}{2}(1-\gamma_5)q$.

Provided $\mathcal{M}$ could be calculated reliably, the experimentally measured m_L-m_S difference puts severe constraints on the unknown parameters, such as t-quark mass and/or K-M angles and phases. Therefore, the K_L-K_S mass difference appears as a sensitive parameter to test new physical ideas and a spectacular example of this is the estimate of the charmed-quark mass[1).

2. Calculation of $\langle\bar{K}^o|O_{\Delta S=2}|K^o\rangle$

Since the hard-gluonic corrections are factorized in (1), one is tempted to insert the complete set of physical states in the product of currents (3):

$$\mathcal{M} = \sum_n \int \frac{d^3p'}{(2\pi)^3} \langle\bar{K}^o|J_\mu|n(p')\rangle\langle n(p')|J^\mu|K^o\rangle = B\,\frac{2}{3}\,f_K^2 m_K^2 \qquad (4)$$

and saturate it with the lowest one, the vacuum[1)], for which $B = 1$. In fact, vacuum saturation has been widely used, although the smallness of other contributions is questionable. Besides, the problem of double counting arises because hard gluons and, say, pions cannot contribute simultaneously for x smaller than some scale $1/\mu$. This means that the one-particle state contributions in (4) should be cut off at $p' \sim \mu$. The precise value of μ is unknown; however, one may try to extract it from, say, the $K^+ \to \pi^+\pi^-$ decay. This decay proceeds through the operator $O_{\Delta I=3/2}$, which transforms as 27 under $SU(3)_{flavor}$, as does $O_{\Delta S=2}$. Actually, assuming SU(3) symmetry, the following relation holds:

$$\langle\bar{K}^o|O_{\Delta S=2}|K^o\rangle = \sqrt{2}\,\langle\pi^o|O_{\Delta I=3/2}|K^o\rangle\ . \qquad (5)$$

One expects that the continuum contributions in (4) will be suppressed[6)] owing to the fact that Regge meson trajectories for 27 are "exotic". Fixing μ for the K^+ decay provides us with a cutoff needed in the calculation of (4). This has been done recently[7)], with a result $B = 1.25$-1.65. It is interesting to note that the r.h.s. of eq. (5) is related to the experimental amplitude for the K^+ decay via PCAC. This fact was used[8)], assuming SU(3) symmetry, to get the value for $\mathcal{M}$ via relation (5), yielding $B \simeq 0.33$.

Instead of saturating the product of currents, one may directly calculate the matrix element of the four-quark operator in quark models, such as the MIT bag model or the harmonic oscillator (HO) model. The MIT bag calculation[9)], being very sensitive to bag parameters, turns out with a wrong sign[10)], and HO calculations[10)] vary in the range $B = 1.44$-2.86.

In summary, the different calculations give results for B which vary in the range from 0.3 to 2.8. The large uncertainties in the calculations are often due to wide cancellations, such as those in the MIT bag model[9,10)]. Large cancellations also appear in the approach of ref. 7, and the large SU(3) symmetry breaking in eq. (5) (which was used in ref. 8) might be expected from the fact that eq. (5) is badly satisfied when saturated with a vacuum.

3. QCD Sum Rules

Having in mind the variety of estimates for $\mathfrak{M}$ and uncertainties involved in calculations, it would be extremely useful to have at least a bound on $\mathfrak{M}$. Recently, an upper bound has been put[11] in the context of QCD sum rules. The method is based[12] on analyticity, unitarity, and general features of QCD. Essentially, the bound is of the form

$$|F(o)| \leq \mathcal{A}(Q^2) \ , \tag{6}$$

where $\langle \bar{K}^o | O_{\Delta S=2} | K^o \rangle$ can be viewed as a value at t = 0 of a scalar form factor F(t) which is a real analytic function in the complex t-plane with a branching cut $4m_K^2 \leq t < \infty$. The function $\mathcal{A}(Q^2)$ is obtained essentially from the two-point function

$$\psi(q^2) = i\int d^4x e^{iq\cdot x} \langle o| T(O_{\Delta S=2}(x)\ O^{\dagger}_{\Delta S=2}(o))|o\rangle \ , \tag{7}$$

with the absorptive part of ψ given by

$$\frac{1}{\pi} \text{Im}\ \psi(t) = \frac{1}{2\pi} \int\!\!\!\!\!\sum_{\Gamma} \langle o|O_{\Delta S=2}|\Gamma\rangle\langle\Gamma|O^{\dagger}_{\Delta S=2}|o\rangle (2\pi)^4 \delta(p-\sum p_{\Gamma}) \ , \tag{8}$$

where the sum extends over all intermediate states Γ with S = 2. Since each state gives a positive contribution, the particular one, $|K^oK^o\rangle$, sets the lower bound. The function (7) obeys a dispersion relation (up to an arbitrary polynomial of the fourth order). Taking five derivatives, one ends up with

$$\mathfrak{F}(Q^2) \equiv -\frac{\partial^5 \psi(q^2)}{(\partial Q^2)^5} = 5! \int_0^{\infty} dt \frac{1}{(t+Q^2)^6} \frac{1}{\pi} \text{Im}\ \psi(t)$$

$$\geq \frac{15}{4\pi^2} \int_{4m_K^2}^{\infty} dt \frac{1}{(t+Q^2)^6} \left(1 - \frac{4m_K^2}{t}\right)^{1/2} |F(t)|^2 \ , \tag{9}$$

where $Q^2 = -q^2$.

If $\mathfrak{F}(Q^2)$ is known, there is a n u p p e r b o u n d for $|F(o)|$!

This might be proved by using the Peierls inequality in (9):

$$\mathfrak{F}(Q^2) \geq (\exp \int_{t_o}^{\infty} d\mu \ln \rho)(\exp \int_{t_o}^{\infty} d\mu \ln|F(t)|^2) ,$$

where $d\mu(t)$ is a normalized measure

$$d\mu(t) = \frac{1}{\pi} \left(\frac{t_o}{t-t_o}\right)^{1/2} \frac{dt}{t}$$

such that $\int^{\infty} d\mu(t) = 1$. The quantity $\rho(t,Q^2)$ is positive definite t_o for $t \geq t_o$. Then the Jensen inequality for analytic functions gives

$$\mathfrak{F}(Q^2) \geq |F(o)|^2 \exp \int_{t_o}^{\infty} d\mu(t) \ln \rho(t,Q^2) ,$$

i.e., an upper bound

$$|F(o)| \leq \frac{2}{3} f_K^2 m_K^2 (t_o \mathfrak{F}(Q^2))^{1/2} \left(\frac{6\pi}{5}\right)^{1/2} \frac{t_o}{f_K^2} \left[1+\left(1+\frac{Q^2}{t_o}\right)^{1/2}\right]^6 . \tag{10}$$

We note that the Peierls inequality follows from the positivity of $\rho(t,Q^2)$. On the other hand, the Jensen inequality is satuarated if $F(t)$ has no zeros in the complex plane.

4. Calculation of $\mathfrak{F}(Q^2)$

The asymptotic contribution (high Q^2) can be easily calculated in perturbative QCD (Fig. 1a). Since our bound in (10) is valid for any Q^2, one could in principle use only the asymptotic contribution for Q^2 large enough. Unfortunately, because of the sixth power in (10), this gives a useless bound, so one is forced to go to lower values of Q^2. This makes troubles since the nonperturbative terms, such as $\langle o|F^2|o\rangle$ and $m_q\langle o|\bar\psi\psi|o\rangle$, although small in themselves, have large coefficients. Fortunately, there is a way how to estimate reliably a low-Q^2 contribution (Fig. 1b). Instead of calculating with quarks and gluons, one could calculate for low Q^2 directly with hadrons. The whole class of hadronic contributions, depicted in Fig. 1b, which are leading*) in the $1/N_c$ expansion could be easily written in terms of polarization tensors:

$$\psi(q^2) = -i \frac{1}{8} \int \frac{d^n k}{(2\pi)^n} \Pi_{\mu\nu}(k)\Pi^{\mu\nu}(k-q) . \tag{11}$$

*) We are not able to set a bound to the contributions neglected. It might be misleading to take for low Q^2 simply the color factor 1/3 which arises for the asymptotic-freedom diagrams.

Using the spectral representation for the two-point function

$$\Pi_{\mu\nu}(k) = (-g_{\mu\nu}k^2+k_\mu k_\nu)\Pi^{(1)}(k^2)+k_\mu k_\nu\Pi^{(o)}(k^2) \ , \tag{12}$$
$$\Pi^{(i)}(k^2) = \int_o^\infty dt \frac{1}{t-q^2-i\varepsilon} \frac{1}{\pi} \text{Im}\, \Pi^{(i)}(t), \quad i = 1,0,$$

and dimensional regularization, one is able to write a rather compact parametric representation for $\psi(q^2)$ and hence calculate $\mathfrak{F}(Q^2)$, which is regular in four dimensions. Insertion of the lowest hadronic contributions, i.e., the K pole and the $(K\pi)_{J=1}$ continuum (which is dominated by the $K^*(898)$ resonance) makes possible a reliable estimate of the overall Q^2-dependence.

The contribution induced by asymptotic QCD from a certain value of $\hat{t}$ onwards has to be added. The value of $\hat{t}$ should be large enough to avoid double counting with hadronic contributions, but not too large; otherwise, the asymptotic continuum would be underestimated. With $\hat{t} \simeq (4m_{K^*})^2$, the optimal bound is obtained at $Q^2 \simeq 0$.

$$|F(o)| \le 11.1 \frac{2}{3} f_K^2 m_K^2 \ , \tag{13}$$

i.e., an order of magnitude larger than the vacuum-saturation estimate. A change in the choice of $\hat{t}$ does not change the bound significantly.

5. Improved Bound

It is possible to improve the bound (10) significantly by using the technique of ref. 12 and some reasonable phenomenological input, i.e., some information about the slope and the convexity of the normalized form factor F(t)/F(o).

The bound in (10) is now changed into

$$|F(o)| \le \frac{2}{3} f_K^2 m_K^2 [t_o \ (Q^2)]^{1/2} (\frac{6\pi}{5})^{1/2} (\frac{t_o}{f_K^2}) [1 + (1+ \frac{Q^2}{t_o})^{1/2}]^6$$
$$\times \{1 + [\rho_1+\lambda_1(Q^2)]^2 + \frac{1}{4}[\rho_2+2\rho_1\lambda_1(Q^2)+\lambda_2(Q^2)]^2\}^{-1/2} \tag{14}$$

where

$$\rho_1 = -4t_o \frac{d}{dt}\frac{F(t)}{F(o)}\bigg|_{t=o}, \quad \rho_2 = 16t_o^2 \frac{d^2}{dt^2}\frac{F(t)}{F(o)}\bigg|_{t=o} + 4\rho_1 \tag{15}$$

and $\lambda_1(Q^2)$, $\lambda_2(Q^2)$ are

$$\lambda_1(Q^2) = \frac{5}{2} - \frac{12}{1 + (1 + \frac{Q^2}{t_o})^{1/2}} , \qquad (16)$$

$$\lambda_2(Q^2) = \lambda_1^2(Q^2) + \frac{1}{2} - 24(1 + \frac{Q^2}{t_o})^{1/2}\left[1 + (1 + \frac{Q^2}{t_o})^{1/2}\right]^{-2} .$$

It is clear from eq. (14) that even a rough knowledge of ρ_1 and ρ_2 might improve the bound significantly. As a matter of fact, the knowledge of the phase shifts for $(K^oK^o)^{I=1}_{J=o}$ suffices to get information about ρ_1 and ρ_2. What is required is that $F(q^2)$ be polynomially bounded in q^2 and that $F(q^2)$ have no zeros in the complex q^2-plane. The former requirement is ensured in QCD, the latter one is, unfortunately, out of our control. Nevertheless, assuming that the $F(q^2)$ has no zeros, one gets ρ_1 and ρ_2. Since phase shifts for K^oK^o have not been measured, one assumes, in addition, that they are equal to the phase shift for $(\pi\pi)^{I=2}_{J=o}$ with an error of $\pm 100\%$. Since ρ_1 and ρ_2 turn out to be rather small compared with λ_1 and λ_2 in eq. (10), we believe that the use of phase shifts is quite justified. The numerical results are given in Fig. 2, with a best bound being

$$|F(o)| \leq (2.0 \pm 0.5) \, \frac{2}{3} \, f_K^2 m_K^2 \quad . \qquad (17)$$

Acknowledgement

I would like to acknowledge very pleasant collaboration with N. Bilić, B. Machet, E. de Rafael, D. Tadić, and J. Trampetić, and very useful discussions with J.F. Donoghue and R.D. Peccei. This work was supported by the SIZ of S.R. Croatia and U.S. National Science Foundation under Grant No. YOR 82/051.

References

1) M.K. Gaillard and B.W. Lee, Phys. Rev. D10 (1974) 897
2) F.J. Gilman and M.B. Wise, Phys. Lett. 83B (1979) 83
3) M.I. Vysotsky, Sov. J. Nucl. Phys. 31 (1980) 797
4) L. Wolfenstein, Nucl. Phys. B160 (1979) 501; C.T. Hill, Phys. Lett. 97B (1980) 275
5) B.D. Gaiser, T. Tsao, and M.B. Wise, Ann. Phys. (N.Y.) 132 (1981) 66
6) V. de Alfaro, S. Fubini, G. Furlan, and G. Rossetti, Phys. Lett. 21 (1966) 576; G. Nardulli, G. Preparata, and D. Rotondi, Phys. Rev. D27 (1983) 557
7) N. Bilić and B. Guberina, Phys. Lett. B, to be published

8) J.F. Donoghue, E. Golowich, and B.R. Holstein, Phys.Lett. 119B (1982) 412
9) R.E. Schrock and S.B. Treiman, Phys. Rev. D19 (1979) 2148
10) P. Colić, B. Guberina, D. Tadić, and J. Trampetić, Nucl. Phys. B221 (1983) 141
11) B. Guberina, B. Machet, and E. de Rafael, Phys. Lett. 128B (1983) 269
12) C. Bourrely, B. Machet, and E. de Rafael, Nucl.Phys. B180 (1981) 157

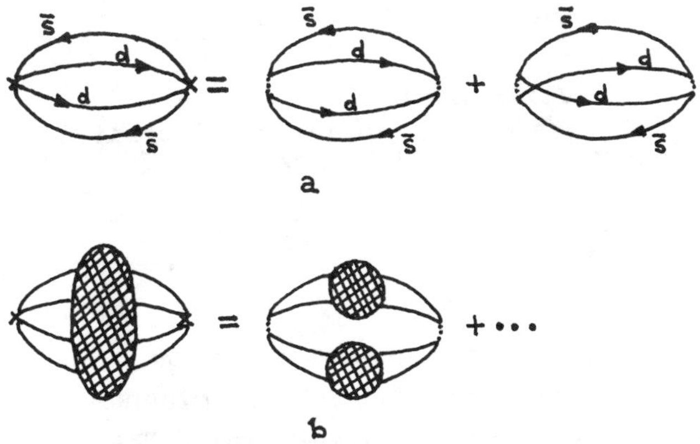

Fig. 1

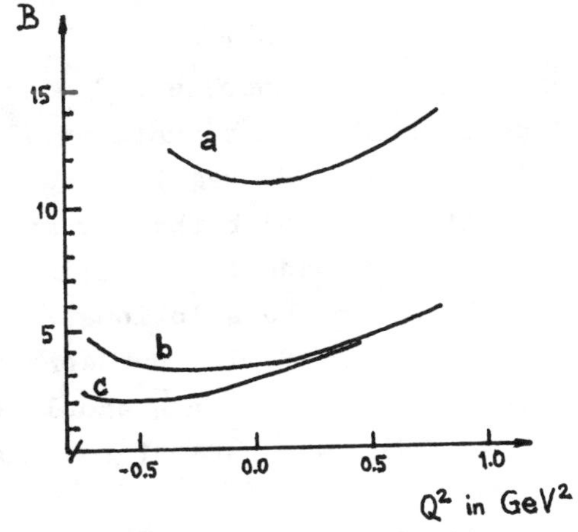

Fig. 2. Curve a corresponds to the bound in (10). Curves b and c correspond to the bound in (14) when the information about ρ_1 (curve b) and about ρ_1 and ρ_2 (curve c) is provided.

BAG-LIKE VACUUM OF QCD

Jerzy Szwed
Institute of Physics, Jagellonian University,
Reymonta 4, 30-059 Kraków, Poland

ABSTRACT

The recently proposed bag-like structure of the vacuum is reviewed. The role of gluon and quark condensates is investigated. The ground state of this scheme is produced by $(q\bar{q}q\bar{q})$ systems with $J^{PC} = 0^{++}$ quantum numbers.

I would like to report on recent work[1,2] concerning the vacuum structure of Quantum Chromodynamics. The approach investigates the consequences of a single assumption which can be formulated as follows:

The QCD vacuum is divided into colourless, finite regions of space, called bags, filled with quark or gluon fields with no colour flux through the bag surface.

One should stress the difference with the bag model[3], where the bag constant B is introduced to stabilize the bags. In the present investigation the solutions to our problem have to be stable from itself. The bag constant, if it appears, is no more a free parameter it should be rather calculable in terms of the QCD parameters, Λ and quark masses.

First attempt along these lines, made by Johnson[4], with no fields inside the bag and only the zero-point energy playing the role, turned out to lead to unstable solutions[5].

Last year Hansson, Johnson and Peterson[1] considered the bag-like vacuum filled with gluonic fields. Before I present their results let me sketch the calculation of the energy density inside a bag.

The energy of a single bag consists of three distinct terms

$$E = E_{kin} + \alpha_s(\Lambda R)[E_{int} + E_{self}] . \quad (1)$$

The first one comes from the solution of the free Maxwell equation inside the bag with the boundary conditions at the bag surface given by the requirement of vanishing colour flux. In the spherical bag approximation we are using, it reads $E = \frac{n\, x_g}{R}$ where n is the number of occupied gluon modes, R - the bag radius and x_g - the mode constant. The next two terms, both proportional to the running coupling constant $\alpha(\Lambda R)$ include the interaction inside the bag. The first one depends on the colour ($\vec{\lambda}$) and spin ($\vec{S}$) configurations of the confined fields $E_{int} = \sum_{i\neq j} m(\vec{S}_i \cdot \vec{S}_j, \vec{\lambda}_i \cdot \vec{\lambda}_j)/R$. The last one, which includes the self-energy interaction, has the form $E_{int} = \frac{e_g}{R}$ with e_g being a constant. This term and its quark analog are being calculated[6] - in what I present they are still treated as free parameters.

Looking at the structure of Eq. (1) one sees that the kinetic energy is repulsive, tending to increase the bag radius. The part proportional to $\alpha(\Lambda R)$ can be repulsive or attractive, depending on the spin and colour configuration. Taking into account the decrease of the running coupling constant with increasing R we obtain a possibility of balancing the kinetic energy by the two interaction terms.

To extract the bag mass from its energy one has to subtract the c.m. momentum which contributes to Eq. (1) due to the static cavity approximation we are using[7]. Dividing the mass by the bag volume we obtain the energy density - the quantity of main interest.

The results concerning 'glueball condensate' were obtained by Hansson, Johnson and Peterson[1]. The dominant contribution, given by the two-gluon bags is shown in Fig. 1 by the short, dashed line. One sees that the outlined scheme produces a minimum in energy density for radii about 1 fm. Secondly, the minimum is negative - 'empty space' is thus unstable against condensation to two-gluon bags (higher number of gluons inside a bag lead to less negative energy densities). Assuming that the gluonic states give dominant rise to the vacuum structure one is able to calculate quantities characterizing the vacuum: the bag constant B and $< G_{\mu\nu} G^{\mu\nu} >$. Carlson, Hansson and Peterson[8] used this scheme to recalculate the low-lying hadron spectrum which came out close to the old bag model prediction[9] where the bag constant was a free parameter.

Our investigation[2] focused on other field configurations, in particular on the role of the quark condensate. I present the results starting from the most interesting case - the $q\bar{q}q\bar{q}$ system in $J^{PC} = 0^{++}$ configuration. Two such states from the SU(3) flavour nonet

$$|udud\rangle \quad \text{and} \quad \frac{1}{\sqrt{2}}\,|s\bar{s}(u\bar{u} + d\bar{d})\rangle \tag{2}$$

are most attractive, producing the energy minimum many times deeper than that of the gluon fields (Fig. 1). They seem thus to dominate the ground state of the theory, within the above approach.

Let me add a few words concerning other configurations. A $q\bar{q}$ pair in $J^{PC} = 0^{++}$ state must be in p-wave and does not produce any significant minimum. For $q^n\bar{q}^n$ with $n \to \infty$ Pauli principle requires again some of the quarks to occupy higher modes which are less attractive. Mixed configurations ($q\bar{q}$ + TM gluon is shown in Fig. 1) do not seem to play important role.

The above remarks produce a definite picture of the

'bagged vacuum'. One can write it in the following form

$$|\phi\rangle = \alpha|u\bar{u}d\bar{d}\rangle + \beta|\frac{1}{\sqrt{2}}\, s\bar{s}(u\bar{u} + d\bar{d})\rangle + \gamma|gg\rangle + \ldots \qquad (3)$$

with α and β being large. Their actual value can be given after calculating the transitions between the states of Eq. (3) which occur already in order $\alpha(\Lambda R)$.

As an exercise we have performed the fit to the non-strange, hadrons ($p, \Delta, \omega, \rho, \pi$) assuming $\alpha = 1$, $\beta = \gamma = \ldots = 0$ in Eq. (3), with two free parameters: Λ and e_q. The resulting values of masses and parameters come out reasonably.

Finally a word of worning: the above approach lacks chiral invariance. This prevents us from calculating the vacuum expectation value $\langle\phi|\bar{q}q|\phi\rangle$ or quark masses.

References

[1] T.H. Hansson, K. Johnson and C. Peterson, Phys. Rev. D26 (1982) 2069.
[2] A. Bialas and J. Szwed, Jagellonian University preprint TPJU-10/83.
[3] A. Chodos, R.L. Jaffe, K. Johnson, C.B. Thorn and V.F. Weisskopf, Phys. Rev. D9 (1974) 3471.
[4] K. Johnson, AIP Conf. Proc. No 59 (1979).
[5] K. Zalewski, Acta Phys. Pol. B12 (1981) 111.
[6] J. Baacke, Y. Igarashi and G. Kasperidus, Dortmund preprint DO-TH 82/13 and CERN preprint TH-3509; J.D. Breit, Columbia preprint CU-TP-229 (1982); S.A. Chin, A.K. Kerman and X.H. Yang, Nucl. Phys. A382 (1982) 355; T.H. Hansson and R.J. Jaffe, preprint MIT-CTP 1026 (1982).
[7] J.F. Donoghue and K. Johnson, Phys. Rev. D21 (1980) 1975.
[8] C.E. Carlson, T.H. Hansson and C. Peterson, preprint MIT-CTP 1020 (1982).
[9] T. DeGrand, R.L. Jaffe, K. Johnson and J. Kiskis, Phys. Rev. D12 (1975) 2060.

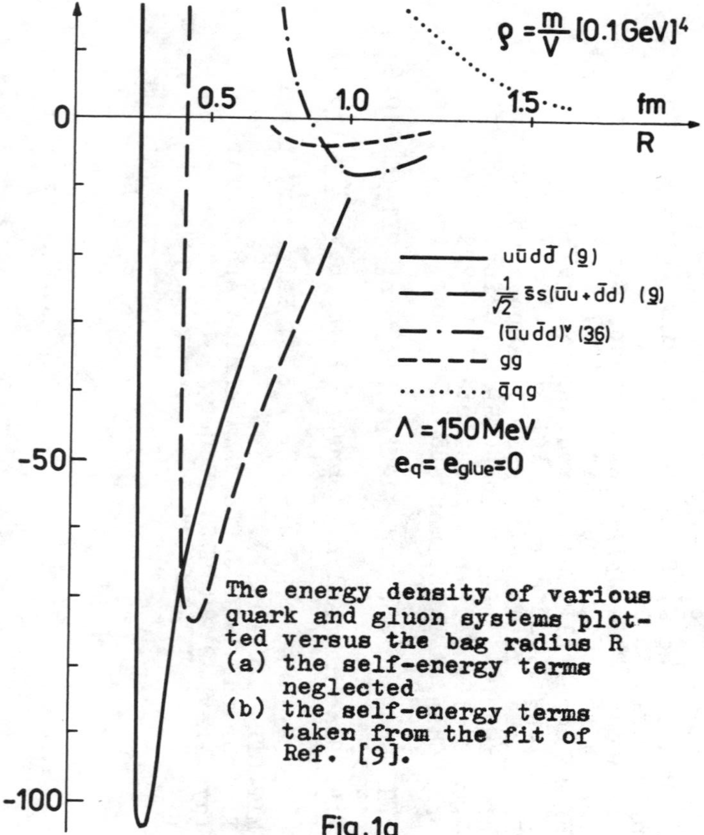

The energy density of various quark and gluon systems plotted versus the bag radius R
(a) the self-energy terms neglected
(b) the self-energy terms taken from the fit of Ref. [9].

Fig. 1a

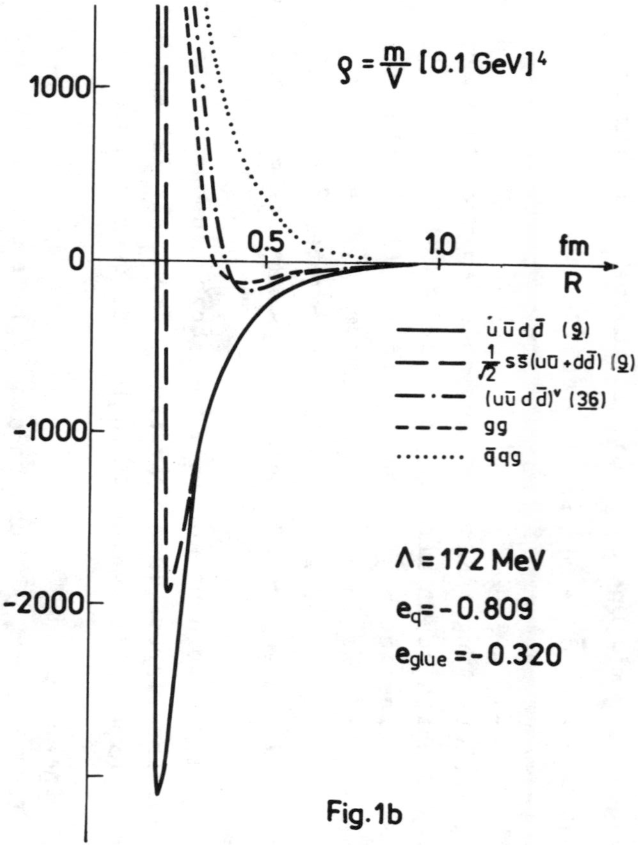

Fig. 1b

SUBSTRUCTURE OF LEPTONS AND QUARKS AND THE PROBLEM OF MASS

Harald Fritzsch
Sektion Physik der Universität München
and
Max-Planck-Institut für Physik und Astrophysik
- Werner Heisenberg Institut für Physik -
Munich (Fed.Rep.Germany)

Recently the weak intermediate bosons have been found in p-$\bar{p}$-collisions at high energies[1]. The masses observed are in good agreement with the values predicted within the standard SU(2) x U(1)-theory. However we should like to remind the reader that the agreement between theory and experiment looks less spectacular if one takes into account that the masses of the weak bosons W and Z are determined by using two input parameters G_F and $\sin^2\theta_W$ (besides the finestructure constant α). Even after the discovery of the W and Z bosons a number of questions remain to be answered, e.g.:

Is the SU(2) x U(1) gauge theory a microscopic theory of the electroweak interactions, or is it merely an effective theory, describing the low energy properties of a more fundamental theory?

Are the weak bosons basic gauge particles like the photon, or are they bound states of certain constituents?

Are leptons and quarks composite and are they made of the same constituents as the weak bosons?

In this talk I shall address these and other related questions, especially the problem of masses[2]. In particle physics there exist two different ways to generate masses:

a) Dynamical mass generation by confinement

Here the mass of a particle is generated by a force between constituents, which becomes strong at sufficiently large distances. Examples: the ρ-meson or nucleon masses in QCD. The masses of the particles are measures of the energy of the fields confined inside a finite volume.

b) Mass generation by spontaneous symmetry breaking

Here a mass scale is introduced by a scalar field which acquires via its self interaction a non-zero vacuum expectation value. For example, in the standard SU(2) x U(1) theory the W-boson mass is introduced via a scalar field whose vacuum expectation value v is of the order of 300 GeV:

$$M_W = \frac{1}{2} g \cdot v \tag{1}$$

$$\frac{G}{\sqrt{2}} = \frac{g^2}{8 M_W^2} = \frac{1}{2v^2} \qquad (v = 246 \text{ GeV}).$$

(g: $SU(2)^W$ - coupling constant; G: Fermi constant).

The question arises whether the W-boson mass is due to a spontaneous breakdown of the SU(2) x U(1) gauge symmetry, or whether it has a dynamical origin. If the first possibility is realized, the SU(2) x U(1) gauge theory may well be the correct theory not only of the electroweak interactions at relatively small energies, but also at energies much above the energy scale exhibited by the Fermi constant (of the order of 300 GeV).

If the W mass is generated dynamically, one expects the W-bosons to be bound states of at least two constituents. No unification of the electromagnetic and weak interactions is achieved. The W-boson will be the ground state of a complicated spectrum of states, just like the ρ-meson is the ground state of the spectrum of infinitely many states in the $\bar{q}q(J^P = 1^-)$ channel. It is this possibility which I would like to address here.

During the progress of physics within the past hundred years it has happened twice that observed short range forces were recognized as indirect consequences of an underlying substructure of the objects considered. Thus the short-range molecular and Van-der-Waals forces turned out to be indirect consequences of the substructure of atoms; they are remnants of the long range electromagnetic forces. Since 1970 something similar has happened to the short-range nuclear force, which has turned out to be a relict of the quark substructure of hadrons and the strong long range color forces between the quarks.

The only short range interaction left in physics which has not been traced back to a substructure and to a fundamental long range force between constituents is the weak interaction. Recently a number of authors has become interested in interpreting the weak force as some kind of "Van der Waals" remnant of an underlying lepton-quark substructure[3)]. The lepton- quark constituents for which I will use the name "haplons" derived from Greek "haplos" (simple) are supposed to be bound together by very strong so-called hypercolor forces which are supposed to be confining forces, presumably described by a non-

Abelean gauge theory (although other types of forces are not excluded). The short range character of the weak interaction arises since the leptons and quarks are hypercolor singlets, but have a finite size. The energy scale provided by the Fermi constant is of the order of 300 GeV; the inverse size of the leptons, quarks and weak bosons is expected to be of the same order, i.e. their radii are of the order of 10^{-17} cm.

If the weak interaction turns out to be a remnant of the hypercolor force, a new interpretation of the relationship between the electromagnetic and weak interaction is required. The W- and Z- bosons cease to be fundamental gauge bosons, but acquire the less prestigious status of bound states of haplons. However the photon remains an elementary object (at least at the scale of the order of 10^{-17} cm, discussed here). As a whole, the SU(2) x U(1)-theory cannot be regarded anymore as a fundamental microscopic theory of the electroweak interactions, but at best can be interpreted as an effective theory, which is useful only at distances larger than the hypercolor confinement scale. It acquires a status comparable to the one of the σ-model in QCD, which correctly describes the chiral dynamics of π-mesons and nucleons at relatively low energies, but fails to be a reasonable description of the strong interaction at high energies.

However I would like to emphasize that at the present time no indication whatsoever comes from the experimental side that leptons, quarks and weak bosons may be bound states of yet smaller constituents. It may well be that the weak force will turn out in the future as a fundamental gauge force, as fundamental as the electromagnetic one and the color force. In fact, interpreting the weak forces as effective forces poses a number of problems which have not been solved in a satisfactory manner. First of all, the weak interactions violate parity, and they do that not in an uncontrolled way, but in a very simple one: only the lefthanded leptons and quarks take part in the charged current interactions. If we interpret the weak interactions as Van-der-Waals type interactions, the parity violation is a point of worry. How should one interpret the observed parity violation? Does it mean that the lefthanded fermions have a different internal structure than the righthanded ones? Or are we dealing with two or several different hypercolor confinement scales, for example one for the lefthanded fermions, and one for the righthanded fermions, such that the resulting effective theory is similar to the left - right symmetric gauge theory, based on the group $SU(2)_L \times SU(2)_R$?

Another point of concern is the fact that the weak interactions show a number of regularities, e.g. the universality of the weak couplings, which one would not a priori expect if the weak interaction is merely a hypercolor remnant. On the other hand it is well - known that the interaction of pions or ρ-mesons with hadrons shows a number of regularities which can be traced back to current algebra, combined with chiral symmetry or vector meson dominance. Despite the fact that both the ρ-mesons and the pions are quark - antiquark bound states for which one would not a priori expect that their interaction with other hadrons exhibits remarkable simple properties (e.g. the universality of the vector meson couplings), the latter arise as a consequence of the underlying current algebra, which is saturated rather well at low energies by the lowest lying pole (either the pion pole in the case of the divergence of the axial vector current, or the ρ- or A_1- pole in the case of the vector or axial vector current).

In the case of chiral SU(2) x SU(2) the pole dominance works very well - the predictions of current algebra and PCAC seem to be fulfilled within about 5 %. The universality of the weak interactions is observed to be valid within 1 % in the case of the couplings of the weak currents to electrons, myons, as well as u,d and s- quarks. Much weaker constraints exist for the heavy quarks. It remains to be seen whether the observed universality of the weak interactions will find an explanation along lines similar to the ones used in hadronic physics.

Here I shall concentrate on models in which the W-bosons consist of a haplon and an antihaplon. Since the observed weak interactions exhibit a symmetry $SU(2)_L$, we assume the existence of two haplons, denoted by the doublet $\binom{\alpha}{\beta}$, which carry hypercolor and electric charge, but no ordinary color. The electric charges are assumed to be: $Q(\alpha) = +1/2$, $Q(\beta) = -1/2$ (see ref. (4)).

The spectral functions at energies much above the hypercolor confinement scale are supposed to be described by a continuum of haplon-antihaplon pairs. At low energies the weak amplitudes will be dominated by the lowest lying poles, which are identified with the W-particles. The latter form the triplet:

$$\begin{pmatrix} W^+ \\ W^3 \\ W^- \end{pmatrix} = \begin{pmatrix} \bar{\beta}\alpha \\ \frac{1}{\sqrt{2}}(\bar{\alpha}\alpha - \bar{\beta}\beta) \\ \bar{\alpha}\beta \end{pmatrix}$$

The experimental data on the neutral current interaction require a mixing between the photon and the W_3 boson (the neutral, isovector partner of W^+ and W^-), which in the standard SU(2) x U(1) scheme is caused by the spontaneous symmetry breaking. Within our approach this mixing is due to the W_3 - γ transitions, generated dynamically like the ρ-γ transitions in QCD (for an early discussion, based on vector meson dominance, see ref. (5,6)). The magnitude of $\sin^2\theta_W$ is directly related to the strength of the γ-W_3 transition. The latter is determined by the electric charges of the W-constituents and by the W wave function near the origin. We suppose that in the absence of electromagnetism the weak interactions are mediated by the triplet (W^+, W^-, W^3), where $M(W^+) = M(W^-) = M(W^3) = O(\Lambda_H)$.

After the introduction of the electromagnetic interaction the photon and the W^3- boson mix. We denote the strength of this mixing by a parameter λ, following ref. (6), which is related to g (W-fermion coupling constant) and the effective value of $\sin^2\theta_W$

$$\sin^2\theta_W = \frac{e}{g} \cdot \lambda .$$

Furthermore one has:

$$M_W = g \cdot 123 \text{ GeV}$$
$$M_Z^2 = \frac{M_W^2}{1-\lambda^2} .$$

The mixing parameter λ is determined by the decay constant F_W of the W-boson, which we define in analogy to the decay constants of the ρ_0-meson ($F\rho$):

$$|W^3> = \frac{1}{\sqrt{2}} \frac{1}{\sqrt{n}} \sum_{j=1}^{n} (\bar{\alpha}_j\alpha_j - \bar{\beta}_j\beta_j) \phi(x)$$

($\phi(x)$: wave function in coordinate space, j: hypercolor index): The current matrix element can be written as

$$<o|j_\mu{}^3|W^3> = \varepsilon_\mu \sqrt{n} \cdot \sqrt{2M_W} \cdot \phi(o) = \varepsilon_\mu \cdot M_W F_W$$

$$F_W = \sqrt{n} \cdot /2 \sqrt{M_W} \phi(o)$$

$$\sin^2{}_W = \frac{e^2}{g} \sqrt{n} \cdot \sqrt{2/M_W{}^3} \phi(o),$$

$$= e^2 / g \cdot F_W / M_W.$$

e.g. $\sin^2\theta_W$ is proportional to the coordinate space wave function of the W-boson at the origin. Taking for example g = 0.65 and M_W = 79 GeV, one obtains F_W = 123 GeV, a value which seems not unreasonable for a bound state of the size 10^{-16} cm.

In the SU(2) x U(1) gauge theory the SU(2) coupling constant g is related to e by the relation $g = e/\sin\theta_W$. In bound state models of the weak interactions discussed here this relation need not be true in general. However it has been emphasized recently[7)] that this relation is approximately fullfilled if the lowest lying W-pole dominates the weak spectral function at low energies. This leads to the relation

$$g = F_W / M_W = e/\sin\theta_W \approx 0.65$$

(we have used $\sin^2\theta_W = 0.22$).

It is interesting to note that many aspects of the bound state models can be derived from a local current algebra of the weak currents. We observe that the lefthanded leptons and quarks form doublets of the weak isospin. The weak isospin charges F_i^W(i = 1, 2, 3) obey the isospin charge algebra

$$[F_i^W, F_j^W] = i\,\varepsilon_{ijk}\,F_k^W\ .$$

Let us assume that these charges can be constructed as integrals over local charge densities $F_{oi}^W(x)$, i.e.,

$$F_i^W(x^o) = \int F_{oi}^W(x)d^3x.$$

Furthermore we suppose that the charge densities obey at equal times the local current algebra

$$[F_{oi}^W(x), F_{oj}^W(y)]_{x^o=y^o} = i\varepsilon_{ijk}F_{o\kappa}^W\delta^3(\vec{x}-\vec{y}).$$

The local algebra is trivially fulfilled in a model in which leptons and quarks are pointlike objects and the weak currents are simply bilinear in the lepton and quark fields. However, if leptons and quarks are extended objects, the situation changes drastically. Currents, which are bilinear in the (composite) lepton and quark fields would not obey the local algebra, just like the currents, which are bilinear in nucleon fields, do not obey the local current algebra of QCD. Thus the local algebra becomes a highly non-trivial constraint. It is fulfilled in the haplon models discussed above, in which the currents are bilinear in α and β.

We consider matrix elements of the weak currents between the various fermion fields. In order to do so, we shall assume that the higher families composed of μ,τ, ... etc. are dynamical excitations of the first family (ν_e, e^-, u, d), without specifying in detail the dynamical structure of these states.

Let us look at the form factors of the left-handed weak neutral current $F_{\mu 3}^L(x)$, i.e., the matrix elements of this current between different lefthanded lepton or quark states, e.g., $<e_L^- F_{\mu 3}(o)\, e_L^->$. Denoting these form factors by $F_e(t)$, $F_\mu(t)$, $F_\tau(t)$, etc., the weak isospin algebra requires a universal normalization at t = 0, i.e., $F_e = F_{\nu_e} = F_\mu = F_\nu = \ldots = 1$. Assuming W dominance to be a reasonably good approximation, we may write for the dependence on the four-momentum transfer t,

$$F_f(t) = \frac{m_W^2}{f_W}\ \frac{f_W^{ff}}{m_W^2-t}\ ,$$

where f denotes any one of the fermions e^-, ν_e, μ^-, ν_μ, etc. From $F_f(o) = 1$, we obtain the universality relation

$$f_W = f_W^{ff} \equiv g\ .$$

The neutral W and, because of the weak isospin algebra, also the charged W bosons couple universally to leptons and quarks, $f_W^{ff} \equiv g$. Thus the universality of the weak interactions follows from the W-dominance.

Let us stress that W dominance is a dynamical approximation of the underlying hypercolour dynamics, which is expected to be valid in the low energy region. At high energies (~1 TeV) lepton-lepton (quark) scattering is expected to show completely new phenomena, like multiple lepton (quark) production, similar to hadron-hadron interactions at high energies. Since universality is valid, we expect W dominance to be a very good approximation in the low energy region. As a consequence, deviations from the predicted charged and neutral boson masses should be small.

If the weak interactions are a manifestation of hypercolor dynamics, the question of SU(2) breaking is again open. One may wonder why the large violation of the weak isospin in the lepton - quark spectrum does not imply a large breaking of the symmetry in dynamical parameters like the W- fermion- coupling constants.

We should like to study the violation of the isospin in the pion dynamics. It is well - known that there exist two different sources of the violation of the isospin in strong interaction: the difference of the quark masses m_u and m_d, and the electromagnetic interaction. Only the second source contributes to the $\pi^+ - \pi^0$ mass difference. If we set $m_u = m_d = m$ and let m go to zero, the pion mass approaches zero as well, provided we neclegt the electromagnetic interaction.

Following the laws of chiral symmetry breaking, one finds:

$$M_\pi^2 = (m_u + m_d) \cdot B + O(m_q^2 \ln m_q)$$

$$B = -\frac{2}{F_\pi^2} \langle o|\bar{u}u|o\rangle$$

where u, d denote the light quark flavors, m_u, m_d the quark masses, $|o\rangle$ the QCD vacuum, F_π the pion decay constant. Typical values are $(m_u + m_d) = 14$ MeV, $B = 1300$ MeV[8].

The electromagnetic self energy of the π^0 vanishes in the chiral limit. The electromagnetic self energy of the charged pion can be calculated to order α in terms of the vector and axial vector spectral functions[8]. Saturating the spectral functions with the ρ- and A_1-poles and using the spectral function sum rules one obtains:

$$(\Delta M_{\pi^+}^2)_{el.} = \frac{3\alpha}{4\pi} \cdot M_\rho^2 \cdot \left(\frac{F_\rho}{F_\pi}\right)^2 \cdot \ln\left(\frac{F_\rho^2}{F_\rho^2 - F_\pi^2}\right).$$

Using the measured values $F_\pi = 132$ MeV and $F_\rho = 204$ MeV, one obtains $(\Delta M_{\pi^+}^2)_{el.} \cong (36.4\ \text{MeV})^2$, which is close to the observed mass difference $\Delta M_\pi^2 = (35.6\ \text{MeV})^2$.

Combining the two relations, denoted above, one finds:

$$M^2_{\pi^o} = (m_u + m_d) \cdot B + \ldots$$

$$M^2_{\pi^+} = (m_u + m_d) \cdot B + \alpha\, M^2_\rho \cdot 0.31 + \ldots$$

In the chiral limit $m_u = m_d = 0$ we obtain $M_{\pi^o} = 0$, $M_{\pi^+} \approx 36$ MeV. As an illustration we consider the case $m_u = m_d = 1$ KeV. One finds $M_{\pi^o} = 1.6$ MeV, $M_{\pi^+} = 36.4$ MeV, i.e. the neutral and charged pion mass differ by a factor of about 23.

We have just found a situation in QCD, which resembles the one in the lepton- quark- spectrum, namely a large isospin breaking despite the fact that for $m_u = m_d$ the isospin is an exact symmetry of QCD. In the chiral limit the π-meson are particles, which in the absence of electromagnetism have zero mass, but have a finite size. Their inverse size is of order Λ.

Including the electromagnetic interaction has the effect of lifting the charged pion mass from zero to the finite value $M_{\pi^+} \approx 0.16 \cdot e \cdot M_\rho \approx 36$ MeV. The neutral pion stays massless. The charged pion mass is of order $e \cdot \Lambda$[QCD], i.e. $e \cdot$ (inverse size of pion).

We note that the π^+ - mass is of electromagnetic origin. The self-energy diagram consists of a charged pion emitting a virtual photon and turning itself into a massive state (ρ, A_1, ...). Due to the chiral symmetry the sum of all these contributions is finite and of order $e \cdot \Lambda$(QCD).

With these preparations in mind, we are ready to consider the lepton quark spectrum. The leptons and quark flavors observed thus far seem to come in three families:

$$\text{I.} \qquad \begin{pmatrix} \nu_e & \vdots & u\ (5) \\ e^-\ (0.5) & \vdots & d\ (9) \end{pmatrix}$$

$$\text{II.} \qquad \begin{pmatrix} \nu_\mu & \vdots & c\ (1{,}200) \\ \mu^-(106) & \vdots & s\ (180) \end{pmatrix}$$

$$\text{III.} \qquad \begin{pmatrix} \nu_\tau & \vdots & t\ (>18{,}000) \\ \tau^-(1784) & \vdots & b\ (4{,}800) \end{pmatrix}$$

The numbers in brackets denote the masses of the particles in MeV. For the light quarks we used typical "current algebra" masses. Various astrophysical constraints require the neutrino masses to be < 100 eV. Looking closer at the fermion mass spectrum one observes the following facts:

a) There exists a well-obeyed hierarchical structure. The mass ratios of fermions belonging to different generations are given by:

$$\frac{m_s}{m_d} \approx 20, \qquad \frac{m_b}{m_s} \approx 27, \qquad \frac{m_\tau}{m_\mu} \approx 17$$

$$\frac{m_c}{m_u} \approx 240, \qquad \frac{m_t}{m_c} \approx 15, \qquad \frac{m_\mu}{m_e} \approx 207 \ .$$

All charged fermions of the first family (e, u, d) are lighter than the ones of the second family (, c, s), and those are lighter than the members of the third family (τ, t, b). Note that, with exception of $\frac{m_c}{m_u}$ and $\frac{m_\mu}{m_e}$ all mass ratios are of order 20.

b) Inside families the mass ratios of charge $\frac{2}{3}$ to charge $(\frac{-1}{3})$ quarks are given by:

$$\frac{m_u}{m_d} \approx 0.6, \qquad \frac{m_c}{m_s} \approx 6.5, \qquad \frac{m_t}{m_b} > 4$$

i.e. the charge $\frac{2}{3}$ quarks of the second and third family are heavier than the corresponding charge$(-\frac{1}{3})$ quarks. This pattern is broken by the quarks of the first generation.

c) The mass eigenstates are not eigenstates of the weak interactions. The corresponding mixing angles (three angles in case of three families) all seem to be relatively small.

d) The lepton-quark mass spectrum looks rather arbitrary. It lacks any approximate symmetry. Wide fluctuations of the mass parameters are observed. Nevertheless it seems that the masses are somewhat correlated with the electric charge. Neutrinos, being electrically neutral, have no (or an exceedingly small) mass; the masses of the quarks of charge 2/3 are much larger that the masses of the quarks of charge -1/3 (except the first family, see b)).

A solution of the fermion mass problem is required to give answers to the following two questions:

a) Why are the fermion masses much smaller than 1 TeV?

b) What is the mechanism responsible for the generation of mass?

We suppose that the answer to the first question is given by a symmetry. On the scale of the hypercolor interaction, both color and electromagnetism can be viewed as small perturbations. We suppose that in the limit where those interactions are switched off the leptons and quarks are massless; one is dealing with 24 massless states. A chiral symmetry (either a continous or a discrete chiral symmetry) is supposed to provide the reason for the absence of mass.

It is supposed that besides the 24 massless fermions an infinite number of other fermions with mass of order 1 TeV or larger exists. For those states we see no reason why a chiral symmetry should be valid. Such a symmetry if it remained unbroken would require a parity doubling of all massive states. We suppose that the chiral symmetry is strongly broken by the hypercolor dynamics in the heavy fermion sector. The observed SU(2) symmetry of the weak interactions is assumed to be a flavor symmetry of the hypercolor interaction.

If the electromagnetic interaction is introduced, the leptons and quarks aquire a finite electromagnetic self energy, where the heavy fermions (mass $\sim$ 1 TeV) serve as intermediate states. The self energy is finite due to the cut off of order Λ_h provided by the finite sizes (of order Λ_h^{-1}) of the leptons and quarks. Note that the leptons and quarks have in particular a finite charge radius of order of Λ_h^{-1}.

Thus far we have mentioned only the electromagnetic perturbation of hypercolor dynamics. In a similar way one may consider the QCD interaction. However the gluonic self energy of a quark is strongly model dependent. In all bound state models of the type considered here the fermions do have a finite charge radius. No finite color radius is implied. In these schemes the color resides on one of the constituents (often a scalar object) of the leptons and quarks. In this case the color self energy can be represented by the renormalized mass of the corresponding constituent, which in general is arbitrary; it may vanish as a result of a symmetry (e.g. as a consequence of an underlying supersymmetry). If the QCD interaction would be an important interaction for the generation of mass for leptons and quarks, the mass difference inside weak doublets would be small compared to the average mass (e.g. $m_t - m_b << \frac{1}{2}(m_t + m_b)$). This is not the case. Instead a very strong dependence of the masses on the electric charges is observed. We conclude: the color force is either excluded from contributing to the lepton or quark masses, or contributes only very little. This has implications for the experimental search for lepton-quark substructure: leptons and quarks are expected to have a charge radius of the order of 10^{-17} cm, but no color radius of this order. Subsequently we shall assume that only the QED interaction is responsible for the fermion mass generation[11].

We analyze the fermion electromagnetic self energy diagram somewhat more in detail[12]. In principle, infinitely many heavy (mass > 1 TeV) states will contribute as intermediate states. Since we have no detailed information about the heavy states there is no way to compute the electromagnetic self energy exactly. However, we expect that the lowest contributing intermediate state will dominate. (Something similar is true in hadron physics: the electromagnetic selfenergy of the pion or the proton is dominated by the lowest intermediate state). Under this assumption the resulting fermion mass matrix reads:

$$M = \frac{\alpha}{\pi} Q^2 K \Lambda_h \begin{pmatrix} |f_1|^2 & f_1^+ f_2 & f_1^+ f_3 \\ f_1 f_2^+ & |f_2|^2 & f_2 f_3 \\ f_1 f_3^+ & f_2 f_3^+ & |f_3|^2 \end{pmatrix} + O(\alpha^2)$$

Q denotes the electric charge of the fermion and K is a parameter of order one, depending on the transition form factors. The elements of the vectors

$$\vec{f} = \begin{pmatrix} f_1 \\ f_2 \\ f_3 \end{pmatrix}$$

are measures of the transitions $<i|j_\mu n>$, where $|i>$ denotes a quark or lepton state, $|n>$ the intermediate heavy state, and j_μ the electromagnetic current. It is useful to rewrite M in terms of the matrix

$$A = \begin{pmatrix} f_1 & f_2 & f_3 \\ 0 & 0 & 0 \\ 0 & 0 & 0 \\ \vdots & \vdots & \vdots \end{pmatrix}$$

The result is

$$M = \frac{\alpha}{\pi} Q^2 K \Lambda_h (A^+ A) + O(\alpha^2).$$

This shows that M is of rank 1, and the diagonalization gives:

$$M = \frac{\alpha}{\pi} Q^2 K \Lambda_h |\vec{f}|^2 \begin{pmatrix} 0 & 0 & 0 \\ 0 & 0 & 0 \\ 0 & 0 & 1 \end{pmatrix} + O(\alpha^2) .$$

Thus in the approximation made above (one intermediate state dominates, $O(\alpha^2)$ terms are neglected) only one family of quarks and leptons aquires a mass. The latter is identified with the third family (t, b, τ). The hierarchical pattern of fermion masses starts to emerge.

As soon as we give up the assumption of the dominance of the fermion self energy by one intermediate state, M ceases to be of rank 1. In the case of 2 intermediate states ($|n\rangle$ and $m\rangle$) the second row of the matrix A ceases to be zero and one finds:

$$A = \begin{pmatrix} f_1 & f_2 & f_3 \\ f_1' & f_2' & f_3' \\ 0 & 0 & 0 \\ \vdots & \vdots & \vdots \end{pmatrix}$$

Now M is of rank 2. Still one eigenvalue of M is exactly zero which means that the third and second family are massive. The magnitude of the fermion mass hierarchy is related to the quality of the dominance of the fermion self energy by one intermediate state, i.e. to the magnitude of f_i/f_i. Finally, if more than two intermediate states contribute, also the third row etc. of A is nonzero, M is of rank 3, and the first generation aquires a mass.

The situation is as follows: We found that the fermion mass hierarchy is related to the quality of the dominance of the fermion self energy by one or several intermediate states. The neutrinos being neutral remain massless to $O(\alpha)$. The quarks obey the following mass relations:

$$\frac{m_u}{m_d} = \frac{m_c}{m_s} = \frac{m_t}{m_b} = \frac{(\frac{2}{3})^2}{(-\frac{1}{3})^2} = 4 \quad .$$

Thus the mass matrices for up and down-type quarks are, up to a facter 4, the same. Therefore, no weak interaction mixing exists in this approximation. The factor 4 between u- type and d- type quark masses as well as the absence of weak mixing is a consequence of the SU(2)- invariance of the transition matrix elements $\langle i|j_\mu|n\rangle$. In order to introduce mixing and departures from relation one has to allow for a violation of the SU(2)-invariance which is caused by electromagnetic effects of order α^2.

An attempt to estimate these effects was made in ref. (12). As a general result we mention that the departures from the relations $m_t : m_b = 4 : 1$ etc. are related to the weak mixing angles. The latter are of order α, e.g. $\sin\theta_C = \frac{3\alpha}{\pi} c\, m_s/m_d$ (c: parameter of order one, depending on the quark formfactors). It is interesting to observe that the weak interaction mixing of heavy quarks is expected to be very small. The heavy quarks t and b are essentially inert with respect to the mixing effects. On the other hand the masses of the light quarks u and d are strongly perturbed by mixing effects, and correspondingly the

Cabibbo angle is exceptionally large. The b - c transition element in the weak mixing matrix is expected to be of the order of 0.05 implying a life time for the B-meson of the order of 10^{-12} s.

In lowest order of α one finds m_t: m_b = 4: 1, i.e. $m_t \approx 19$ GeV (we use $m_b \approx 4.75$ GeV). The higher order corrections cause m_t/m_b to be slightly larger than 4, but significantly less than $m_c : m_s \approx 6...7$. We expect $m_t : m_b \lesssim 5$, i.e. $m_t \lesssim 25$ GeV. If it should turn out that m_t is much larger than 25 GeV, the obvious conclusion would be that also the (t, b)-system is influenced strongly by weak interaction mixing effects, involving one further family of heavy quarks (t', b') with masses significantly larger than the (t,b)-masses. In that case the relation m(t'): m(b') $\approx$ 4...5 should hold, and the B-meson lifetime should be significantly less than the lifetime of the order of 10^{-12} s quoted above.

Finally let me emphasize that the strongly interacting system of W-bosons described here is in its consequences for weak interaction physics in the region 0 ... 100 GeV essentially identical to the SU(2) x U(1) gauge theory. Nevertheless small deviations from the latter are expected, for example in the W- Z- mass spectrum and in the universality of the weak currents. I hope that such small deviations are discovered soon.

Acknowledgement: It is a pleasure to thank the organizers of this meeting right on this beautiful part of the Adriatic coast for their efforts to create an agreeable and stimulating atmosphere during the time of the conference.

REFERENCES

1. G. Arnison et al., Phys. Lett. 112 B (1983) 103.

2. See also: D. Schildknecht, these proceedings.

3. H. Harari and N. Seiberg, Phys. Lett. 98 B (1981) 269
L. Abbott and E. Farhi, Phys. Lett. 101 B (1981) 69
H. Fritzsch and G. Mandelbaum, Phys. Lett. 102 B (1981) 319,
R. Barbieri, A. Masiero, and R. N. Mohapatra, Phys. Lett. 105 B (1981) 369.

4. H. Fritzsch and G. Mandelbaum, see ref. (3), and Phys. Lett. 109 B (1982) 224.

5. J. D. Bjorken, Phys. Rev. D 19 (1979) 335.

6. P. Hung and J. Sakurai, Nucl. Phys. B 143 (1978) 81.

7. H. Fritzsch, D. Schildknecht and R. Kögerler, Phys. Lett. 114 B (1982) 157. See also: R. Kögerler and D. Schildknecht, CERN preprint TH 3231 (1982).

8. See e.g.: J. Gasser and H. Leutwyler, Physics Reports 87 (1982) 77.

9. See e.g.: G.'Hooft, in: "Recent developments in Gauge Theories", Plenum Press, N.Y. (1980), p. 135.

10. See e.g. the class of models, discussed in ref. (4).

11. See also: H. Fritzsch, in: Proceedings of the Int. Conf. Neutrino 82 (June 1982), Balatonfüred, Hungary, A. Frenkel, L. Jenik ed.(Budapest, 1982).

12. U. Baur and H. Fritzsch, The masses of Composite Quarks and Leptons as Electromagnetic Self Energies, Munich preprint MPI - PAE/PTh 37/83 (June 1983).

RADIATION DAMPING IN MAGNETIC MONOPOLE PROCESSES*

Pavao Senjanović

Rudjer Bošković Institute
41001 Zagreb, P.O.B. 1016
Croatia, YUGOSLAVIA

Because of logical connectedness of several papers, and in order to achieve clarity of presentation, I will present a body of work with papers that have the following in common: a) they deal with the infrared problem of the quantum field theory of monopoles and charges (in naive perturbation theory), which we solve in the manner analogous to the one in QED, b) radiation damping in QED carries over here, only, due to the largeness of the magnetic coupling constant, it is a huge effect here, c) this radiation damping is studied as a phenomenon in various situations, such as scattering, pair creation, liberation from a magnetically neutral bound state, the most interesting being the third case, implying a confinement mechanism.

Clearly, if we are to solve the infrared problem, we need a simple description of photon degrees of freedom in QEMD. The one-potential formulation[1)] is ideally suited in this direction. Its Lagrangian is given by

$$\mathcal{L} = -\frac{1}{4} F_{\mu\nu}F^{\mu\nu} + \bar{\psi}\left[\gamma^{\mu}(i\partial_{\mu}-eA_{\mu}) - m_{\psi}\right]\psi + \bar{\chi}(\gamma^{\mu}i\partial_{\mu}-m_{\chi})\chi \ , \tag{1}$$

$$F_{\mu\nu} = \partial_{\mu}A_{\nu} - \partial_{\nu}A_{\mu} - \varepsilon_{\mu\nu\sigma\lambda}(n\cdot\partial)^{-1}\, n^{\sigma}j_{g}^{\lambda} \ , \tag{2}$$

$$j_{g}^{\lambda} = g\bar{\chi}\gamma^{\lambda}\chi \ , \tag{3}$$

$$(n\cdot\partial)^{-1}(x) = \left[-a\theta(n\cdot x)+(1-a)\theta(-n\cdot x)\right]\prod_{i=0}^{2}\delta(\tau^{(i)}\cdot x) \ , \tag{4}$$

where n^{σ} is a fixed spacelike vector ($n^2<0$). From the form of Eq. (2) one can recognize that n^{σ} is the direction in space-time of the frozen string, which is a one-sided Dirac[2)] string for a=1. $\theta(n)$ is a one-sided step function and $\tau^{(0)}$, $\tau^{(1)}$, $\tau^{(2)}$ and n are four mutually orthogonal vectors. a is an arbitrary real number between zero and one.

This formulation has a well-defined Hamiltonian and commutation rules[1)], which we do not display. We have shown[1)] from the operator version of the formulation that our one-potential formulation is equivalent to Schwinger's[3)]

*Supported by a grant from the Croatian Science Foundation.

(for a=1/2) and Zwanziger's (also for a=1/2) formulation.

We pass immediately to Feynman rules, which can be derived, say, from the functional integral formulation of the theory with the Lagrangian given by Eq. (1):

(a) photon-charge-charge ($A-\bar{\psi}-\psi$) vertex

$$-e\gamma_\lambda \ , \tag{5}$$

(b) photon-pole-pole ($A-\bar{\chi}-\chi$) vertex

$$-g\varepsilon_{\mu\nu\lambda\sigma}k^\mu n^\lambda \gamma^\sigma/n\cdot k \ , \tag{6}$$

(c) four-pole vertex

$$\frac{1}{2}\, n^2 g^2 \gamma^\rho_{(1)} (g_{\rho\sigma}-n_\rho n_\sigma/n^2)\left[n\cdot(p_3+p_4)\right]^{-2}\gamma^\sigma_{(2)}+(p_4\to p_1) \ . \tag{7}$$

(c) is equivalent to two standard vertices ($g\gamma_\lambda$) connected by a spurion propagator

$$\frac{1}{2}\, n^2 (g_{\rho\sigma} - n_\rho n_\sigma/n^2)(n\cdot k)^{-2} \ , \tag{8}$$

Note that the Feynman rules are <u>local</u> in momentum space, which greatly facilitates their use.

Having now in our hands the necessary tool, we proceed to solve the infrared problem of QEMD. But before that, we remind ourselves briefly of the situation in QED[5)].

Infrared divergences stemming from soft virtual photons cancel against those coming from soft real photons after they both <u>exponentiate</u> (when we study the problem <u>to all orders</u>). The origin of exponentiation is factorization and photon statistics (1/n!). If A_{n+1} is the amplitude for exchange of, say, n+1 virtual photons, then[5)]

$$A_{n+1} = S(k_{n+1})A_n + R(k_{n+1};k_1,k_2,\dots k_n) \ , \tag{9}$$

where S leads to a logarithmic infrared divergence in k_{n+1} and R is convergent in the infrared region.

A similar factorization rule appears in the probability distribution for emission of soft real photons.

In QEMD, we first consider monopole potential scattering, enabling us to gain insight into the general problem of infrared regularization of processes with monopoles and charges, and even more generally, dyons [6-8)].

The diagrams with charge loops and respective photon insertions are finite in QED[5)]. For pole loops in QEMD the situation is the same, to within singularities from

$$\frac{1}{(n\cdot k)^m} = \frac{a}{(n\cdot k+i\ )^m} + \frac{1-a}{(n\cdot k-i\ )^m}\ , \tag{10}$$

which we have shown to be absent up to two-loop level. We do not display this proof here.

The problem, thus, has been reduced to diagrams with photon insertions on the monopole line.

When the factor

$$-igA_{\nu\sigma} = -ig\,\frac{\varepsilon_{\mu\nu\lambda\sigma}k^\mu n^\lambda}{n\cdot k} \tag{11}$$

is extracted as an overall multiplicative factor and γ^σ is inserted in all possible ways along the monopole line, there result expressions identical to the ones in QED[5], but multiplied by $A_{\nu\sigma}$. Therefore the amplitude for emission of a real soft photon is

$$\bar{R}_\nu = -igA_{\nu\sigma}\left(\frac{p'^\sigma}{p'\cdot k} - \frac{p^\sigma}{p\cdot k}\right)\ . \tag{12}$$

Squaring $\bar{R}_\nu$, using the mass-shell condition $k^2=0$ and

$$k\cdot\left[\frac{p'}{p'\cdot k} - \frac{p}{p\cdot k}\right] = 0\ , \tag{13}$$

we obtain

$$\bar{R}^*_\nu \bar{R}^\nu = -g^2\left(\frac{p'}{p'\cdot k} - \frac{p}{p\cdot k}\right)^2\ . \tag{14}$$

This expression is identical to the one in QED, to within the replacement e→g. The explanation is that a duality transformation which transforms the electron into a monopole changes also photon polarization. This second change is immaterial, as we sum over all polarizations. We emphasize that duality is a symmetry of the theory.

Now for virtual photons, the diagram where both ends of the virtual photon are ending on the monopole line, one shows directly that two graphs involving ordinary photons and spurions combine to yield an effective graph with vertices $V^g_\nu = -ig\gamma_\nu$ and an effective propagator $D^E_{\mu\nu}$:

$$D^E_{\mu\nu} = -\frac{i}{k^2}\left[\eta_{\mu\nu} - \frac{1}{n\cdot k}(n_\mu k_\nu + n_\nu k_\mu) - \frac{n^2}{(n\cdot k)^2}k_\mu k_\nu\right]\ . \tag{15}$$

This multiplies an expression of the form $\Lambda_\mu\Lambda_\nu$ where $k\cdot\Lambda=0$, so we again get an expression as in QED, but with e→g.

We have therefore shown that <u>soft-photon contributions in monopole scattering are finite and factorizable.</u> We can therefore proceed to show <u>exponentiation</u> the same way as in QED.

If we denote the energy loss by ε and external momenta by p and p′, then[5)]

$$\frac{d\sigma}{d\varepsilon} = \exp[2\alpha_g(\text{Re } B + \tilde{B}')]\cdot I\cdot \frac{d\tilde{\sigma}}{d\varepsilon} \quad . \tag{16}$$

In Eq. (16) $\alpha_g = \frac{g^2}{4\pi} = \alpha^{-1}$, B is the contribution of virtual photons

$$B = \frac{i}{8\pi^3}\int \frac{d^4k}{k^2-\lambda^2+i\varepsilon}\left(\frac{2p'_\nu-k_\nu}{k^2-2p'\cdot k} - \frac{2p_\nu-k_\nu}{k^2-2p\cdot k}\right)^2 , \tag{17}$$

and $\tilde{B}$ that of real soft photons

$$\tilde{B} = -\frac{1}{8\pi^2}\int_0^\varepsilon \frac{d^3k}{\omega_\lambda}\left(\frac{p'_\nu}{p'\cdot k} - \frac{p_\nu}{p\cdot k}\right)^2 \quad . \tag{18}$$

$\omega_\lambda = (\vec{k}^2+\lambda^2)^{1/2}$ and λ is the photon mass regulator. I is the genuinely noninfrared contribution of real photons. $d\tilde{\sigma}/d\varepsilon$ is the cross section of the basic process times the infrared convergent virtual photon contribution.

As in QED, one shows:

$$\text{Re } B + \tilde{B} = \frac{1}{2}\left[k \ln \frac{2\varepsilon}{m} + k_1 + k_2\right] , \tag{19}$$

where k, k_1 and k_2 are independent of λ, a crucial result.

Let us turn our attention now to monopole-charge scattering. Using methods analogous to the ones just described, we obtain

$$S_\mu(p) = \frac{2p_\mu - k_\mu}{2p\cdot k - k^2 - i\varepsilon} ,$$
$$\tilde{S}_\mu(p) = \frac{p_\mu}{p\cdot k} , \tag{20}$$

$$\tilde{B} = -\frac{1}{8\pi^2}\int_0^\varepsilon \frac{d^3k}{\omega_\lambda}\{Z^2e^2[\tilde{S}_\mu(p_3) - \tilde{S}_\mu(p_1)]^2$$
$$+ g^2[\tilde{S}_\mu(p_4) - \tilde{S}_\mu(p_2)]^2\} , \tag{21}$$

$$B = \frac{i}{8\pi^3}\int \frac{d^4k}{k^2-\lambda^2+i\varepsilon}\{Z^2e^2[S_\mu(p_3) - S_\mu(p_1)]^2$$

$$+ g^2[S_\mu(p_4) - S_\mu(p_2)]^2\} \quad . \tag{22}$$

The "n-dependent" terms proportional to $egA^{\mu\lambda}$ can be shown to be zero[7].

In general one shows[8]

$$B_{QEMD} = B_{QED}(e_i e_j \to e_i e_j + g_i g_j) \ , \tag{23}$$

$$\tilde{B}_{QEMD} = \tilde{B}_{QED}(e_i e_j \to e_i e_j + g_i g_j) \ , \tag{24}$$

for a general process with N dyons in the external lines: $i,j = 1,\ldots, N$. This is a very suggestive result, showing that our radiation damping respects duality, as only dual invariant combinations of charges appear $(e_i e_j + g_i g_j)$.

The results we have obtained with the superstrong damping are clearly preferred over the Born approximations (+ QED infrared), as the latter do not respect duality and moreover they violate the unitarity bound

$$\frac{g^2}{q^2} = A >> \frac{1}{q^2} = A_o \ , \tag{25}$$

while ours do not, because of the damping.

In Ref. 7), we have included a treatment of processes where magnetically neutral bound states appear. To be specific, we have studied a process with two magnetically neutral states in the initial configuration and a monopole-antimonopole pair in the final configuration (Fig. 1) with

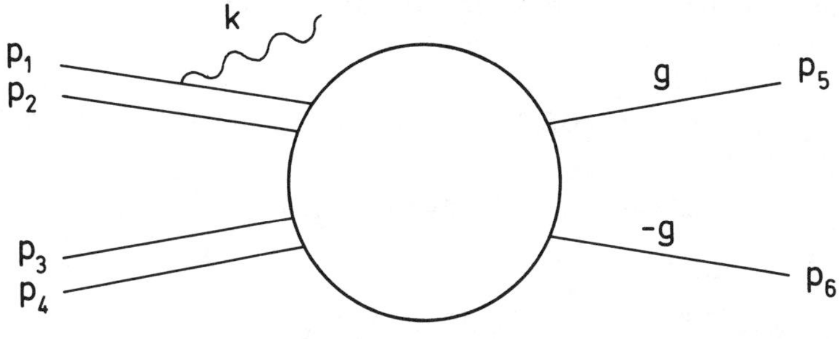

Fig. 1. Monopole pair production from magnetically neutral bound states

a proper treatment of the associated infrared problem and,

again, radiation damping.

The technique we use is the Bethe-Salpeter equation. We illustrate for the case of one constituent with spin 0 and the other with spin 1/2 (the resulting bound state also having spin 1/2; take the case $(e_i g_j - e_j g_i)/4\pi = Z_{ij} =$ = integers, so no dynamical spin).

If we denote the irreducible kernel for the system by $\overline{G}$, we have

$$\mathcal{D}_1 D_2 \chi = \overline{G}\chi \quad , \tag{26}$$

where χ is the Bethe-Salpeter wave function, and

$$\mathcal{D}_1 = i\gamma_\mu \partial_1^\mu - m_1 \quad , \tag{27}$$

$$D_2 = -\Box_2 - m_2^2 \ . \tag{28}$$

In order to describe the interaction of the bound state with the electromagnetic field, we use a method based on the principle of minimal coupling

$$(\mathcal{D}_1 + V_1)(D_2 + V_2)\chi = \overline{G}\chi \ , \tag{29}$$

$$V_1 = -e_1\gamma_\mu A_1^\mu \quad , \tag{30}$$

$$V_2 = -ie_2\partial_2^\mu A_\mu^2 - ie_2 A_\mu^2 \partial_2^\mu - e_2^2 A_\mu^2 A_2^\mu \ . \tag{31}$$

For the moment, we have deleted magnetic vertices, as they can be discussed in a completely analogous manner as electric ones in Zwanziger's formulation[4].

The two-body propagator G satisfies another Bethe-Salpeter equation

$$(\mathcal{D}_1 D_2 - \overline{G})G = 1 \ . \tag{32}$$

In the vicinity of the bound state poles we have the decomposition

$$G_{\alpha\beta}(k,q,P) \approx \left(\frac{i}{\gamma\cdot P-M}\right)_{\alpha\beta} \chi_P(k)\chi_P^\dagger(q) \ . \tag{33}$$

Eq. (29) is solved for

$$\chi = (1 + G\vartheta)^{-1}\chi_o = \sum_{n=o}^{\infty} (-1)^n (G\vartheta)^n \chi_o \ , \tag{34}$$

$$\vartheta = V_1 D_2 + \mathcal{D}_1 V_2 + V_1 V_2 \ . \tag{35}$$

Introducing relative and c.m. coordinates, $Q = p_1 - p_2$,

$P = \frac{1}{2}(p_1+p_2)$, D_2 becomes in momentum space

$$D_2 = -(m_2^2 - M^2 + P\cdot Q - \frac{Q^2}{4}) \ . \tag{36}$$

$P\cdot Q$, upon integration over Q with weight $\chi^\dagger(Q-k)\chi(Q)$ /see Eq. (33)/ produces $P\cdot k$ which is a nonrenormalizable effective vertex. It is infrared finite and will not contribute to radiation damping.

We obtain from GV_1D_2

$$\vartheta_1^\mu = -e_1\gamma^\mu F_1(k^2) \ , \tag{37}$$

$$F_1(k^2) = \int d^4Q(m_2^2-M^2-Q^2/4)\chi^\dagger(Q-k)\chi(Q) \ . \tag{38}$$

We obtain several other nonrenormalizable vertices, and we have shown all of them to be either infrared finite or suppressed in the tight-binding limit $M/m_i \ll 1$. In the infrared region, the effective vertices are, as for point-like objects, minimally coupled (the infrared finite nonrenormalizable pieces proportional to $F_i(k^2)-F_i(0)$ do not contribute). In this case, this confirms a recent conjecture[9].

We, therefore, can proceed with our techniques presented above and we derive a radiation damping factor corresponding to Fig. 1.

$$R = \exp[-e^2f(s/M^2) - g^2f(s/m^2)] \tag{39}$$

m and g are the mass and magnetic charge of the liberated monopole, $s = (p_5+p_6)^2$ and in the kinematic regime where the result can be trusted the function f is positive[6].

The result illustrates partial (but very strong) confinement of monopoles within magnetically neutral bound states owing its origin precisely to the phenomenon of superstrong radiation damping. This confirms the conjecture by Pati[10] for his theory of magnetic preons.

The reader should also note that our results in QEMD complement the result of Drukier and Nussinov[11] for extended monopoles where also exponential superstrong damping is found.

Finally, our treatment of the infrared problem nicely complements recent work done on ultraviolet regularization[12].

References

1) M. Blagojević, D. Nešić, P. Senjanović, Dj. Šijački and Dj. Živanović, Phys. Lett. 79B (1978) 75; M. Blagojević and P. Senjanović, Nucl. Phys. B161 (1979) 112
2) P.A.M. Dirac, Phys. Rev. 74 (1948) 817
3) J. Schwinger, Phys. Rev. 144 (1966) 1087
4) D. Zwanziger, Phys. Rev. D3 (1971) 880
5) D.R. Yennie, S.C. Frautschi and H. Suura, Ann. of Phys. 13 (1961) 379
6) M. Blagojević, S. Meljanac, I. Picek and P. Senjanović, Nucl. Phys. B198 (1982) 427 and references therein
7) M. Blagojević, S. Meljanac and P. Senjanović, Zagreb report, IRB-TP-2-83, to appear in Phys. Lett.
8) Ž. Antunović and P. Senjanović, to appear
9) Unpublished remarks due to M. Veltman, G. 't Hooft, G. Parisi, K. Wilson, L. Susskind, as explained in Ref. 10)
10) J.C. Pati, Phys. Lett. 98B (1981) 40; J.C. Pati, A. Salam and J. Strathdee, Nucl. Phys. B185 (1981) 416; P. Senjanović, Fizika 15 (1983) 165
11) A.K. Drukier and S. Nussinov, Phys. Rev. Lett. 49 (1982) 102
12) C. Panagiotakopoulos, Nucl. Phys. B198 (1982) 303; ibid, J. Phys. A (1983) 133; W. Deans, Nucl. Phys. B197 (1982) 307; G. Calucci and R. Iengo, ISAS Trieste report 72/82/E.P.

SOME ASPECTS OF QUASI NAMBU-GOLDSTONE FERMIONS

Roberto D. Peccei

Max-Planck-Institut für Physik und Astrophysik
- Werner Heisenberg Institut für Physik -
Munich, Fed.Rep.Germany

ABSTRACT

Several important features of quasi Nambu-Goldstone fermions (QGF) are discussed. These include: the expected patterns of QGF for a given breakdown, the low energy interactions among QGF, and the required mass protection mechanisms necessary for identifying phenomenologically quarks and leptons as QGF. Various illustrative models are included.

In a recent letter[1)] Wilfried Buchmüller, Tsotumo Yanagida and I suggested that quarks and leptons may be the quasi Nambu-Goldstone fermions (QGF)[2)] of an underlying supersymmetric preon theory. Since this paper a fair amount of research has been done along these lines, both by ourselves[3,4)] and others[5-12)]. Because this field is so rapidly moving this report, while being based on material I presented at Dubrovnik, has been updated to account for recent developments.

I will concentrate here mainly on those features of QGF which are of immediate physical relevance to the suggestion that quarks and leptons are QGF. These features include: the patterns of QGF for a given $G \to H$ breakdown and what dynamics force one into a given pattern; the concomitant low energy interactions of the QGF, which can signal the compositeness of quarks and leptons; and the mass protection mechanisms necessary for making the idea of quarks and leptons as QGF phenomenologically viable. The models I include here illustrate interesting physical aspects of QGF, but have no real pretense, at this stage, of physical cogency.

If quarks and leptons are composite one must find a dynamical reason for their being light with respect to the compositeness binding scale $\Lambda_{comp} \gtrsim 1$ TeV[13)]. If the underlying preon theory is a strong coupling confining theory one expects all bound states to have masses of $O(\Lambda_{comp})$. Light states can then only be produced as a result of approximate symmetries, which in the limit of their being exact force certain states to be massless.

The idea of quarks and leptons being QGF is based on a direct analogy with pion physics and QCD. Two flavor QCD possesses in the limit of zero quark masses a global $SU(2)_L \times SU(2)_R$ symmetry. This symmetry is spontaneously broken by the vacuum to $SU(2)_{L+R}$. Thus, even though all other states in QCD have masses of $O(\Lambda_{QCD})$, the isotriplet of pions in this zero quark mass limit is massless, because they are the Goldstone bosons of the spontaneous breakdown of $SU(2)_L \times SU(2)_R$ to $SU(2)_{L+R}$. If one has an underlying preon theory which is supersymmetric and in which a global symmetry G is spontaneously broken down to another symmetry H then, independently of the scale of Λ_{comp}, there will appear in the theory massless Goldstone bosons accompanied by certain massless supersymmetric fermionic partners - the quasi Goldstone fermions (QGF).

It is clear that if quarks and leptons are QGF, there is a dynamical reason for their being light. In the limit of exact G and exact supersymmetry the QGF would be massless. However, just as in the case of the pions, once these symmetries are broken quarks and leptons would then acquire some small mass. The situation is, nevertheless, more complicated in the case at hand since there is no evidence yet for any supersymmetric partner of quarks and leptons, with masses less than 15-20 GeV. Therefore realistic models of quarks and leptons as QGF must provide, in addition, dynamical reasons after mass generation for separating in mass the QGF from their bosonic partners. I shall return to this difficult point below, after I discuss some other dynamical features of QGF which make them particularly appealing for constructing models of quarks and leptons.

It is well known that when a global symmetry G is spontaneously broken down to another symmetry group H the number of Goldstone bosons which ensue is precisely equal to the dimension of the coset space G/H. To each of the broken generators of G there corresponds a Goldstone boson. With respect to H, since the Goldstone bosons lie in the G/H pieces of the adjoint of G, the Goldstone bosons transform as "real" representations. That is they transform according to purely real representations or they come in complex conjugate pairs. For the case of supersymmetric theories where a given $G \rightarrow H$ breakdown also generates QGF, the pattern of QGF is, however, not uniquely fixed. What QGF ensue are determined both by the group theory and by the dynamics of the theory. In particular, there is no necessity that the QGF be real with respect to H[14].

I want to briefly discuss the various options available for QGF. The simplest, and most general possibility is that the n Goldstone bosons in a given $G \rightarrow H$ breakdown are accompanied by n QGF. In this (total doubling) case there must exist in the theory also n quasi Goldstone bosons to preserve the supersymmetry. Clearly, in the total doubling case the QGF transform with respect to H as the Goldstone bosons do. That is, they are real with respect to H. Since one knows that quarks and leptons are complex with respect to the standard model group $SU(2) \times U(1)$, in models with total doubling of the QGF - as in the $SU(5) \rightarrow SU(3)_c \times U(1)_{em}$ model of Ref. (1) - either the weak interactions are not fundamental or they act only on a part of H. Alternatively, the low mass spectrum contains mirror fermions which must then be removed, somehow.

However, QGF need not always appear in a total doubling pattern. If under H there exist a pair of complex conjugate representations i and $\bar{i}$ of Goldstone bosons, a perfectly acceptable Goldstone supermultiplet may be constructed by pairing these bosonic states with a QGF transforming as, say, i under H[15]. Roughly speaking, therefore, for a given $G \rightarrow H$ breakdown giving n Goldstone bosons there may arise from n to n/2 (or n+1/2, for n-odd) QGF. In the minimal case of n/2 QGF, all the Goldstone bosons are paired and no quasi Goldstone boson states need to be included to maintain the supersymmetry. For the other cases there are in general quasi Goldstone bosons present besides the Goldstone bosons and the QGF, so that the total number of fermionic and bosonic degrees of freedoms match.

Clearly models with QGF which appear in not totally real representations with respect to H are very intriguing. One may hope in this way to naturally incorporate the chiral nature of quarks and leptons with respect to the weak interactions. An example illustrates this. Consider the breakdown pattern[2,6] $E_6 \rightarrow SO(10) \times U(1)$. The Goldstone bosons transform as a 16 and a $\overline{16}$ of SO(10). In the case of total doubling, there is a set of 16 QGF which are purely left handed and can be identified as the quarks and leptons of one family, but there are also 16 QGF which are their right-handed mirrors. If, however, the QGF are minimal only 16 purely left-handed fermions enter in the theory and no mirroring problem arises.

I have emphasized already that the pattern of allowed QGF depends both on the group theory and on the dynamics. Very recently Lee and Sharatchandra[12] have given a quite general group theoretical prescription for the allowed pattern of QGF for a given $G \rightarrow H$ breakdown. However, whether any of these patterns is realized is a matter of dynamics. Before discussing dynamical issues, let me briefly outline the results of Ref. (12). Lee and Sharatchandra[12] consider the breakdown $G \rightarrow H$ as proceeding in stages $G \rightarrow G_1 \rightarrow G_2 \ldots \rightarrow G_n \rightarrow H$, such that at each stage the coset manifold consists of just one real or a pair of complex conjugate representations. Clearly, if the Goldstone boson representation is real, the relevant QGF must be accompanied also by quasi Goldstone bosons (total doubling). For the case that there are a pair of complex conjugate representations, and only if the coset space G_i/G_{i+1} is Kählerian, then there is the possibility of having a minimal QGF pattern, with no additional quasi Goldstone bosons. In these instances then there is the option of either having a minimal or a doubled case. Each option, through each of the stages from $G \rightarrow H$, leads to a different chain of breakdown. The totality of the QGF patterns are represented by all the possible chains.

The requirement that the coset space be Kählerian for the minimal pattern to emerge is important and needs some explanation. This can be understood as follows: For any supersymmetric model in which there is the spontaneous breakdown of a global symmetry G to H one expects that it should be possible to write a nonlinear supersymmetric Lagrangian which reflects the dynamics of the Goldstone superfields. These nonlinear Lagrangians, in the case that the underlying theory is an ordinary nonconfining field theory can be gotten by integrating out the heavy fields from the theory. However, even in the case of confining field theories one expects that such nonlinear Lagrangians exist for the bound state Goldstone superfields and represent correctly the threshold dynamics of the theory. Zumino[16] has shown that nonlinear supersymmetric Lagrangians can be written in a manifestly supersymmetric way in terms of the chiral and antichiral Goldstone superfields, ϕ and $\bar{\phi}$. Specifically the Lagrangian is just the D-term of some general function of these fields - the, so-called, Kähler potential:

$$\mathcal{L} = K(\bar{\phi}, \phi)\Big|_{\theta\theta\bar{\theta}\bar{\theta}} \quad . \tag{1}$$

It follows from this that the piece of $\mathcal{L}$ which involves only the scalar components of ϕ and $\bar{\phi}$ is

$$\begin{aligned}\mathcal{L}_{scalar} &= -\partial^\mu \varphi^{*i} \frac{\partial^2 K(\varphi^*, \varphi)}{\partial\varphi^{*i}\partial\varphi^j} \partial_\mu \varphi^j \\ &= -\partial^\mu \varphi^{*i}\, h_{ij}(\varphi^*, \varphi)\, \partial_\mu \varphi^j \quad .\end{aligned} \tag{2}$$

The metric h_{ij} appearing in (2) obeys the Kähler conditions:

$$\frac{\partial h_{ij}}{\partial\varphi^{*k}} = \frac{\partial h_{kj}}{\partial\varphi^{*i}} \quad ; \quad \frac{\partial h_{ij}}{\partial\varphi^{k}} = \frac{\partial h_{ik}}{\partial\varphi^{j}} \quad . \tag{3}$$

Therefore one sees that the totality of the massless scalars of a nonlinear supersymmetric Lagrangian can be identified with the complex coordinates of a Kähler manifold. With this point in mind imagine having a particular breakdown $G_i \rightarrow G_{i+1}$, giving some Goldstone bosons and consider the associated nonlinear Lagrangian. If G_i/G_{i+1} is a Kähler manifold, then the nonlinear Lagrangian can be built with only the Goldstone bosons as scalar "coordinates". If, on the other hand G_i/G_{i+1} is not Kählerian, one must add further "coordinates" to the Goldstone bosons so as to span a Kähler manifold on which a nonlinear Lagrangian can be built. These extra "coordinates" are quasi Goldstone bosons. This second option of doubling the available coordinates is always possible. However, the minimal case can only occur if the coset space itself is Kählerian.

As I said earlier, the pattern of QGF emerging from a given theory is determined by the dynamics. In Ref. (3), Buchmüller, Yanagida and I suggested that, unless the underlying theory was chiral asymmetric in some way, one could never obtain a QGF spectrum which was not real. This statement is difficult to prove in general, if the underlying theory is some confining preon theory. However, it can be studied in the context of Lagrangian models. Lerche[17] has examined, in particular, what happens in models where the global symmetry is broken by F-terms and he has verified our conjecture. It may well be that F-term breaking is too restrictive a condition but, at any rate, it is worthwhile briefly discussing Lerche's[17] results, since they illustrate some important points about QGF.

In a Lagrangian model involving various superfields ϕ interacting via a superpotential $W(\phi)$, invariant under a global symmetry G, there may be asymmetric minima where G is broken down to some subgroup H. At these minima, so as to preserve supersymmetry, all F-terms must vanish

$$F(\phi) = 0 . \tag{4}$$

Because Eq. (4) involves only the superfields ϕ and not $\bar{\phi}$ it turns out really that the invariance group at the minimum is not H, but its complex extension H^*. In fact, for this same reason, $W(\phi)$ has also a larger invariance group, G^* not G. If one examines the fermion mass matrix at the superpotential minimum one sees again this possibility of invariance under the complex extension

$$\left.\frac{\partial^2 W}{\partial\phi^i\partial\phi^j}\right|_{\phi=\langle\phi\rangle}(t_a)_{jk}\langle\phi_k\rangle = m_{ij}(t_a)_{jk}\langle\phi_k\rangle = 0 . \tag{5}$$

The above implies that there are zero mass fermions in the theory, associated with generators for which

$$t_a\langle\phi\rangle \neq 0 . \tag{6}$$

However, now t_a is no longer the set of hermitean generators of G but it is extended to include the remaining, antihermitean, generators which turn G into G^*. Only if

$$t_a\langle\phi\rangle \neq 0 \tag{7a}$$

but

$$t_a^+\langle\phi\rangle = 0 \tag{7b}$$

will one not find total doubling. Such a possibility obtains only if one starts with an asymmetric theory. Furthermore, for certain breakdowns, the conditions in Eqs. (7) are impossible to be satisfied and one must have a total doubling pattern of QGF. For instance, for any breakdown in which the commutator of the generators in the coset space yields always a generator in the unbroken subgroup (e.g. $SU(n)_L \times SU(n)_R \rightarrow SU(n)_{L+R}$) it is impossible to have a condition like (7) hold[17].

I should point out that the strong dynamical results obtained above may not be applicable in more complicated models where one has both F and D term breaking. In particular, since D-terms contain both ϕ and $\bar{\phi}$, the invariance under a complex extension of the symmetry group at the potential minimum need no longer hold. These same cautionary remarks apply also to supersymmetric confining gauge theories where spontaneous breakdown of global symmetries are due to condensate formation. It is an open question whether the dynamics of these theories can be mimicked by an appropriate F-term Lagrangian.

Supersymmetric confining gauge theories, of course, are the most reasonable candidates for being the underlying theory which provides one with quarks and leptons as QGF. It is therefore important to try to understand in some way, what might be the allowed pattern of QGF in these theories. An important remark was made, in this connection, by Barbieri, Masiero and Veneziano[7]. They observed that for the spectrum of QGF to be chirally asymmetric (i.e. not totally doubled) it is necessary, in general, that the QGF be part of the set of states needed to match the 't Hooft anomaly conditions[18]. Although there are chiral, but anomaly free, set of states (e.g. $\bar{5}$ + 10 of SU(5)), in most circumstances if the pattern of QGF is chiral asymmetric with respect to H these states will give rise to nontrivial Adler anomalies. 't Hooft has argued[18] that such states can only exist if their anomalies are precisely matched by those computed from the underlying theory.

Barbieri, Masiero and Veneziano[7] illustrated their point with an example based on an $SU(6)_{HC}$ confining group with a global U(6) x U(6)' symmetry which is broken down to $SU(4)_{diag.} \times SU(2)_{diag} \times U(1)^2$. A variety of models also based on $SU(6)_{HC}$ and U(6) x U(6)' but with different breakdown patterns, have been subsequently explored by Greenberg, Mohapatra and Yasue[10]. In the models of Ref. (7) and (10) one finds that, in general, one requires further zero mass fermions to anomaly match than those that are present as QGF. Buchmüller, Yanagida and I[4] have found a class of models in which the fermions which are demanded by the anomaly matching are precisely the QGF. I briefly want to describe these models - in particular the simplest realistic version of them - since some of their features will be important, in a different context, below.

The models discussed in Ref. (4) are based on an $SU(2)_{HC}$ theory which has a U(n) global symmetry which is broken down to U(n-2) x SU(2). The simplest interesting model has n = 6. If n = 6, the coset space U(6)/U(4) x SU(2) has 17 Goldstone bosons associated with it, which transform as (4,2) + ($\bar{4}$,2) + (1,1) with respect to U(4) x SU(2). The QGF associated with this breakdown, which are consistent with anomaly matching, will be seen below to transform as (4,2) + (1,1). That is, in this model there is total doubling of the real representation (1,1) but the Goldstone bosons in (4,2) and ($\bar{4}$,2) are paired with only one QGF representation. So the model has 17 Goldstone bosons, 1 quasi Goldstone boson and 9 QGF, matching bosonic and fermionic degrees of freedom. Assigning the electromagnetic charge as

$$Q = \begin{bmatrix} 1/6 & & & & & \\ & 1/6 & & & 0 & \\ & & 1/6 & & & \\ & & & -1/2 & & \\ & 0 & & & -1/2 & \\ & & & & & 1/2 \end{bmatrix} \tag{8}$$

one sees that the (4,2) QGF have precisely the quantum numbers of one family of lefthanded quarks and leptons. The (1,1) QGF - which we dubbed[4] the novino - is neutral.

The preons in this model are taken to be $SU(2)_{HC}$ doublets, carrying a 6-fold flavor symmetry index p = 1, ... 6 and are described by a chiral superfield ϕ^p_a. The $SU(2)_{HC}$ group is gauged and presumed to confine. The classical invariance of this theory is augmented by an R-symmetry and is therefore

$$G_{class} = SU(2)_{HC} \times U(6) \times U(1)_R \ . \tag{9}$$

Both the preon number U(1) and $U(1)_R$ have strong anomalies with respect to $SU(2)_{HC}$. However, the combination of generators

$$X = T_6 + 3R \tag{10}$$

is anomaly free. This is easily checked since for each preon $T_6 = +1$, while R = -1 or R = 0, depending on whether the preon is fermionic or bosonic. The SU(2) gaugino has R = +1 and being in the adjoint representation of $SU(2)_{HC}$ contributes 4 times more to the $(SU(2)^2_{HC}\ X)$ anomaly than the fermionic preons. Clearly

$$\text{Anom } (SU(2)^2_{HC}\ X) = 6 - 18 + 12 = 0 \ . \tag{11}$$

The quantum symmetry of the model is therefore

$$G_{quant} = SU(2)_{HC} \times SU(6) \times U(1)_X \ . \tag{12}$$

Out of the superfields ϕ^p_a one can construct a unique $SU(2)_{HC}$ invariant composite chiral multiplet

$$\varphi^{pq} = \epsilon^{ab} \left(\phi^p_a \phi^q_b - \phi^q_a \phi^p_b \right) \tag{13}$$

which transforms as a <u>15</u> with respect to U(6). The condensate $\langle \varphi^{56} \rangle \neq 0$ breaks the global symmetry of the preon theory spontaneously and gives rise to bound state Goldstone supermultiplets.

The breakdown induced by $\langle \varphi^{56} \rangle \neq 0$ is clearly

$$SU(2)_{HC} \times SU(6) \times U(1)_X \rightarrow SU(2)_{HC} \times SU(4) \times SU(2) \times U(1)_{\tilde{X}} \ . \qquad (14)$$

Here $U(1)_{\tilde{X}}$ is the linear combination of preon number (for the first 4 preons) and R symmetry, which is unbroken by $\langle \varphi^{56} \rangle \neq 0$, and has no $SU(2)_{HC}$ anomaly:

$$\tilde{X} = T_4 + 2R \ . \qquad (15)$$

The group $H = SU(4) \times SU(2) \times U(1)_{\tilde{X}}$ has nontrivial anomalies at the preon level. These anomalies are matched at the composite level precisely by assuming that the QGF transform as (4,2)+ (1,1) with respect to H. Under H one has fermionic preons which transform as

$$\begin{aligned} \psi_a^p &\sim (4,1,-1) \qquad p = 1,\ldots,4 \\ \psi_a^p &\sim (1,2,-2) \qquad p = 5,6 \\ G_a &\sim (1,1,2) \end{aligned} \qquad (16)$$

with G_a being the gaugino. At the composite level the QGF transform as

$$\begin{aligned} \psi^{pq} &\sim (4,2,-1) \qquad p = 1,\ldots,4\ ;\ q = 5,6 \\ \eta &\sim (1,1,-2)\ . \end{aligned} \qquad (17)$$

Clearly the $(SU(4))^3$ and $\tilde{X}(SU(4))^2$ anomaly match as the $SU(2)_{HC}$ degeneracy at the preon level is replaced by that of the global SU(2) at the bound state level. The $\tilde{X}(SU(2))^2$ anomaly match because the $SU(2)_{HC}$ doublet field ψ_a^p has $\tilde{X} = -2$ while the SU(4) global quartet has $\tilde{X} = -1$. Finally the $\tilde{X}^3$ anomaly require at the underlying level the presence of the gaugino and at the composite level the existence of the novino.

I want to emphasize that this anomaly matching via QGF is <u>not</u> peculiar to the preon theory under discussion which has a U(6) <u>global</u> symmetry. One can easily check that anomalies are matched for any $U(n) \rightarrow U(n-2) \times SU(2)$ breakdown, irrespective of n. This means that the addition of explicit mass terms to the theory, which violate the original U(n) symmetry, still lead to anomaly matching. That is, if one drops from the spectrum of light states the bound states containing a heavy preon, again the relevant QGF match anomalies. This strong dynamical requirement - the persistent mass condition [19] - is <u>not</u> a property of the models based of $SU(6)_{HC}$ and U(6) x U(6') discussed in Refs. (7) and (10). There it is crucial that the global group be U(6) x U(6)'. Adding a mass term which reduces the global U(6) x U(6)' symmetry to U(5) x U(5)' does not lead to anomaly matching.

Although it is possible to find examples of theories where the persistent mass condition does not hold[19], it appear obviously more satisfactory to have this very natural condition to be obeyed. Indeed 't Hooft[18] has argued that this condition is a dynamical necessity in addition to anomaly matching.

I want now to turn to a second interesting aspect of QGF. Namely, the possibility of constructing effective Lagrangians for their low energy interactions. If indeed quarks and leptons are QGF, these Lagrangians should describe the residual interactions for $q^2 \ll \Lambda_{comp}$ which signal their composite nature. In fact, as I will discuss below, it even could be that these effective Lagrangians for quarks and leptons represent the weak interactions that appear in the standard model !

I indicated earlier that associated with any breakdown $G \rightarrow H$ one could construct a nonlinear supersymmetric Lagrangian for the Goldstone superfields which reflected their dynamics. This Lagrangian is, as Zumino showed[16], nothing but the D-term of the Kähler potential (c.f. Eq. (1)). The low energy dynamics is fixed once one knows how to construct this potential. More geometrically, the dynamics is determined by the Kähler metric h_{ij}. There is a direct analogy here with pion physics which I want to mention, both because it illustrates this point and also because it clarifies some important differences between the case at hand and what happens in QCD. Because pions are (approximate) Goldstone bosons they obey specific low energy theorems. These theorems, as Weinberg showed[20], can be reproduced by constructing effective Lagrangians which are invariant under nonlinear transformations of the pion fields in the coset space SU(2) x SU(2)/SU(2). For instance $\pi - \pi$ scattering at threshold is entirely fixed by the Lagrangian

$$\mathcal{L} = -\frac{1}{2}\partial^\mu \pi^i g_{ij}(\pi/f_\pi)\partial_\mu \pi^j \qquad (18)$$

which generalizes the pion kinetic energy by replacing the usual Kronecker metric δ_{ij} by the appropriate metric $g_{ij}(\pi/f_\pi)$ for the coset space. The dynamics is entirely determined by the geometry, except for the scale f_π necessary to make the pion field dimensionless.

In the supersymmetric case there is, however, an important difference. Except in the minimal case, in which the Goldstone superfields contain <u>only</u> Goldstone bosons and QGF but no quasi Goldstone bosons, the effective Lagrangian in Eq. (1) will contain additional information besides that provided by the geometry of the coset space G/H. Putting it another way, in the pion case low energy $\pi - \pi$ scattering is fixed by the geometry of the coset space. QCD only fixes the magnitude of $f_\pi \sim \Lambda_{QCD}$. For the case at hand the effective Lagrangian (1) in general depends on the underlying model in other ways besides the various scales "f_π" for each Goldstone superfield.

One can understand this dependence rather simply. For a non minimal case, the coset space which one needs for the construction of the effective Lagrangian is not G/H, but some complex Kählerian extension. While the metric g_{ij} for G/H can be constructed once one knows how the Goldstone fields transform under G, no such unique construction exists for the metric h_{ij} needed to construct the Kähler potential of Eq. (1). In effect, which extra quasi Goldstone bosons arise and what are their interactions is a function of the underlying theory[3]. It has nothing directly to do with the G/H geometry.

Fortunately, one is not interested in the Kähler potential $K(\bar{\phi},\phi)$ in general but only in the terms of K which are of lowest nontrivial dimensionality. For these terms, the functional arbitrariness of L_{eff} arising from the underlying theory is reflected in the appearance of a finite number of new scales. Therefore, in practice one can determine the principal interactions of QGF without too much arbitrariness[3]. I should note that for the purely Goldstone fields there is no arbitrariness at all, since their dynamics follows from the G/H geometry. It follows therefore that supersymmetry then fixes the dynamics of the QGF, with the only arbitrariness being due to the presence of quasi Goldstone bosons. For a Kähler manifold G/H, minimally realized so that there are no quasi Goldstone bosons, the interactions of the QGF are unique.

If ϕ is a Goldstone superfield, the term in the Kähler potential of Eq. (1) which contains two ϕ's and two $\bar{\phi}$'s gives rise to the first nontrivial interactions among the QGF. It is easy to check that the D-term of this contribution gives a 4 Fermi current-current interaction Lagrangian of the form:

$$\mathcal{L}_{eff} = A_{ijkl}\,\bar{\psi}_{iL}\gamma^{\mu}\psi_{jL}\,\bar{\psi}_{kL}\gamma_{\mu}\psi_{lL}\,. \tag{19}$$

Here the ψ_{iL} are left-handed Dirac QGF. The parameters A_{ijkl}, which are of dimension $(\text{mass})^{-2}$, depend both on the scales associated with each possible Goldstone superfield (the equivalent to f_{π}) and other parameters which depend in detail on the underlying model. Both, this extra freedom and the form of Eq. (19) are extremely suggestive. One is led to speculate that for a given $G \to H$ breakdown, perhaps the underlying theory is such that (19) just reproduces the weak interactions of the standard model[3]. In effect, what one needs if just that Eq. (19) reduce to the $SU(2)_L$ version of current-current interaction. This is because one knows[21] that, after γ -Z° mixing, it is possible from

$$\mathcal{L}_{eff} = \frac{G}{\sqrt{2}}\left[\vec{J}_{\mu}\cdot\vec{J}^{\mu}\right] \tag{20}$$

with $\vec{J}_{\mu}$ an $SU(2)_L$ current, to recover the usual standard model effective $q^2 \to 0$ Lagrangian.

In Ref. (3) we examined two theories which led to the correct spectrum of quarks and leptons for one family, $SU(5) \rightarrow SU(3)_c \times U(1)_{em}$ [1] and $SU(6) \rightarrow SU(4) \times SU(2) \times U(1)$. In both these theories the spectrum of QGF is totally doubled, so that the QGF are real with respect to H. Therefore, if the models are to be realistic the weak interactions must be residual. For the SU(5) case it turns out that A_{ijkl} has very much freedom (6 scales plus 17 other parameters) and one can find a limit in parameter space where Eq. (19) reduces to Eq. (20). However, there is no explanation of why there is an $SU(2)_L$ structure or of quark-lepton universality, since in the model

$$J_\mu^+ = \bar{e}\gamma_\mu(1-\gamma_5)\nu + \xi\,\bar{d}\gamma_\mu(1-\gamma_5)u \tag{21}$$

and ξ is a free parameter which must be fixed by hand to be approximately unity.

The $SU(6) \rightarrow SU(4) \times SU(2) \times U(1)$ model is much better in this respect. Universality is built in because of the SU(4) in H, which acts as a Pati-Salam SU(4)[22], with lepton number being the 4th color. The two representations (4,2) and $(\bar{4},2)$ of QGF each have a scale associated with it, v_+ and v_-. In the limit when $v_- \gg v_+$ the SU(2) in H reduces to an approximate $SU(2)_L$ and the effective Lagrangian one obtains is like (20) but with an additional isoscalar interaction

$$\mathcal{L}_{eff} = \frac{G}{\sqrt{2}}\left[\vec{J}_\mu \cdot \vec{J}^\mu + K\, J_{\mu s} J^\mu_s\right]. \tag{22}$$

To reproduce the weak interaction in the model one must assume that the underlying dynamics is such that, besides $v_- \gg v_+$, there emerges naturally that $K \ll 1$.

The "novino" model of Ref. (4), which I introduced earlier in connection with the 't Hooft anomaly matching, was constructed primarily with a view of reproducing "naturally" the weak interaction. In contrast to the above models where the QGF are totally doubled, in the case of the breakdown $U(6) \rightarrow U(4) \times SU(2)$ one has nearly a minimal set of QGF. Thus it is to be expected that the effective Lagrangian should be much less arbitrary. Indeed a straightforward calculation gives[4], for the quark and lepton sector:

$$\mathcal{L}_{eff} = \frac{1}{8v_1^2}\left[\vec{J}_\mu \cdot \vec{J}^\mu\right] + \frac{(v_1^2 - v_2^2)}{8v_1^4}\left[J_{\mu s} J^\mu_s\right]. \tag{23}$$

Here v_1 and v_2 are the scales associated with the quark and lepton superfield and the novino field, respectively. We see that if these two scales are identical then L_{eff} reduces to the desired $SU(2)_L$ form. This is naturally to be expected in the preon model we discussed where both the quarks and leptons and the novino where constructed as different components of φ^{ab}.

I should mention that getting a theory to have as the $q^2 \rightarrow 0$ L_{eff} that of Eq.(20) no longer really suffices as a criteria to say that the weak interactions are residual. Since the W and Z have now been discovered[23], in the mass range predicted by the standard model, it is also necessary that the preon theory reproduce these results. This follows if one could show that the γ -Z° mixing parameter $\lambda \simeq e/g = \sin\theta_W$. In this case then $M_W = M_Z \cos\theta_W$ obtains and having set the scale of M_W from G_F the right masses ensue, apart from radiative effects. If the underlying theory is such that the J = 1 spectrum of excitation produced has a W and Z boson quite separated from the continuum[25], then vector dominance of the electromagnetic form factor guarantees that $\lambda \simeq \sin\theta_W$. For the "novino" model just discussed, it is not possible to prove that the W and Z are necessarily light. However, because the model has a complementary picture[4] which is nothing but the supersymmetric version of the standard model, this dynamical possibility is by no means excluded.

I should mention that for the breakdown $SU(6) \rightarrow SU(4) \times SU(2) \times U(1)$ in which the QGF are not doubled [9,10] then the effective Lagrangian (23) again applies except that $v_2 = 0$. These models have maximal isoscalar interactions and thus do not reproduce correctly the weak interactions as effective interactions. These interactions must be gauged already at the preon level and one must have that $G_F \gg 1/v_1^2$. Otherwise the residual interactions will spoil the successes of the standard model

Although it is possible to have models where the weak interactions can be gauged, in some sense these models are more complicated than models in which these interactions are purely residual. As I mentioned above, in these circumstances one must make sure that the residual interactions are not too big. Furthermore one must find natural ways to generate the Fermi scale in theories where the natural scale is Λ_{comp} and where phenomenology requires

$$\Lambda^2_{comp} G_F \gg 1 . \qquad (24)$$

Buchmüller, Yanagida and I[25] have been studying a nice model where weak interactions are fundamental, based on the breakdown chain $U(6) \times U(6)' \rightarrow [U(4) \times SU(2)]^2 \rightarrow U(4) \times U(4)' \times SU(2)_{diag}$. The first breakdown provides one with the 16 quarks and leptons of one family plus two "novinos", in exact analogy to the model presented earlier. In the breakdown of $SU(2) \times SU(2)' \rightarrow SU(2)_{diag}$ the assumption is that the QGF spectrum is doubled. If one of the SU(2) is assumed to be gauged in the usual Weinberg Salam way, the condensate which induces the breakdown of $SU(2) \times SU(2)' \rightarrow SU(2)_{diag}$, automatically give masses to the W and Z bosons and the gauginos. Furthermore the whole Goldstone supermultiplet arising from the second breakdown is totally eaten. In effect, in this theory the preon model acts as technicolor. However, to avoid troubles with experiment, the scale associated with the first breakdown, which gives rise to the quarks and leptons, must be much bigger than that of second breakdown, which gives rise to G_F. The correct dynamical question is how does this come about naturally.

This issue can be avoided in a very amusing model introduced in Ref. (3), which is being studied by J. Goity[26]. Here one considers the breakdown of a rather large group $SU(n+8) \to SU(n)_{Tc} \times SU(3)_C \times SU(2)_L \times U(1)$. It is possible to arrange the pattern of QGF so that they include a family of quarks and leptons along with some $SU(n)_{Tc}$ nonsinglet states which are chiral with respect to H. Here the group $SU(n)_{Tc}$ acts as a Technicolor group and it is clear that there is no relation between Λ_{Tc} and Λ_{comp}. If one assumes that Technicolor condensates form which break $SU(2)_L \times U(1)$, it is possible then to generate $G_F \sim 1/\Lambda_{Tc}^2$ and the condition (24) can hold. Residual interactions then do not need to spoil the standard model picture. However, the interactions among the quark and leptons and the technicolor nonsinglet states act effectively as an ETC theory. Once technicolor condensates form, and if supersymmetry is broken, these interactions can give rise to masses for quarks and leptons.

I would like now to turn to the last topic which is of crucial importance if one is to believe that quarks and leptons are QGF. This is the whole issue of mass generation and families. It is unrealistic to try to decouple these two issues. However, since we are still in the infancy of the subject, it may be worthwhile to understand how technically one may generate mass, even in a one family situation. I will begin my discussion, therefore, by focusing only on mass generation, quite apart from the family issue.

To generate mass for the QGF in a given model, it is necessary both to explicitly break the global symmetry G and the supersymmetry. Furthermore, as I have mentioned earlier, in this process one has to be careful that the final remaining mass spectrum has the QGF as lowest mass states, since there is no evidence yet for any kind of supersymmetric partners experimentally. This is tricky since some of the bosonic partners - the real Goldstone bosons - cannot acquire mass until G is broken. So, for example, breaking supersymmetry and not G would give rise to a disastrous phenomenological mass spectrum.

It is an open question at this moment how supersymmetry would be broken in these kinds of models. Perhaps the most natural way would be through some spontaneous breaking triggered by supergravity, but I do not really know. Nevertheless let me associate a scale μ typical for this breaking. Physically we must demand that $\Lambda_{comp} \gg \mu$, if not there is no reason for invoking supersymmetry as an approximate good symmetry in the binding. The above inequality poses some difficulties for models in which one would like to relate the Fermi scale to Λ_{comp}. However, taking an optimistic point of view, in models where the weak interactions are effective one predicts rather light supersymmetric partners to appear. The masses of the QGF and of the bosonic excitations must all be proportional to μ. This follows if the nonrenormalization theorem[27] of supersymmetry applies also in this bound state context. As long as supersymmetry is exact one has that induced self energies are proportional to p^2, so that massless states stay massless.

It is very natural to assume that the global symmetry G gets broken once one turns on some gauge interactions. Hence one expects that the masses of the real Goldstone bosons be proportional to a gauge coupling constant squared, which I will denote generically by α. The QGF masses, on the other hand are not necessarily proportional to α, since there is no necessity for them to vanish in the exact G, but broken supersymmetry limit. These masses, however, depend on the coupling of the QGF with the heavy mass states of the theory, since from massless fermions one cannot generate a mass because of helicity conservation. I will denote the square of this light sector-heavy sector coupling by α_H.

In view of the above considerations, it is easy to convince oneself that the typical masses which the various members of the Goldstone superfield get, after supersymmetry and G breaking, are typically:

$$m^2_{GB} \sim \alpha \mu^2 \ln(\Lambda_{comp}/\mu)$$
$$m^2_{QGB} \sim \alpha_H \mu^2 \ln(\Lambda_{comp}/\mu) \quad (25)$$
$$m_{QGF} \sim \alpha_H \mu \left(\frac{\Delta M}{\Lambda_{comp}}\right) \ln(\Lambda_{comp}/\mu).$$

The logarithmic factors above arise because mass divergences are naturally cut off by the composite scale Λ_{comp}. The additional factor $\Delta M/\Lambda_{comp}$ in the QGF mass formula is there to typify the typical chiral mass splitting in the heavy sector of the theory. Clearly if the heavy states are chirally paired ($\Delta M = 0$) the QGF remain massless because of chirality conservation.

For phenomenological purposes it is necessary that the QGF be less massive than their bosonic partners. This implies that

$$\left(\alpha_H \frac{\Delta M}{\Lambda_{comp}}\right)^2 << \alpha . \quad (26)$$

Unless the QGF have additional dynamical protection, the inequality (26) is not likely to hold. Since the preon theory is presumably a strong coupling field theory one expects $\alpha_H \sim O(1)$. Thus to make the idea viable one needs some sort of chiral protection, so that $\Delta M/\Lambda_{comp} << 1$. This occurs naturally if the unbroken group H contains SU(2) x U(1)[3], since quarks and leptons are forbidden mass by it because of their chiral assignments. However, chirality does not prevent their bosonic partners to acquire a mass.

The inequality (26) should obtain if, as suggested by Barbieri, Masiero and Veneziano[7] the QGF are part of a set which is demanded by anomaly matching. In these cases, the QGF are protected by the chiral symmetries in H from acquiring mass. Indeed, having this double protection, may help in producing really light states. It is also possible that some of the intrafamily mass hierarchies arise[7,10,11] because of the different protection patterns demanded by supersymmetry and/or chirality. In fact, after all these protections are built in, one of the hardest tasks is to generate some masses for the QGF without having to introduce some "seed" chiral breaking term at the preon level. In this sense, the most promising approach, appears to have masses generated via non perturbative (instanton) effects[28,24].

I left the family issue for last, because it is (almost) totally ununderstood. It is possible to construct models in which families appear in a rather mechanical way by using, for instance, the coset space $U(4n_f+2) \rightarrow U(4n_f) \times SU(2)$[4,10]. However, one can in this case paraphrase Rabi and ask "who ordered this coset space ?" There are more ambitious family proposals[10,11], where some of the fermionic families are required because they are QGF and some because of anomaly matching. In general, however, these models end up by having other states besides quarks and leptons, which must be removed from the spectrum.

A nice family model has been studies recently by Kugo and Yanagida [29] based on the coset $E_7/SU(5) \times SU(3) \times U(1)$. This is a Kähler manifold and can give rise to three families of quarks and leptons plus an additional 5-plet (very probably additional states are needed for anomaly reasons[6]). The interesting point of this model is that some form of E_7 naturally arises in N=8 supergravity and so there may be some deeper reasons for considering this coset space. Indeed, since to understand families one probably needs an "orthogonal axis" to the dynamics, the idea of obtaining families from $N > 1$ supersymmetries is worth following up. This idea was suggested a long time ago by Fayet[30] but runs into trouble because it is difficult (impossible ?) to obtain chiral asymmetric patterns.

Although enormous problems remain to be surmounted, the idea of quarks and leptons as QGF appears worthwhile to be pursued. Only time, and hopefully experiment, will tell whether it has any truth in it.

I would like to acknowledge Wilfried Buchmüller and Tsotumo Yanagida for a most pleasant collaboration. As it should be clear, most of what I reported here has arisen from our joint work. I am also grateful to J. Goity, C.K. Lee, W. Lerche and H.S. Sharatchandra for their many insights. Finally I would like to thank the whole organization committee for their efforts, which led to this very nice conference.

References

1) W. Buchmüller, R.D. Peccei and T. Yanagida, Phys.Lett. 124B (1983) 67.
2) W. Buchmüller, S.T. Love, R.D. Peccei and T. Yanagida, Phys.Lett. 115B (1982) 233.
3) W. Buchmüller, R.D. Peccei and T. Yanagida, MPI-PAE/PTh 28/83, Nucl.Phys. B, to be published.
4) W. Buchmüller, R.D. Peccei and T. Yanagida, MPI-PAE/PTh 41/83, Nucl.Phys. B, to be published.
5) A. Buras and W. Słominski, Nucl.Phys. B223 (1983) 157.
6) C-L. Ong, Phys.Rev. D27 (1983) 911; 3044.
7) R. Barbieri, A. Masiero and G. Veneziano, Phys.Lett. 128B (1983) 179.
8) T.E. Clark and S.T. Love, Purdue preprint, PURD-TH-83-10.
9) F. Bordi, R. Casalbuoni, D. Dominici and R. Gatto, Phys.Lett. 127B (1983) 419.
10) O.W. Greenberg, R.N. Mohapatra and M. Yasue, Phys.Lett. 128B (1983) 65 and Univ. of Maryland preprint 220.
11) P.H. Frampton and G. Mandelbaum, Harvard preprint, HUTP-83/A042.
12) C.K. Lee and H.S. Sharatchandra, MPI-PAE/PTh 54/83.
13) For a review, see for example, R.D. Peccei in Gauge Theories for the Eighties (Springer Verlag, Heidelberg 1983), Proceedings of the 1982 Arctic Summer School, Akäslompolo, Finland.
14) This was known long ago, see for example, P. Fayet and S. Ferrara, Phys.Rep. 32C (1977) 249. Models with purely complex QGF have been advocated recently by Ong (6).
15) A technical proviso will be discussed below.
16) B. Zumino, Phys.Lett. 87B (1979) 203.
17) W. Lerche, MPI-PAE/PTh/59/83.
18) G 't Hooft in Recent Developments in Gauge Theories, Cargèse 1979, Eds. G. 't Hooft et al. (Plenum, New York and London, p. 135).
19) J. Preskill and S. Weinberg, Phys.Rev. D24 (1981) 1059.
20) S. Weinberg, Phys.Rev. 166 (1968) 1568.
21) J.D. Bjorken, Phys.Rev. D19 (1979) 335; P.Q. Hung and J.J. Sakurai, Nucl.Phys. B143 (1978) 81.
22) J.C. Pati and A. Salam, Phys.Rev. D10 (1974) 275.
23) M. Denegri, these Proceedings.
24) D. Schildknecht, Proceedings of the 8th International Workshop on Weak Interactions and Neutrinos, Javea Spain 1982.
25) W. Buchmüller, R.D. Peccei and T. Yanagida, in preparation.
26) J. Goity, in preparation.
27) J. Iliopoulos and B. Zumino, Nucl.Phys. B76 (1974) 310; S. Ferrara, J. Iliopoulos and B. Zumino, Nucl.Phys. B77 (1976) 413.
28) S. Weinberg, Phys.Lett. 102B (1981) 401.
29) T. Kugo and T. Yanagida, in preparation.
30) P. Fayet, Nucl.Phys. B113 (1976) 135.

ECHO-QUARKS AND DYNAMICAL SYMMETRY BREAKING

George Zoupanos*)

CERN
CH-1211 Geneva 23
SWITZERLAND

ABSTRACT

A model representative of a class of models in which the colour gauge group is extended and then broken to $SU(3)_C$ is presented. Models of this type naturally accommodate fermions belonging to the usual $SU(3)_C$ representations, as well as exotic ones whose chiral symmetry breaking could produce breaking of electroweak gauge symmetry and radiative current quark and lepton masses.

The determination of the mechanism which produces the spontaneous symmetry breaking of the successful standard electroweak model[1] is of great importance in order to understand fully electroweak interactions. The two mechanisms which have been suggested so far, since they should also provide the model with fermionic masses, became unsatisfactory in one way or another. Firstly, in the breaking of $SU(2)_L \otimes U(1)$ by a Higgs field, which develops a vev of 250 GeV in order to produce enough mass for the vector boson W, even fermions acquire masses from the spontaneous symmetry breaking via Yukawa interactions; there is no prediction about their values or the values of their mixing angles. There also exists a hierarchy problem related to fermion masses, namely, even if the fermion masses are free parameters and can be put in by hand, one has to choose unnaturally small Yukawa coupling constants in order to fit their measured values. Of course, in addition, there exists the well-known hierarchy problem when the $SU(2)_L \otimes U(1)$ is embedded in GUTs. In the second suggestion, the $SU(2)_L \otimes U(1)$ gauge symmetry is broken dynamically. In this scheme, a new interaction, the technicolour interaction[2], has to be introduced; this becomes strong at an energy scale $\Lambda \sim O(\text{TeV})$. The dynamical scenario in the full complexity, which is required in order for fermions to obtain masses, is ruled out because it necessarily involves flavour-changing neutral interactions that predict excessive rates for flavour-changing neutral current processes[3].

Here we are going to discuss another proposal[4] in the direction of dynamical symmetry breaking which is much more attractive than the technicolour scheme, since it requires only ordinary QCD with additional fermions in higher than triplet representation of the $SU(3)_C$ gauge

*) On leave from Physics Department, National Technical University, Athens, Greece.

group. In the original proposals, masses for fermions either were not considered at all, or they were introduced in an unsatisfactory way. Our version of this scenario involves an enlargement of the colour gauge group which breaks subsequently to $SU(3)_C$. In this way, the fundamental fermions, the haplons, of the large colour group become fermions belonging to ordinary representations under $SU(3)_C$ (triplets and singlets), plus new fermions belonging to exotic representations. The fermions which belong to representations $R > 3$, the echo-fermions, can produce dynamical breaking of the electroweak gauge symmetry and also radiative masses for the ordinary fermions.

Let us consider the basis of the conjecture[4)] that a new, very strong interaction, like technicolour, is not necessary if there exist new quarks with representations $R > 3$ under $SU(3)_C$. The strength of the quark-antiquark binding potential based on the approximation of one-gluon exchange is proportional to

$$C_2(R)\ \alpha_s(\mu) \tag{1}$$

where $C_2(R)$ is the quadratic $SU(3)_C$ Casimir invariant of the R representation. The quantity in Eq. (1) is a measure of the effective colour flux linking a quark-antiquark pair at mass scale μ. Thus, quarks belonging to representations $R > 3$ which have bigger Casimir invariants than triplets carry more colour charge and hence interact more strongly than ordinary quarks. The weak coupling régime for ordinary triplet quarks may be a strong coupling régime for quarks in $R > 3$. If chiral symmetry breaking in the triplet sector occurs at $\alpha_S(\mu) = \alpha_S(\mu_3)$ and in the R-plet sector at $\alpha_S(\mu) = \alpha_S(\mu_R)$, then the dynamical mass scales of these two sectors are related by:

$$\frac{\mu_R}{\mu_3} = \exp\left[\int_{\alpha_s(\mu_3)}^{\alpha_s(\mu_R)} \frac{d\alpha_s}{\beta(\alpha_s)}\right] \tag{2}$$

where

$$\mu \frac{\partial}{\partial \mu} \alpha_s(\mu) \equiv \beta(\alpha_s) \simeq b\,\alpha_s^2 + O(\alpha_s^3) . \tag{3}$$

Thus there is an exponential enhancement of μ_R/μ_3 if $\alpha_S(\mu_R) \neq \alpha_S(\mu_3)$, and they are small enough for perturbation theory to be applicable. Of course, a better understanding of chiral symmetry in QCD is needed before one can say that $\alpha_S(\mu_R) \neq \alpha_S(\mu_3)$; however, with the assumption that chiral symmetry breaking depends entirely on the strength of the effective quark-antiquark binding potential, and occurs at some critical value of the flux string tension which is independent of the R representation, one might expect

$$C_2(R)\,\alpha_s(\mu_R) = \text{const.} \tag{4}$$

From Eqs. (2) and (4), one obtains that the scales of triplet and R-plet condensations are related by

$$\frac{\mu_R}{\mu_3} = \exp\left[\int_{\alpha_s(\mu_3)}^{[C_2(3)/C_2(R)]\cdot\alpha_s(\mu_3)} \frac{d\alpha_s}{\beta(\alpha_s)}\right] . \tag{5}$$

With a reasonable range of $\alpha_s(\mu_3)$ between 0.15 and 0.2, and with six flavours in triplet and new quarks in sextet, the ratio μ_R/μ_3 can be made consistent with $F_\pi/f_\pi \sim 2.600$, where f_π is the pion decay constant and F_π is the corresponding one to the new pions. Of course, one may doubt the validity of the assumptions and approximations which are involved in the argument; however, recent lattice calculations support qualitatively the results of the conjecture. In a Monte Carlo study[5] of the lattice SU(2) colour model in the no-fermion-loop approximation, it is found that fermions in different colour representations do condense at exponentially separated mass scales. In the following, we accept the conjecture as being correct.

Next, let us examine a model[6] which has to be considered only as a specific example of a class of models that have similar properties*). The model is based on the gauge group $G = G_C \otimes SU(2)_L \otimes U(1)$, where the strong sector is $G_C = SU(3) \otimes SU(3)$ and the electroweak sector is the standard $SU(2)_L \otimes U(1)$. We impose a discrete symmetry interchanging the two SU(3) subgroups of G_C. The elementary fermions are not identified with quarks. There are quark-haplons, belonging to (3,3) of G_C, that have the following assignments under the $SU(2) \otimes U(1)$:

$$G = (SU(3) \otimes SU(3))_C \otimes SU(2)_L \otimes U(1)$$

$$\begin{aligned} \begin{pmatrix} H^u \\ H^d \end{pmatrix}_L &= \left((3\,,\,3)\;;\; 2\;;\; -1/3 \right) \\ H^u_R &= \left((3\,,\,3)\;;\; 1\;;\; -4/3 \right) \\ H^d_R &= \left((3\,,\,3)\;;\; 1\;;\; 2/3 \right) . \end{aligned} \tag{6}$$

*) I have recently been informed by Baur and Papantonopoulos that Hung has considered another model[7] of this class based on the SU(4) colour gauge group.

Denoting the gauge bosons corresponding to the two SU(3)'s of G_C by A^a_μ and B^a_μ respectively, and writing the quark-haplon field H_{ij} as a 3×3 matrix, we obtain the following strong gauge interaction for the quark-haplons:

$$g_s \, Tr \, \bar{H}^T \gamma^\mu (A_\mu \lambda H + H \lambda^T B_\mu) . \tag{7}$$

Next we demand that G_C breaks down spontaneously to the "diagonal" $SU(3)_C$. This can be done by introducing a complex scalar Higgs belonging to (8,8) and another belonging to (3,3) [6]. It would be interesting to see a symmetry breaking of G_C to $SU(3)_C$ happening via a dynamical mechanism such as tumbling[8]. Unfortunately, the tumbling idea cannot be tested directly in lattice calculations. The reason is that one cannot put chiral fermions on the lattice, while for fermions in non-chiral representations the most attractive channel, according to the tumbling hypothesis, forms singlet condensates which leave the group unbroken.

After spontaneous symmetry breaking of G_C to $SU(3)_C$, a linear combination $V^-_\mu \equiv (A_\mu - B_\mu)/\sqrt{2}$ forms a colour octet of massive vector bosons, while the orthogonal combination $V^+_\mu \equiv (A_\mu + B_\mu)/\sqrt{2}$ emerges as the colour octet of massless gauge bosons of QCD. The quark-haplons decompose into a colour $\bar{3}$ and a colour 6 under the "diagonal" $SU(3)_C$. Naturally, we identify the $\bar{3}$ with ordinary antiquarks and the 6 with new exotic quarks which we call echo-quarks Q. The gauge interactions of quark-haplons given in Eq. (7) can now be expressed as interactions of the ordinary and echo-quarks with the new fields V^+_μ and V^-_μ. These interactions are:

$$g_s \, Tr \, \bar{Q} \gamma^\mu \lambda V^+_\mu Q \tag{8}$$

$$g_s \, \bar{q} \gamma^\mu \lambda V^+_\mu q \tag{9}$$

$$g_s (Tr \, \bar{Q} \gamma^\mu \lambda V^-_\mu q + Tr \, \bar{q} \gamma^\mu \lambda V^-_\mu Q) . \tag{10}$$

The interactions given in Eqs. (8)-(10) have this form before symmetry breaking of G_C determines which combinations of the gauge fields become physical. The symmetry breaking decides which are the massive gauge fields V^-_μ and the massless gluons V^+_μ are just orthogonal to them. The corresponding currents coupled to heavy and massless gluons have to be redefined accordingly[6].

So far, the haplons given in Eq. (6) have produced two triplets of quarks and two sextets of echo-quarks. When echo-quarks are massless, there exists a chiral $SU(2)_L \otimes SU(2)_R$ symmetry which is expected to break down to the diagonal SU(2) when the echo-quarks form condensates at a scale $\mu_6 \sim O(1\ \text{TeV})$. The three resulting Goldstone bosons from the spontaneous breakdown of the global chiral symmetry become longitudinal components of the $W^{\pm}$ and Z^0, which become massive, with masses:

$$\mu_W = g\,F/2$$

$$\mu_Z = (g^2+g'^2)^{1/2}\,F/2 \qquad (11)$$

with $F = 246$ GeV

where g, g' are the coupling constants of the groups $SU(2)_L$ and $U(1)$ respectively, and F is the echo-pion decay constant. The interesting feature of this model is that echo-quarks, being massive after the chiral symmetry breaking, couple to the massless ordinary quarks according to Eq. (10) via the heavy vector bosons V_μ^-. Thus the light quarks obtain a current quark mass according to the mechanism of the figure.

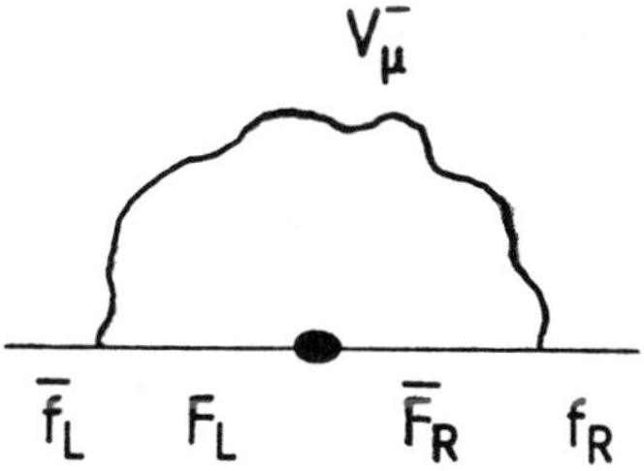

The mechanism for light fermion f mass generation through the exchange of a heavy V_μ^- gauge boson and echo-fermion (F)-antiecho-fermion ($\bar{F}$) condensation.

Next, one could extend the mechanism to leptons. In that case, one could put the lepton-haplons in the $(3,\bar{3})$ representation of $SU(3) \otimes SU(3)$ which in turn is decomposed into $1 + 8$ under $SU(3)_C$. Thus, one can identify the singlets with ordinary leptons and the octets with echo-leptons. The leptons again obtain masses radiatively, and there is an "understanding" of the fact that leptons are lighter than quarks, the reason being that $\mu_8 < \mu_6$ since $C_2(8) < C_2(6)$.

It is worth noting that, in this class of models, the great problem of flavour-changing neutral currents, which ruled out the extended technicolour scheme, does not appear at all. On the other hand, there is no flavour mixing, either. It has been suggested[9] that horizontal interactions could be the source of flavour mixing. We are presently investigating if this idea, which works quite well if spontaneous symmetry breaking comes from Higgs scalars, could also be applied in the present dynamical scenario.

I am grateful to the Organizing Committee for inviting me to this Meeting.

REFERENCES

1) S. Weinberg, Phys. Rev. Lett. 19 (1967) 1264;
A. Salam, Proc. 8th Nobel Symposium, ed. N. Svartholm, Stockholm (1968);
S.L. Glashow, J. Iliopoulos and L. Maiani, Phys. Rev. D2 (1970) 1285.

2) For a review, see: E. Farhi and L. Susskind, Phys. Reports 74C (1981) 277.

3) S. Dimopoulos and J. Ellis, Nucl. Phys. B182 (1981) 505.

4) W.J. Marciano, Phys. Rev. D21 (1980) 2425;
K. Konishi and R. Tripiccione, Phys. Lett. 121B (1983) 403.

5) J. Kogut et al., Phys. Rev. Lett. 48 (1982) 1140.

6) G. Zoupanos, "Fermion Mass Generation and Electroweak Symmetry Breaking from Colour Forces", CERN preprint TH.3586 (1983), to be published in Phys. Lett. B.

7) P.Q. Hung, "Dynamical Generation of Fermion Masses", Fermilab Pub. 80/78-THY (unpublished).

8) S. Raby, S. Dimopoulos and L. Susskind, Nucl. PHys. B169 (1980) 373.

9) G. Zoupanos, Z. Phys. C11 (1981) 27;
E. Papantonopoulos and G. Zoupanos, Phys. Lett. 110B (1982) 465;
G. Zoupanos, Phys. Lett. 115B (1982) 221;
E. Papantonopoulos and G. Zoupanos, Z. Phys. C16 (1983) 261;
K. Tamvakis and G. Zoupanos, Tech. Univ. Athens preprint, to be published in Phys. Lett. B.

PHENOMENOLOGY OF GUTs AND SUSY GUTs

Graham G. Ross
Rutherford Appleton Laboratory
Chilton
Dicot
Oxon

In this talk I would like to review the phenomenological predictions of grand unified theories (GUTs) and their supersymmetric versions SUSY GUTs. By now a large number of GUTs have been investigated and it is impossible to cover all their predictions in detail. For this reason it is useful to organize the predictions using dimensional analysis to write the effective low energy Lagrangian in the form

$$\mathcal{L}^{\text{eff}} = \sum_d c_d \left(\frac{1}{M_x}\right)^{d-4} O^d \qquad (1)$$

where O^d are SU(3)xSU(2)xU(1) invariant and Lorentz invariant operators formed from the light fields (quarks, leptons, gluons, scalars) and d is their (engineering) dimension. M_x is generic for the exchange particle mass responsible for generating a particular operator O^d. The reason this expansion is useful is that the M_x in grand unified theories responsible for rare processes such as baryon number or lepton number violation, is very large so we need only keep the leading term in this expansion.

In Table 1 we list the operators of lowest dimension for a variety of interesting operators.

d	O	B	L	Representative process	Comments
					SU(5) predictions:
4	$\bar{\psi}\gamma_\mu \psi A^\mu$	0	0	Coupling constant[1]	$\sin^2\theta_W = 0.206^{+0.016}_{-0.064}$ $M_x = 3.6^{+3.4}_{-3.2} \times 10^{14}$ GeV

	$m\bar{\psi}\psi$	0	0	mass(2)	$m_d \approx 3m_e$ $m_s \approx 3m_\mu$ $m_b \approx 3m_\mu$
	$\theta F^a_{\mu\nu}\tilde{F}^{a\mu\nu}$	0	0	"strong" CP violation	
					M(GeV)
6	qqql	1	1	$p \to e^+\pi^0$ $n \to e^+\pi^-$	10^{14}
7	$qqql^cH$	1	-1	$n \to e^-K^+$	10^{10}
	$qqql^cD$	1	-1	$n \to e^-\pi^+$	10^9
9	qqqqqq	2	0	$n \leftrightarrow \bar{n}$ $pn \to \pi^+\pi^0$	10^5
10	$qqql^cl^cl^cH$	1	-3	$n \to \nu\nu e^-\pi^+$	10^4
11	qqqlllHH	1	3	$p \to e^+\nu^c\nu^c$	10^4
5	llHH	0	2	ν Majorana mass	10^{11}–10^{15}*
6	$(\bar{d}s)^2$	0	0	$\Delta s = 2$ K^0–$\bar{K}^0$ mixing	Requires $\left(\frac{m_c^2 - m_u^2}{M_W^2}\right) < 10^{-4}$ in standard model.(3) Current bounds(4)
5	$\bar{e}\sigma_{\mu\nu}\mu F^{\mu\nu}$	0	0	$\mu \to e\gamma$ $-\Delta L_\mu = \Delta L_e = -1$	Sensitive to $M \approx 10^8$ GeV
6	$\mu e\bar{e}e$	0	0	$\mu \to e\bar{e}e$	Sensitive to $M \approx 10^3$ GeV

Table 1. Leading dimension operators for various weak processes. M is the order of magnitude mass leading to a nuclear lifetime of 10^{30} yrs with reasonable couplings. *for 10^{-2} ev $\leq m_{\nu_e} \leq 10^2$ ev

The rate at which these processes occur depends on M_x and the coefficient c_d. Let us discuss some of these entries in detail.

d=4

The terms corresponding to d=4 are the coupling constants and masses in the theory. They only depend logarithmically on the scale M_x. The predictions in the minimal SU(5) scheme are given in Table 1 calculated to two loop order. Apart from the ratio m_b/m_τ the predictions for the quark masses[2] are not good and for this reason many people have proposed going beyond the minimal Higgs structure of 5 + 24 multiplets. For example with a 45 of Higgs bosons the correct quark masses may easily be obtained[5]. However the predictions for M_x and $\sin^2\theta_W$ are sensitive to the addition of these bosons, even if they should have masses of $O(M_x)$, the reason being that there are so many of them they affect the β functions significantly. An estimate indicates M_x may vary by a factor of 4 if a 45 of scalars is included[6].

d=6 $\Delta B=\Delta L=1$

In order to construct an uncoloured operator with baryon number we need three quarks. Lorentz invariance of the operator requires that there be conservation of fermion number, so we need another fermion field. Thus the operator of minimum dimension which can mediate proton decay involves four fermion fields and has dimension 6 i.e. in a general Grand Unified theory, proton decay can occur at most at order $1/M_x^2$. To go further it is necessary to construct operators which are SU(3)xSU(2)xU(1) and Lorentz invariant. This must be done using only the low energy fields (including the Higgs scalars) with $M_i \ll M_x$ and derivatives D acting on these fields. SU(2)xU(1) breaking is then automatically included through some of the scalars acquiring (SU(2)xU(1) breaking) vacuum expectation values.

In constructing Lorentz invariant operators that are also SU(2) invariant, it is convenient to introduce the concept of F parity[7]

$$F = (-1)^{2a+2T} \qquad (2)$$

where T is the isospin and (a,b) is the representation under the two SU(2) groups defining the Lorentz group. In Table 2 the F quantum number of the light states are given. Since F parity must be multiplicatively conserved any allowed operator must have F = +1. Thus the only allowed baryon number violating opertor of dimension 6 is qqql (not $qqql^c$). This has B=L=1 and thus

State	(a,b)	T	$F = (-1)^{2a+2T}$
ψ_L	(1/2,0)	1/2	F = +1
ψ_R	(0,1/2)	0	F = +1
ψ_L^c	(0,1/2)	1/2	F = -1
ψ_R^c	(1/2,0)	0	F = -1
γ,g,W,Z D	(1/2,1/2)	0 or 1	F = -1
H	(0,0)	1/2	F = -1

Table 2. F quantum number of the light states and the derivative operator.

dimension six operators automatically conserves (B-L).

There are five possible operators of this type[7,8]

$$O_1 = \varepsilon_{ij}\,\varepsilon_{\alpha\beta\gamma}\,[\overline{(u_L^c)}^{\alpha}\gamma^{\mu}q_L^{\beta,i}][\overline{(\ell_L^c)}^{j}\gamma_{\mu}d_R^{\gamma}]$$

$$O_2 = \varepsilon_{ij}\,\varepsilon_{\alpha\beta\gamma}\,\overline{(u_L^c)}^{\alpha}\gamma^{\mu}q_L^{\beta,i}\,\overline{e_L^{+}}\gamma_{\mu}q_L^{\gamma,j}$$

$$O_3 = \varepsilon_{\alpha\beta\gamma}\varepsilon_{ij}(\overline{(q_R^c)}^{i\alpha}q_L^{j\beta})(\overline{(q_R^c)}^{kj}\ell_L^{\ell})$$

$$O_4 = \varepsilon_{\alpha\beta\gamma}\left((\overline{q_R^c})^{i\alpha} q_L^{i\beta}\right)\left((\overline{q_R^c})^{kj} \ell_L^{\ell}\right) x (\vec{\sigma}\varepsilon)_{ij} \cdot (\vec{\sigma}\varepsilon)_{kl}$$

$$O_5 = \varepsilon_{\alpha\beta\gamma}\left((\overline{d_L^c})^{\alpha} u_R^{\beta}\right)\left((\overline{u_L^c})^{\gamma} e_R\right) .$$

All other operators may be shown equivalent to these by use of Fiertz transformations.

In addition to (B-L) conservation the general set of these operators obey some selection rules[7,8]:

(1) $\Delta S/\Delta B \leqslant 0$. These operators may contain 0, 1 or 2 fields annihilating S quarks but no fields creating s quarks. Processes like $P \to \bar{K}^0 1^+$ or $N \to \overline{K}\, 1^+$ with $\Delta S = \Delta B$ are forbidden.

(2) $\Delta I = 1/2$, $\Delta S = 0$. The $\Delta S = 0$ operators are obtained with q_L^i the mass eigenstates the $\begin{pmatrix} u^m \\ d^m \end{pmatrix}_L$ and u_R, d_R the u_R^m, d_R^m states. Then operator O_4 vanishes. The remaining ones all involve the antisymmetric part of $(\overline{d^c}\ u)$ which is an isoscalar under strong isospin, so the full operator transforms as doublets under strong isospin (i.e. the isospin group of the quark fields only). This immediately leads to the relations

$$\Gamma(p \to 1^+_{L,R}\,{}^0) = 1/2\, \Gamma(n \to 1^+_{L,R}\pi^-)$$

$$\Gamma(p \to \nu_R^c \pi^+) = 2\ \Gamma(n \to \nu_R^c \pi^0) . \quad (4)$$

Ignoring lepton masses we also get

$$\Gamma(n \to e_R^+ \pi^-) = \Gamma(\phi \to \nu_R^c \pi^+) \quad (5)$$

and predictions for inclusive rates

$$\Gamma(p \to e_R^+ X) = \Gamma(n \to \nu_R^c X)$$

$$\Gamma(n \to e_R^+ X) = \Gamma(p \to \nu_R^c X) . \quad (6)$$

If the lepton polarization is not measured these results may be combined in the form

$$\Gamma(p\to l^+\pi^0) = \tfrac{1}{2}\,\Gamma(n\to l^+\pi^-) \geq \tfrac{1}{2}\,\Gamma(p\to\bar{\nu}\pi^+)$$

$$\Gamma(p\to l^+X) \geq \Gamma(n\to\bar{\nu}X)$$

$$\Gamma(n\to l^+X) \geq \Gamma(p\to\bar{\nu}X)\ . \qquad (7)$$

These rules also hold for processes with π replaced by ρ.

Thus it is possible to make definite model independent predictions for nucleon decay based only on the operator product expansion. One may go further by specifying the nature of the process giving rise to these operators(7). Only a limited number of heavy particle scalar exchanges can give rise to them and these are summarized in Table 3.

Exchanged Boson	Spin	SU(3) SU(2) Charge	Quantum numbers	Operators generated
(X,Y)	1	$(\frac{4}{3}, \frac{1}{3})$	$(\bar{3},2)$	$O_1 + O_2$
(X',Y')	1	$(\frac{2}{3}, -\frac{1}{3})$	$(\bar{3},2)$	O_1
X_S	0	$-\frac{1}{3}$	$(3,1)$	O_1, O_2, O_3, O_5
X'_S	0	$-\frac{4}{3}$	$(3,1)$	O_4, O_5
$X''^{\,i}_S$	0	$(\frac{2}{3}, -\frac{4}{3}, -\frac{4}{3})$	$(3,2)$	O_4, O_5

Table 3. Operators generated by exchange of vector and scalar bosons carrying SU(3)xSU(2)xU(1) quantum numbers.

In many models the scalar exchange contribution is small relative to the vector contribution because the Yukawa couplings are related to quark and lepton masses and are small. In this case only two operators, 0_1 and 0_2 occur. Neglecting mixing angles for the moment, the general effective Lagrangian following from a single superheavy vector boson exchange is

$$-L_G = \frac{4G_1}{2} 0_1 + \frac{4G_2}{2} 0_2 + \text{h.c.} \tag{8}$$

SU(5) has only the X and Y bosons of Table 3 so for it

$$-L_{SU(5)} = \frac{4G}{\sqrt{2}} \left(20_2 + 0_1\right) + \text{h.c.} \tag{9}$$

SO(10) has both the X and Y of SU(5) together with new X' and Y' bosons so for it

$$-L_{SO(10)} = -L_{SU(5)} + \frac{4G'}{2} 0_1 + \text{h.c.} \tag{10}$$

If we define $G_2/G_1 = r$, then $r = 2$ for SU(5) with small corrections due to radiative corrections from SU(2)xU(1). In SO(10)[9]

$$r = \frac{\frac{2}{M_X^2}}{\left(\frac{1}{M_X^2} + \frac{1}{M'^2_X}\right)} \tag{11}$$

If $SU(3)xSU(2)_LxSU(2)_RxU(1)$ is the effective theory at low scales then $r \simeq 1$. Note that the operator 0_1 corresponds to creation of a right handed positive lepton or a neutrino, while 0_2 corresponds to creation of a left handed positive lepton. Since $r \leq 2$ in SO(10) the neutrino modes are expected to be relatively enhanced.

Under parity, $0_{e_L^+} \leftrightarrow 0_{e_R^+}$ so that

$$\Gamma(p(\text{or } n) \rightarrow e_L^+ X) = r^2 \Gamma(p(\text{or } n) \rightarrow e_R^+ X) \tag{12}$$

where X is any exclusive or inclusive non strange final state with definite intrinsic parity. This leads the predictions of the type Eq. (7) with the inequality replaced by an equality and $(1+r^2)$ on the right hand side.

The polarization dependence of Eq. (4) implies that polarization measurements in nucleon decay would be a sensitive test of different models (i.e. different r). The polarization of the charged lepton is

$$P(N \to \ell + H_{s(n.s)}) = \frac{1-r^2_{s(n.s)}}{1+r^2_{s(n.s)}} \tag{13}$$

for either strange (s) or non-strange (n.s.) final states.

The prediction of the expected rate of proton decays requires a definite model and an estimate of the operator matrix elements. The case of the minimal SU(5) model has been reviewed here by Prof. Berezinski and gives

$$\tau_{p \to e^+ \pi^0} = 4.5 \times 10^{29 \pm 1.7} \text{ yrs.} \tag{14}$$

The main uncertainty in this prediction applies to the scalar sector and what is assumed for the scalar masses. For example if the heavy scalars have a mass of 10^{-2} M_X rather than M_X then M_X is reduced by a factor of 3/4 corresponding to a threefold increase in τ_p[6]. However a change in the mass for these heavy scalars also affects the operator anomalous dimensions in two loop order and a recent calculation has shown they actually decrease τ_p by 1/6[10]. Take together these effects give a decrease of 1/2 in τ_p. Thus the uncertainty in the mass of the scalars introduces only a small net uncertainty to τ_p and always reduces the lifetime from that given in Eq. (14).

If we add the 45 of scalars needed to improve the quark mass predictions the estimate for the proton lifetime may be dramatically changed. They can affect M_X by a factor of 2.8 leading to a 60-fold increase in the proton lifetime[6] (these effects on the two loop anomalous dimensions has not been computed). However they may have an even more dramatic effect for now there is no direct connection between the mixing angles necessary to predict proton decay and the Kobayashi-Maskawa mixing angles. Thus τ_p may be increased by a factor $(\frac{1}{\cos\beta})^2$ where β is an unknown mixing angle[11]. As a result the value for τ_p in SU(5) is not accurately known once we go beyond the minimal Higgs scheme. In SO(10) the mixing angles are not related to the Kobayashi-Maskawa angles although one might suppose that the mixing between families is small[9]. SO(10) and all generalizations of SU(5) have much greater uncertainty in the proton lifetime not just for the unknown mixing angles but also because the value of M_X may vary enormously because there may be intermediate scales of symmetry breaking which affect the radiative corrections giving the β functions needed to predict M_X.

Nucleon decay through higher dimesnion operators

Operators with dimension greater than 6 may violate (B-L) conservation and may mediate proton decay to interesting new channels (see Table 1). However because of the additional mass suppression of these operators (cf Eq. (1)), it is necessary that this proceed through superheavy bosons with a mass less than in the d = 6 case. If this is the case one must be careful that the leading dimension operators do not occur, even in higher order, for they would then be expected to be the dominant terms. This can be avoided if the dangerous bosons which can generate the dimension 6, $\Delta B = \Delta L = 1$ operators are absent or superheavy ($> M_X$). Indeed the allowable bosons follow from the quantum numbers of Table 3[7]. They are

$Y_S = (3,1,-\frac{2}{3})$ or $(3,3,-\frac{1}{3})$ and

$$Z_S = (3,2,-\tfrac{1}{6}) \text{ or } (3,2,-\tfrac{7}{6}) \;. \tag{15}$$

Baryon number violation mediated by Y_S and/or Z_S will violate B-L and can generate the baryon number operators of Table 1.

Neutrino masses

Beyond SU(5) a new feature, characteristic of almost all generalizations of SU(5), arises. This is the presence of a new right handed neutrino ν_R which can combine with ν_L to form a Dirac fermion. As a specific example in SO(10) the mass matrix is[11]

$$(\nu_L \bar{\nu}_R) \begin{pmatrix} \phi_{126}(15) & \phi_{10}(5)+\phi_{120}(5) \\ \phi_{10}(\bar{5})+\phi_{120}(\bar{5}) & \phi_{126}(1) \end{pmatrix} \frac{\nu_L}{\nu_R} \;.$$

The vacuum expectation value of $\phi_{126}^{(1)}$ leaves SU(5) invariant and is expected to be larger than M_x. The off diagonal elements are expected to be of order of the associated up quark masses (with only a ϕ10 they are equal). The expectation value of $\phi_{126}(15)$ is expected to be small[11] of order m_q^2/M_x. Thus the mass matrix becomes

$$(\nu_L \bar{\nu}_R) \begin{pmatrix} \sim \frac{m_q^2}{M_x} & m_q \\ m_q & M_x \end{pmatrix} \begin{pmatrix} \nu_L \\ \bar{\nu}_R \end{pmatrix} \tag{16}$$

with mass eigenstates $\nu_L + \varepsilon\nu_R$ and $\nu_R + \varepsilon\nu_L$ where $\varepsilon = m_q^2/M_x$ and masses $\sim m_q^2/M_x$ and $\sim M_x$ respectively. An interesting case arises in the minimal SO(10) scheme. Because there is no fundamental 126 Higgs in the theory the diagonal entries of the neutrino mass matrix arise only radiatively[12] at $O(\frac{\alpha}{\pi})^2$ through the two loop diagrams of Fig. 1 giving an effective 126

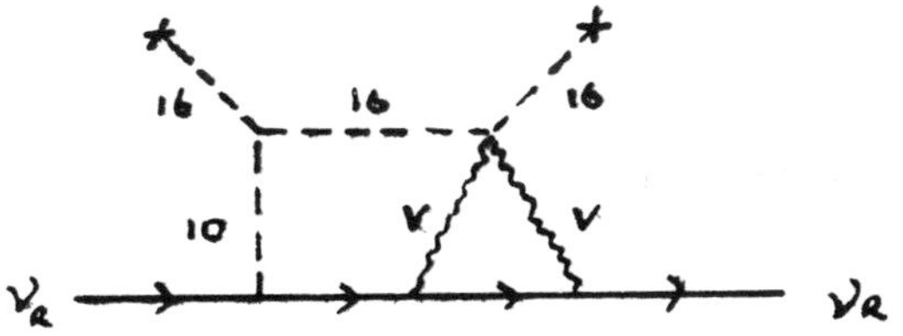

Fig. 1. Diagram generating a Majorana mass for ν_R in minimal SO(10) model.

coupling. This generates a Majorana mass for ν_R of order $(\frac{\alpha}{\pi})^2 M_{X'}$ which, when substituted in Eq. (16), gives heavier neutrino masses. Also, because the couplings giving the neutrino Dirac masses are proportional to the up quark masses of the equivalent flavour, we get the mass predictions

$$m_{\nu_i} = m_{u_i} \frac{1}{\varepsilon(\frac{\alpha}{\pi})^2} \frac{M_W}{M_{X'}} \simeq 10^{-7} m_{u_i} \tag{17}$$

where ε is associated with the couplings in Fig. 1, taken to be $\simeq \frac{1}{10}$ in estimating the magnitude of m_{ν_i}. This gives masses

$$m_{\nu_e} \simeq 1 \text{ ev}$$

$$m_{\nu_\mu} \simeq 100 \text{ ev}$$

$$m_{\nu_\tau} \simeq 1 \text{ kev} \tag{18}$$

Another possible source of large neutrino masses comes from the $d = 5$, $\Delta B = 0$ $\Delta L = 2$ operators. These clearly do not occur if (B-L) is conserved. In SO(10) (B-L) is a generator and is broken at some scale[9]. In some breaking schemes the group $SU(2)_L \times SU(2)_R \times U(1)_{B-L}$ remains a good symmetry until the (possibly low) scale M_R. In this model the electric charge

$$Q = T_{3_L} + T_{3_R} + \frac{(B-L)}{2} \quad . \tag{19}$$

At energy scales E such that $M_W < E < M_R$, SU(2)xU(1) is still a good symmetry so

$$\Delta(B-L) = -2\Delta I_{3_R} \quad . \tag{20}$$

Thus the scale of (B-L) breaking is related to the scale of parity breaking. As a result in such models the neutrino gets a Majorana mass from the d = 5 operators of order[13]

$$m_\nu \approx \frac{M_q^2}{M_N} \tag{21}$$

where now M_N is related to M_R, the scale of L-R breaking. This case, for $m_N > 150$ GeV, give neutrino masses in the ev to Mev range, the precise numbers depending on the details of the Yukawa couplings. The heavier neutrinos, presumably ν_μ and ν_τ are unstable so provided the lightest is < 100 ev the cosmological bounds will not be violated[14].

<u>$d = 9 \;\; \Delta B = 2 \;\; \Delta L = 0$</u>

The dimension 9 operators in Table 1 can lead to several interesting $\Delta B = 2$ processes. The most interesting are $n-\bar{n}$ oscillations and nuclear decay via $n-\bar{n}$ annihilation[15]. If we parameterize the effects of such a term by a Majorana mass term for the neutron

$$-L_{n\bar{n}} = \delta m \; n^T C n + h.c. \tag{22}$$

In free space $n-\bar{n}$ oscillations will occur with characteristic time

$$\tau_{n\bar{n}} = \frac{1}{\delta n} \quad . \tag{23}$$

For nuclear decay, the amplitude for annihilation is clearly proportional to $\frac{1}{\tau_{n-\bar{n}}}$ so the nuclear annihilation rate has the form

$$\Gamma_{nuc} = \frac{a}{m_N \tau^2_{n\bar{n}}} \tag{24}$$

where m_N supplies the needed dimensions and a is a parameter describing the necessary wave function overlap probability. For a lifetime > 10^{30} yrs and $a = 10^{-2}$ Eq. (24) implies[15]

$$\delta m < 10^{-20} \text{ev and } \tau_{n\bar{n}} > 10^5 \text{ secs} \quad . \tag{25}$$

Such oscillation times may just be observable in reactor experiments.

In order to generate such a term through a dimension 7 operator we need $CM_N^6/M^5 = \delta m$ where C is the operator coefficient dependent on the couplings needed to generate the opeator and M_N and M are the nuclear mass and exchange boson mass respectively. In specific models[15] C arises through multiple Yukawa couplings and is very small $C \simeq 10^{-10}$. Thus the rate Eq. (25) requires a B violating interaction with scale $M \sim 10^4$ GeV. As we have seen it is possible such interactions occur without conflicting with the bounds from proton decay. However there is a problem in cosmology with baryon number production in the early universe which is usually ascribed to baryon number violation in (B-L) conserving interactions. In this case a $\Delta B = 2$, $\Delta L = 0$ interaction associated with such a low scale would be expected to destroy at late times any pre-existing baryon number[7]. This argument would allow for a single additonal source of baryon number violation at scales < M_X if it conserves the combination B+aL with $a \neq 0$, for in this case baryon number excess satisfying $B = -aL$ will be stable. It does not allow, however, for the $\Delta B = 2$, $\Delta L = 0$ process needed to mediate $n-\bar{n}$ oscillation.

Supersymmetric grand unified models

We turn now to a discussion of the phenomenology of SUSY-GUTs. The operator analysis of Eq. (1) may be applied in this case too but because of the new supersymmetric partners with low mass ($\lesssim 0\,(M_W)$) there are many more operators to be included. The light states needed for a supersymmetric version of the standard model are given in Table 4 [16]. In Table 5 we list some of the interesting operators for a SUSY-GUTs.

Conventional State	(J)	Supersymmetric State	(J)	Name
$\binom{u}{d}_L\ u_R\ d_R$	$\frac{1}{2}$	$\binom{\tilde{u}}{\tilde{d}}_L\ \tilde{u}_R\ \tilde{d}_R$	0	Squarks
$\binom{\nu}{e}_L\ e_R$	$\frac{1}{2}$	$\binom{\tilde{\nu}}{\tilde{e}}_L\ \tilde{e}_e$	0	Sleptons
$G_\mu^{a=1..8}$	1	$\tilde{G}^{a=1..8}$	$\frac{1}{2}$	Gluinos
$W^\pm_\mu, Z_\mu$	1	$\tilde{W}^\pm_\mu, \tilde{Z}_\mu$	$\frac{1}{2}$	Winos, Zino
γ	1	$\tilde{\gamma}$	$\frac{1}{2}$	Photino
$\begin{pmatrix} H_1^+ \\ H_1^0 \end{pmatrix} \begin{pmatrix} H_2^0 \\ H_2^- \end{pmatrix}$	0	$\begin{pmatrix} \tilde{H}_1^+ \\ \tilde{H}_1^0 \end{pmatrix} \begin{pmatrix} \tilde{H}_2^0 \\ \tilde{H}_2^- \end{pmatrix}$	$\frac{1}{2}$	Higgsinos

Table 4. States needed in the supersymmetric version of the standard model. In addition there must be chiral supermultiplets to break supersymmetry.

Dimension d	Operator	Process	Comments
4	$[\bar{\psi} e^{gv} \psi]_D$	Coupling constant and mass renormalizations [17,18]	In minimal SUSY-SU(5) $M_x = 1.5\times10^{16}$ GeV

	$[m\psi\psi]_F$		$\sin\theta_W = .233$ $m_{q_i} \simeq 3m_{\ell_i}$ (18,19,20)
	$[W^\alpha W_\alpha]_D$	θ parameter	Insensitive - Not renormalized in supersymmetric theory
4	$(qqq)_F$ $(lll)_F$ $(l\bar{q})_F$ $(l\phi)_D$	$\Delta B=1\ \Delta L=0$ $\Delta B=0\ \Delta L=3$ $\Delta B=0\ \Delta L=1$ $\Delta B=0\ \Delta L=1$	Sensitive to arbitrarily high mass - must be absent in viable theory
5(6)	$(qql)_F$	$\Delta B=\Delta L=1\ \tau_p = 10^{31}$ yrs for	$M_{\tilde{W}}=M_W, M_{\tilde{q}}=10^3$ GeV, $M_{H_x} = M_x$
5(5)	$[ll\phi\phi]_F$	$\Delta B=0\ \Delta L=-2$	
7(9)	$[qqqqqq]_F$	$\Delta B=-2\ \Delta L=0$ eg $n-\bar{n}$	
5(6)	$(\bar{d}s)^2{}_F$	$\Delta S=2$, $K^0-\bar{K}^0$ mixing(20)	$\dfrac{\Delta m_{\tilde{q}_i}^2}{m_{\tilde{q}_i}^2} < 10^{-3}$ (20)
5(6)	$[\bar{\mu}e\bar{e}e]_F$	$\Delta L_\mu=-\Delta L_e=-1, \mu\to 3e$	

Table 5. Interesting supersymmetric SU(3)xSU(2)xU(1) and Lorentz invariant operators in a SUSY-GUT. In brackets are shown the leading dimension operator for the particular process in an ordinary GUT (cf Table 1).

Now these operators must be supersymmetric as well as SU(3)xSU(2)xU(1) and Lorentz invariant. Thus the operators are F and

D components of products of chiral superfields[21]. These are supersymmetric by construction. The F and D components contain various combinations of the fermion (ψ_i) and scalar components (ϕ_i) of the chiral superfields Φ_i. The F term is defined by

$$O(\Phi_i)_F \equiv \frac{\partial^2 O}{\partial\Phi_i \partial\Phi_j}\bigg|_{\Phi_k=\phi_k} \psi_i \psi_j \tag{26}$$

The D term is slightly more complicated. We will be interested mainly in its four fermion component

$$O(\Phi_i, \Phi_i^+)_D \equiv \frac{\partial^4 O}{\partial\Phi_i \partial\Phi_j \partial\Phi_k^+ \partial\Phi_\ell^+}\bigg|_{\substack{\Phi_m = \phi_m \\ \Phi_m^+ = \phi_m^+}} \psi_i \psi_j \psi_k^+ \psi_\ell^+ \tag{27}$$

Let us discuss some of these terms

<u>d = 4 Mass and coupling constant renormalization</u>

Because a SUSY-GUT involves new light supersymmetric particles it is necessary to compute the values for the grnd unification mass and $\sin^2\theta_W$. The initial ratios of the couplings and hence $\sin^2\theta_W$ are unchanged in going to a SUSY-GUT because we still have the same assignment of states to a GUT representation. However the radiative corrections will differ for now we must include loops containing the new states, the gauginos, the squarks, etc. It is easy to compute the expected size of the corrections at one loop assuming all heavy particles have a mass $\approx M_X$[17]. The SU(3)xSU(2)xU(1) effective couplings depend on M_X via

$$\alpha_i(\mu) = C_i + \frac{1}{6\pi} b_i \ln(\frac{M_X}{\mu});\ i = 1,2,3 \tag{28}$$

Then

$$M_X = \mu \exp\left[6\pi(b_2 + \frac{5}{3} b_0 - \frac{8}{3} b_3)^{-1}(\frac{1}{\alpha_{em}(\mu)} - \frac{8}{3}\frac{1}{\alpha_3(\mu)})\right]$$

$$\sin^2\theta_W = \frac{3}{8} + \frac{\frac{5}{8}(b_2 - b_0)}{(b_2 + \frac{5}{3} b_0 - \frac{8}{3} b_3)} \left(1 - \frac{8}{3} \frac{\alpha_{em}(\mu)}{\alpha_3(\mu)}\right) . \qquad (29)$$

The values of b_i are easily calculated using their definitions in Eq. (28). The results for the standard model are $b_3 = 27-4N_G$, $b_2 = 18-4N_G$, $b_0 = -4N_G$ giving, for a value of $\Lambda = 150$ Mev, $\sin^2\theta_W = 0.23$ and $M_X = 4 \times 10^{16}$ GeV. (For comparison the SU(5)b_i were $b_3 = 33-4N_G$, $b_2 = 22-4N_G$, $b_0 = -4N_G$). The result for M_X is about 20 times the SU(5) value. The reason for this is principally due to the decrease in b_3 compared to he SU(5) value which comes about mainly because the supersymmetric theory requires an SU(3) adjoint of fermions, the gluinos. Due to their large charge they contribut significantly to the β function and because they are fermions they contribute a negative amount to β_3 making the theory less asymptotically free. The value of M_X is, very roughly, the scale at which α_3 equals α_2. Since β_3 is reduced, α_3 varies more slowly; and thus it takes longer for this equality to be achieved. Hence M_X is increased. This can be compensated by speeding up the rate of evolution of α_2 so the value of M_X depends on the number of light Higgs particles included. For example(17) adding the light Higgs SU(2) singlets to mimic a lepton family brings M_X back to the usual SU(5) value and lowers $\sin^2\theta_W$ by 0.015.

Including the two loop corrections gives(18) the best values for $\sin^2\theta_W$ and M_X in the minimal supersymmetric extension of SU(5) for $\Lambda_{\overline{MS}} = 160$ Mev.

$$M_X = 7.7 \times 10^{15} \text{ GeV}$$

$$\sin^2\theta_W = 0.236 \quad . \qquad (30)$$

The renormalization of quark and lepton masses is also sensitive to the change in the unification scale(18,19,20). It also requires evaluation of an additional contribution to the anomalous dimension coming from gaugino contributions to the wave function renormalization. Remarkably the two effects almost cancel leaving predictions close to the SU(5) values (see Table 5).

Baryon and lepton number violation in SUSY-GUTs

To aid the construction of these operators we work with the basis

$$q_{L\alpha ia},\ l_{Lia},\ u_{R\alpha a},\ e_{Ra},\ H_{Li},\ \overline{H}_{Li} \qquad (31)$$

where α, i and a label the colour, flavour and generation. Then, suppressing all but the helicity index it is straightforward to check that the leading dimension 4 supersymmetric operators which are SU(3)xSU(2)xU(1) invariant and violate baryon and/or lepton number are[22,20]

$$(l_L H_L^c)_D,\ (l_L l_L e_R^c)_F,\ (l_L q_L d_R^c)_F,\ (d_R d_R u_R)_F,\ (e_R^c H_L H_L)_F \qquad (32)$$

For example the first operator is $\varepsilon^{ij} l_{Li}(H_L)^c{}_j$. It carries no colour indices, so is clearly $SU(3)_c$ invariant. The SU(2) indices are contracted to form an SU(2) invariant and the weak hypercharge sums to zero. The dimension of the operator is 4, two coming from two chiral fields and two from the D projection.

Dimension 4 operators, if present in a given theory, are not suppressed by any inverse powers of M_X^2. This would imply proton decay proceeds too fast for although the operator $(d_R d_R u_R)_F$ always contains squarks it can contribute to proton decay by coupling the squarks to quark fields. For example the $qq\tilde{q}$ component contributes to the $qq q\tilde{\gamma}$ or $qqq\tilde{G}$ light operator via the graphs of Fig. 2. These would contribute to proton decay with amplitude α $1/M_{\tilde{q}}^2$ which, since $M_{\tilde{q}}$ = 0 (1 Tev), are unacceptably large. There are two possibilities which avoid this problem. The first is that $\tilde{\gamma}$, $\tilde{G}$ and $\tilde{g}$ are too heavy for proton decay to proceed. In this case there are no

$\Delta B = 1$, $\Delta L = 0$ operators that can be constructed using light fields (light enough to be relevant for

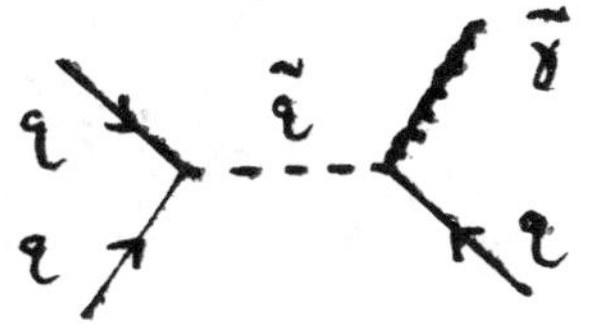

Fig. 2. Born diagram generating the $qqq\tilde{\gamma}$ amplitude from a component of the $(qqq)_F$ operator.

proton decay) and the operator may not contribute to proton decay (provided there are no $(l_L q_L d_R^c)_F$ terms). It will, however, contribute to $\Delta B = 2$ processes through higher dimension operators and we will consider this later. The second possibility is that this operator does not occur in a specific model as the result of a (discrete) symmetry[22]. For example, if we ask that our theory should be invariant under change of sign of the matter fields (quark and lepton supermultiplets), none of these dimension 4 terms would arise. This operation is often referred to as R parity[21].

In fact the minimal SU(5) model is invariant under R parity and lepton violating processes proceed by at most dimension 5 operators[22]. Models which respect R parity will also have the property that the new supersymmetric states must be produced in pairs. For the component fields R parity is defined to be +1 for every particle of the standard model and −1 for their supersymmetric partners. Then R parity is multiplicatively conserved, which means conventional states cannot produce an odd number of new states and the new states cannot decay only into conventional ones.

However there are possibilities for discrete symmetries other than R parity[24]. For example $q \to -q$, $u \to -u$, $d \to -d$, forbids the $\Delta B = 1$ operator $(d_R d_R u_R)_F$ while allowing the lepton number violating terms. Alternatively lepton number may be preserved by $l \rightarrow -l$ and $e \rightarrow -e$ leaving only $(d_R d_R u_R)_F$ which then need not mediate proton decay via the graph of Fig. 2 if $\tilde{\gamma}$ is heavy. Because of this uncertainty we should not, perhaps, rule out the possible presence of a dimension 4 term in the Lagrangian. They will allow a variety of rare processes. For example a combination of $(l_L l_L e_R^c)_F$ and $(l_L q_L d_R^c)_F$ can mediate decays of the form $K_L \rightarrow \mu^+ e^-, \mu^- e^+, e^+ e^-, \mu^+ \mu^-$.

Nucleon decay in SUSY GUTs

If, as in the minimal SUSY GUT, R parity is a good symmetry the only dimension 5 operators that may be constructed are of the form(22)

$$O_A = (\varepsilon_{\alpha\beta\gamma} u^{\alpha}_{Ra} u^{\beta}_{Rb} u^{\gamma}_{Rc} e_{Rd})_F$$

$$O_B = (\varepsilon_{\alpha\beta\gamma} \varepsilon_{ij} \varepsilon_{kl} q^{\alpha i}_{La} q^{\beta j}_{Lb} q^{\gamma k}_{Lc} l^{l}_{Ld})_F \, . \tag{33}$$

Being dimension 5 they are only suppressed by one power of mass because the graphs generating these operators involve a fermion, not a boson, propagator as, for example, in Fig. 3. We will estimate the magnitude of their coefficient in a specific model shortly but first let us consider the general operator structure.

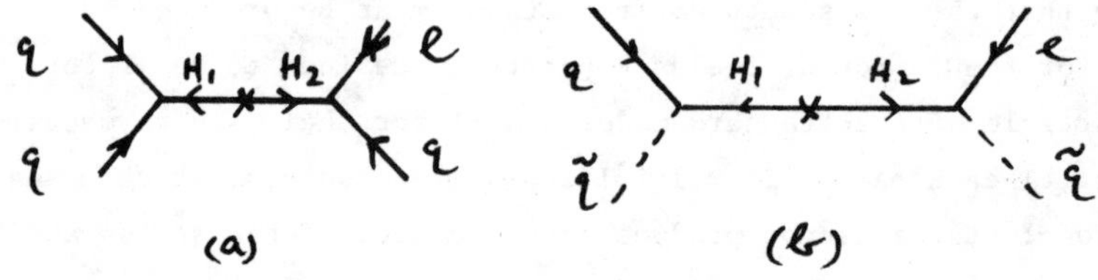

Fig. 3. (a) Supergraph generating the operator $(qqql)_F$. (b) The important component graph in Fig. 3(a). The x denotes a mass insertion.

The first operator O_A does not contribute to proton decay because it must be antisymmetric in generation indices a and b and must contain a charm or top superfield(23). Since these are SU(2) singlets, radiative corrections cannot change their flavour so the final dressed operator always contains a top or a charm quark. The operators O_b can contribute to proton decay through the graphs of Fig. 4.

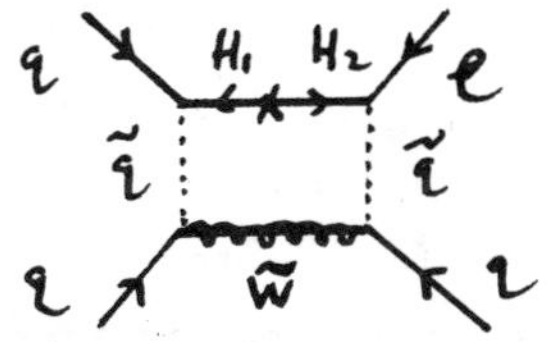

Fig. 4. A typical diagram converting via gaugino exchange an operator involving squarks and sleptons to one involving quarks and leptons alone.

It turns out only Winos give nonzero contributions leading to the form(23)

$$L_{eff} = b^0 \; c^d_{abc} \; [\tfrac{1}{2} O^4_{abcd} - 3O^3_{abcd} + 3O^3_{bcad}] \tag{34}$$

where c_{abcd} is the coefficient of the original operator $(O_B)_{abcd}$ and b^0 results from performing the loop integral in Fig. 3

$$b^0 = \left(\frac{g_2^2 m_{\tilde{W}}^2}{256\pi^2}\right) [f(m_{\tilde{q}}, m_{\tilde{q}}, m_{\tilde{W}}) + f(m_{\tilde{q}}, m_{\tilde{q}}, m_{\tilde{W}})] \tag{35}$$

where

$$f(m_1, m_2, m_3) = \frac{1}{m_2^2 - m_3^2} \left(\frac{m_2^2}{(m_1^2 - m_2^2)} \ln\left(\frac{m_1^2}{m_2^2}\right) - \frac{m_3^2}{(m_1^2 - m_3^2)} \ln\left(\frac{m_1^2}{m_3^2}\right) \right) . \tag{36}$$

The four fermion operators are given by

$$O^4_{cuc\mu} \equiv [(\bar{c},\bar{s}')\tau_i \begin{pmatrix} 0 & 1 \\ -1 & 0 \end{pmatrix}\begin{pmatrix} u \\ d' \end{pmatrix}][(\bar{c},\bar{s}')\tau_i \begin{pmatrix} 0 & 1 \\ -1 & 0 \end{pmatrix}\begin{pmatrix} \nu_\mu \\ \mu \end{pmatrix}]$$

$$O^3_{cuc\mu} \equiv [(\bar{c},\bar{s}') \begin{pmatrix} 0 & 1 \\ -1 & 0 \end{pmatrix}\begin{pmatrix} u \\ d' \end{pmatrix}][(\bar{c},\bar{s}') \begin{pmatrix} 0 & 1 \\ -1 & 0 \end{pmatrix}\begin{pmatrix} \nu_\mu \\ \mu \end{pmatrix}]$$

and analagous operators involving the other generators. d'(s') is the Cabibbo rotated d(s) quark.

Note that our original operators of Eq. (33) were formed from "current" eigenstates of quarks and squarks and leptons and sleptons. In deriving the final form of the L_{eff} it is necessary to convert these to mass eigenstates using the Kobayashi-Maskawa mixing angles for the quarks and the equivalent form of rotations for the squarks and sleptons. However, since supersymmetry is broken at low energies, the Kobayashi-Maskawa angles for squarks need not be the same as those for quarks. For leptons, since the neutrinos are massless, there are no mixing angles but the sneutrinos are expected to be massive so in the slepton sector we will need a new set of mixing angles too. However there are strong constraints on the mnass differences Δm^2_{sq} between squarks and Δm^2_{sl} between sleptons following from the need to suppress flavour changing neutral currents. These require $\Delta m^2_{sq}/m^2_{sq}$ and $\Delta m^2_{sl}/m^2_{sl}$ should be much less than 10^{-3}[20]. As a result the squark and slepton mixing angles may, to a first approximation, be neglected in calculating the graphs of Fig. 3 because the Kobayashi-Maskawa mixing matrices V_{ij} always occur in the combination

$$V_{fi} \frac{1}{(m_i^2-p^2)} V^*_{if'} \simeq \frac{\delta ff'}{m^2-p^2} + O(\frac{\Delta m^2}{m^2}) \tag{38}$$

where m^2 is the mass^2 of the propagating squark or slepton.

The L_{eff} of Eq. 34 contains the baryon number violating terms that mediate proton decay. In order to make a specific prediction for the expected decay modes it is necessary to estimate the matrix elements of the quark operators when taken between physical hadronic states. In Table 5 we give the relative decay rates resulting from a non-relativistic SU(6) analysis of Salati and Wallet taken from an analysis of Ellis et al[23]. Other analyses of Chadha and Daniel[25] are in general agreement with this result. The qualitative features are easy to understand, as we discussed above, the indices a, b and c cannot be the same. As a result they always involve the second or third generation and thus favour decay into strange particles. Decay rates into non-strange final states are suppressed by an additional factor of $\sin^2\theta_c$.

Dominant operator	$p\to\bar{\nu}K^+$	$p\to e^+K^0(\mu^+K^0)$	$p\to\bar{\nu}K^{*+}$	$p\to e^+K^{*0}$	$n\to\bar{\nu}K^0$	$n\to\bar{\nu}K^{*0}$
$c^{e(\mu)}_{cuu}(s^0)$	1	1/4	0(1/25)	0(1/400)	1/4	0(1/16)
$c^{e(\mu)}_{tuu}(s^2)$						
$c^{e(\mu)}_{ucc}(s^2)$	1/4	0	0(1/16)	0	1	0(1/25)
$c^{e(\mu)}_{uct}(s^4)$						
$c^{e(\mu)}_{utt}(s^6)$						
$c'^{e(\mu)}_{uct}(s^4)$	0(1)	0	0(1/100)	0	0(1)	0(1/100)

Table 5. Relative decay rates. The decay rates into K^* are suppressed by kinematic factors. The relative decay rates for the c'^{ℓ}_{uct} case depend on unknown Cabibbo-Kobayashi-Maskawa mixing angles. Indicated in parentheses at the left are the number of small angle factors suppressing the decay rates due to the different operators.

Nucleon decay in the minimal SU(5) SUSY GUT

To estimate the expected decay rate and the dominant operator of those shown in Table 5 it is necessary to specify the model and calculate the coefficient c^{α}_{abc}. This has been doe for the minimal SUSY GUT(23).

The expected rate for $p \to \bar{\nu}_\mu K^+$ is (using SU(16) for the spin-flavour wave functions),

$$\Gamma \approx 4 \left(\frac{m_c m_s m_p^2}{2\sqrt{2} v_1 v_2 M_{H_X}}\right)^2 b^{0^2} A^2 \sin^4\theta (1.39 \times 10^{27})\ y^{-1}$$

where b^0 is given by Eq. 35, v_1 and v_2 are the expectation values of H_1^0 and H_2^0, and A is the enhancement factor coming from summing the large logarithmic corrections from gauge loop corrections

$$A = \left[\frac{\alpha_s(1\ \mathrm{GeV})}{\alpha_3(m_c)}\right]^{2/9} \left[\frac{\alpha_3(m_c)}{\alpha_3(mb)}\right]^{6/25} \left[\frac{\alpha_3(m_b)}{\alpha_3(m_t)}\right]^{6/23}$$

$$\left[\frac{\alpha_3(m_t)}{\alpha_3(M_W)}\right]^{2/7} \left[\frac{\alpha_3(M_W)}{\alpha_3(M_X)}\right]^{4/3} \left[\frac{\alpha_2(M_W)}{\alpha_2(M_X)}\right]^{-3} \left[\frac{\alpha_1(M_W)}{\alpha_1(M_X)}\right]^{-1/66}$$

A is ≈ 15 with the parameters chosen as in Eq. 30. For $M_{H_X} = M_X$ and $\tau_p = 10^{31}$ years this implies

$$b^0 \approx \frac{1}{3} \times 10^{-8}\ \mathrm{GeV}^{-1} .$$

For $m_{\tilde{q}} \approx m_{\tilde{l}} >> m_{\tilde{W}}$ this means

$$\frac{m_{\tilde{W}}}{m_{\tilde{q}}^2} < 10^{-5}\ \mathrm{GeV}^{-1}$$

where $M_{\tilde{W}}$ is the Majorana mass for the Wino. Even for $M_{\tilde{W}} \approx O(M_W)$, the current experimental limit on $p \to \bar{\nu} K^+$ or $n \to \bar{\nu} K^0$ of $\tau_p > 0.6 \times 10^{31}$ years can be satisfied provided $m_{\tilde{q}} > 3$ Tev, not an unreasonably large value.

Proton decay in non-minimal models

It is possible to prevent proton decay from proceeding via the dimension 5 operators[22]. For example if there were no mass term connecting H_1 and H_2 in the minimal model the graph of Fig. 5 would not exist and the coefficient of the dimension 5 baryon number violating operator would vanish.

If dimension 5 operators are absent, proton decay will proceed only through dimension 6 operators generated by superheavy vector or Higgs scalar exchange. If these masses are as large as predicted in the standard model then in this case proton decay will be invisible. It is possible that M_X is lower (through, for example, a different light Higgs structure[17]) and then proton decay could proceed via vector boson exchange as in standard SU(5). In theories of the geometric hierarchy type with a large scale μ^2 of supersymmetry breaking in the gauge nonsinglet sector there are possibly significant contributions coming from dimension 6 operators of the type $[qqqlx]_F$. This gives a term $\tilde{q}\tilde{q}\tilde{q}\tilde{l}F_X$ where F_X is the supersymmetry breaking scale μ^2. Since $\frac{\mu^2}{M_X} \approx O(M_W)$ these operators contribute at order $(\frac{M_W}{M_X})\tilde{q}\tilde{q}\tilde{q}\tilde{l}$ and so can be comparable to dimension five terms[26].

Another possibility is that Higgs scalars may be anomalously light and enhance dimension 6 operator contributions[27]. For example with the Higgs triplets in the standard model of mass $O(10^{11})$ GeV proton decay will proceed through dimension 6 operators at a rate $\tau_p \approx 10^{31}$ years. Being Higgs mediated the decay modes are still expected to be into the heaviest states possible but the operator symmetry differs from that of the dimension 5 operators and the modes $p \to \mu^+ K^0$, $\nu_\mu K^0$ are expected to be comparable. As in the SU(5) case, beyond the minimal model there are many possibilities and it is important to look for as many decay channels as possible.

Other processes in SUSY GUTs

The operator analysis may be straightforwardly extended to any other rare processes. In Table 5 we list the more interesting operators together with the dimensions of the leading order terms in nonsupersymmetric models. Clearly there are differences as in proton decay which will lead to new predictions for the expected rates. For example if the operator $(qqq)_F$ is present it can mediate $\Delta B=2$ processes such as $n-\bar{n}$ oscillations at a rate $\propto 1/m_{\tilde{q}}^2$ which is very large. However such a term will run into the cosmological difficulties discussed above.

Of course the most direct test of supersymmetric models will be to find one of the many supersymmetric states predicted in Table 4. These states have definite couplings and their expected production and decay mechanics are known. Once the threshold for producing a pair of such new states is crossed they should be easily produced and detected(28).

REFERENCES

(1) H. Georgi, H. R. Quinn and S. Weinberg, Phys. Rev. Lett. 33 (1974) 451; C. H. Llewellyn Smith, G. G. Ross and J. Wheater, Nucl. Phys. B177 (1981) 263; S. Weinberg, Phys. Lett. 91B (1980) 51; P. Binetruy and T. Schucker, Nucl. Phys. B178 (1981) 293, 307; L. Hall, Nucl. Phys. B178 (1981) 75.

(2) A. J. Buras, J. Ellis, M. K. Gaillard and D. V. Nanopoulos, Nucl. Phys. B135 (1978) 66; M. S. Chanowitz, J. Ellis and M. K. Gaillard, Nucl. Phys. B128 (1977) 506, D. A. Ross and D. V. Nanopoulos, Nucl. Phys. B157 (1979) 273.

(3) M. K. Gaillard and B. W. Lee, Phys. Rev. D10 (1974) 897.

(4) For a review of the experimental and theoretical situation see

(5) P. H. Frampton, S. Nandi and J. J. G. Scanio, Phys. Lett. 85B (1979) 255; H. Georgi and C. Jarlskog, Phys. Lett. 86B (1979) 297.

(6) G. Cook, K. Mahenthappa and M. Sher, Phys. Lett. 91B (1981) 369; L. Ibanez, Nucl. Phys. B181, (1981) 105.

(7) S. Weinberg, Phys. Rev. Lett. 43 (1979) 1566; Phys. Rev. D22 (1980) 1694.

(8) F. Wilczek and A. Zee, Phys. Rev. Lett. 43 (1979) 1571. G. Segre and H. A. Weldon, Phys. Rev. Lett. 44 (1980) 1737. L. F. Abbott and M. B. Wise, Phys. Rev. D22, 2208.

(9) H. Georgi, Particles and Fields 1974, ed. C. E. Carlson (AIP, NY, 1975) p. 575; H. Fritzsch and P. Minkowski, Ann. Phys. 93 (1975) 193.

(10) M. Daniel and J. A. Penarrocha, Phys. Lett. 127B (1983) 219.

(11) C. Jarlskog, Phys. Lett. 82B (1979) 401. H. Georgi and D. V. Nanopoulos, Phys. Lett. 82B (1979) 392; Nucl. Phys. B155 (1979) 52; B159 (1979) 16. R. Barbieri, D. V. Nanopoulos, G. Marchio and F. Skrocchi, Phys. Lett. 90B (1980) 91. M. Magg and Ch. Wetterich, Phys. Lett. 94B (1980) 61. See also Prof. Berezinski's talk.

(12) E. Witten, Phys. Lett. 91B (1980) 81.

(13) See for example, G. Senjanovic, Nucl. Phys. B135 (1979) 334 and references therein.

(14) For a recent review see D. N. Schramm and K. Freese, University of Chicago preprint 1983.

(15) V. A. Kuz'min, JETP Letters 12 (1970) 228. R. E. Marshak and R. N. Mohapatra, Phys. Lett. 91B (1980) 222; Phys. Rev. Lett. 44 (1980) 1316; Phys. Lett. 94B (1980) 183.

(16) N. Sakai, Z. f. Phys. C11 (1981) 153; S. Dimopoulos and H. Georgi, Nucl. Phys. B193 (1981) 150.

(17) L. Ibanez and G. G. Ross, Phys. Lett. 105B (1981) 439.

(18) M. B. Einhorn and D. R. T. Jones, Nucl. Phys. B196 (1982) 475; W. Marciano and G. Senjanovich, Phys. Rev. D25 (1982) 3092.

(19) D. Nanopoulos and D. A. Ross, Phys. Lett. 118B (1982) 99.

(20) J. Ellis, D. V. Nanopoulos and S. Rudaz, Nucl. Phys. B202 (1982) 43.

(21) For a review see P. Fayet and S. Ferrara, Physics Reports 32C, 251.

(22) S. Weinberg, Phys. Rev. D26 (1982) 287.
N. Sakai and T. Yanagida, Nucl. Phys. B197 (1982) 533.
S. Dimopoulos, S. Raby and F. Wilczek, Phys. Lett. 112B (1982) 133.

(23) P. Salati and C. Wallet, Nucl. Phys. B209 (1982) 389.
J. Ellis, J. S. Hagelin, D. V. Nanopoulos and K. Tamvakis, Phys. Lett. 124B (1983) 464.

(24) L. Hall and M. Suzuki, Lawrence Berkeley Laboratory Report (1983).
M. Bowick, M. Chase and P. Ramond, Phys. Lett. 128B (1983) 185.

(25) S. Chadha and M. Daniel, Rutherford Laboratory preprint RL-83-056 (1983).

(26) J. P. Derendinger and C. A. Savoy, Phys. Lett. 118B (1982) 347.
N. Sakai, Phys. Lett. 121B (1983) 130.

(27) D. V. Nanopoulos and K. Tamvakis, Phys. Lett. 110B (1982) 449;
M. Srednicki, Nucl. Phys. B202 (1982) 327.

(28) See, for example, J. Ellis and G. G. Ross, Phys. Lett. 117B (1982) 397. P. Fayet in "Quarks, leptons and supersymmetry" ed. by J. Tran Thanh Van, Proceedings of the Seventeenth Rencontre de Moriond (1982) p 483. C. Kane, "Experimental Searches for Supersymmetric Particles", talk presented at 4th Workshop on Grand Unification, Philadelphia (1983).

SUPERSYMMETRY, SUPERGRAVITY AND THEIR PHENOMENOLOGICAL IMPLICATIONS

R. BARBIERI

Dipartimento di Fisica, Università di Pisa
INFN, Sezione di Pisa, Italy

1. The naturalness of the Fermi scale

The standard electroweak model is receiving a spectacular confirmation with the finding of the intermediate vector bosons at the CERN $p\bar{p}$ collider [1]. The growth of the integrated luminosity will render this confirmation more and more neat.

Within the context of the standard model, the interest is focused now on the problem of the physical origin of the Fermi scale $G_F^{-1/2}$, or of the W and Z masses. From an experimental point of view this corresponds to the search for the Higgs boson. As it is well known, the standard model with a physical Higgs particle lighter than about 1 Tev and heavier than a few Gev (or more for a large top quark mass $m_t \gtrsim M_W$) is a consistent perturbative theory up to very high energies. The extrapolation, which is limited only by the non asymptotically free nature of the theory, could reach even the Planck scale, where in any case gravity should come in.

Infact, is this smooth extrapolation of the standard model to be expected on physical grounds? To clarify this central issue let me recall the salient features of the potential for the $SU(2)$-doublet φ

$$V(\varphi) = -\mu^2 \varphi^+\varphi + \lambda (\varphi^+\varphi)^2 \tag{1}$$

which gives rise to

$$\langle\varphi\rangle = \begin{pmatrix} 0 \\ \frac{\mu}{\sqrt{2\lambda}} \end{pmatrix} . \tag{2}$$

The parameter μ sets the scale of the weak interactions through

$$(\sqrt{2}\, G_F)^{-1/2} = \frac{\mu}{\sqrt{2\lambda}} = 246 \text{ Gev} \tag{3}$$

and it gives the mass of the physical Higgs particle

$$m_S^2 = 2\mu^2 . \tag{4}$$

We can look now at the theory at an energy scale $\Lambda >> \mu$. In the Lagrangian of the standard model relevant at those energies a small dimensionless parameter appears, namely μ/Λ. Is there anything wrong with that? A scale fixing parameter - and μ is the only such parameter in the standard model - should sooner or later enter into the theory. Furthermore the standard model includes many other small parameters, starting from the Yukawa coupling of the electron $g_e \simeq 2 \times 10^{-6}$ and spanning a large range of values. Clearly, even though we may not like the small numbers in a fundamental Lagrangian, we are not, or not yet, at the point where we can ban them at all.

We must however observe a striking asymmetry between μ/Λ and these small parameters, practically all the other parameters of the standard model. Precisely with the only exception of μ/Λ, letting any one of them go to zero increases the symmetries of the Lagrangian. Both the gauge and the Yukawa couplings have this property. Their status is therefore rather satisfactory. Although we cannot compute them, their smallness is protected by the nearby symmetry. This guarantees the multiplicative character of all renormalization effects: the size of the quantum corrections is kept under control. Even for the ambitious program of computing the small parameters from a completely natural Lagrangian, with no small number at all, this seems a useful intermediate step.

What can be said[2)] then of μ/Λ, if we stick at the above "naturalness" criterium? A symmetry is indeed gained as $\mu \to 0$ provided, at the same time, one switches off all the couplings of the Higgs scalar. Demanding therefore that μ/Λ should not get lower than these dimensionless couplings, an upper limit is obtained on the energy Λ up to which the standard model can be safely and "naturally" extrapolated.

A more quantitative extimate of this maximal energy is obtained by considering the one loop contribution to

$$\mu^2 \equiv - \frac{dV}{d\varphi^+\varphi} \Big|_{\varphi^+\varphi=0} \tag{5}$$

where V is now the one loop Coleman Weinberg[3)] effective potential. In general one has

$$\mu^2 = \mu^2(<\Lambda) + \mu^2(>\Lambda) \tag{6}$$

where we have separated the contribution $\mu^2(<\Lambda)$ coming from the loop integral cut off at $k^2=\Lambda^2$ and the rest $\mu^2(>\Lambda)$, which includes also the bare contribution and in general all the effects of unknown physics at higher energies $E>\Lambda$.

In terms of the tree level squared masses $M_J^2(x)$ that the various particles of spin $J=0,\frac{1}{2},1$ would obtain if $\langle\varphi^+\varphi\rangle = x$, one gets

$$\mu^2(<\Lambda) = - \sum_J (2J+1)(-1)^{2J} \frac{dM_J^2}{dx} \left[\frac{\Lambda^2}{16\pi^2} + \frac{M_J^2}{64\pi^2}\left(2 \lg \frac{M_J^2}{\Lambda^2} + 1\right)\right]\Bigg|_{x=0} \tag{7}$$

where terms of order M_J^2/Λ^2 have been neglected. The quadratic growth of $\mu^2(<\Lambda)$ with Λ is a well known phenomenon. The coefficient of the dominant quadratic term, in the standard model, is given by

$$\frac{1}{16\pi^2} \sum_J (2J+1)(-1)^{2J} \frac{dM_J^2}{dx}\Big|_{x=0} =$$
$$= \frac{G_F}{8\sqrt{2}\pi^2}\left(6M_W^2 + 3M_Z^2 + \frac{3}{2} m_S^2 - 4\sum_F m_F^2\right) \simeq 6\times10^{-3} . \tag{8}$$

In getting the numerical result I have neglected the unknown contribution from the scalar as well as from the fermions (with the top quark giving possibly the only sizeable effect).

Barrying accidental cancellations, wich are not justified on the basis of any symmetry, I assume now that $|\mu^2|$ is of the order of, or

it is lower-bounded by, the quadratic term in Λ.
On account of Eqs (7,8), and taking $\lambda \lesssim e$ one finally gets

$$\Lambda \lesssim 2 \text{ TeV} . \tag{9}$$

By adopting the mentioned "naturalness" criterium, this should be taken as an order of magnitude estimate of the "Naturalness Breakdown Mass Scale" of the standard model. On these grounds a change of the physical regime is to be expected above this energy scale[2).

Suppose that we insist on the description of the Fermi scale in terms of a weakly coupled fundamental scalar field that gets a non vanishing vacuum expectation value. The virtue of the "naturalness" criterium is that it allows not only to set a limit on Λ, but also to select the extension of the standard model needed to enlarge its natural domain. Eq (7), which has general validity, suggests as a necessary condition that the equation

$$\frac{d}{dx} \sum_J (2J+1)(-1)^{2J} M_J^2(x) \Big|_{x=0} = 0 \tag{10}$$

hold as a consequence of a symmetry principle rather than of an accidental cancellation. Because of the $(-1)^{2J}$ factor, related to the different statistic, a compensation is required between the fermionic and bosonic contributions. This calls for a symmetry of fermionic nature[4)]. On the other hand, for a large class of supersymmetric Lagrangians[5)], one has[6)]

$$\sum_J (2J+1)(-1)^{2J} M_J^2(x) = 0 \tag{11}$$

as an identity in x. In such theories it can in fact be shown that $\mu^2 (<\Lambda)$ has no quadratic dependence on Λ not only at the one loop level but to all orders of perturbation theory[7)]. Within the context of the <u>weakly coupled fundamental Higgs model</u>, the naturalness criterium for the Fermi scale leads almost unavoidably to supersymmetry.

The coefficient of the Λ^2-term in the curvature of the scalar potential is set to zero in the supersymmetric Lagrangians by having the contribution of the bosons identically cancelled within each supermultiplet by the fermionic contribution. This occurs because of the relations between the couplings constants

$$g_J^2 \equiv \frac{dM_J^2}{dx}\bigg|_{x=0} \tag{12}$$

and independently from the values of the masses themselves M_J^2 at x=0. What does depend on the masses is the logarithmic or the finite piece in Eq (7), which also should not give a too large contribution to $\mu^2(<\Lambda)$. This bounds the squared mass splittings at x=0, ΔM_i^2 within each supermultiplet. Infact, for degenerate supermultiplets the r.h.s. of Eq(7) vanishes identically and, on the other hand, no natural relation occurs between couplings and masses of different supermultiplets, at least in perturbative elementary theories. As an order of magnitude bound, for a coupling g_i of the i-th supermultiplet to the Higgs scalar, one gets

$$\frac{g_i^2}{32\pi^2}\,\Delta M_i^2 \lesssim O(G_F^{-1}) \,. \tag{13}$$

Within N=1 supersymmetry any known particle should find its superpartner with a mass consistent with the bound (13).

2. Spontaneous supersymmetry breaking and supergravity

In the theories of physical interest supersymmetry cannot be exact. In order not to loose any predictive power and not to disturb everybody's aesthetic sense, the breaking of supersymmetry should be spontaneous. The relevant concepts here areanalogous, with some cave ats, to the ones encountered in the spontaneous breaking of a bosonic symmetry. The supersymmetry spinor-vector current J_μ^α couples to the vacuum a massless fermion, ψ_g, the goldstino

$$J_\mu^\alpha = M_S^2 (\gamma_\mu \psi_g)^\alpha + \ldots \tag{14}$$

with an order parameter M_S^2. This parameter enters into to the low energy theorem of spontaneously broken supersymmetry[8)]

$$\Delta M_\nu^2 = G_i M_S^2$$

relating the squared mass splitting of the i-th supermultiplet to its coupling G_i to the goldstino.

A classification of a priori interesting situations can be attempted according to the value of the supersymmetry breaking scale

$$\begin{aligned} &\text{i)} \quad M_S^2 = O(G_F^{-1}) \\ &\text{ii)} \quad M_S^2 \gg G_F^{-1} . \end{aligned} \tag{15}$$

In the first case[8)] (supersymmetry restored together with the electroweak symmetry) the goldstino should be subtancially coupled($G_i \sim g_{gauge}$, g_{yukawa}) to normal matter to raise, according to Eq (15), the masses of the unseen superpartners. The massless goldstino has only effective weak interactions since it connects a light particle (say a quark or a lepton) with its heavy superpartner. The typical scale of the spectrum of such a theory is the Fermi scale itself and only quarks and leptons (not their partners) should be anomalously light because of the related chiral symmetries.

The problem with this approach is essentially the mass relation implied by Eq(11) at $\chi = \langle x \rangle$, which was used to cure the quadratic Λ-dependence of the curvature of the potential. The known fermions are too light to compensate the boson contribution in the mass sum rule. The introduction[8] of new supermultiplets all leaving within the Fermi scale and of new gauge interactions brings in additional problems (unwanted minima, triangle anomalies, etc.) rather than solve the difficulties.

In the alternative[9] approach (i), supersymmetry is broken at much higher energies than the weak interaction scale. Suppose that the theory contains an extra scale $M \gg G_F^{-1}$, such that

$$M_S^2 = M\, G_F^{-1/2} . \tag{16}$$

In this case the goldstino field must be very weakly coupled to normal matter in order not to make Eq(15) inconsistent with the bound(13). These couplings go like $G_i \sim O(G_F^{-1/2}/M)$. On the other hand the goldstino can - infact it must - be substancially coupled to supermultiplets which have a very small coupling $g_i \sim O(G_F^{-1/2}/M)$ to the Higgs doublet. These supermultiplets, normally sitting at M, have large mass splittings, $\Delta M_i^2 = O(M_S^2)$, and can give a sizeable contribution to the mass sum rule 11) other than the one of the normal supermultiplets. Otherwise they do not disturb the physics at lower energies. This is how the difficulty of the mass sum rule is overcome.

In my opinion the real interest of this situation lies in the fact that it can be naturally implemented in supergravity[5] with M identified with the Planck mass M_P. I will not describe here how this is done; a detailed exposition and list of references can be found for example in Ref. 10. I shall rather illustrate in a simple and self-contained example how the mass sum rule gets modified in broken supergravity.

The starting point is the Deser-Zumino Lagrangian[11] for the goldstino field ψ_g coupled in a locally supersymmetric way to the gravitino spin-$\frac{3}{2}$ field ψ_μ. For the purpose of the argument one only needs the terms in the Lagrangian which are quadratic in the fields

$$\mathcal{L} = -\frac{1}{2}\varepsilon^{\mu\nu\rho\sigma}\bar{\psi}_\mu \gamma_5 \gamma_\nu \partial_\rho \psi_\sigma - \frac{1}{2}\bar{\psi}_g \not{\partial} \psi_g + m\left(\bar{\psi}_\mu \sigma^{\mu\nu}\psi_\nu + \sqrt{\frac{3}{2}}\,\bar{\psi}_g \gamma\cdot\psi - \bar{\psi}_g \psi_g\right) + \ldots \tag{17}$$

with the gravitational constant put equal to 1. One can check directly that this Lagrangian is invariant under

$$\delta\psi_g = \sqrt{6}\, m\, \epsilon(x) \tag{18}$$
$$\delta\psi_\mu = 2\partial_\mu \epsilon(x) + m\gamma_\mu \epsilon(x)$$

where $\epsilon(x)$ is an anticommuting spinor. Notice that I have already imposed the Deser-Zumino relation[11)] between the supersymmetry order parameter M_S^2 (the coefficient of $\epsilon(x)$ in the transformation of the goldstino field) and the gravitino mass

$$M_S^2 = \sqrt{6}\, m \tag{19}$$

which has allowed the cancellation of the cosmological constant*.

---

* This is an unnatural adjustment of parameters. It may have to do with the fact that gravity, - and N=1 supergravity -, is not yet a consistent quantum theory. On the other hand the idea[12)] that the cosmological constant of the basic Lagrangian is not necessarily small since it may not be the same as that derived from astrophysical and cosmological considerations does not seem to apply here. We are assuming that a possible dynamical explanation of the vanishing cosmological constant can be incorporated in the models under study without modifying their "low-energy" consequences.

With a special choise of gauge, the goldstino field can be eliminated from (17) and one remains with a massive spin-$\frac{3}{2}$ gravitino (Super-Higgs effect)[13,11].

We want to couple now a chiral supermultiplet made of a scalar φ and a Majorana spinor χ to the sistem described by the Lagrangian(17). One may think of adding to (17) the free kinetic terms for φ and χ and the minimal Noether current coupling

$$\frac{1}{2}\bar{\Psi}_\mu\,(\not{\partial}\hat{\varphi})\gamma^\mu\chi \qquad\qquad (\hat{\varphi} = \mathrm{Re}\,\varphi + i\gamma_5\,\mathrm{Im}\,\varphi).$$

This is however not enough. Invariance is obtained up to cubic terms in the fields under the transformations (18) and

$$\begin{aligned}\delta\varphi &= \frac{1}{2}\,\bar{\epsilon}(x)\,(1+\gamma_5)\chi \\ \delta\chi &= \frac{1}{2}\,(\not{\partial}\hat{\varphi}^*)\,\epsilon(x) - \frac{m}{2}\,\hat{\varphi}\,\epsilon(x)\end{aligned} \tag{20}$$

if one adds to (17) the Lagrangian for the chiral multiplet

$$\begin{aligned}\mathcal{L}^{c.m.} = &-\frac{1}{2}|\partial_\mu\varphi|^2 - \frac{1}{2}\bar{\chi}\not{\partial}\chi + \frac{1}{2}\bar{\Psi}_\mu(\not{\partial}\hat{\varphi})\gamma^\mu\chi \\ &+ \frac{m}{2}\,\bar{\Psi}\cdot\gamma\,\hat{\varphi}^*\chi - \frac{m^2}{2}|\varphi|^2 .\end{aligned} \tag{21}$$

The important point to notice is the appearance of the mass for the scalar field equal to the gravitino mass, whereas the fermion has remained massless. For the single chiral supermultiplet (φ,χ) one has

$$\sum_J (2J+1)(-1)^{2J} M_J^2 = m^2 . \tag{22}$$

Generalizations of this example can be implemented in closed supergravity Lagrangians invariant to any order in the gravitational coupling[13, 14]. Eq (22) is a special case of a general mass sum rule in broken supergravity with vanishing cosmological constant[13].

Let us come back to the general problem now. In the general Lagrangian a universal supersymmetry breaking mass term for all the scalars in chiral supermultiplets is obtained[15]. This is not the only effect at low energy of the supergravity couplings. One also gets a supersymmetry breaking in the scalar potential. In minimal supergravity models the effective Lagrangian for the light chiral supermultiplets (φ_i, χ_i) at low energy relative to the supersymmetry breaking scale acquires the form[15-19]

$$\mathcal{L} = \mathcal{L}(\text{glob. susy}; f) - \frac{m^2}{2}\varphi_a^* \varphi_a + m\left[(A-3) f(\varphi) + \varphi_a \frac{\partial f}{\partial \varphi_a} + \text{h.c.}\right] \tag{23}$$

where the first term is the globally supersymmetric Lagrangian depending on an arbitrary superpotential f and the breaking term in the scalar potential, also proportional to the gravitino mass m, is totally specified in terms of f a part from the dimensionless parameter A[16].

The Lagrangian (23) is the basis for the model building and for the phenomenological applications. From a general point of view the explicit supersymmetry breaking terms in (23) are special cases of more general breaking terms[20] which are soft in the sense that they preserve the ultraviolet properties of the globally supersymmetric Lagrangian at the level of the quadratic divergences. This is what is needed to keep under control the dominant corrections to the curvature of the scalar potential, as explained in the previous Section. On the other hand, the special form acquired in the minimal models by the supersymmetry breaking terms, is most welcome since more general soft breaking terms can lead in principle to unwanted phenomena, like, e.g., flavour and CP violations by strong interactions.

3. Phenomenological implications

Based on the type of Lagrangians(23), explicit supersymmetric models[10] have been constructed with the standard $SU(3)\times SU(2)\times U(1)$ group as well as with grand unified groups (mostly $SU(5)$). A salient feature, - distinctive among the various models -, is the breaking of the electroweak symmetry occurring either at the tree level (Tree Level Models)[15, 21] or from renormalization group loop corrections (Loop Correction Models[22, 23]). In the latter case one basically relies on a heavy top quark mass ($m_t \gtrsim M_W$), whose large Yukawa coupling drives the Higgs mass negative at exponentially lower energies $(\sim M_W)$ relative to the scale ($\sim M_P$) where the parameters of the original Lagrangian(23) are defined. In the following I choose to illustrate an $SU(3)\times SU(2)\times U(1)$ model[15] with tree level breaking of the $SU(2)\times U(1)$ factor.

The light chiral superfields are the quarks and leptons, a pair of Higgs doublets of opposite ypercharge H, H_c and an averall singlet Y. The LCM may try to avoid the introduction of the singlet Y, although this makes life a bit more difficult. The pair of Higgs doublets is needed anyway to describe the $SU(2)\times U(1)$ breaking. The superpotential f which is considered is the most generale one consistent with gauge invariance, Baryon and Lepton number conservations*, and renormalizability. This defines completely the model with the caveat that the minimal Lagrangian(23)is not strictly renormalizable: logarithmic divergences appear in higher loops. This calls for the introduction of counter terms corresponding to the terms of the most general softly broken Lagrangian, but with a size estimated from the radiative corrections themselves cut off at $\Lambda \lesssim M_P$. With small couplings in f (I take a "light" top quark $m_t < M_W$), I do not know of cases where these divergent non minimal terms are large and I will neglect them in the following.

The salient features of the spectrum which do not depend upon the details of the parameters in f are:

i) There is a charged w-ino, - a fermion partner of the W -, which is lighter than the W itself[24]. Its mass gets close to the W-mass as the gravitino mass decreases ($m \gtrsim 20\,GeV$), whereas it becomes light

$$m(\tilde{\omega}) \simeq \frac{M_W^2}{m} \tag{24}$$

for an heavy gravitino ($m \lesssim 300\,GeV$. The other w-ino is heavier than the W.

---

* It is annoying that the introduction of scalar quarks and leptons allows to write down $SU(3)\times SU(2)\times U(1)$ renormalizable couplings which violate B and L. This might call for an enlargement of the gauge group. A left-right extension from $SU(2)_L \times U(1)$to $SU(2)_L \times SU(2)_R \times U(1)$ would work.

ii) The masses of the two scalar particles associated with any (Dirac) quark or lepton, f, are related to m_f and m according to[15,17)]

$$\mu^2_{f,\pm} = m^2 + m_f^2 \pm 2b\, m\, m_f \tag{25}$$

b being a model dependent parameter of order unit. The charged scalar component in H, H_c, not eaten by the W, is substancially heavier than the W itself.

iii) In the neutral fermion sector there is always a Majorana spinor $\tilde{z}$ lighter than the Z, with a mass

$$m(\hat{z}) \simeq \frac{M_Z^2}{m} \tag{26}$$

for $m \gg M_W$. The remaining part of the neutral fermion sector (3 more Majorana spinors a part from the photino) is more model dependent, as it is the spectrum of the neutral scalar H, H_c sector.

iv) In the model there are light gluinos ($\tilde{g}$) and a light photino ($\tilde{\gamma}$). At the tree level they are massless. They pick up one loop radiative masses[10)] which appear too small ($\lesssim$ 1 Gev) to be consistent with observation and/or, in the case of a stable photino, with cosmological limits[23,25)]. Do we need here a small deviation from the minimal models? Non minimal models indeed allow an explicit mass term for the gauginos in the Lagrangian(23). A preferable way out comes from possible one loop contributions from the exchange of new heavy fermion-boson supermultiplets which contribute as

$$(\delta m(\tilde{g}), \delta m(\tilde{\gamma})) = \left(c\frac{\alpha_s}{4\pi}, Q^2\frac{\alpha}{4\pi}\right) m \tag{27}$$

for a colour Casimir operator C and a charge Q of the virtual particles. These contributions are there in grand unified extensions of the model and the various representations are large enough to give sizeable contributions to the gluino ($\delta m(\tilde{g}) \simeq 10 \div 50$ GeV) and the photino ($\delta m(\tilde{\gamma}) \simeq 2 \div 10$ GeV) masses. If asked, I could only recommend the search for "light" gluinos and for a "light" probably stable photino.

The couplings of all these new particles to the photon and the gluons are of course dictated by their charge and colour. Also the Yukawa like couplings to the photino and gluinos of the matter supermultiplets (quarks, leptons, and their partners) are fixed by charge and colour. In general the couplings of the new particles to the W and the Z is complicated by possible mixings in the mass matrices between fields of different weak isospin and ipercharge. In the models under consideration and, I guess, in all other models (like LCM) this mixing is negligible for scalar partners of quarks and leptons with opposite helicity:also their couplings to the W and the Z are therefore fixed. In conclusion what is model dependent, or at list dependent on the value of the masses, are the W and Z couplings of the fermionic gaugino-Higgsino sector.

From what has been said about the spectrum and the couplings of the new particles predicted in supersymmetric models, are there concrete chances of seeing any of them in the decay products of the W and Z bosons? (In no way I want to imply that this is the only possibility to look for them, but I have of course in mind the opportunity offered presently by the $p\bar{p}$ collider at CERN).
I think that these chances exist. I am assuming that the problem of the photino and gluino masses can be solved as I have indicated without modifying substancially the other conclusions.

Probably the best signatures for the detection of the new particles in the W and Z decays would be offered in the case of a light gravitino, m = 20 ÷ 30 Gev, admittedly a small window in the range of all possible values (20 Gev $\lesssim$ m $\lesssim$ 300 Gev). In this case the allowed decay modes

$$W^{\pm} \rightarrow (se)^{\pm} + (s\nu) \tag{28a}$$

$$Z \rightarrow (se)^{+} + (se)^{-} \tag{28b}$$

would feed[25,26] the same final states

$$p\bar{p} \rightarrow e + X \tag{29a}$$

$$p\bar{p} \rightarrow e^{+}e^{-} + X \tag{29b}$$

which are looked for at present to establish the very existence of the W and the Z through their conventional decay modes. The largely dominant decay modes of the scalar electron and of the scalar neutrino should in fact be

$$\begin{aligned} se^{\pm} &\rightarrow e^{\pm} + \tilde{\gamma} \\ s\nu &\rightarrow \nu + \tilde{\gamma} . \end{aligned} \tag{30}$$

The important point to notice[26,27] here is the substancial difference in the charge asymmetry if the final lepton is produced through the conventional decay mode versus the supersymmetric decay mode. In Fig. 1 a tridimensional view is given[26] of the cross sections for the process (29a) as functions of the transverse momentum and laboratory angle of the electron in the case of the conventional W-decay mode (Fig. 1a), for the separate supersymmetric mode (Fig. 1b) and for the sum of the two cross sections for minimal values of the se and sv masses, 20 Gev, both equal to the gravitino mass (Ffg 1c) Sea parton contributions as well as standard QCD corrections are included. The cross sections for the process(29b)via Z production and subsequent decay through(28b)have also been studied[28]. A selection of the events of the type(29b)with a missing transverse energy allows a discrimination of the interesting events versus the conventional Drell Yan background.

An increase of the gravitino mass, ($m \gtrsim 40$ Gev), and so of the scalar lepton and quark masses will close the allowed phase space for the above processes. This should however open more and more the channel

$$W^{\pm} \to \tilde{\omega}^{\pm} + \tilde{\gamma}$$

with a branching ratio

$$R(\tilde{\omega}^{\pm} + \tilde{\gamma}) = \frac{\Gamma(W \to \tilde{\omega} + \tilde{\gamma})}{\Gamma(W \to e + \nu)}$$

given in Table 1. At $m \gtrsim 1.5\ M_W$ the following other channels should open

$$W^{\pm} \to \tilde{\omega}^{\pm} + \tilde{z}$$
$$Z \to \tilde{\omega}^{+} + \tilde{\omega}^{-}$$

with sizeable branching ratios* (the decay $Z \to \tilde{\omega}^{+}\tilde{\omega}^{-}$ is normalized to $Z \to \nu\bar{\nu}$).

---

* For related numbers see Ref(29).I thank M. Mangano for help in computing Table 1.

TABLE 1

m	40 GeV	150 GeV	300 GeV
$R(\tilde{\omega}^{\pm}+\tilde{\gamma})$	0.1	0.5	0.8
$R(\tilde{\omega}^{\pm}+\tilde{z})$	—	1.2	3
$R(\tilde{\omega}^{+}+\tilde{\omega}^{-})$	—	3.7	4.5
$m(\tilde{\omega})\simeq m(\tilde{z})$	60 GeV	35 GeV	20 GeV

These figures are encouraging even though the fact that the main decay mode of $\tilde{\omega}$ and $\tilde{z}$

$$\tilde{\omega} \to \tilde{\gamma} + \text{hadrons}$$

$$\tilde{z} \to \tilde{\gamma} + \text{hadrons}$$

will make the detection of the gaugino - Higgsino decays of the W and Z more difficult than the detection of the scalar decay modes. The final states in $p\bar{p}$ collision will consist of broad jets with unbalanced momentum.

Finally, the overall widths of the intermediate vector bosons. Disappointly enough the ratio $\Gamma(W)/\Gamma(Z)$ is equal within a few percents to the same ratio in the standard model and it is practically independent from the value of the gravitino mass m. The absolute widts do depend on m, with the ratio

$$\Gamma(W)/\Gamma(W;\ \mathrm{standard})$$

varying from 1,5 at m $\simeq$ 20 Gev to 1,3 at m $\simeq$ 300 Gev and passing through a minimum value $\sim$ 1 when the phase space of the scalar decays is closed (m $\simeq$ 40 Gev) and the ω-ino, photino mode starts being open.

4. Conclusions

A central problem in our field is the physical origin of the Fermi scale. A consequence of the probably unorthodox point of view that I have taken in this talk is that the search for the Higgs scalar field may not be the basic tool to shed light on this issue. Of course I am not disputing the fact that the Higgs phenomenon is the correct description of the breaking of the electroweak symmetry. I believe however that the adoption of the naturalness criterium described in Sect 1 has far more reaching consequences. At the moment we can think of two alternative ways to incorporate the Higgs picture in a natural framework. One possibility is to try to relate the Fermi scale to a new strong interaction (technicolour, composite models, etc.). The main drawback of this view is, in my opinion, a technical one, namely our present inability to make strong interaction calculations. The alternative possibility is the one described in the talk where the standard perturbative techniques are at work. As in the standard model, the Higgs particle is still a weakly interacting fundamental field, but surrounded by a pletora of new particles which cannot be too elusive. Some of them might show up in the decay fragments of the newly found intermediate vector bosons. What a sign of liveliness for our field if this would turn out to be true!

Acknowledgements

I am deeply indepted to L. Maiani with whom I have discussed practically all the points contained in this paper, and to S. Ferrara, L. Girardello, A. Masiero and H. Nilles for several useful conversations.

5. References

(1) G. Arnison et al., Phys. Lett. 122B, 103 (1983);
G. Banner et al., Phys. Lett. 122B, 476 (1983);
G. Arnison et al., CERN preprint EP/83-76 (1983).

(2) G. t'Hooft, lectures given at the Cargèse Summer Institute (1979).

(3) S. Coleman and E. Weinberg, Phys Rev D7, 1888 (1973).

(4) S. Weinberg, Phys. Rev D13, 3333 (1976);
L. Maiani, Proc. Summer School of Gif-sur-Yvette, (IN2P3, Paris, 1980), p. 3;
M. Veltman, Acta Phys. Pol. B12, 437 (1981);
E. Witten, Nucl. Phys. B188, 513 (1981).

(5) For a review of supersymmetry sec P. Fayet and S. Ferrara, Phys. Rep. 32, 249 (1977); for supergravity sec P. van Nieuwenhuizen, Phys. Rep. 68, 189 (1981).

(6) S. Ferrara, L. Girardello and F. Palumbo, Phys. Rev. D20, 403

(1979).

(7) W. Fiscler, H. Nilles, J. Polchinski, S. Raby and L. Susskind, Phys. Rev. Lett. 47, 757 (1981).

(8) P. Fayet, Unification of the Fundamental Particle Interactions, eds. S. Ferrara, J. Ellis and P. van Nieuwenhuizen (Plenum Press, New York, 1980), p. 587.

(9) R. Barbieri S. Ferrara and D.V. Nanopoulos, Z. Phys C13, 267 (1982) and Phys. Lett. 116B, 6 (1982);
M. Dine and Fisher, Nucl. Phys. B204, 346 (1982);
J. Ellis, L. Ibanez and G. Ross, Phys. Lett. 113B, 283 (1982);
S. Dimopoulos and S. Raby, Los Alamos preprint LA-UR-82-1982 (1982);
S. Polchinski and L. Susskind, Phys. Rev. D26, 3661 (1982).

(10) For review and an exhaustive list of references see R. Barbieri and S. Ferrara, CERN preprint TH. 3547 (1983) to appear in "Surveys in High - Energy Physics".

(11) S. Deser and B. Zumino, Phys. Rev. Lett. 38 (1977) 1433.

(12) S.W. Hawking, Nucl. Phys. B144 (1978) 349.

(13) E. Cremmer, B. Julia, J. Sherk, S. Ferrara, L. Girardello and P. von Nieuwenhuizen, Phys. Lett. 79B (1978) 231; Nucl. Phys. B147 (1979) 105;
E. Cremmer, S. Ferrara, L. Girardello and A. von Proyen, Phys. Lett. 116B (1982) 231; CERN preprint TH-3348 (1983).

(14) E. Witten and J. Bagger, Phys. Lett. 115B (1982) 202; Princeton preprints (1982).

(15) R. Barbieri, S. Ferrara and C. Savoy, Phys. Lett. 119B 219 (1982).

(16) H. Nilles, M. Srednicki and D. Wyler, Phys. Lett. 120B,346 (1983)

(17) E. Cremmer, P. Fayet and L. Girardello, Phys. Lett. 122B, 41 (1983).

(18) L. Hall, J. Lykken and S. Weinberg, Austin preprint UTTG-1-83 (1983).

(19) S. Soni and H. Weldon, Pennsylvania preprint (1983).

(20) L. Girardello and M. Grisaru, Nucl. Phys. B194, 65 (1982).

(21) R. Arnowitt, A.H. Chamseddine and P. Nath, Phys. Rev. Lett. 49, 970 (1982).

(22) J. Ellis, D.V. Nanopoulos and K. Tamvakis, Phys. Lett. 121B, 123 (1983);

L.E. Ibanez, Universidad Autonoma de Madrid preprint FTUAM/82-8 (1982);

(23) L. Alvarez-Gaume, J. Polchinski and M.B. Wise, Harvard preprint HUTP-82/A063 (1982).

(24) S. Weinberg, Phys. Rev. Lett. 50, 387 (1983).

(25) H. Goldberg, Northeastern Univ preprint NUB 2592 (1983);
L. Krauss, Harvard Univ preprint HUTB-83/A009 (1983).

(26) R. Barbieri, N. Cabibbo, R. Maiani and S. Petrarca, Rome preprint n. 348 (1983).

(27) R. Barnett, K. Lackner and H. Haber, SLAC preprint PUB-3105 (1983).

(28) N. Cabibbo, R. Maiani and S. Petrarca, Rome preprint n.355(1983).

(29) A. Chamseddine, Pran Nath, and R. Arnowitt, Harvard preprint HUTP-83/A040 (1983).

NEW VACUUM FORMATICN AND BUBBLE EVOLUTICN IN THE EARLY UNIVERSE

V.A.Berezin,V.A.Kuzmin,I.I.Tkachev

Institute for Nuclear Research of the Academy of Sciences of the USSR,60-th October Anniversary Prospect 7a, Moscow II7 3I2, USSR

Effects of gravitation on decay of a metastable state in the early Universe are investigated.It is found that the decay is not possible under certain conditions which involve parameters of a field theory and a sign of a curvature of a cosmological model. The corresponding constraints are the most essential in the case of (locally) supersymmetric models. The relation is found between an amount of inflation and a temperature after reheating. The equations are investigated of a new phase bubble wall motion as well as the behaviour of old phase remnants and domains.

A great attention has been paid recently to studies of vacuum phase transitions in the early Universe. Due to the large unification mass scale of fundamental interactions, $M_X \sim 10^{14} - 10^{18}$ GeV, a significant role in phase transition process could be played by gravitation.

A full account of general relativity effects in phase transition phenomena seems to be a rather complicated problem and as a matter of fact this question is not yet investigated properly up to now despite of its importance. In particular,gravitational effects are usually neglected in studies of new phase bubble nucleation during decay of a metastable state in the Universe. The account of these effects was carried out only in the case of the decay of a pure vacuum state in ref. / I /. At some conditions gravitation makes the probability of vacuum decay smaller and it can even stabilize the false vacuum, preventing vacuum decay altogether / I /. The account of effects of gravitation is also of importance at studies of inflationary scenarios / 2 /. It was found in ref./ 3 / that the decay of a metastable vacuum with account of general relativity effects could proceed via simultaneous transition of the whole Universe into the state of the maximnm of effective potential rather than by means of isolated bubbles nucleation.

In the present paper we restrict ourselves by the consideration in the framework of general relativity of dynamics of the evolution of space regions occupied by different phases assuming that the transient layer between phases is rather thin. We shall carry out a detailed consideration only for spherically symmetric surfaces of phase separation. We shall consider both time-like (TL) and space-like (SL) surfaces of phase separation.

The shape of the TL surface of phase separation determines in particular the motion of bubble walls.One encounters with such a problem studying three following physically different situations: new phase bubbles surrounded by the old phase,remnants of the old phase surrounded by the new phase and, finally, considering the domain structure.

I. The decay of a metastable state in the Universe proceeds by means of new phase bubble nucleation in the interiors of the old phase. Thus the problem of the investigation of phase transitions consists of two parts. First, one needs to know the probability of new phase bubble nucleation and, second, it is necessary to study the subsequent evolution of arising bubbles. In a pure vacuum case both these problems combines in one as follows: the motion of nucleatedbubble is given by the analitic continuationinto the real time of the Euclidean configuration described the process of subbarrier tunneling /1,4/. In paper /5/ it was found the probability of thermodynamical formation of a new phase bubble. However, the problem of the bubble grow requires in this case a special treatment. Up to now there was no consistent approach to this problem in the literature devoted to study of phase transitions. Usually the process of new phase bubble evolution is treated similarly to the detonation wave propagation /6/, so called "condensation discontinuities" /6/. In the paper /7/ similar approach has been proposed for investigation of phase transitions in the early Universe. However, the detonation wave approximation is valid only for nonsingular surface of phase separation. Remind that a surface of phase separation is called singular if the tensor of energy-momentum surface density on the shell is not equal to zero. In a number of cases the surface of phase separation can not be treated as nonsingular. For example, the shell separating two phases with pure vacuum equations of state is singular. Another example is the shell describing a "vacuum burning" /8 /.

Here we investigate the equations of motion of a singular shell. In particular these equations describe a bubble grow in a pure vacuum case as well as detonation wave propagation.

2. The bubbles nucleate, expande and collide till the universe will be filled with the new phase. The phase transition may, in principle, not to complete. Such a situation arises when the rate of cosmological expansion exceeds the bubble nucleation rate /IO/. Nevertherless phase transition did complete and the percolation in old phase was ceased provided we do not live in a single bubble (visible part of the Universe may be in one bubble in the case of GUT phase transition /II/). Thus the old phase remnants are isolated and there exists the remnant of certain maximal size. Black holes in the Universe may originate from such remnants /I2/. Here we consider only sphe-

rically symmetric remnants of old phase. The spherization may be coused by the surface tension.

3. Of interest also is an investigation of the domain structure in the universe /I3-I5/, in particular of the domains with different gauge symmetry groups /I4/ and of CP-domains /I5/, the latter playing important role in baryon excess generation in the Universe /I6/. The flat domain walls were considered in ref./I3/. The domain boundaries form however the closed surfaces when the abundance of one phase is smaller than that of another phase (the corresponding volume fraction is given by percolation theory). Such an isolated domain may be treated approximately as the spherically symmetric bubble.

The physical content of a space-like hypersurface of phase separation differs essentially from that of time-like hypersurface the latter being described a real motion of bubble walls. In what follows we enumerate several situations when a space-like junction seems appropriate.

4. A phase transition which proceeds through isolated bubbles nucleation,collisions and subsequent thermalization but finishes very rapidly (almost instantly).

5. A phase transition which proceeds by means of Hawking-Moss mechanism /3/.

6. A materialization of a new phase inside one (large) bubble.

7. A phase transition in the framework of the new inflationary scenario /II/.

In the cases 4 and 5 the matching is carried out across the Universe,while in cases 6 and 7 we are restricted by the bubble dimensions. In the cases 5 and 6 we match two phases, the transition between them being quantum tunneling process. Therefore the applicability of SL junction to these cases is unclear. Though this junction may proved to be rather unphysical we shall nevertheless formally investigate it too. In the case 7 we pay no attention to the quantum transition process and consider the whole region of space-time where occurs the slow classical rolling of the field fluctuation (during which vacuum energy does not change practically).as the region still occupied by the old phase. We attribute to the transient layer the region where the system rolls down rapidly to the minimum of the potential and then oscillates, the kinetic energy of the field being transformed into the particle energy. The duration of both latter stages is of the order I/M_X, that is much smaller than even dimensions of visible part of the Universe. Therefore it is quite natureal to use here the thin-wall formalism.

Our investigation of the hypersurfaces of phase separation will be based on the thin shell formalism in general relativity /I7,I8/.

The line element of spherically symmetric hypersurface in the TL case may be written as

$$dl^2 = d\tau^2 - \rho^2(\tau)d\Omega^2 , \tag{Ia}$$

while in the SL case we have

$$dl^2 = -dq^2 - \rho^2(q)d\Omega^2 , \tag{Ib}$$

where $d\Omega$ is a solid angle element. The form of this surface is determined by the conditions derived from Einstein equations for a singular spherically symmetric shell (the formalizm is described in ref./I7,I8/):

$$[K_2^2] = \epsilon\, 4\pi S/M_{Pl}^2 , \tag{2a}$$

$$[K_0^0] + [K_2^2] = \epsilon\, 8\pi S_2^2/M_{Pl}^2 , \tag{2b}$$

$[K_i^j]$ being the discontinuity of the K_i^j component of the shell's outer curvature tensor; $S \equiv S_0^0$, $\epsilon = +1$ for a TL hypersurface and $S \equiv S_1^1$, $\epsilon = -1$ for a SL hypersurface respectively, where

$$S_i^j = \lim_{\delta\to 0} \int_{-\delta}^{\delta} dn\, T_i^j , \tag{3}$$

S_i^j is the surface density of energy-momentum tensor on the shell and n is the coordinate measured in the direction of the outer normal to the hypersurface. Tensor S_i^j can be shown to take the following form in the pure vacuum case

$$S_i^j = S\,\delta_i^j . \tag{4}$$

The tensor S_i^j has the same structure in the case of SL hypersurface of phase separation for arbitrary equation of state under conditions of homogeneity and isotropy, while the "vacuum burning" phenomenon requires the following structure /8/:

$$S_0^0 = 0 , \quad S_2^2 = S_3^3 \neq 0 . \tag{5}$$

We shall denote all the quantities before the phase transition by the index "b" and those after the transition by the index "a" ; correspondingly the indices "in" and "out" will be used for the quantities inside and outside the bubble.

I. DECAY OF METASTABLE STATE

In the general case of a first order phase transition spacetime is described by different metrics inside and outside the new phase bubble. The same is true as concerns the Universe before and after the phase transition. The phace separation surface should obey Einstein's equations so one has to match metrics on this hypersurface. The form of this hypersursurface in the TL case gives the bubble walls motion the investigation of which we leave to the next section. In this chapter we consider only the possibility of junction of the metrics on the hypersurface separating the phases. In such a way the decay probability of a metastable state can not been obtained, however we can find the range of parameters of a theory at which it should vanish. One has to consider the junction on both time-like and space-like surfaces of phase separation.

2.I. Time-like junction

We first consider the TL junction. Calculating the outer curvature tensor for the TL shell in spherically symmetric metric of general form

$$ds^2 = e^{\nu} dt^2 - e^{\lambda} dr^2 - r^2 d\Omega^2, \qquad (6)$$

$$\nu \equiv \nu(t, r), \quad \lambda \equiv \lambda(t, r)$$

we obtain

$$K_2^{\,2} = -\sigma \sqrt{\rho_\tau^2 + e^{-\lambda}} / \rho, \qquad (7a)$$

$$K_0^{\,0} = -\sigma \left[\rho_{\tau\tau} + \rho_\tau^2 (\lambda' + \nu')/2 + \nu' e^{-\lambda}/2 \right] (\rho_\tau^2 + e^{-\lambda})^{-\frac{1}{2}} - \sigma \dot{\lambda} \rho_\tau e^{\frac{\lambda - \nu}{2}}, \qquad (7b)$$

where $\rho_\tau \equiv \frac{d\rho}{d\tau}$, $\lambda' \equiv \frac{\partial \lambda}{\partial r}$, $\dot{\lambda} \equiv \frac{\partial \lambda}{\partial t}$, $\sigma = \pm 1$.

The case $\sigma = +1$ corresponds to increasing radii r in the outward direction while $\sigma = -1$ indicates the opposite case. Thus, for given inner and outer metrics σ determines the global geometry (i.e. how is the inner geometry sticked together with the outer one). Substituting (7) into Eq. (2) one can obtain the equation of motion of the shell determining $\rho(\tau)$ and find σ. Here we are not interested in the explicit form of the function $\rho(\tau)$ but shall investigate the general junction conditions. We find that at certain conditions the junction is impossible. Such a situation may arise if the sign of σ_{out} (or σ_{in}) following from the Eqs. (7) does not agree with the given geometry of an outer (inner) region. It follows immediately from Eq. (2a) that $\sigma_{out} > 0$ if

$$\exp(-\lambda_{in}) - \exp(-\lambda_{out}) > 16\pi^2 (S_0^{\,0})^2 \rho^2 / M_{Pl}^4 . \qquad (8)$$

Correspondingly $\sigma_{out} < 0$ at the opposite sign of the inequality (8). One may easily write also similar inequalities for σ_{in}

Consider the case of homogeneous isotropic space described by the Robertson-Walker-Friedmann metric:

$$ds^2 = dt^2 - a^2(t) \left[\frac{dr^2}{1 - kr^2} + r^2 d\Omega^2 \right]. \qquad (9)$$

This metric can be easily represented in the form (6). Using Einstein equations we obtain:

$$\exp(-\lambda) = 1 - 8\pi \varepsilon \rho^2 / 3 M_{Pl}^2 , \qquad (10)$$

ε being energy density inside (outside) the bubble. For further convenience let us introduce the following notation:

$$\xi \equiv M_{Pl}^2 \left[\varepsilon_{out}(t_{out}) - \varepsilon_{in}(t_{in}) \right] / 6\pi (S_0^{\,0}(\tau))^2 . \qquad (11)$$

The correspondense between ξ and σ's which follow from conditions (8) is shown in Table I, where we represented also the scematic views of corresponding spatial sections.

Table I.

	σ_{IN}	σ_{OUT}	SPATIAL SECTION (SCHEMATIC)		
			$K_{OUT} = +1$	$K_{OUT} = -1$	$K_{OUT} = 0$
$\xi > 1$	+1	+1	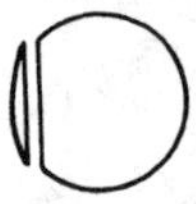		
$-1 < \xi < 1$	+1	-1	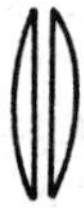	JUNCTION	
$\xi < -1$	-1	-1	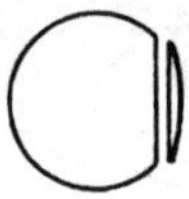	IMPOSSIBLE	

We see that the case $K_{out} = +1$, $\xi < -1$ can be reduced to the case $K_{out} = +1$, $\xi > 1$ by exchanging the outer and inner regions i.e. these two cases are physically equivalent. The same is true for $\xi < 0$ and $\xi > 0$ cases when $-1 < \xi < 1$,so it is sufficient to consider the $\xi \geq 0$ case. Note that in the case of of spherically symmetric domains created in a course of spontaneous breaking of discrete symmetry (e.g. for CP domains /I5/) one has just $\xi = 0$. As one cah see from Table I the junction is not always possible. In the closed Universe (k = +I) the junction is possible at any value of ξ ,so one can not obtain any constraints on parameters of (quantum field) theory. In the open Universe (k = -I) the junction is possible only if $\xi > 1$. However there may take place situations requiring additional analysis, when coordinates (9) with k = -I do not describe all the space-time but its part only. In these coordinates the junction is again impossible at $\xi < 1$, however, this does not mean yet that the metastable state does not decay. It may be simply that the new phase bubble is nucleated in such a way that it goes out of the scope of the coordinate set (9). Let us explain this by considering as an example the junction of two metrics with pure vacuum equations of state, i.e. two deSitter metrics with different $\mathcal{E}$'s but $\mathcal{E} > 0$. In the pure deSitter world (without bubbles) with $\mathcal{E} > 0$ one can always choose the coordinate t in such a way that the section t = const will be open or spatially flat. However, one needs two such coordinate systems to cover all the manifold. At $\xi < 1$ the junction in terms of these coordinates is impossible, while it may be easily shown that the junction of two deSitter metrics with $\mathcal{E} > 0$ is possible at any ξ. It is sufficient to note that such a metric can be written in the form (9) with k = +I and this coordinate set covers all the space-time. Thus, we see that the junction is always possible in coordinates with k = +I but it is impossible in coordinates k = -I, k = 0 at $\xi < 1$. This property has also the following meaning. While it is meaningless to ask whether the "pure" deSitter world is open or closed because there is no preferable frame of reference, in the Universe containing at least one bubble such a preferable frame of reference does appear. Namely, at $\xi < 1$ one can introduce only such coordinate t in the whole spacetime for which the section t = const is closed, i.e. the Universe containing a vacuum bubble is closed.

Let us put now $\mathcal{E}_{out} = 0$, i.e. the Universe without a buble is being a Minkowsky world which is described by one coordinate set of the type (9) with k = 0. We see that gravitation stabilizes such a vacuum with respect to decay into the states with negative energy density if $\xi < 1$. This particular result was obtained in ref /I/ using completely different approach. It was found /I/ that the probability of decay of a pure vacuum state equals to zero at $\xi < 1$ if $\mathcal{E}_{out} = 0$, in agreement with our constraints following from thejunction conditions.

Thus, the conclusion about the stability of a system with $\xi < 1$ may by done always if the coordinates (9) with k = -I describe all the spacetime. Therefore such a conclusion may be done, for example, with respect to the Universe filled with radiation only (in this case the metric with k = -I is inextendable /I9/).

In order to obtain from Table I the constraints on the decay of a metastable state of the Universe in terms of parameters of the model of quantum field theory one has yet to find the relation between the times t and τ in (II). Fortunately, in practically interesting cases this procedure is unnecessary because of the large difference between $\mathcal{E}$ and S^2/M_{Pl}^2 at $\xi \leqslant 1$. Let us consider for example the supersymmetric SU(5) model with low scale of supersymmetry breaking, $M \ll R_{GUT}^{-1}$, where R_{GUT} is the radius of confinement during the grand unified phase (in the case of the SU(5) model $R_{SU(5)}^{-1} \sim 10^9$ GeV). In such a theory (as generally in any theory where the barrier between phases disapperas at low temperatures) a strong coupling occurs at $T \sim R_{GUT}^{-1}$ and this is when the phase transitions occurs /20/, energy density then being equal to $\varepsilon = \pi^2 N_{eff} R_{GUT}^{-4}/30$ where N_{eff} is the total number of effectively massless degrees of freedom ($N_{eff} \sim 200$ in the minimal SU(5) model). In the wall energy density at least at early stages of the bubble expansion the vacuum contribution dominates. Thus we obtain that in the non-closed Universe in such a case the transition is possible only if

$$S_0^0 \lesssim \sqrt{\pi N_{eff}/180}\, M_{Pl} R_{GUT}^{-2} \sim 10^{37} (GeV)^3 . \qquad (I2)$$

The constraints on decaying vacuum parameters following from the Table I may be useful in studies of any stages of the Universe evolution and not only of the very early ones. In ref./2I/ the constraint $\xi > 1$ derived in ref./I/ for the particular case $\varepsilon_{out} = 0$ was used to show the stability of the present $\Lambda = 0$ Universe against the decay into the states with negative energy which arise in the framework of supergravity models (all the states arising in the model of ref./2I/ satisfy the condition $\xi < 1$). It should be noted,however,that the Universe state is not in fact pure vacuum. Therefore,using the results of the present paper we may conclude that the decay probability of such a state could not equal zero in closed universe (though it should be extremely small). In the open Universe the states considered in /2I/ is undoubtedly stable for it satisfies the condition $\xi < 1$.

Of particular interest is the vacuum dominated case. Namely, let the Universe at high temperatures be the radiation-dominated and be described by the metric (9) with k = -I. Let further at a certain temperature there to begin the epoch of domination of a metastable vacuum and the parameters of a (field) theory to be such that $\xi < 1$. Will there occur a phase transition in this case or not? We belive that the answer to this question depends on the global space-time structure at the epoch preceeding the vacuum dominating stage (see,however /3/).

I.2. Space-like junction

Let us now proceed to consider the junction on the SL hypersurface. Straightforward calculations of $K_i{}^j$ for spherically symmetric SL hypersurface Σ show that in this case $\sigma_a \sigma_b = \text{sign}\, dt_a/dt_b$ (remind that in the case of TL hypersurface we had $\sigma_{in}\sigma_{out} = \text{sign}\, d r_{in}/d r_{out}$). Therefore, if we do not allow for time direction to reverse after the phase transition we must require the signs of σ_a and σ_b to be the same. The tensor $K_i{}^j$ for SL hypersurface may be obtained from $K_i{}^j(\tau)_{TL}$ given by Eq.(7) by the continuation $K_i{}^j(q)_{SL} = i K_i{}^j(iq)_{TL}$. Here we consider the isotropic homogeneous case with the metric (9), therefore $S_i^{\,j} = S\,\delta_i^{\,j}$ S = const and it may be shown that only one of Eqs.(2a), (2b) is independent. It is convenient to take the Eq.(2a):

$$\sigma_b\sqrt{\rho_q^2 - 1 + \frac{8\pi}{3}\frac{\mathcal{E}_b}{M_{Pl}^2}\rho^2} - \sigma_a\sqrt{\rho_q^2 - 1 + \frac{8\pi}{3}\frac{\mathcal{E}_a}{M_{Pl}^2}\rho^2} = -\frac{4\pi\rho S}{M_{Pl}^2}. \qquad (13)$$

Let us introduce the quantity ζ defined as

$$\zeta \equiv (\mathcal{E}_b - \mathcal{E}_a)M_{Pl}^2 \,/\, 6\pi\,(S_1^{\,1})^2 . \qquad (14)$$

The time direction does not reverse at crossing over a SL hypersurface if $|\zeta| > 1$ while it reverse if $-1 < \zeta < 1$.

First we consider the junction between two phases connected by the tunneling process (see n.5 and n.6 in the Introduction). In a pure vacuum case we found no constraints on metastable vacuum decay from the SL junction because here we may not worry about time direction. We can not calculate S in this case directly but we may suppose that it is equal to $S_o^{\,o}$ due to O(4) invariance of the euclidean vacuum solution /22/. Considering the non-vacuum case we require the time not to change its direction at crossing a SL hypersurface. Then a decay of a metastable state is possible only if $\zeta > 1$.

Let us consider now the cases 4 and 7. The Eq.(13) in this case has to be understood as the condition on parameters after the phase transition. Besause of homogeneity and isotropy the hypersurface of phase separation is just the surface of constant t, where t is the cosmological time (9). In proper coordinates the equation of such a hypersurface is $\rho_q^2 = 1 - k\rho^2/a^2$ and the Eq.(13) takes now on the form:

$$\sqrt{\frac{8\pi}{3}\frac{\mathcal{E}_b}{M_{Pl}^2} - \frac{kT^2}{N^2}} - \sqrt{\frac{8\pi}{3}\frac{cT^4}{M_{Pl}^2} - \frac{kT^2}{N^2}} = -4\pi S M_{Pl}^2 , \qquad (15)$$

where cT^4 is the radiation energy density, $N = Ta$, $N^3 = s\frac{3}{4c}$, s being the coordinate entropy density. For the inflationary scenario to work it is necessary to have $N > 10^{28}$ /2/. Thus, the Eq. (15) relates the amount of inflation with the temperature after the reheating. In general the value of k in Eq. (15) is not fixed. However, when the comlete metric is O(4) invariant the metric inside the new phase bubble is of the open type (k = -1) /1,10/. In the new inflationary scenarious the fluctuation passes the stage of vacuum expansion. One has therefore to expect that in this case the visible part of the Universe is described by (9) with k = -1. The contributions to S come from the rapid rolling down to the minimum of potential and from subsequent particle creation processes. The first contribution can be easily calculated and equals to $S = -\sqrt{2\lambda}\,\varphi_o^3$,where φ_o is the equilibrium value of the scalar field, λ being the quartic coupling constant entering the potential as $\lambda\varphi^4$. The second contribution requires special consideration.

2. GROWTH OF NEW PHASE BUBBLES

In general the process of new phase bubble expansion is determined essentially by the structure of the tensor S_i^j. In the present paper we shall analyse, accounting for gravity, only those consequences which follow from Eqs.(2a) (7a),(I0),i.e. we shall consider the case when both interiors of the bubble and the space - time outside are described by the metric (9). In the pure vacuum case this is the complete set of equations. In a non-vacuum case the motion of the shell is not determined by the Eq.(7a) only, so one has to consider both Eq.(7a) and Eq.(7b). However, even here we may obtain rather important conclusions considering the Eq. (7a) only.

Squaring twice equation

$$\sigma_{in}\sqrt{1+\rho_\tau^2-\frac{8\pi}{3}\frac{\varepsilon_{in}(t_{in})}{M_{pl}^2}\rho^2}-\sigma_{out}\sqrt{1+\rho_\tau^2-\frac{8\pi}{3}\frac{\varepsilon_{out}\rho^2}{M_{pl}^2}}=\frac{4\pi S_0^0\rho}{M_{pl}^2} \quad (I6)$$

we obtain

$$\dot\rho^2=B^2\rho^2-1\ , \quad (I7)$$

where

$$B^{-1}=\frac{3S_0^0(\tau)}{\sqrt{(\varepsilon_{out}+\varepsilon_{in}+6\pi(S_0^0)^2/M_{pl}^2)^2-4\varepsilon_{in}\varepsilon_{out}}}\,. \quad (I8)$$

In the pure vacuum case ε's and S are constants (see about S below, 2.I), and the quantity B^{-1} detrmines the bubble radius at the rest moment in the frame system connected with the shell and coincides with the bubble radius at its materialization moment /I,4/.

Let us find now the equation of motion of the bubble in coordinates of inner or outer region. In both cases this equation looks identically, so we omit the index out (in) remembering that the corresponding quantities carry this index. The equation to be found is as follows

$$\frac{dR}{dt}=\frac{\sqrt{(\frac{8\pi\varepsilon}{3M_{pl}^2}-\frac{K}{a^2})(1-\frac{K\rho^2}{a^2})}\pm\sqrt{(B^2\rho^2-1)(B^2-\frac{8\pi\varepsilon}{3M_{pl}^2})(1-\frac{K\rho^2}{a^2})}}{\rho a(B^2-K/a^2)}\,, \quad (I9)$$

where $\rho=aR$.

For simplicity let us consider this equation in particular case of spatially flat world, i.e. put in Eq.(I9) k = 0 (which is a good approximation at any k if the buble sise is much less than dimentions of the Universe):

$$\frac{dR}{dt}=\frac{1}{a}\sqrt{1-\frac{8\pi}{3}\frac{\varepsilon}{M_{pl}^2B^2}}\sqrt{1-\frac{1}{B^2\rho^2}}-\frac{1}{\rho B}\sqrt{\frac{8\pi}{3M_{pl}^2}\frac{\varepsilon}{B^2}}\,, \quad (20)$$

A light readial geodetic would be described in the coordinates (9) by the equation $dR/dt = 1/a$. The bubble shell (20) will move along the light geodetic only in the case $1/B = 0$ or, equivalently, $S_0^0 = 0$. Moreover, the shell velocity during expansion does not even tend to the coordinate velocityofof light. This is the consequence of two following factors:

I. The shell velocity in the coordinate space does not tend to velocity of light due to medium thermal properties During the shell motuon in a thermal medium the metric remains homogeneous and isotropic only in the case of a shell of a rather special structure. We shall consider later the case of arbitrary S_i^j in the limit $M_{Pl} \to \infty$.

2. The asymptotical shell velocity in the coordinate space differs from velocity of light due to the Hubble expansion of space /23/. This statement is valid for any equation of state of matter, so that in particular case of a pure vacuum we have

$$\frac{dR_{out}}{dt_{out}} \xrightarrow[\rho \to \infty]{} \frac{1}{a}\sqrt{1 - \frac{8\pi}{3}\frac{\mathcal{E}}{M_{Pl}^2 B^2}} \, . \tag{2I}$$

Note that in a vacuum case in contrast with the thermal one only coordinate velocity of the shell does not tend to velocity of light. The proper velocity (I7) does tend to velocity of light ($\rho_\tau \to \infty$) never being however equal to it.

In GUT's with $M_X \ll M_{Pl}$ the velocity (2I) differs only slightly from velocity of light. This however may not be so if the wall energy contribution is essential which may take place for example in supersymmetric GUT's. Moreover, $dR_{out}/dt_{out} \to 0$ if $\xi \to 1$, i.e. the coordinate volume of such bubble does not increase.

It is important to know the value of the asymptotical velocity of the shell in estimates of number density of produced monopoles /24/, in studies of percolation problem in phase transitions /I0/ etc.

2.I Bubble expansion in a thermal medium. The $M_{Pl} \to \infty$ limit.

Let the energy-momentum tensor of a medium be that of homogeneous isotropic ideal liquid both inside and outside the bubble

$$T_{\mu\nu} = (\varepsilon + p) u_\mu u_\nu - g_{\mu\nu} p \, , \tag{22}$$

ε and p being proper energy density and thermodynamical pressure respectively, u_μ being 4-velocity of a medium element. Then equation of motion for the shell takes in the limit $M_{Pl} \to \infty$ the form /8/ :

$$\frac{dS_0^0}{d\tau} + \frac{2\pi}{\rho}\left(S_0^0 - S_2^2\right) = \left[\frac{(\varepsilon + p)\, u}{1 - u^2}\right]_{out} - (out \to in), \tag{23a}$$

$$\frac{S_0^{\,0}\,\varrho_{\tau\tau}}{\sqrt{1+\varrho_\tau^2}} + \frac{2\,S_2^{\,2}\sqrt{1+\varrho_\tau^2}}{\varrho} = \left[p + \frac{(\varepsilon+p)\,v^2}{1-v^2}\right]_{in} - (in \to out), \quad (23b)$$

where u and v are 3-velocities of external and internal media relative to the shell, respectively.

In the case of a plane front ($\varrho \to \infty$) the left hand sides of the Eqs.(23) tend to zero provided $\dot{\varrho} \to$ const (such a solution exists if $(\varepsilon + p)_{out} \neq 0$). Then Eqs.(23) are reduced to the well known detonation wave equations.

It is seen from Eqs.(23) that two phases with pure vacuum equations of state $(\varepsilon + p)_{in} = (\varepsilon + p)_{out} = 0$ can be matched across a singular shell only, $S_i^{\,j}$ having the form (4). Then it follows from Eq.(23a) that S = const.

If the state of an internal medium is not the vacuum one, i.e. $(\varepsilon + p)_{in} = T s$, then there exists a solution to the Eqs.(23) with surface energy-momentum tensor of the form (5). Due to relation $S_0^{\,0} = 0$ the energy released during the bubble expansion can not be converted to the kinetic energy of bubble walls but is completely transformed into energy of the internal medium.Such a pdocess may be called "a vacuum burning" (see details in ref /8/).

3. OLD PHASE REMNANTS AND DOMAINS

Till now we considered the evolution of a new phase bubble immersed into the old phase. This picture corresponds to the very beginning of the phase transition. The formal description of the intermediate stage of the transition would be extremely complicated, so we omit it and proceed to consider the final stage. Suppose that at a certain moment there occurs the percolation through the new phase (or through one of new phases in the case of the domain structure) . Moreover, suppose that beginning from a certain moment there is no percolation through the old phase , i.e. there exists at the time the remnant of the old phase of finite maximal size. We may believe that such a moment was in any case during the phase transition with the breaking of the Weinberg-Salam electroweak group. The percolation through the old phase should also be absent beginning from a certain moment in the GUT phase transition if only we do not live inside one inflated bubble /II/.

A shape of a remnant at the beginning is very angular and it reminds an amoeba. However, after a certain time has passed , at least some of these remnants will take a spherical form (in particular due to surface tension effects) and we may think about such remnants of old phase as spherical bubbles.

Such a bubble differs however essentially from a spontaneously nucleated bubble of a new phase. Namely, an old phase remnant may have nonzero total mass. Of course, this mass appears not at once but after settling of appropriate boundary conditions at infinity (during this process a part of energy is carried away by gravitational and electromagnetic radiations). Thus, the case of old phase remnants is reduced to the problem of a spherically symmetric bubble in the outer space with the Schwarzschild metric. We shall consider here a pure vacuum case but for generality we shall take that an external vacuum may possess nonzero energy density and a remnant may carry a charge. Then the metric both inside and outside the bubble has the form

$$ds^2 = f dt^2 - \frac{1}{f} dr^2 - r^2 d\Omega^2, \tag{24}$$

where inside the bubble we have

$$f(r) = 1 - \frac{8\pi}{3}\frac{\varepsilon_{in} r^2}{M_{Pl}^2},$$

while outside

$$f(r) = 1 - \frac{8\pi}{3}\frac{\varepsilon_{out} r^2}{M_{Pl}^2} - \frac{2m}{r M_{Pl}^2} + \frac{g^2}{r^2 M_{Pl}^2}.$$

Note that this metric has already the form (6) with $e^{\nu} = e^{-\lambda} = f$. So we arrive at the following equation of motion of of bubble walls under consideration

$$\sigma_{in}\sqrt{1+\rho_\tau^2 - \frac{8\pi}{3}\frac{\varepsilon_{in}\rho^2}{M_{Pl}^2}} - \sigma_{out}\left(1+\rho_\tau^2 - \frac{8\pi}{3}\frac{\varepsilon_{out}}{M_{Pl}^2}\rho^2 - \frac{2m}{M_{Pl}^2\rho} + \frac{g^2}{\rho^2 M_{Pl}^2}\right)^{1/2} = 4\pi S_0^0 \rho / M_{Pl}^2 . \tag{25}$$

We find solving Eq.(25) with respect to m :

$$m = \frac{g^2}{2\rho} + \frac{4\pi}{3}(\varepsilon_{in} - \varepsilon_{out})\rho^3 + 4\pi\rho^2 S \sigma_{in}\left(\rho_\tau + 1 - \frac{8\pi}{3}\frac{\varepsilon_{in}\rho^2}{M_{Pl}^2}\right)^{1/2} - 8\pi S^2\rho^3/M_{Pl}^2 . \tag{26}$$

The relation (26) is also the equation of motion of the shell. It can be solved with respect to ρ_τ , however the resulting equation is too cumbersome in the case of a charged shell, so we write it down for the case $g = 0$ only:

$$\rho_\tau^2 = B^2\rho^2 - 1 + \frac{m}{\rho}\left[\frac{1}{M_{Pl}^2} + \frac{\varepsilon_{out} - \varepsilon_{in}}{6\pi S^2}\right] + \frac{m^2}{16\pi^2 S^2 \rho^4}, \tag{27}$$

where B is given by (18). Both forms of equation of motion (26) and (27) are proved to be useful.

One can easily see from Eq.(27) that the junction hypersurface is O(4) invariant in imaginary time when $m = 0$, the invariance being lost at $m \neq 0$. Therefore, calculating the probability of spontaneous creation of a spherical ring of a new vacuum with an old vacuum remnant at the center of the ring, the remnant having a nonzero mass, one has to take into account that the Euclidean solution is at most O(3) invariant (in contrast with the calculations of the probability of new vacuum bubble creation for which we have thus proved the validity of the assumption about O(4) invariance used essentially in ref /I/).

Let us consider now the equations of motion in the form (26). It is easy to understand the meaning of all the terms in the right hand side of Eq.(26). The first term gives a potential energy of a charged shell, the second one is the difference between old and new vacuum energy densities, the third one gives the kinetic energy of a shell, the forth one is the energy of gravitational self-interaction of a shell. Let us show that a charged shell has a point of stable equilibrium.

<u>Theorem</u>. A shell has an equilibrium point if the equation

$$\frac{\partial m}{\partial \rho}(\rho, \rho_\tau)\Big|_{\rho_\tau=0} = 0 \tag{28}$$

has a solution at some value of ρ , say ρ_0 . At $\frac{\partial m}{\partial \rho_\tau^2}\Big|_{\rho_\tau=0} > 0$ the equilibrium state is stable if the function $m(\rho, \rho_\tau=0)$ has a minimum at the point ρ_0 , while at $\partial m/\partial \rho_\tau|_{\rho_\tau=0} < 0$ the equilibrium is stable if this function at ρ_0 has a maximum.

<u>Proof</u>. A point is an equilibrium point for the shell if conditions $\rho_\tau = 0$ and $\rho_{\tau\tau} = 0$ are satisfied simultaneously. We have

$$\frac{dm}{d\tau} = \rho_\tau \left(\frac{\partial m}{\partial \rho} + 2\, \frac{\partial m}{\partial \rho_\tau^2}\, \rho_{\tau\tau} \right) . \tag{29}$$

Since m is the integral of motion, we have for any $\rho_\tau \neq 0$

$$\frac{\partial m}{\partial \rho} + \frac{2\partial m}{\partial \rho_\tau^2}\, \rho_{\tau\tau} = 0 \ . \tag{30}$$

Thus, at $\rho_{\tau\tau} = 0$ one has $\partial m/\partial \rho = 0$. The point $\rho_\tau = 0$ has the same property by virtue of continuity of the equations of motion. Therefore, an equilibrium point is a solution to the equation (28). The equilibrium point is stable if $\rho_{\tau\tau} < 0$ at $\rho > \rho_0$, while $\rho_{\tau\tau} > 0$ at $\rho < \rho_0$. It is easy to see from Eq.(30) that at $\partial m/\partial \rho_\tau^2|_{\rho_\tau=0} > 0$ the equilibrium point is stable if at this point the function $m(\rho, \rho_\tau = 0)$ has a minimum, while at $\partial m/\partial \rho_\tau^2|_{\rho_\tau=0} < 0$ the state is stable if this function has a maximum at the equilibrium point.

In the particular case of the Eq.(26) one has $\partial m/\partial \rho_\tau^2|_{\rho_\tau=0} > 0$ if $\sigma_{in} > 0$ and $\partial m/\partial \rho_\tau^2|_{\rho_\tau=0} < 0$ if $\sigma_{in} < 0$.

Let us consider now as a simple example a charged shell in the particular case when one may neglect S . It is easy to find the radius of a stable configuration

$$\rho_0^4 = g^4/8\pi(\varepsilon_{in} - \varepsilon_{out}) \tag{3I}$$

and its mass

$$m = \frac{2}{3} g^2/\rho_0 \; . \tag{32}$$

At $g^2 \gg 1$ the radius of the stable configuration is much larger than its Comptonlength I/m , so our treatment of the configuration as a classical one is quite appropriate. One example of such a configuration is well known: it is a magnetic monopole.

Consider the field φ^i , i = I,2,3 transforming as a triplet with respect to group SU(2). Let the field direction in isotopic space coincide with the direction of the radius in configurational space and φ^i tend at $\rho \to \infty$ to its vacuum averaged value. The field φ^i at the center of such a configuration equals to zero. Therefore $\varepsilon(\rho \to \infty) = 0$ and $\varepsilon(0) \sim M_X^4$. The electromagnetic field far from the center reproduces the field of a magnetic monopole with the charge $g = 2\pi/e$, where e is electron charge /24/. We may now treat the monopole problem in a thin-wall approximation , i.e. we may regard that all the field φ^i variation is concentrated around a certain value of radius ρ_0 . Then Eqs.(3I), (32) describe the magnetic monopole in the thin-wall approximation and one obtains for the monopole mass $m_M \sim M_X/\alpha$, where α is fine structure constant.

In principle one can construct other charged configurations too, for example, islands of the SU(4)x U(I) phase in SU(3)x SU(2)x U(I) symmetrical vacuum /I4/. Such a remnant may carry a charge with respect to group SU(2) since generators corresponding to the weak intermediate bosons are broken in SU(4)x U(I) vacuum while they are not broken in SU(3)x SU(2)x U(I).

If the shell radius at the rest moment does not coincide with ρ_0 which is the solution of Eq.(28) but differs from it not very much then the shell with oscillate around that state. At other initial conditions the shell may proceed either to regime of unrestricted expansion or collapse. During a phase transition there may arise of course rather different conditions for the remnants. Let us proceed now to study the relation between initial conditions and geometry of spacetime.

Let us introduce the variable ξ as in Eq. (II) and the new variable η as

$$\eta \equiv (m - g^2/2\rho) M_{Pl}^2 / 8\pi^2 S^2 \rho^3 \; . \tag{33}$$

Signs of σ_{in} and σ_{out} in these variables (and therefore the global geometry of spacetime) are completely determined. The relation of σ with the variables η and ξ is given in Table 2. The signs of σ 's may in general change during the shell motion. This may however occur in T-regions of spacetime only. Therefore the shell classification in accordance with the signs of σ is unique at the moment when the shell crosses the R-region only, however it is sufficient for the construction of the global geometry.

Table 2.

		σ_{in}	σ_{out}	SPATIAL SECTION (SCHEMATIC)
A	$\eta+\xi>1$	+1	+1	
B	$-1<\eta+\xi<1$	+1	-1	
C	$\eta+\xi<-1$	-1	-1	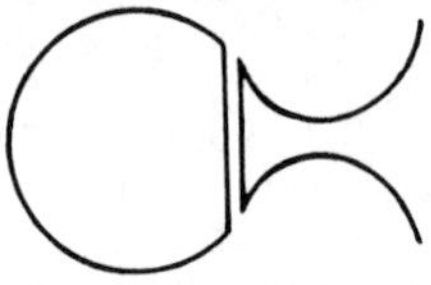

In the case A (table 2) we have $\sigma_{out}>0$ and the shell crosses R_+- region. In such a case the shell forms a black hole if initial conditions permit the shell to collapse. The collapse with formation of a charged black hole is possible in the case $\mathcal{E}_{out}=0$ only if $m \geq g M_{pe}$. A neutral shell collapses always at the final stage of it's evolution in the case $\mathcal{E}_{out}=0$ (i.e. in the case of pure Schwarzschild outer metric).

Suppose now that in the course of phase transition a magnetically charged remnant of the old vacuum has been formed and it has a mass large enough to collapse and to form a black hole. This black hole then evaporates. However, evaporation of charged black holes differs from that of neutral black holes, namely a temperature of charged black hole increases at first, achieved its maximum and then decreases. The evaporation stops when mass of the hole decreases to the value $m=g M_{pe}$. Thus unusual magnetic monopoles may exist which which in fact are magnetically charged black holes with masses

$$m = 2\pi M_{pe} / e \,. \tag{34}$$

A stability properties of such a black hole require special consideration. It may be thought that it will prove to be unstable, decaying on usual black hole and usual magnetic monopole.

In the cases B and C the shell crosses R_--region. Any shell crossing the R_- -region forms a wormhole.

Let us consider now neutral remnants of the old vacuum in more details. If such a remnant has mass obeying the following condition

$$m > M_c \equiv M_{pe}^3 / 3\sqrt{8\pi \mathcal{E}_{out}} \,, \tag{35}$$

then outer metric has no horizons /25/. Such a shell will expand infinitely. At $m < M_c$ the outer metric has two horizons, an event horizon being at $\rho = \rho_H$,and a cosmological horizon being at $\rho = \rho_c > \rho_H$ /25/. Possible trajectories of the shell in Schwarzschild -deSitter metric in the case $m < M_c$ are shown in Fig.I.

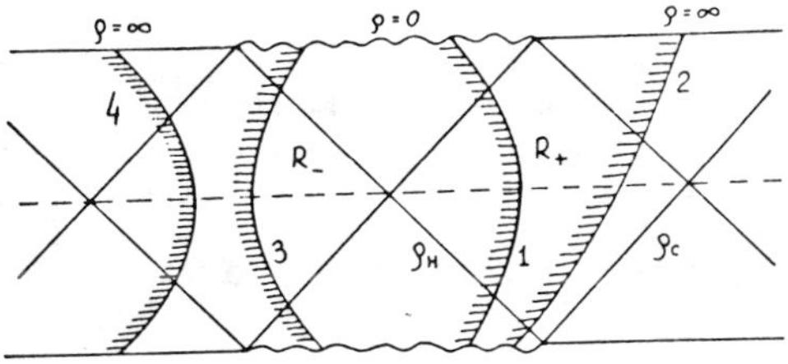

Fig.I. Path of the shells on the Penrose diagram of the Schwarzschild-deSitter geometry. A space-like hypersurface represented by the dashed line is shown schematically in Table 2.

The shells I and 2 cross a R_+ -region and shells 3 and 4 cross R_- -region.

A trajectory of any shell has either a turning point ($\rho_\tau = 0$) or a point with $\rho_{\tau\tau} = 0$. Fig.2 shows a dependence of a Schwarzschild mass of a bubble upon the value of radius at turning point (curveI) and upon the value of radius at the point where $\rho_{\tau\tau} = 0$ (curve2). For definiteness we have drawn them for the case $\mathcal{E}_{in} = \mathcal{E}_{out} = 0$. It is seen that the curve 2 intersects the curve I at the extremum point of the latter one what is in accordance with the theorem proved. Only solid part of the curve I corresponds to black holes,all other parts giving us the wormholes.

In general the mass spectrum starts from zero both for

black holes and wormholes. It may be shown however that the mass of any shell crossing a R_+ -region is bounded from above when $\xi < 1$ (Fig.2 illustrates well this property in the case $\mathcal{E}_{in} = \mathcal{E}_{out} = 0$ corresponding to $\xi = 0$).

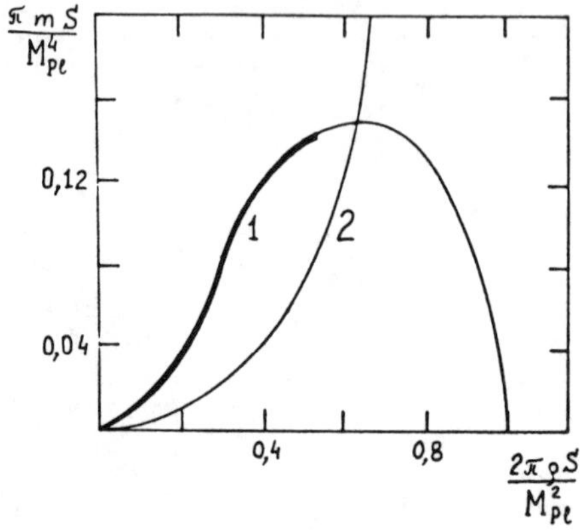

Fig.2. Dependence of the bubble mass upon shell size at the rest moment in the case $\mathcal{E}_{in} = \mathcal{E}_{out} = 0$ (curve I). The curve 2 represents the dependence of bubble mass on the value of size where the resultant forse vanishes for the shells which do not possess rest points. The solid parts of the curves correspond to the black holes while other parts of the curves correspond to wormholes.

Indeed, let the shell crosses R_+ -region, then we have $\eta(\rho) > 1 - \xi$ (see Table 2). In R-regions $\rho > \rho_H$, so for ρ in R_+ -region we have $\eta(\rho_H) > \eta(\rho) > 1 - \xi$. Further, we have $\rho_H \geq 2m/M_{Pl}^2$ in the case of Schwarzschild-deSitter metric, i.e. shell can cross R_+ -region only when $\eta(2m/M_{Pl}^2) > 1 - \xi$, i.e.

$$m < m_c / \sqrt{1 - \xi}\,, \qquad m_c \equiv M_{Pl}^4 / 8\pi S. \tag{36}$$

Thus, a black hole mass is bounded by the value $m_c \sim (\frac{M_{Pl}}{M_G})^3 M_{Pl}$ when wall energy dominates ($|\xi| \leq 1$) and by the value $m_c \sim (M_{Pl}/M_G)^2 M_{Pl}$ when vacuum energy dominates ($|\xi| \geq 1$). In the above formulae M_G is the unification mass scale. For GUT black holes with $M_G \sim 10^{15}$ Gev we obtain $m < 10^{27}$ GeV in the case of vacuum energy domination and $m < 10^{35}$ GeV in the case of wall evergy domination. Black holes with masses in this range have evaporated long ago. At present there are evaporating the black holes with masses of order 10^{39} GeV.

Consider now the phase transition resulting in the

breaking of Weinberg-Salam electroweak gauge group. In this case a vacuum energy dominates. Consequently, the maximal mass of a black hole created in a course of this phase transition is less than 10^{53} GeV ~ 10^{-4} $M_\odot$. An observation of black holes with such masses would be in favour of its formation fromremnants of old cosmological vacuum withunbroken electroweak symmetry.

It may be shown similarly to (36) that the mass of a wormhole of type B at $\xi < -1$ is also bounded by

$$m < m_c / \sqrt{-1-\xi} \, . \tag{37}$$

Note also that for a shell having a turning point we may give the following criterion : if the shell radius at turning point obeys the inequality

$$\rho < \rho_c \quad , \quad \rho_c \equiv M_{Pl} / 4\pi \sqrt{(S^2/M_{Pl}^2 + \mathcal{E}_{in}/6\pi)} \, , \tag{38}$$

then an object is formed during a phase transition which collapses towards a black hole, otherwise ($\rho > \rho_c$) we are dealing with a wormhole.

We are grateful to V.A.Matveev, V.A.Rubakov , M.E.Shaposhnikov and A.N.Tavkhelidze for the interest in the work and useful discussions.

REFERENCES

I. S.Coleman,F.De Luccia.Phys.Rev. D2I (I980) 2205.

2. A.H.Guth.Phys.Rev. D23 (I98I) 347
A.D.Linde.Phys.Lett. I08B (I982) 382
A.Albrecht,P.J.Steinhardt.Phys.Rev.Lett. 48 (I982) I220

3. S.W.Hawking,I.G.Moss.Phys.Lett. IIOB (I982) 35.

4. S.Coleman. Phys.Rev. DI5 (I977) 2929.

5. A.D.Linde. Phys.Lett. 70B (I977) 306;
Nucl. Phys. B2I6 (I983) 42I.

6. L.D.Landau and E.M.Lifshitz. Fluid Mechanics , Pergamon Press, London I959.

7. P,J.Steinhardt. Phys.Rev. D25 (1982) 2074.

8. V.A.Berezin,V.A.Kuzmin,I.I.Tkachev.Phys.Lett. 124B (I983) 479.

9. V.A.Berezin,V.A.Kuzmin,I.I.Tkachev.Phys.Lett. I20B (I983) 91.

IO. A.H.Guth,E.Weinberg. Phys.Rev. D23 (I981) 876,
Nucl.Phys. B2I2 (I983) 32I.

II. A.D.Linde., in ref. /2/.

I2. K.Sato,M.Sasaki,M.Kodema and K.Maeda. Prog.Teor.Phys. 65 (I98I) I443.

I3. Ya.B.Zeldovich,I.Yu Kobzarev,L.B.Okun.ZhETF 6I (I974) 3

I4. V.A.Kuzmin,M.E.Shaposhnikov,I.I.Tkachev.Phys.Lett.
IO2B (I98I) 397.
Z.Phys.C I2 (I982) 83.
I5. R.W.Brown,F.W.Stecker.Phys.Rev.Lett. 43 (I979) 3I5.
V.A.Kuzmin,M.E.Shaposhnikov,I.I.Tkachev.Phys.Lett.
IO5B (I98I) I67.
I6. A.D.Sakharov. Pisma ZhETF 5 (I967) 32.
V.A.Kuzmin. Pisma ZhETF I3 (I970) 335.
A.Yu.Ignatiev, N.V.Krasnikov,V.A.Kuzmin,A.N.Tavkhelidze
Phys.Lett. 76B (I978) 436.
I7. W.Israel. Nuovo Cim. 44B (I966) I,
48B (I967) 463.
I8. C.W. Misner,K.S.Thorne,J.A.Wheeler. Gravitation,
W.H.Freeman and Company,San Francisco I973.
I9. S.W.Hawking,G.F.R.Ellis. The Large Scale Structure of
Space-Time, Cambridge Univ.Press. I973.
20. D.V.Nanopoulos,K.Tanvakis. Phys.Lett IIOB (I983) 449.
2I. S.Weinberg. Phys.Rev.Lett. 48 (I982) I776.
22. V.A.Berezin,V.A.Kuzmin,I.I.Tkachev., in Proc.of the
2nd seminar on Group Theoretical Methods in Physics,
Zvenigorod, I982, Gordon and Breach,in press.
23. A.H.Guth,S.-H.Tye. Phys.Rev.Lett. 44 (I980) 63I.
24. A.M.Polyakov, Pisma ZhETF 20 (I974) 430.
G.t'Hooft. Nucl.Phys. B79 (I974) 276.
25. G.W.Gibbons,S.W.Hawking. Phys.Rev. DI5 (I977) 2738.

SOLUTION TO THE GAUGE HIERARCHY PROBLEM IN LOCALLY SUPERSYMMETRIC GRAND UNIFIED THEORIES

Mariano Quirós

Instituto de Estructura de la Materia
Serrano, 119 - Madrid-6
SPAIN

ABSTRACT

Higgs colour triplets contained in the $\underline{5}+\underline{\bar{5}}$ representation of SU(5) get large masses (10^{10}GeV) from non-renormalizable terms, which are naturally present in locally supersymmetric grand unified theories, while their weak partners, SU(2) doublets, remain light without any fine-tuning of parameters. The $\underline{50}+\underline{\overline{50}}$ representation of SU(5) is involved and the relevant coupling in the superpotential is $(\underline{\overline{50}})(\underline{24})^2(\underline{5})$. No $\underline{75}$ representation (disastrous for cosmological scenarios) is needed.

1. The gauge hierarchy problem in SUSY GUTS.

The gauge hierarchy problem of grand unified theories (GUTS) is to understand why and how the Higgs weak doublets are light while their colour triplets partners are heavy. The difficulty of this splitting arise from the fact that both of them are contained in the $\underline{5}$ representation of SU(5) which is decomposed, with respect to SU(3)xSU(2)xU(1), as: $\underline{5} = (\underline{3},\underline{1},-2)+(\underline{1},\underline{2},3)$. Colour triplets mediate proton decay, so that they cannot be lighter than 10^{10} GeV, while SU(2) doublets are going to break SU(2)xU(1) at the weak interaction scale, so that they cannot be heavier than 10^2 GeV.

The introduction of supersymmetry SUSY into GUTS has proved to be a giant step toward the solution of the triplet-doublet splitting. The "no renormalization" theorems[1)] guarantee that a Higgs doublet which is light at the tree level remains light to all orders in perturbation theory. The splitting of doublets from triplets then becomes a tree level problem. (There are exceptions in both globally and locally supersymmetric theories which include light SU(3)xSU(2)xU(1) singlets[2)]).

For SUSY GUTS based on SU(5), solutions to the tree-level splitting have been proposed by different authors. We shall review them in what follows.

a) The fine-tuning method.

It was introduced by Dimopoulos and Georgi[3)]. They used the following chiral supermultiplets: H(5), H'($\bar{5}$) and Σ(24). Their contribution to the superpotential is : $\delta f = H'\Sigma H + 3/2m\ H'H$. Along the SU(3)xSU(2)xU(1) direction, $\Sigma = \omega$ diag (1,1,1,-3/2,-3/2), if m is fine-tuned to the value $m=\omega$, the doublet remains massless while the triplet takes a mass $O(\omega)$. This method is unnatural (although technically possible) because m and ω must be adjusted to the same value until the fourteenth decimal place.

b) The sliding singlet method.

Introduced by Ibáñez and Ross[4]. An extra SU(5) singlet ϕ is added and the relevant superpotential is : $\delta f = H'\Sigma H + 3/2H'\phi H$. If the vacuum expectation value (VEV) $<\phi>$ is adjusted (up to the fourteenth decimal place) to the value of ω, then the doublet mass does not exceed 10^2 GeV. This method is also unnatural since $<\phi>$ need to be fine-tuned.

c) The extra $\tilde{U}(1)$ method.

Introduced by León, Quirós and Ramón-Medrano[5]. The gauge group is $U(5) \simeq SU(5) \times \tilde{U}(1)$. The superpotential is $\delta f = H'\Sigma H$, where Σ is the adjoint (25) representation of U(5). In the SU(5)x$\tilde{U}$(1) decomposition, Σ can be written as $\Sigma = \sigma - 1/5\ \mathrm{tr}\Sigma$ where σ is the 24 representation of SU(5) and $\mathrm{tr}\Sigma \equiv \phi$ is an SU(5) singlet. The supersymmetry conditions choose naturally a value of $<\phi>$ such that the doublet remains massless. No fine-tuning of parameters is needed. However, other problems arise from the fact that U(5) is not semisimple: i) The unification is lost in a way; ii) Extra anomalies associated to $\tilde{U}$(1) must be exorcised; iii) To allow the inclusion of supergravity the flat space lagrangian must be R-invariant[6].

d) The 75-method.

Introduced by Masiero, Nanopoulos, Tamvakis and Yanagida[7]. The chiral superfields are θ(50), θ'($\overline{50}$) and S(75), and their contribution to the superpotential is $\delta f = M_\theta \theta'\theta + \lambda\theta' SH + \lambda' H' S\theta$. The Higgs fields H and H' couple to quark and lepton fields in the usual way. The 75 is supposed to get a VEV which breaks SU(5) to SU(3)xSU(2)xU(1) at a scale M_X. The same VEV will provide a mass term which mixes the colour triplets in H and H' with those in θ and θ'. However there is no weak doublet in the 50 and, so, the weak doublets in H and H' remain massless. All components of θ and θ' have a bare mass M_θ (larger or equal to M_X) and so remain heavy after SU(5) breaks to SU(3)xSU(2)xU(1). Since the only modifications of the theory are at the GUT scale, this seems like a harmless and elegant solution. Unfortunately, it drastically conflicts with cosmological scenarios based on SUSY GUTS. In fact it is essential to have a potential barrier between the SU(5) and SU(3)x xSU(2)xU(1) phases which is not higher than Λ^4, where Λ is the confinement scale in the SU(5) phase, typically about 10^9 GeV. Since a mass term for a symmetry breaking field with VEV V contributes a term of order m^2V^2 to the barrier, we must require $m < \Lambda^2/V$ which is, at most, a few TeV. This means that the zero hypercharge components of the $\underline{75}$, four colour octets, must be very light, with a mass much less than M_X. (This comes from the SU(3)xSU(2)xU(1) decomposition $\underline{75} = (\underline{1},\underline{1},0)+(\underline{8},\underline{3},0)+$ $+(\underline{3},\underline{1},10)+(\underline{3},\underline{2},-5)+(\underline{\bar{3}},\underline{1},-10)+(\underline{\bar{3}},\underline{2},5)+(\underline{\bar{6}},\underline{2},-5)+(\underline{6},\underline{2},5)+(\underline{8},\underline{1},0)$). But this means that there is no Λ at all! The presence of these new light particles in the SU(3)xSU(2)xU(1) phase change the renormalization group equations and prevents perturbative unification.

None of the above methods are completly satisfactory. In the next Section we present the natural solution to the gauge hierarchy problem in supergravity theories.

2. The gauge hierarchy problem in local SUSY GUTS.

When the GUT is coupled to N=1 supergravity, there is no reason to take renormalizable superpotentials. In fact the most natural choice will be to take the most general non-renormalizable superpotential. This will provide the solution to the triplet-doublet splitting problem in all cosmologically acceptable local SUSY GUTS[8,9,10]. The superpotential can be written as[11]:

$$f = M_\theta \theta'\theta + \theta' H(\lambda_1 M^{-1}\Sigma^2 + \lambda_2 M^{-2}\Sigma^3 + \dots) + H'\theta(\lambda_1' M^{-1}\Sigma^2 + \lambda_2' M^{-2}\Sigma^3 + \dots)$$

where $M = M_P/\sqrt{8\Pi} = 24\text{x}10^{18}$ GeV and Σ is a light 24. Once Σ acquires a VEV breaking SU(5) to SU(3)xSU(2)xU(1), the weak doublets in H and H' will remain massless, while the colour triplets will have a mass matrix whose eigenvalues are $O(M_\theta)$ and $O(M_X^4/M^2M_\theta)$. The most natural case will be when $M_\theta = M$, $M_X \simeq 2\text{x}10^{16}$ GeV. Then the mass of lighter triplets is 10^{10} GeV. In this case the Higgs colour triplets can be used to generate the baryon number of the universe after the SU(5) to SU(3)xSU(2)xU(1) transition, which occurs at a temperature of order Λ.

In ref. (11) we have checked that when Σ gets a VEV in the SU(3)x xSU(2)xU(1) preserving direction, the colour triplets get a non-vanishing mass term. The proof uses the tensor structure of the 50 : $\theta_{abcd} = -\theta_{bacd} = -\theta_{abdc} = \theta_{cdab}$, $\theta_{abcd}\epsilon^{abcef} = 0$. The only part of $\underline{24}\text{x}\underline{24}$ which contributes to the coupling $\theta_{abcd}\epsilon^{abefg}\Sigma^c_e\Sigma^d_f H'_g$ is contained in the $\underline{75}$ representation:

$$S^{cd}_{ef} = \Sigma^c_e\Sigma^d_f - \Sigma^d_e\Sigma^c_f - \frac{1}{12}[\mathrm{tr}(\Sigma^2)(\delta^c_e\delta^d_f - \delta^d_e\delta^c_f)]$$

$$+ \frac{1}{3}[(\Sigma^2)^d_f\delta^c_e + (\Sigma^2)^c_e\delta^d_f - (\Sigma^2)^c_f\delta^d_e - (\Sigma^2)^d_e\delta^c_f] .$$

In this way one can easily check that replacing Σ by diag(2,2,2,-3,-3) results in non-zero mass terms $\theta_3' H_3 + \theta_3 H_3'$ for the colour triplets.

Let us conclude by stressing that this mechanism of producing triplet-doublet splitting:

i) Is a possible origin of the <u>intermediate scale</u>, $\Lambda \simeq 10^{10}$ GeV, useful for cosmological baryon asymmetry and proton decay.

ii) Does not destroy <u>perturbative unification</u>. In fact the only light components of $\underline{24}$ are $(\underline{8},\underline{1},0)+(\underline{1},\underline{3},0)+(\underline{1},\underline{1},0)$ which do not destroy the renormalization group equations[12].

iii) Does not destabilize the <u>gauge hierarchy</u>. Since the coupling $H'\Sigma H$ is not present, the light singlet ϕ is not coupled to the doublets, $H_2'\phi H_2$, and to the triplets, $H_3'\phi H_3$. The one-loop contribution giving to Higgs doublets a mass proportional to the scale of breaking of local SUSY $(m_{3/2}M)^{1/2}$ does not exist and the gauge hierarchy remains stable.

REFERENCES

1. J. Wess and B. Zumino, Phys. Lett. 49B (1974) 52.
   J. Iliopoulos and B. Zumino, Nucl. Phys. B76 (1974) 310.
   S. Ferrara, J. Iliopoulos and B. Zumino, Nucl. Phys. B77 (1974)413.
   S. Ferrara and O. Piguet, Nucl. Phys. B93 (1975) 261.
   M. Grisaru, W. Siegel and M. Rocek, Nucl. Phys. B159 (1979) 420.
2. J. Polchinschi and L. Susskind, Phys. Rev. D26 (1982) 3661.
   H.P. Milles, M. Srednicki and D. Wyler, Phys. Lett. 124B(1983)337.
   A.B. Lahanas, Phys. Lett. 124B (1983) 341.
3. S. Dimopoulos and H. Georgi, Nucl. Phys. B193 (1981) 150.
4. L. Ibáñez and G.G. Ross, Phys. Lett. 110B (1982) 215.
5. J. León, M. Quirós and M. Ramón-Medrano, Nucl.Phys. B222 (1983)104.
6. R. Barbieri, S. Ferrara, D.V. Nanopoulos and K. Stelle, Phys. Lett. 113B (1982) 219.
7. A. Masiero, D.V. Nanopoulos, K. Tamvakis and T. Yanagida, Phys. Lett. 115B (1982) 380.
8. D.V. Nanopoulos, K.A. Olive, M. Srednicki and K. Tamvakis, Phys. Lett. 123B (1983) 41.
9. C. Kounnas, J. León and M. Quirós, Phys. Lett. B (1983),to appear.
10. C. Kounnas, D.V. Nanopoulos and M. Quirós, Phys.Lett.B (1983),to appear.
11. C. Kounnas, D.V. Nanopoulos, M. Quirós and M. Srednicki, Phys Lett. B (1983), to appear.
12. C. Kounnas, A.B. Lahanas, D.V. Nanopoulos and M. Quirós, CERN preprint (in preparation).

LIST OF PARTICIPANTS

E.W. Anderson, CERN, Geneve, Switzerland

J. Balog, Institute of Theoretical Physics, Eötvös University, Budapest, Hungary

R. Barbieri, Istituto di Fisica, Pisa, Italy

A. Barroso, CERN, Geneve, Switzerland

U. Baur, Max-Planck-Institut für Physik und Astrophysik, München, BR Deutschland

V.S. Berezinsky, Academy of Sciences of the USSR, Institute for Nuclear Research, Moscow, USSR

N. Bilić, Rudjer Bošković Institute, Zagreb, Yugoslavia

E. Buturović, Institut za fiziku, Sarajevo, Yugoslavia

F. Csikor, Institute of Theoretical Physics, Eötvös University, Budapest, Hungary

V. Damjanović, Institut za fiziku, Prirodno-matematički fakultet, Beograd, Yugoslavia

M. Damjanović, Institut za fiziku, Prirodno-matematički fakultet, Beograd, Yugoslavia

M. Davier, Laboratoire de l´Accelerateur Lineaire, Centre d´Orsay, Orsay, France

D. Denegri, CEN Saclay, DPHPE - SECB, Gif-sur-Yvette, France

J.F. Donoghue, Commonwealth of Massachusetts, University of Massachusetts, Department of Physics and Astronomy, Amherst, USA

J.O. Eeg, Fysisk Institutt,Universitetet I Oslo, Norway

E. Fiorini, Istituto di Scienze Fisiche "Aldo Pontremoli", Università degli Studi di Milano, Milano, Italia

E. Fischbach, Physics Department, Purdue University, West Lafayette, Indiana, USA

H. Fritzsch, Max-Planck-Institut für Physik und Astrophysik, München, BR Deutschland

H. Galić, Rudjer Bošković Institute, Zagreb, Yugoslavia

J.F. Grivaz, Laboratoire de l´Accelerateur Lineaire, Centre d´Orsay, Orsay, France

B. Guberina, Rudjer Bošković Institute, Zagreb, Yugoslavia
G. Heise, Köln, BR Deutschland
R. Horvat, Rudjer Bošković Institute, Zagreb, Yugoslavia
D. Horvat, Faculty of Electrical Engineering, Zagreb, Yugoslavia
T. Hübsch, Zavod za teorijsku fiziku, Prirodoslovno-matematički fakultet, Zagreb, Yugoslavia
E. Hujdur, Unis Electronic, OOUR IRC, Mostar, Yugoslavia
A. Ilakovac, Zavod za teorijsku fiziku, Prirodoslovno-matematički fakultet, Zagreb, Yugoslavia
F. Jegerlehner, Theoretische Physik, Fakultät für Physik, Universität Bielefeld, Bielefeld, BR Deutschland
Z. Kaliman, Pedagoški fakultet, Rijeka, Yugoslavia
D. Kekez, Rudjer Bošković Institute, Zagreb, Yugoslavia
J. Krstič, Institut za fiziku, Beograd, Yugoslavia
D.F. Kusnezov, Institut für Kernphysik der Kernforschungsanlage Jülich, Experimentale Kernphysik II, Jülich, BR Deutschland
V.A. Kuzmin, Academy of Sciences of the USSR, Institute for Nuclear Research, Moscow, USSR
J. Leon, Consejo Superior de Investigaciones Cientificas, Instituto de Estructura de la Materia, Madrid, Spain
W. Lerche, Max-Planck-Institut für Physik und Astrophysik, München, BR Deutschland
P. Lipari, Syracuse University, Department of Physics, Syracuse, USA
W. Lucha, Institut für Theoretische Physik, der Universität Wien, Wien, Austria
D. Lust, Max-Planck-Institut für Physik und Astrophysik, München, BR Deutschland
N. Mankoč, VTOZD Fizika, Univerza E. Kardelja, Ljubljana, Yugoslavia
T.N. Massey, Institut für Kernphysik der Kernforschungsanlage Jülich, Experimentale Kernphysik II, Jülich, BR Deutschland

S. Meljanac, Rudjer Bošković Institute, Zagreb, Yugoslavia

R.A. Meyer, Institut für Kernphysik der Kernforschungsanlage Jülich, Experimentale Kernphysik II, Jülich, BR Deutschland

K. Mursula, University of Helsinki, Department of High Energy Physics, Helsinki, Finland

V.A. Novikov, ITEP, Moscow, USSR

G. Paić, Rudjer Bošković Institute, Zagreb, Yugoslavia

S. Pallua, Zavod za teorijsku fiziku, Prirodoslovno-matematički fakultet, Zagreb, Yugoslavia

R.D. Peccei, Max-Planck-Institut für Physik und Astrophysik, München, BR Deutschland

I. Picek, Rudjer Bošković Institute, Zagreb, Yugoslavia

K. Pisk, Rudjer Bošković Institute, Zagreb, Yugoslavia

A. Purišić, Gradjevinski školski centar "Z. Brkić", Zagreb, Yugoslavia

M. Quiros, Consejo Superior de Investigaciones Cientificas, Instituto de Estructura de la Materia, Madrid, Spain

E. de Rafael, Centre de Physique Theorique CNRS, Centre de Luminy, Marseille, France

M. Roos, Research Institute for Theoretical Physics, University of Helsinki, Helsinki, Finland

G.G. Ross, Rutherford Appleton Laboratory, Chilton, Didcot, Oxfordshire, Great Britain

M. Rosina, VTOZD Fizika, Univerza E. Kardelja, Ljubljana, Yugoslavia

H.R. Rubinstein, Weizmann Institute of Physical Sciences, Department of Nuclear Physics, Rehovot, Israel

F. Scheck, Institut für Physik, Universität Mainz, Mainz, BR Deutschland

K. Schilcher, Institut für Physik, Universität Mainz, Mainz, BR Deutschland

G. Senjanović, Brookhaven National Laboratory, Upton, N.Y., USA

P. Senjanović, Rudjer Bošković Institute, Zagreb, Yugoslavia

A. Serdarević, Institut za fiziku, Prirodno-matematički fakultet, Sarajevo, Yugoslavia

A. Smailagić, International Centre for Theoretical Physics, Trieste, Italy

H. Steger, Max-Planck-Institut für Physik und Astrophysik, München, BR Deutschland

S. Stenlund, Department of Philosophy, Uppsala University, Uppsala, Sweden

Z. Stipčević, Institut za fiziku, Prirodno-matematički fakultet, Sarajevo, Yugoslavia

J.Z. Szwed, Jagellonian University, Institute of Physics, Krakow, Poland

A. Šokorac, Institut "Boris Kidrič", Vinča, Beograd, Yugoslavia

D. Tadić, Zavod za teorijsku fiziku, Prirodoslovno-matematički fakultet, Zagreb, Yugoslavia

J. Trampetić, Max-Planck-Institut für Physik und Astrophysik, München, BR Deutschland

D. Vranić, Rudjer Bošković Institute, Zagreb, Yugoslavia

Z. Wanyun, International School for Advanced Studies, Trieste, Italy

Z. Was, Jagellonian University, Institute of Physics, Krakow, Poland

M. Wirbel, Institut für Theoretische Physik, der Universität Heidelberg, Heidelberg, BR Deutschland

V.I. Zakharov, ITEP, Moscow, USSR

G. Zoupanos, CERN, Geneve, Switzerland

N. Zovko, Rudjer Bošković Institute, Zagreb, Yugoslavia